Stana Nenadić

OBSERVATIONS

IN HUSBANDRY

OBSERVATIONS

IN

HUSBANDRY.

By EDWARD LISLE, Esq;

LATE OF

CRUX-EASTON, in HAMPSHIRE.

Satis mirari non possum, quòd animi sibi quisque formatorem præcepto-
remque virtutis è cœtu sapientium arcessat; sola res rustica, quæ sine
dubitatione proxima & quasi consanguinea sapientiæ est, tam discentibus
egeat quam magistris. Adhuc enim scholas rhetorum, & geometrarum,
musicorumque, vel, quod magis mirandum est, contemptissimorum vitio-
rum officinas, gulosius condiendi cibos, & luxuriosius fercula struendi,
capitumque & capillorum concinnatores non solum esse audivi, sed & ipse
vidi: agricolationis neque doctores qui se profiterentur, neque discipulos
cognovi. Cùm etiam, si prædictarum artium civitas egeret, tamen, sicut
apud priscos, florere posset respublica; nam sine ludicris artibus, atque
etiam sine causidicis olim satis felices fuere futuræque sunt urbes; at sine
agricultoribus nec consistere mortales, nec ali posse manifestum est.

COLUMELLA, lib. 1.

THE SECOND EDITION.

IN TWO VOLUMES.

VOL. II.

LONDON:

Printed by J. HUGHS, near Lincoln's-Inn-Fields:
For C. HITCH and L. HAWES, J. RIVINGTON and J. FLETCHER, in
Pater-noster-row; W. SANDBY, in Fleet-street; J. RIVINGTON, in
St. Paul's Church-yard; and R. and J. DODSLEY, in Pall-Mall.

M DCC LVII.

Complete set - ISBN 0 576 53185 5
This volume - ISBN 0 576 53211 8

Republished in 1970 by Gregg International Publishers Limited
Westmead, Farnborough, Hants., England.

Printed in Offset by Kingprint Limited
Teddington, Middx., England.

OBSERVATIONS
IN
HUSBANDRY.

FATTING of CATTLE.

§. 1. **T**HO' grass of a middling good-ness may raise a beast to be half fat, yet such grass, tho' the bite be never so deep, may not be able thoroughly to fat-ten him, but he will stick

Grass, tho' plenty of it, from poor land, not good to fat oxen.

there, or mend but very little; for tho' a lean beast will feed greedily till he is half fat, yet afterwards he will grow nice, and require to be tempted with sweeter meats; otherwise he will not feed beyond hunger: therefore persons ought to consider their land, and have a care how they resolve on fatting of cattle, because they think they have plenty of grass and a good bite.— Nor does it follow, because French-grass, hop-clover, or rye-grass will fat, that therefore such grasses, when they grow on poor ground, will do the same, tho' the cattle may have a full bite; therefore such ground ought to be appli-ed to the breeding of cattle.

A 2 §. 22. Dr.

FATTING of CATTLE.

§. 2. Dr. Sloan says, fol. 84.—The true way of fatting cattle, as I was informed by the graziers of Jamaica, is by bleeding them in the jugular vein, (which will stop of itself) and then purging them with aloes, or sempervive-leaves cleared of their outward skins. - Much the same method is often used by some graziers in the north, especially if their grounds raise a bullock very fast, as I suppose the land in Jamaica may do. Dr. Sloan says, the less nourishment the grass affords. the bigger the paunches of the beasts that feed on it; so that. the bellies of cattle, in dry times, in hot countries, are as big as if they were with young.—It would be the same with all sorts of cattle in England also, if you starved them.

§. 3. I was saying to Mr. Bachelour of Ashmonsworth, that I approved of cutting a young bull before his being put to fatting ; he seemed to wonder at it, and said, that he, and all the neighbourhood used to fat a young bull without gelding him, and they supposed, except he was not fatted till the next year, he would fat the better for it, and he was sure it was so of a ram, and to keep him till the year after would not pay charges.

§. 4. In fatting a bullock in Hampshire in the winter they use, by the latter end of October, when the goodness of the grass is gone, whereby he became half fat, to give him hay, and then to finish him with corn and hulls ; but they ought to be wheat hulls ; those are much the best ; and it is much better to give him threshed corn than oats in the straw ; for of them he will make great waste.

There is nothing cheaper, to raise a fatting-bullock with, than ground-barley mixed with chaff.

§. 5. A Wiltshire grazier shewed me a three-year-old bull in January 1698, which he had gelt a fortnight before Michaelmas, and had then in fatting, along with a heifer ; for, he said, they would fat

more

more kindly together, and it would very much improve their meat. His way was, to drive the new-made ox and the heifer to house on nights, and there give them their supper, and in the morning their breakfast, and then let them out to fodder with the milch-cattle; for keeping them warm in the cold nights did much favour their fatting.

§. 6. About the beginning of November, when *Time of buying in lean beasts.* it may be supposed the graziers have disposed of many of their high-fat oxen, and the plough-man has sowed his crop of wheat, and casts off oxen, then will the markets be open for lean oxen, which the graziers buy to eat up the * oughts, and rowety * leavings. grass the high fat oxen had left; and then with straw or hay they keep them in a thriving condition till spring, when they begin to fat them; but from the beginning of November to the middle of December is the chief time of selling them.

§. 7. A stalled ox in the winter, if he be kept to *Quantity of hay a stalled ox will eat.* hay only, will eat at least a load every two months.

§. 8. I asked Mr. Biffy how long an ox would *How long an ox is in fatting.* take to be fat; he said, a good ox must be in good case at May-day, when he is put to grass to be fatted, if he is designed to be got fat by Allhallowtide, which is about six weeks before Christmass; nor will he be fat then with outsome hay: but, if any grazier should order his grazing so, as not to get his oxen fat by that time, but must be haying all the winter,—unless beef be at three-pence halfpenny or four-pence per pound, he can get nothing by it. --I asked him how then it came to pass that we had any ox-beef in the markets at the latter end of winter; he said, some people were no wiser; but there were often beasts put to fatting, that would not be sat so soon as others, and some people overstand their markets by setting themselves a price, under which they will not sell, hoping beef will be dearer, and at last are forced to sell; then there are cows that come in with-calf unfeasonably, and they must be fatted, be it when it will.

§. 9. Farmer Lavington of Wiltshire says, that a heifer, that has never been bulled, will not take fatting fo well as if she had ; but if she has had a calf, or has warped, she will fat very well, though not bulled, when she was turned to fatting.—But Mr. Clerk of Leicestershire says, it is not safe to trust to her fatting without having her bulled.

Of fatting a heifer that has not been bulled.

§. 10. I asked Mr. Clerk how soon a calf would make beef; he said, a cow-calf would make very pretty beef at three years old, but, if killed sooner, they called it beviss ; nor would an heifer prove in fat till that time, not being past growing ; for which reason steers will not be beef till four or five years old, because they will be fo long growing ; therefore it is only profitable for those countries to fat steers that plough them.

How soon a calf will be beef.

§. 11. I had an old black cow brought a calf in the beginning of July, the cow being high in case : the question was, whether I should keep her over the winter, for fake of her winter's-milk, she having calved late in summer, or should make the best I could of fatting her, she being in case. So I asked the farmer's wife, if such a cow, being old, would give milk all the winter; she replied, according as she should take bull ; the sooner she took bull fo much sooner her milk would dry up.—Now she, being high in case, would soon take bull ; fo I looked on myself as answered.

The sooner a cow goes to the bull the sooner her milk dries —therefore to be fatted.

§. 12. An old cow, or an old sheep, will not fat near fo well with hay as with grass.

Mr. Clerk of Leicestershire said, he commonly gave a bull, or an old beast, when they were got pretty well in flesh, (if corn was cheap) ground-oats and ground-barley ; he said, it would improve them much ; he gave it them dry, and it would make them drink abundantly.

Ground-oats or barley to fat an old beast.

Mr.

Mr. Putchin, and Mr. Oldershaw of the same county assured me, they knew of nothing so good to plim a horse, or an old cow, as the tails of the malt, or the larger malt-dust; the proportion was, to boil two quarts of malt-tails in six or eight quarts of water, and to give it two or three times a day: — it would, they said, fat an old cow in six weeks time, so that she would feel very well to the butcher, but then, said they, she would deceive him; for it cannot be expected that flesh blown up so soon should carry any quantity of tallow withinside.

Malt-tail-ings or dust.

§. 13. Falling into company with an ancient butcher, I asked him, what ground he judged best for giving tallow to a beast. He said, old grass-ground, if fat, though lying high and dry, would do very well towards Midsummer, but it would then fall off, at which time the lower and moister pastures would tallow much better: he said, such pastures were good for tallowing all the year round.

What ground best to make a beast tallow

§. 14. It has been found by experience, that turnips do not fat cattle well after Christmass; they grow hollow and sticky; but they will do very well for folding sheep.

Turnips not good to fat cattle after Christmass.

§. 15. A butcher came to buy an old cow of me; she was near fat: it was October the 13th, anno 1702; he said, if he bought her, he would keep her till Christmass in aftermass-grass, for my broad-clover would raise her no higher. —I said, I thought so too; for the broad-clover leaf, being so very broad, held a dew on it, at this time of the year, all day long, whereby the cattle fed half on water; besides, the juice of that grass was too watery at this season; but the meadow-aftermass is soon rid of the dew, within three hours of the morning, and does not hold it like broad-clover. This I learned by having occasion to carry some aftermass broad-clover hay to dry, and to spread it abroad, which I found was to no purpose on a broad-clover ground;

Broad-clover not fit to fat cattle after October.
Meadow-aftermass best.

A 4   and

and yet I did it with good fuccefs on the rye-grafs, though of a deeper bite than the broad-clover.—A farmer of my neighbourhood coming afterwards, afked the above butcher's father, whether it was beft to fat a cow in broad-clover or meadow-erfhe at this time of the year. The old man faid, the meadow-aftermafs was abundantly the better, and gave my reafon for it, without knowing what had paffed between his fon and me.

Hop and broad-clover hay not good to fat large cattle. See Graffes, § 16.

§ 16. Farmer Sartain faid, he had experienced, that hop-clover and broad-clover hay would not prove a bullock in fatting;—But quære, whether this may not only hold good in the great oxen of Wiltfhire.—Surely fmall beafts, fuch as are in our hilly-country, may do very well with thofe forts of hay.

Meadow-aftermafs beft.

§. 17. I afked Mr. Biffy what aftermafs would raife a beaft in autumn fo as to finifh him; he faid, in the fpring almoft any ground will raife a bullock, the fap being then flufh; but it muft be the aftermafs of good ground only, when September and October come, that will hold a bullock, and carry him on when near fat; for though, by hayning up a ground early, after mowing or fummer-feeding, there may feem to be a great bite of grafs in it, yet, if fuch ground, by reafon of it's poverty, fhould fall off of it's ftrength in September and October, which may be feen by the dying away, or the fading colour of the grafs, it is loft on fuch a bullock.

If one has natural aftermafs-grafs able to keep up a bullock from September to Chriftmafs, it will pay for keeping an almoft fat bullock or cow, if fhe be not too forward with calf; and the reafon is, becaufe there is but a fmall part of England that have natural aftermafs at that time of the year, fit to fat with, in proportion to the fummer-clover every one has fit for that purpofe; befides ox-beef is not then come in, and cows are generally too forward with calf.

§. 18. I

§. 18. I asked Mr. Bissy if French-grass hay was fit to fat a bullock with; he said, the Somersetshire graziers going to London had often assured him, that, if French-grass was cut early in flower, it would fat cattle very well till towards spring, but then it grew too dry.

Of French-grass hay to fat a bullock.

§. 19. By discoursing with Mr. Bissy about winter-fatting, I find by his experience, and the neighbourhood's, who have kept the account, and weighed the hay, that a good heifer put up to winter-fatting on hay would eat at least two hundred weight of hay per week, which at thirty shillings per ton, or eighteen-pence per hundred weight, will come to three shillings per week, and at that rate her fatting for twenty weeks will cost three pounds, and in less time a heifer, that is not very forward when put up to hay, cannot be fatted; yet at this rate, if beef sells well in the spring, some advantage may be had, but gain cannot be depended on by such practice.—How comes it then, said I, to pass, that heifer-beef is so frequently to be had in the spring? Because, said he, we graziers have sometimes the mischance to have a heifer warp, that would otherwise have been beef at Christmass, but casting her calf put her at least ten weeks backward, and, to make the best of her, we must keep her on to fatting. Sometimes we are disappointed by a heifer's or a cow's calving sooner than we expected, perhaps in December or January, and thence she would go dry; such we must therefore fat, and, being fed with hay, she makes early beef in the spring.

What quantity of hay will fat an heifer.

§. 20. Fourteen pound weight of hay is the constant allowance on the road, to every fat beast that is drove to London; they that entertain cattle fling fourteen pound of hay for each beast into the rack in the evening, when they come into the inn, which is to serve also next morning for their breakfast; so that half a ted, i. e. seven pound of hay, is supposed

Allowance of hay to a fat beast on the road.

sufficient

sufficient for a fat ox's bait at night, and the same in the morning.

Of beasts that are over-drove.

§. 21. The cattle, that in hot weather come to London in droves, are many of them heart-broken, and so heated, and tired off their spirits, that, if they were not killed they would die ; and those whose feet bear not the journey well, do so waste their juices through the fatigue, that, when they are killed, they will not stiffen.—The reason is, because they have so emptied themselves of their juices that their joints will remain loose and flabby ; — and thus we may observe, the plimming of meat in boiling argues the youth of it, i. e. it's fulness of juice, and it's shrinking argues the contrary.

Cattle handle best when warm, &c.

§. 22 Mr. Clerk, Sir Ambrose Phillipps's tenant, says, when he drives cattle to Smithfield, if he has a chapman that is eager, as soon as his cattle take up their stand, if he can he will deal with him ; for cattle handle to the best advantage when warm, and their fat when heated is mellower, and softer, than after they have stood to cool.

One may be more deceived in the condition of a fat beast in good quick-springing grass than in a coarse pasture, because the fine grass may plim him faster than it can make good sound meat of his flesh.

Of old cow-beef.

§. 23. An experienced butcher observed to me, that a young beast would eat well half fat, but an old cow, and but half fat, was not eatable ; for the whole body of such a cow ought to be filled with new juices.

Old cow-beef generally comes in about St. Simon and Jude, which is the latter end of October, or later ; for old cows are not apt to take bull so soon as young ones, and so do not make the earliest cow-beef.

Old cows tallow best on the inside.

§. 24. The butcher killed a fat cow for me, of four years old ; I saw her opened, and she proved very fat withinside, and very fat on the back. — He said,

said, it was common for a young cow to be fat on the back, but very rarely to tallow well in the inside; but old cows generally tallowed best withinside, but not so well on the back.

§. 25. If a cow seeming high in case should bring forth a small calf, it argues, the cow thrives in tallow; and if a good cow, middling in case, produces a great calf, there cannot at that time be any foundation for tallow.

Sign of a cow's tallowing well.

§. 26. I was at Gausuns in Wiltshire with farmer Pain and Mr. Biffy: they agreed that an old cow, though she would not weigh so well in the quarters as a young one, yet she would tallow better. — But farmer Pain said, to his certain knowledge, an old ewe would not do so; what tallow an old weather might yield he knew not. — However he was sure, that the best mutton, and that for which the butcher would give me most, was a sheep of two year, or two year and a half old; such mutton would spend and weigh best. I objected, that such sheep, not having done growing, would not be fat. He said, he never found it so: he bade me look at the ewes with their lambs, that he then had with him; the ewes are but two years old, and I hope, said he, to have them all with the butcher in a little time.

Old cows tallow best.

§. 27. In discourse with farmer William Sartain of Wiltshire about the choice of a bullock for fatting, and when his bones lay well, he said, an understanding butcher might get more money by an ugly mishapen bullock than one whose bones lay well, because those bones that lie ill, carry more fat than they seem to do; therefore, if a bullock handles well in the places they make trial of, that is only to be regarded.

Marks of a good bullock for fatting.

§ 28. If a cow carries a deep navel, or her navel springs or struts forth when she is fat, it is a very good, and almost a certain sign that she will die well, that is, that she is full of tallow.

Signs of a cow's tallowing well.

If

Id. of an
ox.

If an ox be full at the cod, when bought lean, or springs and struts forth full in the cod, when fat, it is a good sign that he will tallow well.

Marks of a
good ox—
among the
antients.

§. 29. [a] Varro, Columella, and Palladius are, in the main, pretty well agreed in the characters they have given us of a fine ox, which are as follow —— Symmetry of parts; stout sound limbs; a body large and somewhat long (close and short, says Columella) and well ribbed; horns bending a little inward like a crescent, stately, strong, and in colour inclining to black; a broad curled forehead; large black eyes; great hairy ears (or, as Markham translates it, rough within); flat cheeks; spreading nostrils; snub nose; blackish lips; neck thick, long, and muscular, with vast dewlaps, swagging down almost to the knees; deep brisket; buttocks round and full; sides and paunch strutting and capacious; a strait flat back, or a little swayed; a tail brushing his heels, the lower part of it thick with hair, and a little frizzled; nervous and well set his legs, and

[a] Hæ pecudes sint bene compositæ, integris membris (grandibus, Colum.) oblongæ, amplæ, (corpore denso brevique, Colum.) nigrantibus cornibus (proceris et robustis, Colum. sine curvaturæ pravitate lunatis, Pallad.) latis frontibus (et crispis, Colum.) oculis magnis et nigris, pilosis auribus (hirtis, Colum. magnis, Pallad.) compressis malis, sublimisve, apertis naribus, labris subnigris, cervicibus crassis, et longis, (et torosis. Colum.) a collo palearibus demissis (amplis, et pene ad genua, Colum.) latis humeris (vastis, pectore magno, Colum.) bonis clunibus (rotundis, Colum.) (capaci et tanquam implente utero, lateribus porrectis, dorso recto planoque, vel etiam subsidente, Colum.) caudam ut habeant profusam usque ad calces, inferiorem partem frequentibus pilis subcrispam, auribus (nervosis, Pallad. brevioribus potius quam longis, Colum.) rectis genibus, eminulis, distantibus inter se, pedibus non latis (unguis magnis, Colum. et Pallad.) neque ingredientibus qui displodantur, nec cujus ungulæ divaricent, et cujus ungues sint pares,—et leves, says Varro, but that term must rather refer to the cow than the ox.—Corium attactu non asperum et durum, colore potissimum nigro, dein rubeo, tertio helvo, quarto albo; mollissimus enim hic, ut durissimus primus.

                                        rather

rather short than long; his knees strait, somewhat knotted, or embossed, and standing wide from each other ; a foot not very broad, the claws large and of an equal size, not standing apart, nor liable to accidents by inclining inward ; his hide smooth and sleek to the touch, it's colour black, as the most eligible, because it denotes the beast to be of the hardiest kind, next to that red, then flesh-colour, and lastly white, which is the tenderest of the four. The colours Columella and Palladius most approve of are red and brown.

A beast should have a large hoof or foot, and large long legs : this is a sign, that, when he is fat, he will weigh well. A spiny-legged beast never pays the grazier so well as the former. *Id. for fatting among the moderns.*

A beast should not be leather-throated, that is, have his skin hang down deep under his throat ; but should have a thin neck : the former is observed never to prove so well

A beast should be deep in his gascoigns, which mounts him high in the hinder parts, and makes him weigh well.

A beast should be wide between both huckle bones, which gives room for his filling : such a beast, when fat, will be sure to weigh well.

A beast should be deep in the brisket, that is, from the upper part of the shoulder to the lower part of the neck ; for then he will fill well with fat.

A beast should be short ribbed, that is, the rib and the flank should meet close : some beasts either want a rib, or have a false rib, which is so called, because it is very little, or lies deep within ; this is a great disflight, by which means the flank will pitch and fall in.

When a beast is fat, he will shew himself to the eye to be so by a roll of fat as big as one's fist, which when he walks, moves itself forwards before his

shoulder :

shoulder : such a roll of fat may likewise be seen in his flank. Luxuriat toris, says Virgil.

Sign of a good cow. See Bulls and Cows, §. 1. &c.

§. 30. A cow has a good udder, when her teats are at equal distance, and pretty wide asunder ; when the teats are near together, there is danger of losing one of them ; as her teats ought not to be very small, so neither ought they to be too big ; for such are called windy teats.—When a cow's udder hangs full in leather, and in wrinkles behind, it is an argument the vessel is large to receive milk, whereas some cows, tho' they might give ever so much milk, have no vessel for it.

Mr. Clerk of Leicestershire says, after all that has been said, if he can buy a cow cheap, he will buy her against the rules and shape above described, and she may sometimes pay as well as any.

Signs of a good beast.

§. 31. Being at Holt in Wilts, I fell into discourse with Mr. Bissy, and having a mind to be more particularly informed in this branch of the grazier's business, I asked him what were the signs and tokens of a good beast ; those by which he chose them when he went to fairs ; for he had just been saying, that there were many beasts in a fair, which were in show twenty shillings better than some others, and yet not so valuable as those that seemed to be so much less worth : nay, he said, there were many fat beasts in Smithfield-market, twenty shillings more in weight than some others, and of the same age too, and the lighter beast the more preferable at the same price.—He therefore said, that, in an ox the experienced graziers had a particular regard not to buy one that had a long and heavy dewlap, or merry-thought, which hung down under his throat, nor one that had a thick jaw, nor heavy small eyes, nor that was thin in the buttocks : they commonly observed, he said, that those beasts, which had most of these properties, paid least for

their

their fatting, nor did they take it kindly; for they were apt not to take fat in all parts proportionably alike. We love to choose those beasts which have not too thick a hide, but of a middling thickness; for the grain of the beef of a thick-hided ox is apt to be coarse, and yet we do not covet a very thin hide neither. The north-country oxen, said he, are generally thick-hided, nor will they in Smithfield sell so dear as North-Wiltshire oxen will do: the sweetness of our beef is esteemed greater than their's, and we can out-sell them one hundred weight in seven.—— We choose an ox with a light head, thin and close jaws, full and lively eyes, not thin on the rump, but that has a thin and short dewlap, and as little under the throat as may be; such an ox is likely to thrive much faster than one of the contrary shape, and to carry fat in all pieces equally, which is a great advantage to the butcher; for then, the coarse pieces will sell well. A light bony head in a sheep is also a good sign, but in a cow a long and heavy dewlap is not so much regarded.——Then I went with him down to his grounds, and was shewed two oxen which answered the above differences and characters.—— Taking notice of a particular ox, he said, he was half fat, and began to gather flesh, which might be as soon perceived in the cod as any where; for there they soon begin to shew their thriving, and so does a weather-sheep. —— I observed myself the cod to be truss, and extended round as big as my fist; whereas, in the lean oxen in the field, the cod was lank, and made little shew.——He says, all fat beasts are apt to be too hot; therefore a fatting-bullock, if he be kept out of the wet, cannot be kept too cool, and for that reason it does very well for one side of the fatting-houses to be open; for, if a fatting-bullock be too hot, he will be apt to * peal: but for lean beasts, they could not be kept too warm.

* the hair will come off.

§. 32. I

§. 32. I find by Mr. Alyff of Oxenleaze, Wilts, that the largeneſs of the cod of a fat ox is a great beauty, and the bigger it is, proportionably a ſign of his fatting the better ; and he is very poſitive in it, that oxen that work make the beſt beef, and die kindlier, and are inwardly fatter than thoſe that never worked, and ſays, (it being a phraſe he often uſed) that they divide better in the joints, and piece better under the cleaver, when quartered-out by the butcher ; whereas the unworked-beef does not ſo eaſily divide, and (as he terms it) eats coarſe and livery.——I told him, I had often heard the graziers affirm as much, but it did not ſeem reaſonable to me, becauſe, as country farmers and labourers had much greater ſtrength than gentlemen of the ſame bulk, by means or the exerciſe of all the ligatures and cords of their bodies, which became thereby ſtronger and tougher, ſo I thought that muſt be the caſe of the ploughed ox ; and ſeeing their fleſh and ours is but a bundle of pipes, tubes, or fiſtular parts faggotted together, full of heterogeneous juices, I could not conſequently ſuppoſe, but the fleſh of a worked ox muſt be tougher than the fleſh of an unworked ox.

Alſo of a worked and unworked ox.

§. 33. Markham, lib. 1. fol. 62.——for an ox to feed, adviſes, that he ſhould as much as might be, be ever luſty and young of years, or, if old, yet healthful and unbruiſed, which you may know by a good tail, and a good piſſel ; for, if the hair of one or both be loſt, he is then a waſter, and will be long in feeding. If you would chooſe a fat beaſt, handle his hindmoſt rib, and, if it be looſe, and ſoft, like down, then it ſhews the ox to be outwardly well fed ; ſo do ſoft huckle-bones and a big notch round and knotty ; if his cod be big and full, it ſhews he is well tallowed, and ſo doth the crop behind the ſhoulders.

Marks of a beaſt when fat, or for fatting.

Mr.

Mr. Serjeant Webb's bailiff came to me in the beginning of November, 1713, to buy my lean oxen, that I wanted to cast off to the grazier. He found fault with some that their bones did not lie right in two respects, viz. that they were thin in their buttocks behind, i. e. that their buttock, or britch-bone did not spread, and stand out wide; from whence, he said, they would not prove, nor fill up in their buttocks behind, so as to look well to the grazier.

Again, there were two of them that had a rib wanting on each side, or a rib less in the flank than they should have, viz. the first rib next to the buttock: note, though this defect commonly goes, and is known by the expression of a rib wanting, yet a juster expression is, that such a beast has a short rib, which sinks or falls inward, and does not bear outward, as the rest do, so that in the handling one cannot get to feel all of it, but the lower part seems lost, and therefore it vulgarly carries the name of a lost rib.

There was another bullock he excepted against, because the bottom bushy part of his tail was lost, having but little hair on it, which was to him a token that he had been over-worked.

In two or three he disliked their hair's staring, or standing on-end, on the ridge of their back, another argument of their hard labour.

I asked Mr. Dark, a great grazier in Wiltshire, what marks he looked on as promising in beasts to be bought for fatting; he said, a beast with thick horns was by no means liked by graziers: and a thick head was an ill mark amongst them; a beast with large ribs weighed well; a close-ribbed beast, with quarters that lay well, they liked to buy, and not a thin flat-ribbed beast.

§. 34. A butcher bought a heifer half fat of me to kill: he said, she would not pay for keeping, for A thick hide a bad sign.

fhe was thick-hided, and fuch beafts would not prove.—I obferved the hide feemed to fit loofe, and the hair to ftare more than ordinary, or look like beggars-plufh.

Upon the beft inquiry I could make of Mr Biffy, farmer William Sartain, and others in Wiltfhire, they do not think the Welch-cattle of North-Wales and the cattle of Shropfhire fat kindly ; for they are thick-hided, efpecially the burs, i. e. the oxen ;— and it is to be noted, that the thicker hided the cattle are the longer they are in fatting.—And it is gene-rally to be obferved, that the cattle of North-Wales are black cattle.—But Mr. Biffy fays, that in South-Wales, as in Glamorganfhire, they have thin-hided cattle, which are much on the red and brown co-lour, and that they get their breed from Gloucefter-fhire; they will fat very kindly.——Mr Biffy tells me, the more northerly the cattle are bred, by means of the cold, the thicker are their hides ; for in Leicefterfhire, Derbyfhire, and Yorkfhire, the hide of a large ox may fell for thirty fhillings, becaufe of it's thicknefs, and being fit to make ben-leather for the foles of fhoes ; whereas the hide of an ox in North-Wiltfhire, &c. though as big as the other, will not fetch above fifteen fhillings ; but fuch an ox will notwithftanding fell for more than a north-country ox will do, becaufe the meat is finer, and the beaft will yield more tallow ; for the finer the hide the finer always the meat.---I put the queftion to farmer William Sartain, young John Sartain &c. ——what difference there might be in Smithfield-market between the price of a north-country ox, and a North-Wiltfhire ox of the fame weight; they faid two pounds in ten pounds, but the hide of the north-country ox would yield a third penny more in value.

Rules for the hill-country grazier.

§. 35. If a farmer intends to graze cattle in a hill-country farm, fuch as mine in Hampfhire may be, thefe these three things are especially to be regarded; First, to raise a good quantity of French-grass for hay and aftermass.—Secondly, to turn a good quantity of hill-country meadow into rich pasture, by feeding it, dunging it, or other manure; to make it fit for raising the bullock or heifer in the spring, when he comes first from hay into grass-lease, and to receive him with a vigorous aftermass, when other grasses, as clovers, and French-grass aftermass goes off.—Thirdly, to have hovels in your bartons, inclosed with close court walls, to shelter your cattle in the winter from wind and rain. All these three things are necessary and uniform, and do correspond one with another; without them grazing must be carried on very defectively, and to little profit by the hill-country farmer.

By the methods here prescribed, in order to the fatting of cattle, plenty of French-grass hay will enable the grazier to buy in barren beasts before the spring-grass comes, when it is most likely they will be cheap, and may be bought to the best advantage, allowing the value of the hay they may eat in consideration with the purchase; and if by winter-hayning some meadow-ground, (after it has been fed close, but has been kept high in heart, by feeding it and foiling it,) you can early in the spring, by April or sooner, have a bite to take off such grazing beasts from hay to grass, it will be very advantageous before the clovers can be ready, which are seldom so in the hill-country till a week or fortnight within May;—and by hayning-up such meads for an aftermass, which towards the end of the summer are in very good heart, you'll support your bullock, and carry him on when the spirit of the other grasses fail.—Then such cattle as are unfinished being brought to French-grass hay, and tied up under hovels, or coverings, and within court walls, will proceed in thriving by being secured from the wind and rain,

B 2   and

and the tedious hill-country rimes, that often continue whole winter-days, all which makes fatting-cattle brought from grafs to pitch, and wafhes them out.---Befides, if you have not plenty of French-grafs hay, you cannot in winter make the beft of a milch-cow that warps, or of a cow that towards the latter end of winter you may perceive proves barren, or of a fat cow that cafts her calf before you kill her.

------I mention here the neceffity of French-grafs hay only, and not of clover hay, becaufe I fuppofe the ·hill-country farmer, who provides ftore of French-grafs hay, will be wife enough not to mow the clovers, but to feed them, to improve his lands, for the hill-country farmers have generally fo much land for their money, that all they can do is little enough to keep their arable land in fuch heart, as for their profit it ought to be in.

If the foregoing cautions are not obferved, the ill confequences that will follow muft be fuch as thefe ; ------if the firft of the three foregoing cautions is difregarded, your cattle cannot at any time of the year be made fat as they ought to be, and then you muft be under neceffity of felling them half fat, of which neceffity the buyer never fails to take the advantage; and fell them you muft, notwithftanding the profpect of prices rifing in a month or two never fo much; and you'll commonly find, that you fhall have nothing for the meat they have eat whilft they have been fatting. ------ In the fecond place, we will fuppofe that very few will be fo unwife, as to begin to fat a beaft in October with hay, and fo to hay him throughout the winter ; but we may reafonably fuppofe, that warping beafts and barren heifers, &c. may, and commonly are begun to be fatted with hay from Chriftmafs, in which cafe, though hay be plenty, yet if an early fpring-grafs be wanting, fuch cattle muft be hayed at leaft till the middle of May ; for till then, in the hill-country, the clovers will not give

give a beaft a bite, and then commonly, where the
mafter is at a lofs and difappointed, the goods fuffer
before his eyes before he can make the beft of them,
and in this cafe he fhall find a beaft vifibly pitch
before he can find a purchafer for him.——Again,
if early fpring-grafs be wanting, you cannot begin
fummer-fatting of cattle, nor can buy a barren heifer till towards the middle of May, and then they
are commonly very dear; and in the hill-country
from fo late a beginning the fummer-grafs will hardly fat a beaft, the ground falling early off it's
ftrength, being generally poor;—— and then, if
you have not a quick-growing aftermafs treafured
up, by keeping fuch ground as was formerly meadow in good heart for that purpofe, it is plain you
muft again run into the firft evil;——and if you
have fuch an aftermafs, you will again often be
wanting hay in November, and December, to finifh
fummer-fatted beafts; fo that plenty of hay is always neceffary, &c.—— And laftly, though you
have both hay and grafs, if you want winter fhelter
the cattle muft fuffer.

PROPOSALS for FATTING CATTLE in the hill-country, and firft of the BARREN HEIFER.

§. 36. It is propofed (1.) That the meadows of
the farm, which generally in a farm of an hundred
pounds per annum hold to no greater proportion
than from twelve to twenty acres, be laid to pafture
for the fatting purpofe.

(2.) That from feven to ten acres be yearly fowed to hop-clover, for the firft fpring-grafs for the
fatting of beafts.

(3.) That the good pafture you have made of
ground beft inclined to natural grafs, by chalking
and dunging, &c. may receive the barren heifers,
(for I fear it will not be good enough, nor deep
enough

enough fed for the oxen) and this made pasture, having been hayned from the latter end of January, or the middle of February, I suppose may by the end of April have got a good head of grass.

(4.) Your barren heifers must, from the time they may have been supposed to have eaten up this made pasture, be kept in your meadows till they come to the slaughter.

All fatting-cattle, whether lambs, sheep, barren cows, or oxen, do require a regular and proportionable progression from coarser to better food, as they grow more and more into good flesh; otherwise, when half fat, they will go back, and you will not without great difficulty raise them again, which will be a great loss, nor will such beef spend kindly.

Against the time he buys in his heifers, a gentleman who would make a good hill-country grazier (for I do not suppose it to answer but to such who kill their own beef in their family) ought to take care to be provided with an over-plus stock of middling good hay or of winter-vetches, or of barley-straw and autumn-grass mixed together, layer and layer of each, be it whatever it will; it ought properly to be better than barley-straw; for he is to suppose he has bought barren heifers which have been kept all winter to straw;—if they have been kept better, i. e. to straw and rowet, there is still the greater reason for him to mend their keeping;— and he is from the time of buying to consider, that he ought to begin to raise them in flesh; for the better case they are in against they are turned to spring-grass, they will take to fatting the kindlier, and bear their first scouring the better.—If he could turn them into a field, for an hour or two in the day, where there is a little rowet, it would do well, and to have change of the abovesaid dry meats would keep them the better to their stomachs.

PROPOSALS

PROPOSALS for FATTING OXEN, in the hill-country.

§. 37. The times of turning off oxen to fatting are two in-the-year, which in feveral refpects anfwer the publick conveniency, viz.

(1.) The firft is about May-day, when the labour of the ox is pretty well over for the fpring-feafon, the fpring-corn being then generally all fown.

(2.) The fecond time for turning oxen to fatting is the beginning of winter, i. e. from the firft of October to the middle of November, which falls out again very luckily; for then the winter-corn, i. e. wheat, and winter-vetches, are generally all fowed throughout England, and the plough-man's hurry relaxes.

At both thefe times the grazing gentleman, who defigns to kill for his table all the year round, muft turn oxen to fatting.——We will firft begin to dif-courfe of the fpring-fatting, which is the moft chargeable to the hufbandman, [and therefore he ought to expect a better price, and a fuitable re-turn;] for oxen turned out at May-day will hard-ly get fat till Chriftmafs, and, if not turned out till June, will not be fat till March, April, or May, which again falls out very opportune-ly; becaufe from Chriftmafs till the latter end of May cow-beef is very fcarce, and is generally fupplied by ox-beef; but then it is obvious, that when an ox gets half, or three quarters fat by or before winter, he muft be fupported and carried on by a great quantity of hay, and that very good; for the beaft will then grow nice.

The other time of entering an ox into fatting is, as beforefaid, in October and November, when he is alfo turned off from the plough; and the gentleman, my young hufbandman, muft be informed, that it is

wafte

waſte to lay very good, much more the beſt of hay before ſuch an ox ; for coming hungry and poor to it, he will devour abundance, and will eat up the fatteſt hay without paying for the coſt and charges of it.—The moſt you can propoſe by this method is to get him fat by July, inſtead of September, or October; during all which interval of time heifer-beef will be plenty, and will ſink the price of ox-beef ; therefore ſo chargeable a method will not quit coſts.

What the grazier therefore in this caſe ought to do, is as follows : he ſhould bring his ox eaſily and gently into good fleſh by a rowet, that he ought to have hayned his grounds up to for that purpoſe, and of which rowet he ought to give him the worſt firſt, except it be of ſo ſour a kind as to want the cor-rection of the winter-froſts before he will eat it, of which kind ſtubble-rowet commonly is, and in ſuch caſe that muſt be reſerved till then, or rather for young beaſts, and milch-cow cattle.—He ought to give him variety of dry meat along with his rowet, in which he ought to conſult his tooth by flinging be-fore him, by changes, each ſort of good ſtraw, giving now and then a lock of winter-vetches, or coarſe hay, but of every thing good in it's kind, i. e. ſweet, and well made, and thus the ox ought to be carried on throughout the winter.—Againſt March comes he ought to have better hay ; not only becauſe the rowet may be ſuppoſed to be all gone, but alſo becauſe the ox mending in fleſh grows nicer, and will be weary of dry meat, through the tediouſ-neſs of being foddered ſo much with it during the winter ; therefore his hay muſt be mended ; for not proceeding is going back.—Againſt April, if poſſi-ble, a ſhort head of graſs ſhould be got for him in your paſture-grounds for cow cattle, by hayning the paſture in February, that he may have graſs along with his hay, as before ſaid in the fatting of barren

heifers ;

FATTING of CATTLE.

heifers;—and against May a head of hop-clover must be in readiness, in the hill-country, to receive him into his first full grazing, as is also said of fatting the barren heifer; for it is not to be supposed the meadows of the hill-country, which according to this scheme are to be converted to pasture, can be fit before the first of June to entertain a grazing-ox; and it is also to be noted, that in the hill-country, in the month of May, hop-clover will not afford a good bite for an ox, or a cow, unless the autumn-bud be hayned, and preserved from being fed by sheep: in the month of May, if it should prove a cold and dry spring, the fatting-oxen and cows must also with their hop-clover, if it be short, have good hay given them, if they will eat it.—Note, fatting in the hill-country, if you hay in the winter, is more chargeable than in the vale, not only because hay is dearer there, but also because the winter-season begins a month sooner, and holds a month later in the hill-country than in the vale.

Thus you see what disadvantages the hill-country gentleman lies under, who would kill a bullock once a month, or three weeks, more than a grazier of the vale does; for the first must, in a manner, by forcing nature, provide rowet and several sorts of grasses in their due order, exactly accommodated to the season of the year, besides winter-meat, &c.—Whereas, for the latter all may be procured in a natural course, with but a very little care and trouble.

Now I doubt not but by this time the reader is provided with a fatal objection, and will tell me, I have forgot the taking care to provide one of the most material and difficult ingredients to be had in the hill-country for fatting of cattle, viz. proper grass, in a sufficient plenty, and yet on all occasions I have before prescribed it.—I do acknowledge I

should

ſhould make a very great, and ridiculous blunder, without an ample proviſion in this caſe ; I muſt therefore lay it down as a principle, that a hill-country grazier goes to work without his tools, who does not lay down from fifty to an hundred acres of land proper for it to French-graſs, not only on the account of making up the deficiency of the meadows, not laid down to paſture, being converted to other uſes, but alſo to anſwer many other demands ; for in-ſtructions in which matter, I refer to the chapter on French-graſſes, &c. [b]

T U R N I P S.

Liming good for turnips.

§. 1. [c] **O**Bſerving that the turnips, which one of my tenants was cutting, were wormy, I told him, they would have been leſs ſo, in caſe he had limed his ground. — He ſaid, that laſt year (1702) he limed one part of his ground, and thoſe turnips were much freer from worms than theſe ; — and, ſaid I, much ſweeter too, I believed. — He an-ſwered, he never had ſweeter turnips, nor carrots, than from that ground, and he did believe that liming was the occaſion of it.

Dunging turnips in Norfolk.

§. 2. [d] Mr. Heron of Norfolk aſſures me, that they dung their turnip-land as much as may be, even to that degree, that their dry-land meadows are quite impoveriſhed by it.

[b] See the articles—Bulls and Oxen—Cows and Calves.
[c] To deſtroy the caterpillar, Mr. Miller ſays the ſureſt method is, to turn a large parcel of poultry into the field ; which ſhould be kept hungry, and turned early in the morning into the field : theſe fowls will ſoon devour the inſects, and clear the field.
[d] Dung and tillage together, ſays Mr Tull, will attain the ne-ceſſary degree of pulverization in leſs time than ploughing can do alone ; therefore dung is more uſeful to turnips, becauſe they have commonly leſs time to grow than other plants.

TURNIPS.

§. 3. I had difcourfe with Mr. Pawlet of Leicefterfhire, who deals in great quantities of turnips; it
was Auguft the 7th, 1699—he fays, when turnips
are fowed after Midfummer they are generally counted out of danger of the fly:—This fly is like to a
weevil breeding in malt, with hard wings; there is
no danger of it after the turnip-leaf begins to grow
rough, which will be in a fortnight's time after
fowed, if they come up well. He fows a pound and
half of feed on an acre, and fo, as I find, do all the
gardeners in thofe parts; for the more are fown on
an acre the more chance they have to efcape the flies.
— There are, he fays, four forts of turnips; viz.
the white turnips, the red or blue turnips, the yellow
turnips, and the long turnips; for fale the gardeners
deal only in the firft two forts;—that the fly lays
more feverely on the leaves of the red or blue fort
than on the white; that turnips fhould be fowed in
dry weather, or elfe they cannot be raked or harrowed in well; that they muft have a fhower of rain to
come up in; that though it is true the rain beats
downs and deftroys the fly that would devour them,
yet it makes thofe flies that out-live it cruelly hungry; fo that it is after fuch rain that the turnip-leaves
are moft eaten. He fays, there is fo much moifture
in the ground before Michaelmafs, that you never
need to doubt the feed fown in Auguft or after.

4. §. Mr. Scamwell affures me, if I ftrew tobacco-
duft over the land where any greens, as lettuce, &c.
are fet, (fuppofe a pound to an acre) the fly will not
come to thofe greens. Quære, if not a good way to
fow turnip-feed with tobacco-duft.—I am told if you
mix powder-brimftone with your turnip-feed it will
preferve them from the fly.—Mr. Worlidge in his
treatife, called Two treatifes, fays, that the greateft

---

e Mr. Miller adds two forts, viz.—the rufty-black, and the
green turnip.

enemies

enemies to turnips are the flies, which about the
fowing-time, by the fun's influence, are generated in
the ftubble that remained in the field, where you
now fow your feed ; for it is obferved, that an eafy
ploughing and fudden fowing thefe feeds makes the
turnips more apt to be thus deftroyed, than a well
dreffing and more leifurely fowing ; for this deprives
thefe vermin of their fhelter and fuftenance, fo that
they generally die before the feeds come up. The
feeds being foaked in foot-water, and fowed, the
bitternefs they have attracted from the foot is faid to
be a fecurity againft birds, flies, and infects.——New
burn-beaked ground fowed with turnips has been
obferved to efcape the fly more than other land, and
fome ftrew afhes on their turnips in gardens to preferve them from this infect.

§. 5. Mr. Bachelour told me, that I might depend on it, this was fo cold a country, that, if I
fowed turnips the latter end of Auguft, I fhould not
fo much as have leaves, and therefore I ought to fow
them by Midfummer: he faid, he had known it tried.

§. 6. I told a famous gardener, that I had heard it
faid, if turnips were fowed when the wind was in the
north, or north-eaft, that no turnips would come up.
——The caufe of that, he faid, muft chiefly be, becaufe fuch wind, which naturally parched the ground
and dried up all moifture, was at that time accom-
panied with drought ; but he doubted not, though
turnips were fown in fuch wind, if rain came afterwards, they would come up well.—I have alfo heard,
faid I, that if turnips were fowed in rain, and a hot
gloom came afterwards, that no turnips would come
up.——He faid, the reafon of that, he thought, muft
be, becaufe the ground, by fuch a fudden heat after
wet, was made ftarky, fo that the turnips could not
get through ; and may not, faid he, charlock, and
other weeds be deftroyed by the fame accident ?——
And indeed I cannot but agree with him ; for if it
                                              be

Turnips to
be fowed
early in a
cold coun-
try.

Why tur-
nips fowed
when the
wind is
northerly,
or in a hot
gloom,
may not
come up.

be obferved, you will find the turnip does not come up with it's feed-leaves, upright, picked, and fharp, as many feeds do, but with broad indented feed-leaves, and the ftem that carries it's head being but tender, no wonder if it cannot pierce through the cruft of earth, when it is hardened.——Here the wifdom of God is to be admired, who, having ordered feed-leaves not fharp-pointed or fpiked, but broad, or many, and indented, and fo not fit to force upwards, has caufed them to bend their heads downwards, and fo to get through the earth by their bended ftalk.

§. 7. I am of opinion the way to have large turnips is to preferve fome of the largeft turnips for feed; for from fuch feed do the largeft turnips proceed; whereas the feed bought of gardeners comes of their fcattered feed, which, running up thick, does not head, nor produce a feed that will carry a large turnip.—It is the fame of afparagus, fays Quinteny. *Caution —to preferve the beft feed.*

§. 8. Mr. Cheflin of Leicefterfhire having been very fuccefsful in turnips, I afked him, whether he did not fow about a pound and an half on an acre; he faid, his was cold land, for which reafon he fowed rather more. *Quantity of feed on an acre.*

§. 9. As the lefs folid the rinds of all feeds are the larger the fibres, and as the lefs fpirit and oil is contained in them they do the lefs refift vegetation, and confequently putrefaction, and the fooner begin growing, or are malted in the ground, fo fuch feeds may be expected, if they come not up in a few days (as turnip-feed in four or five days) to be either burften with too much rain, or malted for want of moifture, and conveniency to fet them on growing; for fuch feeds, of the nature above defcribed, are fufceptible of a great deal of moifture, and therefore, when fown in the drieft time, though they meet not with moifture enough to fet them on growing, feldom fail of being malted, becaufe the *Of turnip-feed burfting with too much rain.*

very

very relaxing quality which is in all earth, together
with the dew of the night, are sufficient for that
purpose.   Yet, as to the bursting the vessels of the
turnip-seed by plethory caused by too much rain, it
may be noted, that some have observed a glut of
rain to have fallen on the turnip-seed, soon after
they have sown it, without any such ill effect, and
others have found that such speedy rains have burst
the vessels, and turned the flour of the seed into a
mucilage.——In these two different cases, as I judge,
the following distinctions should be made, viz. in
case the turnip-seed be sown for the sake of roots in
June or July, while the ground is hot with the sun,
and has at the time of such heat been glutted with
rain, or that a glut of rain immediately falls on such
sowing the turnip-seed, i. e. the same day, or the
night after it was sown; in such case I easily conceive,
the turnip-seed being very susceptible of moisture,
the seed-vessels may imbibe the rain to so great a
degree as to be distended thereby, and be bursten
with the heat that rarifies such moisture;——but in
case the seed be not sown till about the middle or
latter end of August, when it is sown chiefly for
the herbage, the ground being generally cooler,
and not heated like a hot-bed to force up the seed so
quickly, yet moist enough, when driest at that time
of the year, to set the turnip-seed on growing without rain, in such case, especially if rain does not fall
under two days after the turnips are sown, it is probable the seed may have had so much time to swell
gradually in the ground before the rain comes, that
it may be past such danger; and this is the best account I can give of the aforesaid diversity.

Id. and of   As for the above reasons turnip-seed is subject
other seeds. either to be malted, or to corrupt, it may not be
improper to add here, that the same reasons may
hold for the same effect in many other seeds, as the
medic-grass, the vetch, &c.——which the Rei rusticæ

ticæ scriptores order to be soon covered, because
they are soon corrupted ; for whether a hasty rain
may come suddenly on them as they lie above ground
before they can be harrowed in, or they lie on the
ground exposed to the scorching sun before they are
covered, it seems in both cases, for the same reason,
they may either be malted by the scorching heat
of the day, and the giving damps of the night, or,
being first scalded by the sun, and a sudden rain
coming on them whilst above ground, they may imbibe the moisture the faster, and so burst with a plethory, and this more likely than if they were first
covered, or than after they have lain wet in the
ground, because, in the first case, the too much wet
they receive as they lie above ground carrying not
so much of spirit, or vegetable juices, or volatile
salts of the earth along with the water, the nib, or
germen is not so much impregnated therewith, as to
be pushed forward into the act of vegetation, but
the nib or plant of the seed is swelled, and drowned,
and bursts in the vessels by receiving too much water without a spirit sufficient to actuate and protrude
the vegetable parts, &c.——In the second case, the
seed lying on the ground, if the scorching sun lies on
it, it's vessels, being thereby shrunk, do, on a hasty
rain following, imbibe the moisture to a greater degree than otherwise, and to a bursting ; ——and I
must now acquaint the reader, it has not a little ex-
ercised my thoughts in the reflection what should be
the reason why hop-clover and broad-clover seed
should often come up so partially in the same field,
where the nature of the earth has been the same, the
season the same, and the tillage the same ; yet I
have had some lands in the same field, and that more
than once, where the clover has not come up at all,
or but sparingly, when at the same time it has come
up in another part of the ground very prosperously.
I am not able to account for it otherwise than that

I sus-

I suspect we have sometimes sowed some of the clover-seed, as is usual, after the day's-work of harrowing has been over, in order to cut out work for the horses the next day, and then rain has fallen in the night, or the next day, so as to hinder the harrowing the seed in for a day or two, or sun-shiny, or windy weather has come, so as to dry the seed, and we have neglected to heal it with the harrows next day, other business intervening, and so the seed has perished. I must confess I cannot advance this beyond a probable hypothesis for want of having kept a diary of the fact, therefore leave the reader to make the best he can of the hint I give.——— [f] Pliny says, caution must be used in sowing the medic-clover, which ought to be covered in as soon as sowed, lest it should be burnt up.

Of sowing turnips on a peas-ersh
§. 10. Farmer Miles says, he has often known, where peas have proved rank, so as to have made the ground mellow, that turnips have been sown thereon, as soon as the peas were removed, and harrowed-in without ploughing, and it has had very good success.

Of turnip-seed lying a year in the ground.
§. 11. My gardener affirms, if turnip-seed be dropped, and in digging covered over with earth, he has the next year found such seed fresh and good, and, when the earth was turned back again, it has grown, and produced good turnips.—I asked him how that could be, since it is said, if turnips be sown, and no rain falls in some short time, the seed will die and never come up.—He said, that was true ; for when it lies on the top of the earth, and but just harrowed-in, if nine or ten days hot weather come upon it, it will never come up, but in this it was turned a spade deeper under ground.

The time of houghing.
§. 12. The Newtown-men, who houghed my turnips this year (1707) having made it their business

[f] De medica cavendum, ne aduratur, terrâque protinus integi debet. Plin. lib. 18 fo. 288.

for

for many years to hough turnips, affures me, that it is beft to hough turnips as foon as they have four leaves, that is, as they explain it, the two feed-leaves, and the two fucceeding leaves, provided they are grown big enough to be out of danger of being buried in houghing.

§. *13.* In houghing turnips I fuppofe care ought to be taken to hough thofe up that are deepeft rooted in the earth, and to leave thofe that grow upon, and moft out of the earth, without much regarding their bignefs, inafmuch as they that lie on the ground, and have room to grow, will quickly be the biggeft turnips.

Manner of houghing turnips.

§. 14. A dry feafon is the beft for houghing turnips, becaufe neither the weeds nor the turnips houghed up will be fo apt to grow again.

A dry fea-fon beft for houghing turnips.

§. *15.* I am apt to think the beft way to manage turnips (the feed of which is impatient of growth, and apt to burft in too much wet, as alfo to corrupt, if the ground be fo dry as only to give it a damp, but not wet enough to fet it on growing) is, firft to harrow the ground fine, then to roll it with a roller big enough to break the little clods, and fo to let it lie till the next rain ; then the ground being mellow, to fow the feed, and harrow it in with fhort-tined harrows, which may not open the ground too deep, nor bury the feed ; then roll it again with an one-horfe roller, in order to keep the moifture in the ground as deep as the feed may lie ; for the furface of the ground muft not be dried before the feed can ftrike root, which may be in two days and two nights, and yet the furface of the earth muft be fo fine, and fo lightly compreffed, that the feed may fpear through.—The myftery of the fuccefs or mifcarriage of a crop of turnips confifts in thefe four things, viz. firft in the feed's not lying too deep; fecondly, in it's not lying too wet which it cannot eafily do if har-rowed-in fhallow, for the furface of the earth is foon

Beft way of managing turnip feed.

dry; thirdly, in it's not lying too dry; and fourthly, in it's lying in a fine bed.

Turnips ought, in clay-land, to be but just harrowed in with a bush, as light as may be, that the turnip-root may grow upon the ground; for it will not be able to grow to it's dimensions within the clay-ground, or can it, if it be checked in it's growth by a stiff ground, be sweet, because, for want of room, the exuberancy of it's juice will make it knotty and sticky.

I have often considered the nature of turnips, particularly with relation to the soil of our hilly-country, and do think we are like to be deprived of that benefit others have from turnips, because our ground is so cold and backward in it's production, that we can never expect to sow a crop of turnips after a crop of hot-spur peas; for in the first place hot-spur peas will be late ripe with us, and, if we could rid that crop by the middle of June, yet that is too late to sow turnips with us, on account of the drought that reigns over us at that time, nor would turnips have time enough, in so cold a country as our's is, to grow to perfection.—If we sow in the beginning of May, the turnip will not feed with us the same summer; so that it is plain we cannot have two crops the same summer, but the crop of turnips, which is hazardous, must stand in the room of a crop of corn.—The best way I can propose for a crop of turnips in our country is, to winter-fallow the second or third year's clover-ground, which will be rather too poor to bear a crop of barley without the soil of folding, and then to sow turnips the beginning of May, and if they succeed, you will have all the May-showers to forward them, and time enough, if the first sowing fails, to try again, and, if you should not succeed at last, the ground will be very sufficiently, and excellently well husbanded to plough again, and sow winter-vetches in August: all things considered here is the least loss every way, as I could demonstrate.

§. 16. With

§. 16. With us at Crux-Easton, turnips will be sweeter in white than in our clay-ground, as I have observed in a garden-pot with one part of it clay-land, and the other white down-land : always from the white-land there comes a very sweet turnip, but from the clay-land a rank turnip that the people cannot eat ;—I suppose, if a ground consisted of these two sorts of land, the sheep would lie on the turnips of the white-land. White-land better than clay for turnips, in regard to their sweetness.

But notwithstanding this. January 10th (anno 1698) going to Holt by Burbage I asked a farmer whether white lightish land might not bear turnips, and he said, by no means, it was the worst sort of land of all for them ; the blackish sandy earth, or redish sandy earth were the best.—Another farmer I met with afterwards said the same, and they agreed the best time for sowing them was about St. James's-tide. [Note, if they are sowed earlier in the summer, the sun will ripen them, and bring them on so fast, that they will be apt to run to seed.] Charlock, rape, and turnip-seed are not easily distinguishable, and sheep will eat of the rape-roots as well as of the turnip-roots, and it is of the same nature, and the some sort of land agrees with it ; only the rape-root does not grow so large as the true turnip-root does ; yet many farmers about Burbage buy of it to sow. White-land bad for turnips. Also of rape-roots.

§. 17. Mr. Cooper of Berkshire sowed four acres of turnips last summer (anno 1699) and ploughed them up at spring, and sowed the ground to peas ; and the little dwarfish turnips that were left behind uneaten, notwithstanding his ploughing them up, took root again, and were then in great quantities run to seed, and had much damaged his crop of peas ; but the seed being dropped he intended, after the peas were off, to harrow them in. Turnips, if not clean eaten, may take root again after ploughing.

§. 18. Being in company with Mr. Gouch, a Norfolk gentleman, we discoursed about the turnip-husbandry of Norfolk : I could not find that they Of the han-berry, a distemper among so turnips.

fo much valued the harm the fly did to their turnips, while they were young and tender in the leaf, as they did a diftemper or difeafe that fell on the roots of their turnips, which they called the hanbery, alluding it feems, as he faid, to the like diftemper in a horfe's heel, which was a warty excrefcence, that would fometimes grow to the bignefs of one's fift, and that fome years this diftemper would take whole fields, and, after it began to grow in the turnips, they would never thrive.—No one, he faid, could ever find out the caufe of this difeafe.—I told him, I thought it muft proceed from the egg of a worm or fly that was laid in the turnip, in the place where it had been bit, and the little maggot lay in the hollow place, which, with it's tail continually working circularly, formed the juice of the turnip into a round excrefcence about itfelf, in which it continued growing, like that of the oak-apple [*].

GRASSES.

[*] After blaming the practice of putting a flock of fheep into a large ground of turnips without dividing it, by which they will deftroy as many in a fortnight as would keep them a whole winter, Mr. Tull proceeds to give an account of the three manners of fpending turnips with fheep, which are common to thofe drilled, and to thofe fown in the random way.

The firft manner now in ufe is, to divide the ground of turnips by hurdles, giving them leave to come upon no more at a time than they can eat in one day, and fo advance the hurdles farther into the ground daily, until all be fpent ; but we muft obferve, that they never eat them clean this way, but leave the bottoms and outfides of the turnips they have fcooped in the ground. Thefe bottoms people pull up with iron crooks made for that purpofe ; but their cavities being tainted with urine, dung, and dirt from their feet, tho' the fheep do eat fome of the pieces, they wafte more, and many the crooks leave behind in the earth, and even what they do eat of this tainted food, cannot nourifh them fo well as that which is frefh and cleanly.

The fecond manner is to move the hurdles every day, as in the firft ; but, that the fheep may not tread upon the turnips, they pull them up firft, and then advance the hurdles as far daily as the turnips are pulled up, and no farther: by this means there is not that wafte made as in the other way ; the food is eaten frefh

and

GRASSES.

§. 1. BY my own observation I am sensible, that, as the sort of grass every ground bears (which is best discovered by it's ear or panicle) is a certain indication of the nature of the soil, so by the thinness of the culm, which carries the ear or panicle, and the shortness of the ear or panicle compared to what you may observe it to be in other grounds, you may make a right estimate of the goodness or poverty of any ground carrying such or such a sort of grass; for the reason holds as well in this case as it does in corn; therefore it is very necessary for our husbandman to understand the English pasture, and meadow-grasses. *Grasses indicate the nature and goodness of the soil.*

§. 2. The cow-quake grass, or gramen tremulum, though a very poor and slender grass, is no indication of poor land where it grows; for Mr. Ray *The cow-quake grass*

and clean, and the turnips are pulled up with less labour than their pieces can be.

The third manner is to pull them up, and to carry them into some other ground in a cart or waggon, and there spread them every day on a new place, where the sheep will eat them up clean, both leaf and root. This is done when there is land not far off, which has more need of dung than that where the turnips grow, which perhaps is also too wet for sheep in the winter, and then the turnips will, by the too great moisture and dirt of the soil, spoil the sheep, and, in some soils, give them the rot; yet such ground will bring forth more and larger turnips than dry land, and when they are carried off and eaten on ploughed ground in dry weather, and on green-sword in wet weather, the sheep will thrive much better; and that moist soil, not being trodden by the sheep, will be in much the better order for a crop of corn; and generally, the expence of hurdles and removing them being saved, will more than countervail the labour of carrying off the turnips.—They must always be carried off the ground for cows and oxen, which will be fatted by them, and some hay in the winter.

says,

says, it is the moſt common graſs of any in all the
paſture grounds throughout England, Hoc genus in
paſcuis per totam Angliam vulgatiſſimum eſt : in
omnibus quas unquam luſtravit Cluſius regionibus
prata multis locis veſtit. Fo. 1274.

§. 3. The gramen parvum repens purpureâ ſpicâ,
or ſmall creeping graſs, is no indication of bad
ground, though a very bad graſs : Ray ſays, vol. 2.
fo. 1266. it is very common in paſtures.—It ſeems to
have a great ſweetneſs in it.—The ſame may be ſaid
of the gramen criſtatum, for that alſo abounds every
where in our meadows and paſtures. It is in Engliſh
called ſmooth creſted graſs.

§. 4. As I conceive, it may be laid down for a general rule, that all ſuch plants as are perennial will
bear ſowing as well at autumn, i. e before winter, as at
ſpring, provided they are ſowed early enough to take
good root before winter, the difficulty lying here ;
for they are plants that will endure many winters ;
thus may you ſow rye-graſs, broad-clover, hop-
clover, French-graſs, &c.

I happened to carry out in my dung ſome winnow-
ings of clover-ſeed, and laid them on two ridges of
land where I had ſowed wheat : the clover came up
very thick at harveſt ; but was not ſo rank as the
barley-clover, it being kept down by the wheat.— It
was a very wet, but not a hard froſty winter ; but
from hence I do infer, that clover-ſeed will endure
the winter, nor will it feed the next ſummer, nor
damage the wheat.

§. 5. This day, being the 30th of May (anno
1707) walking in the fields at Mr. Raymond's I obſerved that the ſeed-veſſels, or cups of all the ſeveral
ſorts of graſſes in the meadows, gape in their flowering-time, ſo that the miſtreſs or plume (from whence
the flower ariſes, which is the firſt principle of the
ſeed, and no bigger than the point of a needle) may
eaſily be conceived to be hurt by bad weather, ſuch

as

Small
creeping
graſs and
ſmooth-
creſted
graſs.

Perennial
graſſes may
endure the
winter.

Of the
gaping of
the ſeed-
veſſels.

as blights, mildews, rain, &c. I also obſerved the
ſeed-veſſels of the barley to gape.

I impute the great quantity of graſſes this ſummer, 1705, to the advantage of the great drought
the graſs-flowers had in flowering-time, the farina-
ceous or flowering ſeeds on the ſtamina not having
been waſhed off by rain.

§. 6. Hop-clover and broad-clover graſſes ſeem
to my eye, by their deeper colour the ſecond year
than the firſt, not to be ſo ſweet a food then as in the
firſt year, when they are brighter coloured. *Of the nature of hop
and broad-
clover.*

§. 7. As broad-clover falls off of it's ſweetneſs
after Midſummer (as elſewhere hinted) and will not
then fat ewes and lambs, as natural graſs in a good
paſture will do, ſo I doubt not but all graſſes do
abate of their ſweetneſs and ſpirit at that time of the
year. *Graſſes
abate of
their ſweet-
neſs after
Midſum-
mer.*

§. 8. Varro ſays the medic ſeed ought to be ſowed
in the morning after the dew is off; and no more
ought to be ſowed than can be covered-in by the
harrows the ſame day; for, if not covered, the leaſt
wet may deſtroy it. *Of the
medic ſeed.*

Poſt ſecundam diei horam vel tertiam ſpargendum
eſt, cum jam omnis humor ſole ventove deterſus eſt,
neque amplius projici debet quam quod eodem die
poſſit operiri, nam, ſi non inceſſit, quantulocunque
humore prius quam obruatur corrumpitur.—I believe this ſeed, as well as vetches, and other grain
that come up in the ſhorter time, takes in moiſture
very faſt, and is apt therefore, if not ſowed dry, to
burſt and corrupt. [h]

C 4

§. 9. I

_____

[h] The medic or Luſerne ſo much extolled by ancient writers
had not been long introduced into England, and was very little
known in the time of our author. Mr. Tull's deſcription of it is
as follows. " It's leaves reſemble thoſe of trefoil : it bears a blue
" bloſſom very like to double violets, leaving a pod like a ſcrew,
" which contains the ſeeds about the bigneſs of broad-clover,
" tho' longer and more of the kidney ſhape. It's tap-root pene-
" trates

Hop and
broad-
clover not
natives of
England.

§. 9. I have often fufpected, that the hop-clover and broad-clover we fow was not of Englifh extraction, becaufe it will not laft above two years with us, if mowed, and but three years if we feed it as fparingly as poffible, and fow it in the beft land we have; therefore I thought thefe feeds might have been brought from Flanders, where, as natives, they might laft many years;—but I am now (anno 1707) convinced from Mr. Ray, and from the nature of thofe plants: Mr. Ray, in his Hiftory of Plants, vol. 1. fo. 944, calls the broad-clover we fow—the larger purple meadow trefoil;—and fhews the manifeft differences between it, and our red honeyfuckle, and fays,—it grows in paftures, but lefs frequent than the common purple trefoil, and is alfo fown in fields as food for cattle, and by fome called common clover-grafs: and the fame author, in his Synopfis Stirpium Britannicarum, fo. 194, carries on the comparifon farther, and fays, it is not fo durable as the leffer purple meadow trefoil, nor does it like that fow itfelf.—And of the hop-trefoil, vol. 1. fo. 949. he makes but two forts, and fays, the bigger, which is that we fow, grows in the fields among the hedges, efpecially in gravelly or fandy foils.—I do indeed conceive, that none of thefe trefoils are long-lived, not only becaufe

"trates deeper into the earth than any other vegetable it pro-
"duceth."—He is of opinion however, from fome reafons he there mentions, that there is no hope of making any improvement by planting it in England, in any manner practifed by the antients or moderns, and relates the great expence and pains the Romans were at to raife it; but to thofe, who are defirous of making the experiment, he recommends his new Horfe-hoeing Hufbandry as the only method to obtain it. Mr. Miller calls it an extreme hardy plant, and is pofitive it will fucceed well in England, but feems to agree with Mr. Tull, that it cannot be cultivated here to any good purpofe by the old method of hufbandry; for the rules he lays down for it's culture are all according to Mr. Tull's manner, by the drill, and the hoe-plough. See his directions at large under the article.—Medica.

they

they have tap-roots poorly maintained by fibres (of which those we sow have fewer, and are less nourished by the capillary roots than the others, they being pretty well matted) but also because I find the white honeysuckle, the purple, and the lesser hop-clover to increase and decrease yearly in a manifest manner, according as you improve or impoverish your ground; if you improve it with manure or ashes, you may raise a great quantity of it, I judge, from the seed, but if you mow it, and with-hold your dung, it will die away in two or three years time. — The * white honeysuckle, I think, ought chiefly to be *Dutch managed by manures, where it likes a ground, be- clover. cause it is sweet food, and by it's trayling stalks takes root at the joints, and matts extreamly, and soon over-runs a ground, and is therefore, I believe, the longest liver.

§. 10. The more stony your ground is the more To sow reason to sow clover, because thereby the barley stony land. may be the better raked up; inasmuch as either hop or broad-clover will bear-up the barley from the stones, but rye-grass, it seems, is not serviceable on that account.

§. 11. I find that broad-clover, sowed on strong Broad-clay-land, which is apt to run to sword, is not so clover runs apt to run to grass, if mowed, as when fed; for grass when when it is mowed, the clover-grass runs so rank, that fed than it shades and depresses the natural grass, which it mowed. cannot do when fed; besides, the feeding of cattle brings a soil to it, which encourages the natural grass, but kills the broad-clover; for, where the cow-dung lies, the broad-clover will turn white and rot underneath it, and dunging of sown-grasses, such as saint-foin, instead of enriching them, brings on the natural grass.

§. 12. It seems to me a very great difficulty how Inquiry in-to account for the growing or not growing of why broad-broad-clover, whether sowed in the spring, or at clover often autumn fails.

autumn with a wheat-crop ; for I have often observed some lands in the same ground to fail, where
the nature of the soil has been the same.—On the
utmost reflection I can make, I do conclude, that
sometimes, where fields are sown with wheat and
broad-clover, the clover has failed on account of
the coldness and wetness of the ground, and I make
the same judgment of broad or hop-clover sowed
with oats, especially if sown early in the spring,
when, though the land may not be too cold, neither
in it's own nature, nor through rain, &c. for oats,
yet it may be so for clover-seed.—And though
white-ground in it's own nature be dry and warm,
yet it is hollow and light, and, being also poor, the
cold of the spring often pierces it, and so in such grounds
the hop-clover as often dies as in cold clay-ground.
—And it often happens, that three or four acres in a
large ground may fail by being sowed wetter than
the rest, by the falling of rain, which might put a
stop to the sowing of the oats for two or three days,
and then you may be obliged to sow again before
the ground may be dry enough for the clover-seed,
though it may do well enough for the oats.—Note
therefore for the future to observe more critically
whether this diversity does not hold.—From hence
seems to arise the cause, why broad-clover seldom
succeeds so well with black oats as with white, because they are sowed early, and while the ground is
cold, and therefore the more care ought to be taken.

Of feeding
broad-clo-
ver.
§. 13. The autumn-clover, which shoots up at
the beginning of September, arising from a young
bud, and being full of sap as well as of but a short
length, is easily fed and maintained throughout the
winter, and therefore to be saved by being hayned ;
but the first year's clover, which comes up among
the corn, or the growth of aftermass-clover, being
before autumn grown to a good length, requires too
much nourishment (when nature is withdrawing it's
strength

it's ftrength in order to form and nourifh the buds
of the next fpring) to be maintained during the
winter, and therefore ought to be fed down, becaufe otherwife it would die on the ground.

§. 14. I left a patch of French-grafs for feed, and Caution to
favourgrafs
after brit-
ting.
See §. 27.
it britted much ; I foon eat down the aftermafs, and
hayned it from the middle of Auguft, or the beginning of September, for the next fummer's crop : the
2d of October (anno 1704) I went to fee whether
the brittings came up, or not ; I found they came
up very thick on the ground, with their feed-leaves,
and eftablifhed trefoil leaves, and with farther foboles prepared at the roots for the next year, and I
believed they would do well, not having been fed
otherwife than as above ; for this feeding of the
aftermafs, to eat down the rowet, that the brittings
might grow, did them good. A day or two after I
obferved broad-clover and hop-clover in their feed-
leaves, and their trefoil-leaves, very plentiful from
brittings ; therefore the favouring fuch grounds a
month after britting, and in rains, advifeable.

§. 15. Broad-clover of the firft year, i. e. after Firft year's
clover
makes the
beft early
grafs for
horfes.
the ftubble, is forwarder in it's growth, and fprings
fafter than the fecond year's growth will do ; therefore, if you would have early grafs for your horfes,
a crofs of the firft year's growth is fitteft for them.—
The fibres of the roots of the young clover are more
fpungy than thofe of the fecond year's growth ; the
glands alfo of the former are tenderer, and more
eafily admit of the philtration of the juices through
them than the latter do, and therefore the young
bud fprouts fafter than that of the next year's
growth.

§. 16. Having faid fomething of the great fervice Of broad-
clover of
the fecond
year's
growth for
fatting cat-
tle in the
fpring. Vid.
Fatting of
cattle, §. 17.
of twenty or thirty acres of broad-clover to fupport
great cattle in a dry feafon, in July and Auguft,
when there is more efpecially a ftop to vegetation
for a month or five weeks, I have this fpring (anno
1719)

1719) found such twenty or thirty acres of broad-clover, of the second year's growth, of equal service to what it had been in July and August; for this year my broad-clover supported my great cattle from the middle of April to the middle of May. —— As I found the broad clover of the said grounds beneficial the former year in July and August, so without the same relief this spring my great cattle must have starved; for my fodder-straw was gone by the middle of April, and no rain had fallen for five weeks before, and the wind had been north and easterly for six weeks, so that no grass of any other kind did wag, and yet the twenty acres of broad-clover did from Mid-April to Mid-May maintain twenty-three yearlings, and eight steers of four years growth, besides a great many hogs, and yet the pasture grew on them, and run more and more to a head every day, though early in the spring the sheep had fed it down bare, so that the ground was not hayned till the beginning of April, and the wind, as well as drought, opposed the growth of the grass.

Of broad-clover, it's use.

§. 17. Amongst the many advantages of sowing broad-clover one is, that it will grow during the fore-part of the winter, and will support a few fatting-sheep, giving them a little hay with it, and without the grass being injured by them, provided you keep only a few in a large extent of ground, that they may not be forced to bite too close ; whereas hop-clover will make no such advances in the winter months as to serve such an end or purpose : this is a good conveniency to a country gentleman, who would fat his own mutton in the winter.

Broad-clover loves moist ground.

§. 18. As I remember, Ray says, that the true broad-clover grows wild in moist fat meadows; therefore it is no wonder that it should succeed well when sowed in moist, spewy, and springy cold arable. —— At Holt there is so cold and springy a clay, that

that the farmers used not to sow it, either to barley,
oats, or peas, and would but now and then clap in a
few beans; but farmer Isles (before, or about the
year 1716) sowed it to broad-clover, and it got a
very thick swarth, and carried a deep green colour,
and yet the ground was not laid round, but was
laid down flat.

Farmer Lavington of Wiltshire was of opinion, *Id. black,*
that a black, sandy, mellow land was the best ground *sandy, mel-*
for broad-clover, and that the old broad-clover hay *low land.*
was as good as old meadow hay, only in foddering
the leaves of the clover were apt to fall off, and so it
made more waste than the other.———Mr. Raymond
said, the broad-clover hay was so luscious, that neither sheep nor cows liked it so well as common meadow hay;---but farmer Lavington replied, he found
not but that with change they liked it as well as the
best hay.

§. 19. It often happens, that, when dry springs *Of clover*
and summers follow after the sowing of clover-gras- *in dry*
ses, they will come up in a blade, and die away *springs.*
again without any sign of a blade appearing at harvest, and yet about that time on the following summer a thick blade shall appear above ground, and
produce a good crop: this happens when the blade
only was killed by the drought; but the root had
escaped, and so sprung up again when rain came.---
When the blade appears in the spring, tho' it dies
away again, you may have hopes of it's reviving,
but, if it never appeared, there can be no hopes at
all.

§. 20. A Gloucestershire gentleman shewed me *Sickly clo*
his broad-clover, and said, some part of it had been *ver should*
dunged, and was the better for it;---but, when I had *be fed,*
examined it, I found the land to be of a wet, cold *healthy*
nature, and I suspected that most part of that which *mowed.*
was not dunged was killed by the wet, and I believed much of the other was killed by the dung; but
it

it is true, so much of it as escaped grew the thicker
and ranker for it, being supported by the dung, as
by a cordial, against the wet. This broad-clover
turned yellow ; therefore, if it did not recover it's
colour, especially if it put forth fresh buds at the
root, I thought he should feed it down, though if it
recovered of it's sickly look, it ought to be mowed.

§. 21. I have heard say, that broad-clover would
not come again where the cows had dunged, and I
do believe it, especially where it falls broad on the
grass ; for I have turned up such cow-dung, and
found the broad-clover under it perfectly whitened,
and rotted by the dung, which roots I suppose were
forced by the dung in such a manner as thereby to
be killed, as it fares with kitchen-plants.

§. 22. November the 5th (anno 1703) I cut up
several roots of broad-clover, and found the top of
the root divide itself into many tufts, as the French-
grass root does, through the center of which tufts
the new soboles are formed, and issue out ; I found
at this time of the year most of the soboles formed
for the next year grown enough to be bit off by the
sheep, which I conclude must put nature very backward, and cause her to form another centrical bud
within the foldings of that bit off ; therefore great
favour ought to be shown to such grasses at this time
of the year ; —— but as for rye-grass, and other such-
like grasses, though their roots divide themselves into tufts, from the center of which also, as through a
sheath, the new spires of grass spring up, yet it is
but of one continued spring of grass, not made up
of dissimilar parts, and so it has no leafy head to be
taken off, to so great damage as the French-grass
has ; but being bit off, it has similar succedaneous
parts, which carry on it's growth, and so winter-

feeding does not hurt it.

§. 23. My men were fallowing up a field that had
been two years sowed to broad-clover : I wondered

to

to fee fuch abundance of flender carrotty-roots turned up by the plough, and ftaring an-end; I plucked at them and drew fome of them up, and found
they were the broad-clover roots; I meafured them,
and found moft of them to be eleven inches long in
the tap-root: it is evident from hence of what confequence the depth and ftrength of the foil is as well
to broad-clover roots as to carrots and parfnips, and
to hop-clover too; for quickly after I dug up a hop-
clover root of two years growth; it was in pretty
good ftrong ground, and I found it to be in length
about fix inches, and very thick, when compared
with a root or two of the fame year's growth; I
pulled another root of hop-clover, in a piece of
white-land, in the fame ground, but it was very
flender and weak compared with the other, and not
fo long.——From hence it is plain, as has been before obferved, that in good land the clover is neither
hurt by the fun, nor tore up by the cattle, as it is in
poor land: it is alfo apparent, from the deep penetrating of it's tap-roots, how neceffary it is their
mold fhould be made fine and eafy to them when
they are fown. I alfo examined the rye-grafs, and
I found it confifted of an innumerable number of
fhort hairy capillary roots, and confequently feeds
on the fat furface of the ground, and therefore at
Midfummer, when ground is burning, it foonelt
burns, and is beft and chiefeft in the fpring, and at
autumn; nor need ground be fo fine, nor fo deep,
nor fo rich for it, as for either French-grafs or clover. Rye-grafs improves for a year or two, or
three years; whereas the clover dies away, and dif-
improves the furface of the land, tho' indeed it improves yearly by pafturing of cattle, by the heat of
the fun, and by the moifture of both rain and dew.

§. 24. The flourifhing condition of plants is no
argument for the agreement of the ground with
them,

The good
condition
of the plant
no argu-
ment that
ground is
proper to
perfect the
feed.

them, in case the seed of such plants be the fruit for
sake of which they were sown; or, as before observed, the plant is the hardiest part, and will often flourish in a soil much too cold to bring the seed of it to
perfection; thus I can have rank barley-straw, and
rank broad-clover grass on my clay-grounds, where
the seed of each will be cold and thin, nor will they
come to due perfection.

Id. and in-
ferences. It is plain from the reasons aforesaid, that the
seed-part of the seed is the tenderest part of it, and
that the plant, or herbaceous part of the seed, is the
hardiest part of it; so that one need not be so very
curious in changing the seed of any grain, tho'
somewhat degenerated, when you sow not to produce seed, but only to raise the grassy or herbaceous
part of the plant. Therefore what gore or winter-
vetches, tills, or clover-grass you may sow only for
fodder for cattle will do very well from seed of
your own growth, taking this caution, that every
year you buy new seed for what you intend to let
run to seed, and wherewithal to sow your crops the
succeeding year; except indeed you raise seed of
winter-vetches of your own saving, it is impossible,
if you sow a great quantity of them, to procure seed
time enough to sow so early as that grain requires to
be sown; so remiss are farmers in threshing out their
winter-vetches for the market.

Aftermass
of broad-
clover bad
hay in the
hill coun-
try. §. 25. Our Hampshire hill-country is so cold,
that the broad-clover aftermass ripens very indif-
ferently, and the juices of it are very cold and sour;
so that if the hay made of it sods a little in the wet,
though housed afterwards never so dry, it becomes
tasteless: this I had experience of in the year 1711;
when I had such hay that had taken wet, but was
recked very dry, and came out in good order; yet
the cow-beasts would not eat it for change so well as
straw, but made waste of it; and the calves would
not

not touch it; yet I could see nothing more than ordinary in it, but that it had lost it's colour and smell, but was neither wet nor finnowy.

§. 26. I have observed, that if a summer proves dry, hop-clover will not hold above one year; either the sheep, feeding it close, pull it up by the roots, or else the root not striking deep has no shade, and so is burnt up by the sun. — But I have a great presumption, that that evil would be remedied, if we laid our grounds down in good heart to hop-clover; for then the root would strike deep, and would neither be injured by feeding at stubble-time, nor by the heat of the sun in summer.

Hop-clover, it the summer proves dry, lasts but one year.

§. 27. Mr. Townsend of Caln, in Wilts, tells me, that thereabouts they make great advantage of ploughing the aftermass of the broad-clover into the ground the second year, and then sowing wheat on it:—they roll it down, he says, and some, who have sheep, tread it down before they plough on it.

Management of broad-clover in Wilts.

§. 28. The extraordinary fineness of the wool, about All-cannons in Wiltshire, is imputed to the richness of their arable land, which bearing continual ploughing, the grass that springs up in the fallows is thereby always young and tender, as proceeding from annual seeds, not from old roots: it holds as a general rule in grasses of all sorts, that the younger the root the sweeter the grass. So broad-clover, and hop-clover, and rye-grass too, are much sweeter the first year than the second; it seems therefore to be good husbandry in the hill country of Hampshire to plough-in the second year's broad and hop-clover, because, as it is coarser the second year than the first, so it must be very coarse feed in the hill-country, where it is often four the first year.

The younger the root the sweeter the grass.

§. 29. It seems to me, that in the vale, where land is good, and lies warm, and brings the broad-clover forward, and where they sow wheat late (the latter end of October, or after) they may plough-in the

Of ploughing-in clover in the vale and hill-country.

the broad-clover pretty early in the spring, viz. by
the middle of May, it having been hayned up early
for that purpose; for by that time there may be a
good burden, being ploughed-in, to improve the
ground with, and there will be time enough to sow
it, either on the second, or on the third earth; for
the clover will have time to rot by Michaelmass;
but in the hill-country, where both the land and the
air are cold, and consequently cannot bring the
broad-clover forward to a good head early enough
in the spring, and where we sow wheat very early
(in August, or the beginning of September) I do
not see how we can have a burden of broad-clover
on the ground early enough in the spring to have
time, when ploughed-in, to rot, and to give the
ground any more than one earth before seed-time.
—Therefore, in the hill-country, I rather advise to
feed the broad-clover early in the spring, and then
hayn it up, so that a good burden may be ploughed-in by the latter end of July, taking a dry time for
doing it, in order to sow wheat on the back of it,
i. e. on one earth in August, or by the middle of
September at fartheft.

§. 30. Amongst other advantages of sowing broad-
clover beyond hop-clover one is, that, as I have
observed, few thistles, docks, or other trumpery of
weeds come up in my broad-clover grounds, in
comparison of what come up in the grounds sown
with hop-clover; for the broad-clover spreading,
and covering the ground so much more than hop-
clover does, it kills the weeds; it also grows taller
than hop-clover, and runs up to a good height the
second year's growth, which hop-clover does not,
and is a great means to suppress weeds. The
growth of weeds in my hop-clover cannot be imputed to the foulness of the feed, because I used milled-
feed.

Advantage of broad-clover beyond hop-clover.

§. 31. Mr.

§. 31. Mr. Herrick affured me from experience, that, if, on their rich land in Leicefterfhire, broad-clover was fown, when the ground was intended to be laid down for a long time to natural grafs, the broad-clover would, when it decayed, prevent the ground from fwording to natural grafs.—This may very well be in fuch grounds as naturally run to grafs, as the rich lands of Leicefterfhire do, inafmuch as the broad-clover may deftroy the very roots of the natural grafs, and kill the feedlings that may lie in the ground, and would come up, were they not checked.

Broad clover bad in land laid down to grafs in Leicefterfhire.

§. 32. The poorer the ground is the clofer you ought to feed down the fown-graffes: broad-clover and hop-clover ought to be fed down almoft clofe to the root; for, if either broad-clover, or hop clover grafs be fown on white-land, or be out of proof by the poverty of the ground, and you let them run but to a full-grown leaf, it will be of a foliomort colour, and fpeckled with black fpecks, which is a blight occafioned by the weaknefs of the ground, and fuch graffes, efpecially hop-clover, will eat bitter, and therefore the grafs of fuch ground fhould be always kept fed down clofe with fheep; for, if you let it run up high enough for a bite for a cow, no cattle will eat it; fo the rule holds, as well in fown as natural graffes, the poorer the ground is the clofer to feed them down.

The poorer the ground the clofer you muft feed fown grafs.

§. 33 If broad-clover, or hop-clover has a fmall, thin, unfappy leaf, or looks of a foliomort colour, and is out of proof, whatever the nature of the ground be, and tho' generally kind for corn, yet truft not fuch a ground at it's firft breaking up, neither to wheat, peas, nor barley, for it will difappoint you; rather choofe to fow it to vetches, and if they prove well, you may then promife yourfelf a good crop of barley: this I have found by experience to be true.

If clover be thin and fickly when broke up, fow vetches.

D 2

§. 34. If

Hop-clo-
ver after-
mass comes
to nothing,
if sown
with broad-
clover.
Hop-clo-
ver short
lived.

§. 34. If hop-clover and broad-clover be sowed together, and mowed, the hop-clover aftermass will come to nothing; consequently the aftermass of the broad-clover must be thinner.

§. 35. I conclude that the hop-clover common-ly sowed is not long-lived where it grows wild, not above two or three years, as Mr. Ray says, in areno-sis & sabulosis (which I have often observed) be-cause in all sorts of soils that I have known it to be sowed in, as well sandy as gravelly, I never heard that it lived above two or three years.

Hop-clo-
ver prefer-
red to
broad-clo-
ver.
See §. 30.

§. 36. Notwithstanding what I have said of the advantages of broad-clover beyond hop-clover, yet I know many farmers are of opinion that hop-clover is much sweeter feed than broad-clover; and particu-larly one assures me, if a ground be sowed half and half of each, the cattle will never touch broad-clover till the hop-clover is eat quite bare.—He judged the broad-clover to be a sour feed; for, said he, if cattle were put into a field of it, they would pare away the sour grass round the hedges quite to the earth before they would begin on the broad-clover; but he said, the broad-clover hay was much better for either great cattle or sheep than hop-clover hay, which nevertheless was good feed for sheep, if well housed, but the broad-clover hay was full as good as any other hill-country hay.

Caution to
sow twenty
or thirty
acres of
broad clo-
ver for fat-
ting beasts
in the hill-
country.
V. Fatting
of cattle, §.
17.

§. 37. Though I think it answers my purpose, as well as others in the hill-country, to sow hop-clover rather than broad-clover, yet it is very neces-sary for me every year to sow from twenty to thirty acres of broad-clover, to supply me for a short time with grass for my great cattle, when other grasses are either not so forward in the spring as to pasture them, or have been burnt up in a hot summer, and so have expired till they revive in af-termass; for instance, broad-clover may be very useful to usher in the other spring-grasses for a fort-night

night before hop-clover will be high enough to afford a bite for great cattle, and, if you mow the broad-clover, the aftermass will be of great use, when the vigour of the hop-clover is spent, as also that of the natural grasses, which will come in turn after the hop-clover, and will hold till after the hop-clover is gone ; the aftermass of the broad-clover will then fall in turn to support that great stock of cattle maintained hitherto by hop-clover and natural grass, which you could not otherwise have maintained, had you not had such a quantity of broad-clover aftermass, or French-grass aftermass, to receive them till the aftermass of the hill country meadows, or the natural grass pastures, could be of growth enough for that purpose.

§. 38. The farmers are very apt to say, that broad-clover impoverishes land, but hop-clover does not.—This, as it seems to me, must be understood, if they are both mowed ; for then, broad-clover being double the burden, no wonder if thereby the ground be doubly exhausted ; on the other hand, both being fed, it should seem, broad-clover maintaining twice the cattle that hop-clover will, acre for acre, it should doubly improve the ground ; but, to abate of that, it may be objected, that hop-clover being undeniably the sweeter feed consequently makes the richer dung, and therefore, being but half the quantity in burden, yet being fed, may improve ground as much as broad-clover. —Cold clays are not fit however for hop-clover, and it appears to me, that the best barley ground is the best hop-clover ground. *Hop and broad-clover compared, and which most enriches land.*

§. 39. I have observed, according to the forwardness or backwardness of the spring, that about the beginning of May the hop-clover will have run it's length to it's first flowering, and then it begins to be pasture for cows and young beasts, and from thence it continues on flowering, joint by joint, *Hop-clover good feed for beasts till the 9th of June.*

D 3 as

as the neſt of bud-bloſſoms proceed on in growth, ſtill leaving a bloſſom behind on the laſt joint on a ſtalk below, and thus it will continue to do till about the eighth, or, as it did this year (1718) till the ninth of June, about which time it will have compleated it's height, and the topmoſt bloſſoms will then wither and run to ſeed ; all which time, being about ſix weeks, the hop-clover graſs is very hearty for all great cattle, and they will eat it freely till about the 8th or 9th of June, tho' the bloſſoms of the loweſt joint are ſeeded ; ſo long as the ſeeds continue ſoft and green, and do not turn blackiſh, ſo long the ſtalk alſo will retain good ſap ; ſo until this time the hop-clover graſs may be depended on for paſture for all ſorts of great cattle ; ſheep alſo will eat of it thus long very well, and will bite deep of the ſtalk.

Hop-clo-ver ſeed judged of by it's ſmell.

§. 40. [i] It may be known, whether the hop-clover out of huſk is too much kiln-dried or not, as well by it's ſtrong fragrant ſmell as by it's colour and taſte ; for it has a ſtrong rich ſmell, if not overheated.

Hop-clo-ver roots torn out of the ground by winter-feeding with ſheep, and infe-rence.

§. 41. Walking in the hop-clover ground of the ſecond winter's growth on the 26th of January (anno 1702) I obſerved more particularly than I had done before, that not only many hop-clover roots had been drawn out of the ground by the ſheep, and lay without any hold at all, but half the hop-clover tufts alſo were more or leſs drawn out of the ground, ſome for inſtance half out, others not ſo much, but in general they were all of them jogged or looſened, which was occaſioned by the ſheep's being kept hard on them, and often biting in laſt ſummer's and this winter's feeding, but more eſpe-cially in this laſt winter, which proving very wet,

---

[i] Mr. Miller ſays, in the choice of broad-clover ſeed that which is of a bright yellowiſh colour, a little inclining to brown, ſhould be preferred, but the black rejected as good for little.

the

the roots were the more loosened or drawn out;
besides by the great vacancies among the tufts of
the clover, compared with the first thickness they
appeared in after harvest, it was visible vast quantities had perished in the aforesaid manner before the
second winter ; nor can it but stand to reason, that
by their roots being thus shaken, and half drawn out
of the ground, they must be much weakened in
their growth, and kept backward, no less than trees
are that suffer by such loosening at their roots.——
This is therefore a strong inducement to me to think
summer-fatting of sheep more profitable than a win-
ter-breeding stock, whereby the winter charges of
the latter is altogether avoided, and the clover, being winter-hayned for the summer-fatting, four times
the quantity may be expected to be well-grown and
deep-rooted, and, such fatting-sheep being to be
well kept, there will be no danger of their much
injuring the clover in the summer.

§. 42. Mr. Webb of Mountain-farley sowed the
wild white and red broad-clover, or honeysuckle, and it
holds the ground and decays not : he says, it is prac-
tised in Sussex, and that he had his seed from thence.

Of wild white and red broad-clover or honey-suckle. See §. 45.

§. 43. [k] The melilot-leaves are generally nicked
in the edges by some insect that knaws them : Mr.
Bobart and I were looking on a plant of it in his
garden, that was so bit ; —— he said, he never
saw a plant of it but what had it's leaves bit in
that manner.——This cannot always be done by
a worm in the same manner the peas are, for
there were many collateral branches of it at Mr.
Bobart's, which stood a foot and an half high, and
had shot after it was out of the reach of the worm :

Of the melilot—nonsuch.

[k] They, who are desirous of being acquainted with the culture of the melilot-trefoil, or nonsuch, may consult Mr. Miller's
Dictionary, under the article—Melilot.   I believe there was
very little of it sown in the fields in our author's time, nor is it
yet grown common.

quære

quære therefore what insect this must be.—It has also the name of trifolium caballinum in Italy, because horses are particularly fond of it—it seems it is an annual plant.

§. 44. Some will have the rattle-grass to be called louse-wort, because it makes the cattle lousy. Ray, vol. 1. fol. 769. and Synopsis, fol. 162. In pratis sterilioribus.

Of louse-wort.

§. 45. The broad-clover grass, which of late years (anno 1707) had obtained some credit, as a longer living grass than the common broad-clover, and is sown under the name of cow-grass, I find to be the common purple-trefoil, or honeysuckle trefoil, as described by Mr. Ray, vol. 1. fol. 944. distinguished from the great purple meadow-trefoil, which has always hitherto been sowed by the country farmers, and I doubt not but always will; for by experience I find the other not to yield half the burden, nor indeed, in poor ground, such as in our hill-country we commonly lay down to grass, to be a longer liver than the common sort: —but both sorts being natural to some lands, I doubt not but they will continue more years therein than when sown in poor land, or in a soil not so agreeable to the genius of the plant.

Of the honeysuckle trefoil.

§. 46. Mr. Holyday, a considerable clothier in Wiltshire, was giving me an account, in the year 1707, that the Spanish wool was always troubled with a burr, and that, in cleansing some of the foulest of it, there came off more coarse foul wool than ordinary, so that he was tempted to lay it on his meadow-ground, to improve it, which brought forth a strange sort of grass, that had lasted ever since, it being many years ago. It was, he said, a three-leaved grass, and brought forth yellow flowers, and abundance of burrs with seeds in them.—I found this to be one of the annual medics I had in my garden, with burrs for the seed-vessels, and by it's

Of the lesser medic-trefoil, yellow blossomed.

seeding

feeding every year, I suppose, it maintained itself in his ground ; but what I take notice of it for, is this, he assured me, in picking the Spanish fleeces there were none but had more or less of the burrs in them, which is an argument to me, that the Spaniards sow much of this trefoil, it not being a native of their country,. but brought from Persia.——Quære if it may not be a very sweet feed to breed fine wool.—— It seems to me in the leaf to taste sweeter than hop-clover : I went to see this trefoil, and found it to be the lesser medic-trefoil that had small burrs ; —but I since find by the clothiers, that the Spanish wool has been coarser for thirty years last past than formerly, which may be occasioned by their sowing these grasses.

§. 47. Notwithstanding the great character the Rei rusticæ scriptores give of the cytisus, or shrub-trefoil, for food for all sorts of cattle and fowls, and Pliny says,—it is not in danger of being hurt by heat, or hail, or snow, non æstuum, non grandinum, non nivis injuriam expavescit, yet the use of this trefoil is not to be transferred into our clime ; for Mr. Bobart assured me, that the plant will not bear our winters, unless housed in a green-house. *Of the cytisus, or shrub-tre-foil.— Medicago, Miller.*

Columella commending the cytisus for it's great use for cattle and fowl, says, there is no climate in which this shrub will not grow plentifully even in the poorest foil, neque est ulla regio, in qua non possit hujus arbusculæ copia esse vel maxima, etiam macerrimo solo, fol. 187.— It will not, as above noted, endure our winters in England.

§. 48. One of my tenants told me, rye-grass was what they coveted in the Isle of Wight beyond hop-clover ; for, said he, the rye-grass will bear the winter, and keep to a good head, which the clover will not do : I have had, added he, an acre and a half of rye-grass upon tolerable good ground, which I have hayned up from Michaelmass until within a week *Rye-grass.*

week of Candlemafs, and from thence to the middle of April it has kept fifteen ewes and fifteen lambs.

Though I difapprove of dunging French-grafs and clover, for reafons noted before, yet it is proper to dung rye-grafs ; for it makes the roots of that tillow, and mat on the ground, to the utter deftruction and fuppreffion of the couch-grafs.

Mr. Ray fays of the gramen foliaceum, or rye-grafs ; it is a perennial plant, with jointed roots, and propagates itfelf by fending forth fibres from it's joints, fol. 1263.—— And becaufe it's roots do farther propagate, I doubt not but it may be kept alive, by dunging it, many years longer than we ufually do, or by refrefhing it with foil, when after two or three years it begins to decay.

As rye-grafs does not improve land as other graffes do, fo it may be prefumed, if Dr. Woodward's doctrine be true, the rye-grafs roots, being very like the roots of oats, barley, and wheat, may feed on the fame falts of the earth that the roots of thofe grains do, and that the orifices of the rye-grafs roots confift of the fame angles with thofe of the faid grains.

Rye-grafs generally lafts but three years : Mr. Lawrence, near Upcern, Dorfet, told me, that he had as much rye-grafs feed on eighteen acres of land as was worth twenty pound, and after the feed was threfhed out, the hay was better than oat-ftraw fodder.—I faw a reek of it in his backfide, and an oat-ftraw reek, which were both laid open to the cattle, and they would not touch the ftraw, but had made fuch an hole into the rye-grafs hay-reek, that it was ready to fall.—He faid, if it was mowed green, and not for the lucre of the feed, it was excellent good for cattle.—He fells the feed for twenty-two pence, and two fhillings per bufhel; and fows three bufhels on an acre.

Mr.

Mr. Oxenbridge ſhewed me ſome of his rye-graſs hay, and I thought it was very fine hay ; he looked on it, he ſaid, as his choiceſt fodder for his ſheep : —he mowed it when in the flower.

Farmer Ryalls of Dorſetſhire affirmed, he had known experienc'd farmers ſay, that the very hee-graſs, after mowing the rye-graſs the ſame year it was ſowed, being ploughed-in, was as good as dunging, and would pay for the ſeed.

I find all farmers from experience do agree, that notwithſtanding rye-graſs will maintain as many cattle on an acre as hop-clover will do, yet it does not improve land for corn like hop-clover.—This muſt proceed from one of the following two reaſons, or partly from them both : viz. Firſt, the rye-graſs conſiſting of a multitude of matty fibres, which run on the ſurface of the ground, they gird and hold it ſo together, that when ploughed, they cannot be diſentangled from it's earth, which cannot therefore be made to work fine.—Secondly, the fibrous thready roots of rye-graſs having great likeneſs to thoſe of wheat and barley, as alſo the ſpiry graſs-leaf being much like the blade of thoſe grains, it may well be ſuſpected, that the rye-graſs roots ſuck ſimilar juices from the earth with the roots of thoſe grains, and ſo they may rob each other of their ſpe-cific nouriſhment proper to them ; whereas, the roots of hop and broad-clover being like a carrot, and their leaves different from the blade of corn, they neither gird the earth together, nor feed on the ſame juices the aforeſaid grains are believed to do ; for in all reſpects otherwiſe rye-graſs ſhould more improve the ground than hop-clover, not on-ly as it feeds more cattle, but alſo as it keeps down all weeds, which hop-clover does not.

A farther reaſon why rye-graſs is not ſo natural to produce a good crop of corn as clover is, may be, becauſe rye-graſs and darnel are by many her-
baliſts

balifts ranged, as baftard forts of corn, amongft the claffes of corn : the roots of rye-grafs are fweet and juicy, promifing nothing of ftrong concoctedfalts ; whereas the roots of clover are very hot and tart, which argues that they have drawn to them and digefted many nitrous and falt parts, which, when rotten in the earth, may well impregnate it. — Quære about the roots of peas-halm, and of the halm of vetches ; for I much fufpect thofe roots to communicate to the earth the fame benefit that clover-roots do, and a greater benefit than only by mellowing it.

Of mowing clofe to the ground for the fake of the feed. §. 49. All plants with piked flowers, as faintfoin, and which carry a gradation of flowers one above another, on the fame fpike, put forth the lowermoft bloffoms on the fame fpike firft, which go into feed in the fame order, till at laft the topmoft buds flower and feed ; and of plants which bear many flowers on a gradation of joints, as the pea, hop-clover, common crow-foot daify of the field, &c. I obferve the lowermoft bloffoms on the joints blow and feed firft ; and I do fufpect, that all thofe plants which carry their bloffoms on in a fucceffive gradation of joints, have thofe feries of joints all at firft included in a huddle in one fmall pod ; at leaft it has been fo with many, as I have obferved, and as before noted of the pea ; which clufter of bloffoms ftill advance upwards, leaving a joint bearing bloffoms behind, and fo on : thus it is in hopclover ; on which when it is in flower, the cattle for a fhort fpace of time feed but fparingly, and on the uppermoft parts, and topmoft flowers, becaufe, the flowers on the lowermoft joints being run to feed, the feeds eat bitter, which the cattle diflike. — From hence it is obvious, that fuch grafs mowed for feed ought to be mowed clofe to the ground, and the ftones to be well rolled down ; elfe the beft of the feed, growing on the lowermoft joints, will be loft,

§. 50. It

§. 50. [1] It is evident, that where French-grass is sown, on those parts of each field, where the earth is weak, shallow, and poor, there the French-grass will first decay.

§. 51. Being

[1] Mr. Miller says, this plant, if sown upon a dry, gravelly, or chalky soil, will continue eighteen or twenty years; but, if it be sown upon a deep, light, moist soil, the roots will run down into the ground; and in a wet season the moisture will rot the roots, so that it seldom lasts above two years in such places. This is esteemed one of the best sorts of fodder for most cattle, and is a great improvement to shallow chalky hills, upon which it succeeds better than in any other soil, and will continue many years. Mr. Lisle and Mr. Tull both agree with Mr. Miller in regard to it's being damaged by wet, but Mr. Tull will by no means allow that a shallow chalky soil is most proper for it. As he has wrote very largely on the culture of this plant, I imagine the following extract from his work may be agreeable to the reader.

EXTRACT from Mr. Tull, chap. 12. of St. Foin, or Sain Foin,—Sanum fœnum, Sanctum fœnum, or French-grass.

There is a vulgar opinion, that St. Foin will not succeed on any land, where there is not an under stratum of stone or chalk, to stop the roots from running deep; else, they say, the plants spend themselves in the roots only, and cannot thrive in those parts of them which are above the ground. — I am almost ashamed to give an answer to this.—'Tis certain that every plant is nourished from it's roots (as an animal is by his guts) and the more and larger roots it has, the more nourishment it receives, and prospers in proportion to it. St. Foin always succeeds where it's roots run deep, and, when it does not succeed, it never lives to have long roots; neither can there ever be found a plant of it, that lives so long as to root deep in a soil that is improper for it.—An under stratum of very strong clay, or other earth, which holds water, makes a soil improper for it; because the water kills the root, and never suffers it to grow to perfection. If there be springs near (or within several feet of) the surface of the soil, St. Foin will die therein in winter, even after it has been vigorous in the first summer, and also after it hath produced a great crop in the second summer.—The lighter the land the seed will come up from the greater depth, but the most secure way is, not to suffer it to be covered deep in any land, for the heads (or kernels when swoln) are so large, and the necks

(o1

§. 51. Being at Holt, I was told by Mr. Bailey and Thomas Miles (the winter having been exceeding wet) that the wet winter had killed abundance of French-grafs round about the country, especially where

(or strings that pafs from the hufks to the heads) fo weak, that, if they lie much more than half an inch deep, they are not able to rife thro' the incumbent mold ; or, if they are not covered, they will be malted [a] .——The worft feafons to plant it are the beginning of winter and in drought of fummer : the beft feafon is early in the fpring.——It is the ftronger when planted alone, and when no other crop is fown with it : the worft crop that can be fown with it is clover or rye-grafs ; barley or oats continue but a little while to rob it ; but the other artificial graffes rob it for a year or two.——The qualities following are figns by which to choofe good feed— viz. the hufk of a bright colour, the kernel plump, of a light grey or blue colour, or fometimes of a fhining black ; —— yet the feed may be good, tho' the hufk is of a dark colour, if that is caufed by it's receiving rain in the field, and not by heating in a heap, or in the mow ; and, if you cut the kernel off in the middle, crofs-ways, and find the infide of a greenifh frefh colour, it is furely good ; but, if of a yellowifh colour, and friable about the navel, and thin, or pitted, thefe are marks of bad feed. It's manure is foot, peat-afh, or coal-afh. The firft winter is the time to lay it on, after the crop of corn is off.—[Note, other good farmers there are, who fay no afhes or manure fhould be laid on St. Foin till it has been fowed two years, for it will force it too much, and the crop will not laft fo many years if afhes be fowed as Mr. Tull directs.] — Be fure to fuffer no cattle to come on the young St. Foin the firft winter, after the corn is cut that grows amongft it ; their very feet would injure it, by treading the ground hard, as well as their mouths by cropping it : nor let any fheep come at it, even in the following fummer and winter.—St. Foin is more profitable either for hay or feed than meadow grafs, for the latter, if not cut in good weather, is fpoiled, and yet it muft be cut in it's proper feafon, which is but one, whereas there are four feafons for cutting St. Foin, and if you are difappointed in the firft of thefe, you may ftay till the fecond, and fo on ; befides, the hilly ground whereon St. Foin is chiefly planted, is more commodious for drying the hay, has lefs of the morning and evening

[a] Mr. Lifle differs from him in this, and advifes, if the ground work light and fine, to fow St. Foin under furrow. See—Of fowing St. Foin.

dews

where it was near the clay,—and I found it to be
ſo ; therefore neither cold nor wet land are .proper
for French-graſs.

§. 52. Being

dews than the low meadows. The four times for cutting it are,
—firſt, before bloſſoming,—ſecondly, when in flower,—thirdly,
when the bloſſoms are off,—and fourthly, when the ſeed is ripe.
He commends the firſt of theſe, which he calls virgin hay,
much before the others for keeping working horſes in good
caſe, or fatting ſheep in winter, and prefers it even to beans,
peas, and oats. He adds however that this ſort of hay is not
to be had from poor ground, that is not cultivated, or manured
with peat-aſhes, ſoot, or the like.—The ſecond, or that which
is cut in it's flower, according to the moſt common practice,
tho' inferior to the firſt, yet far exceeds all other kinds of hay
commonly known in England.—The third, which is cut when
the bloſſom is gone or going off, tho' greater in bulk, is much
leſs valuable than the former two, and, after theſe three, you
have a fourth chance for good weather when the ſeed is ripe.

To make St. Foin hay.——A day or two after it is cut,
when dry on the upper ſide, turn the ſwarths two and two together, oppoſite ways, and the ground will require leſs raking.
Make them up into little cocks the ſame day they are turned, if
conveniently you can ; for when it is in cock, a leſs part of it
will be expoſed to the injuries of the weather than when in
ſwarth.——Dew, being of a nitrous penetrating nature, enters
the pores of thoſe plants it reaches, and during the night poſ-
ſeſſes the room from whence ſome part of the juices is dried out :
thus it intimately mixes with the remaining ſap, and when the
dew is again exhaled, it carries up moſt of the vegetable ſpirits
along with it, which might have been there fixed, had they not
been taken away in that ſubtle vehicle. If St. Foin be ſpread
very thin upon the ground, and ſo remain for a week in hot
weather, the ſun and dew will exhauſt all it's juices, and leave
it no more virtue than is in ſtraw. Therefore it is beſt to keep
as much of our hay as we can from being expoſed to the dews,
while it is in making, and we have the better opportunity of
doing it in this than in natural hay, becauſe we may more ſafe-
ly make it in larger cocks, for St. Foin cocks (tho' twice as big
as cocks of natural hay) by the leſs flexibility of the ſtalk admitting the air, will remain longer without fermenting.——
When the firſt cocks have ſtood one night, ſpread two, three,
or more together in a freſh place, and, after an hour or two,
turn them, and make that number up into one cock ; but
when the weather is doubtful, let not the cocks be thrown or
ſpread, but inlarge them, by ſhaking ſeveral of them into one,
and

§. 52. Being at Mr. Jeremy Horton's in Wiltshire, there were there Mr. Anthony Methwin and
Mr. Holdway, clothiers, but experienced farmers,
and I afked them if they dunged their French-grafs ;
they

and thus hollowing them to let in the air, continue increafing
their bulk, and diminifhing their number daily, until they be
fufficiently dry to be carried to the reek. The beft hay I ever
knew in England, was of St. Foin, made without fpreading,
or the fuh's fhining on it. This way, tho' it be longer ere
finifhed, is done with lefs labour than the other.——If St.
Foin be laid up pretty green, in fmall round reeks, with a large
bafket drawn up the middle, to leave a vent-hole for the moifture
to tranfpire, it will take no damage. Thefe reeks, as foon
as the heating is over, ought to be thatched ; and all St. Foin
reeks, that are made when the hay is full dried in the cocks,
ought to be thatched immediately after the making them.

The feed is good for provender, and three bufhels of it, fome
fay, will go as far in nourifhing horfes, as four bufhels of oats.
All cattle are greedy of it ; I have known hogs made very good
pork with it, but whether it will fat them well for bacon, I
have had no trial.—— The threfhed hay alfo, when not damaged by wet, has been found more nourifhing to horfes than coarfe
water meadow hay, and, when cut fmall by an engine, is much
better food for cattle than chaff or corn. —— It requires fome experience to know the proper degrees of ripenefs, at which the
feeded St. Foin fhould be cut, for the feed is never all ripe together, and, if we fhould defer cutting till the top feeds are
quite ripe, the lower, which are the beft, would fhed, and be
loft. —— The beft time to cut is, when the greateft part of
the feed is well filled ; the firft-blown ripe, and the laft-blown
beginning to be full.——The colour of the kernel is grey or
blueifh when ripe, and the hufk, that contains it, is of a brown-
ifh hue, but both of them continue perfectly green for fome time
after full grown, and, if cut in this green plight, will ripen afterwards, have as good a colour, and be as good in all refpects as that ripened before cutting, add to which, there will
be lefs danger of it's fhedding.

St. Foin feed fhould not be cut in the heat of the day, while
the fun fhines out ; for then much, even of the unripe feed,
will fhed in mowing : therefore, in very hot weather, the
mowers fhould begin to work very early in the morning, or
rather in the night ; and, when they perceive the feed to fhatter,
leave off, and reft till toward the evening. After cutting we
muft obferve the fame rule as in mowing it, viz. not to make
this hay while the fun fhines. —— Sometimes it may, if the feed
be

they said, by no means; Mr. Holdway said, they looked on it in Gloucestershire, that dung did little good to French-grass, the dung chiefly encouraging bennet-grass, and couch-grass.—Mr. Methwin said,

be pretty near ripe, be cocked immediately after the scythe : or, if the swarths must be turned, let it be done while they are moist, not two together, as in the other hay aforementioned. If the swarth be turned with the rake's handle, 'tis best to raise up the ears first, and let the stub-side rest on the ground in turning ; but, if it be done by the rake's teeth, then let them take hold on the stub-side, the ears bearing on the ground in turning over. It is commonly rain that occasions the swarths to want turning, or otherwise, if the swarths are not very great, we never turn them at all ; because the sun or wind will quickly dry them.——Sometimes, when we design to thresh in the field, we make no cocks at all, and but only just separate the swarths in the dew of the morning, dividing them into parts of about two feet in each part. By this means the St. Foin is sooner dried than when it lies thicker, as it must do, if made into cocks : but, if it be cocked at all, the sooner it is made into cocks the better ; because, if the swarths be dry, much of the seed will be lost in separating them, the ears being entangled together : when moist the seed sticks fast to the ear ; but, when dry, will drop out with the least touch or shaking.

Of threshing St. Foin there are two ways, the one, in the heat of the day, while the sun shines, in the field, the other in the barn. Of the former, the best manner is, to have a large sheet pegged down to the ground, for two men to thresh on. Two persons carry a small sheet, and lay it down close to a large cock, and with two sticks, thrust under the bottom of it, gently turn it over, or lift it up upon the sheet, and carry, and throw it on the great sheet ; but, when the cocks are small, they carry several at once, thrown upon the little sheet carefully with forks ; those which are near they carry to the threshers with the forks only, as fast as it is threshed, one person stands to take away the hay, and lay it into a heap, and sometimes a boy stands upon it, to make it into a small reek of about a load. As often as the great sheet is full, they riddle it thro' a large sieve to separate the seed and chaff from the broken stalks, and put it into sacks to be carried into the barn to be winnowed. Two threshers will employ two of these little sheets, and four persons in bringing to them, and when the cocks near them are threshed, they remove the threshing sheet to another place.——The sooner these threshed cocks are removed, and made into bigger

ſaid, he would not believe Mr. Holdway, who had
formerly told him ſo, but dunged ſome of his
French-graſs, and found that the dung nouriſhed a
natural graſs, and cauſed it to come up upon the
ſurface

reeks, the better; and, unleſs they be thatched, the rain will
run a great way into them, and ſpoil the hay; but they may be
thatched with the hay itſelf, if there be not ſtraw convenient for
it.

The better the ſeed eſcapes the wet in the field, the ſooner it's
own ſpirits will ſpoil it in the granary barn. Seed threſhed in
the field, without being ever wetted, if immediately winnowed,
and a ſingle buſhel laid in a heap, or put into a ſack, will in a
few days ferment to ſuch a degree, that it will loſe it's vegetative
quality; the larger the heap the worſe; but I have known it
lie a fortnight in ſwarth, till the wet weather has turned the
huſks quite black: then threſhed in the field, and immediately
put into larger veſſels, holding about twenty buſhels each, and
this ſeed has, by being often wet and often dry, been ſo exhauſted of it's fiery ſpirits, that it remained cool in the veſſels,
without ever fermenting in the leaſt; and then it grew as well
as any did that was ever planted. To prevent the fermentation
abovementioned many ſpread it on a malt-floor, turning it often,
or, when the quantity is ſmall, upon a barn-floor, but much of
it is ſpoiled even this way; for it will heat, tho' it be ſpread but
an handful thick, and they never ſpread it thinner: beſides,
they may miſs ſome hours of the right times of turning it, for it
muſt be done very often; it ſhould be ſtirred in the night as well
as the day, until the heating be over; and yet, do what they can,
it never will keep it's colour ſo bright, as that, which is well
houſed, well dried, and threſhed in the winter; for in the barn
the ſtalks keep it hollow; there are few ears or ſeeds that touch
one another, and the ſpirits have room to fly off by degrees, the
air entering to receive them.———The only way I have found to
imitate and equal this, is to winnow it from the ſheet; then lay
a layer of wheat-ſtraw (or, if that be wanting, of very dry
threſhed hay); then ſpread thereon a thin layer of ſeed, and thus
layer upon layer, ſix or ſeven feet high, and as much in breadth,
then begin another ſtack; let there be ſtraw enough, and do not
tread on the ſtacks. By this means the ſeed mixing with the
ſtraw will be kept cool, and come out in the ſpring with as
green a colour as when it was put in, and not one ſeed of a
thouſand will fail to grow when planted. I have had above
one hundred quarters of clean ſeed thus managed in one bay of
a ſmall barn. We do not ſtay to winnow it clean before we lay
it

surface of the ground, but it did not enrich the French-grass;—nor does it stand to reason it should, the faint-foin root running down so deep into the ground that dung cannot reach it; yet it will make the stalks a little prouder, but will neither make the root to tillow, nor matt.

§. 53 On the second of November (anno 1703) I looked into my French-grass, to see the method of it's progression in it's growth; I pulled up some roots of it, and washed them, and I saw plainly, that at the top the root divided itself into many tufted branches, which tufts carried a few branches or grassy divisions, which closed together, all folding, at the bottom of the tuft, one within another: in the center of these tufts were the soboles or mistresses wrapped up by the said folding branches, which soboles were designed for the spring-shoot. In some

Of the growth of French-grass, and caution not to feed it after August.

it up in straw; but only pass it thro' a large sieve, and with the van blow out the chaff, and winnow it clean in the spring. —— This field-threshing requires extraordinary fine sun-shiny weather, and therefore, in most summers, it is but a small part of the day in which the seed can be threshed clean out. They, who have but a little quantity, carry it into a barn early in the morning, or even in the night, while the dew is on it; for then the seed sticks fast to the ear: as it dries, they thresh it out, and if they cure it well, have thus sometimes good seed, but generally the hay is spoiled.—There are two misfortunes that attend carrying it in without threshing. If carried in the dews or damp, the hay is sure to be spoiled, if not both hay and seed, and, if taken up dry, the seed comes out with a touch, and the greatest part is lost in pitching up the cocks, binding and jolting in carrying home. To avoid this dilemma he relates a contrivance, which is intricate and impracticable to common farmers, and therefore I omit it.

Rats and mice are great devourers of this seed, and will take the kernels out so dextrously, that the hole in the husk shuts itself up when the seed is out of it: but, if you feel the husk between your finger and thumb, you will find it empty; also a sackful is very light. Incurious persons have sowed such empty husks for several years successively, and, none coming up, concluded their land improper for St. Foin.

tufts

cufts the foboles were better grown than others, according to the vigour of the tuft : thefe tufts taken up with the roots feem to ftand off at a little diftance from the roots, fo as (being fed in the winter, by fheep efpecially) to be obnoxious to be bit off, and fo the foboles, the hopes of the fpring, may be loft ; but, if your obferve them whilft in the ground, thefe tufts are fo clofely feated, and let into the very ground, that the foboles in the bottom of the tufts do not feem fo much expofed, but only the leafy branches round about the tufts, which are well grown, and not dependent on the foboles ; for, if they are bitten off, the hopes of the fummer-crop feems to be deftroyed. Great regard ought therefore to be taken, in winter-feeding of this grafs, by obferving how far the foboles are advanced upwards, and whether within the power of the fheep to bite them off or not, before they are put into it. Befides thefe foboles, mentioned to be fituated in the center of each tuft, there appears here and there an eye, or a bud, in the upper part of the root, but juft to be difcovered, not fo big as a pin's head, which in all likelihood makes but a very weak branch the next year, but grows ftronger and ftronger every year, and thickens, as wexing into tufts, ftronger and ftronger, according as frefh foboles may annually arife out of the center of thofe of the laft year's growth. Thus it feems, that what is but a foboles this year, thickens the tuft next year, and in it's center carries a new foboles, which grows ftronger the more the tuft thickens ; by what appears, the old fpreading-branches of the French-grafs, fuch as have grown up after the feeding of the aftetmafs till September, being of the nature of the winter-vetch, will endure the winter, and be the moft vigorous branches of the next fummer, if not fed. And whereas fome fay, you ought not to feed French-grafs after Chriftmafs, it feems they do

well

well that feed it no longer, but they who feed it not at all after August do better.

§. 54. I observed by digging up French-grass roots, that their decay proceeds from the same cause that the decay of the broad-clover roots does, and that in clay-land they decay soonest; this decay is occasioned by the fibres perishing, and then the canker takes the top, and eats downwards.

Of the decay of French-grass.

§. 55. After French-grass is mowed, if you are resolved to winter-feed it, I look on the following to be the best manner, first, to eat down all the wild natural grass with sheep, that being fine and green, by virtue of being shaded by the French-grass, but will burn away if not eaten, and it ought also to be kept down; secondly, to feed down the remaining part of the French-grass, which the scythe has left, but, after these are eaten, I would advise, that it should be hayned till towards September, because the roots of the French-grass running down great depths are apt, till summer is over, to draw a great quantity of sap, and, if during the months of June and July, especially if rain should fall, they should put forth grofs buds, and tender shoots, and the cattle should crop them off, the root might chance to be choaked by a plethory, whereas about September the roots cease to draw in such plenty of juices, and begin to be quiet, and, if the branches should then be eaten off, the roots will not be so over-charged as to want branches to empty their redundancy of juices into.

Best manner of winter-feeding French-grass.

§. 56. The reason why many plants are to be killed by often cropping, and yet the natural pasture-grass no wife suffers by it, I conceive, is, because the leaf of the natural grass is a continued spire, and, when it is bit, lengthens itself out again by growth, and receives all the affluence of sap in the root; and in case it could be bit below the leafy spire into the ground sheath, yet in the tuft,

Some plants killed by cropping, others not, and the reason.

from

from the same root, are a multitude of issues monthly and weekly breaking out, enough to receive the
sap from the roots, so that the roots cannot be
choaked by a plethory.   Now, the plants, which
are to be killed, by being cropped at spring and at
Midsummer, are those, which being full of sap, at
those times only do make issues of shoots, which
being cut off, the channels consequently are taken
away, and the exuberancy of the sap must burst the
root-vessels and kill the plant.   Some plants there
are, such as hop-clover, broad-clover, and other
trefoils, which may be said to partake of both na-
tures aforesaid; for the trefoil, being bit off from
it's pedestal or stalk, does not grow again, (as the
spires of common grasses do) that is, out of the same
stalk do issue forth no new trefoil buds ; therefore it
seems good husbandry to suffer the trefoil-leaf to
come to some maturity before it is bit ; but again,
on the other hand, it has a property common with
pasture-grass, which is, to be continually putting
forth buds and issues, one under another, from it's
roots, capable to receive all redundancy of sap ; for
which reason it is not killed by often cropping.

French-
grass after-
mass not
equal to
natural
grass for
fatting
sheep.

§. 57. At Holt in Wiltshire, walking in the
French-grass with farmer Miles, I asked him, whether he found the French-grass aftermass good for
fatting of sheep ; he said, it was neither so good,
nor would prove them so well as English grass; for
the sheep would pick up the English grass from
amongst it before they would heartily fall on the

Not to feed
it after
Christmass.

French-grass.—He said, the sheep might feed the
aftermass of the French-grass till towards Christmass without hurting it, and after that the hurt it
received was not from the winter, nor by the frosts,
but because about that time, or soon after, it might
spring and shoot up, and to take off that early shoot
in the cold weather was that which might hurt it ;

for

for by. the side of such early shoot a little dwindling shoot would spindle.

§. 58. Mr. Short Baily assured me, that sheep will feed very well on French-grass hay, and make little waste.—Mr. Randolph says, the sheep will eat French-grass hay till it be above three years old, but then it grows too stemmy.—Mr. Raymond says, in their country their sheep eat French-grass hay very clean, if the grass be cut before it blows out in flower. *Of French-grass hay for sheep.*

§. 59. Mr. Anthony Methwin thought, that foddering of cattle in French-grass would do it as much harm as winter-feeding. — Mr. Short Baily was of a different opinion, unless you turn in great cattle, which might tread it too deep; but he was confident, that folding or foddering with sheep would do it a kindness. *Different opinions on foddering in French-grass.*

§. 60. I have observed, where natural grass comes up near a hop-clover or broad-clover root, that such root will be but of short continuance, and will insensibly vanish and die away before any of the rest of the clover-grass in the same field, about which no natural grass comes up ; which makes for what is said by gardeners of those grasses, viz. that they and weeds impoverish the ground, and draw away the nourishment from the plants. — Natural grass consists of innumerable matty fibrous roots, which, without doubt, running on the surface of the ground, must feed on the nourishment which the clover should have ; and these grasses do, I believe, so far rob the roots of trees of their nourishment, that the gardeners, who advise orchards to be ploughed up, among other advantages to the roots of the trees, think likewise, that those trees may find a farther advantage by having such grasses destroyed from the surface of the ground. *Natural grass destroys other grasses.*

E 4   § 61. The

§. 61. The strength and spirit of rowety grass is observed, after the first snow that falls, if it lies a while on the ground, to go off very much, and to have little proof in it, to what it had before the falling of the snow.

The more you improve your grounds, the more rowet you will have after the corn is cut; for the stubble-land will carry a good grass to maintain cattle, till it is ploughed up again, and this will both save hay, and keep you from a necessity of threshing out corn to a disadvantage of price.

There is often a rowet in grounds, which your own beasts, as being used to sweeter grass, will not eat, or sometimes the growing season of the year may not afford them opportunity to eat: in this case it will seldom be proper to buy in hungry beasts to eat it up; for they may either be dear, or, when they have eat up your rowet, you will not know what to do with them, they not deserving your sweeter meat; therefore in this case I hold it to be more proper to plough-in the rowet, for the improvement of your land.

§. 62. The grass which country-people call the hooded-grass, or lob-grass, is apparently of but little value; for it grows up in a single culm to a root, without grassy leaves, or herbage about it's roots; it generally grows on the poorest sort of ground; no wonder then, that so much of the seed of this is commonly seen among the rye-grass seed that is sold; for the lands, that are sowed with rye-grass, are generally poor in nature, and impoverished farther by corn; so these grounds are apt to yield abundance of lob-grass, for the bearing of which I hardly find any ground too poor: and I have observed, that poor ground will naturally carry a little crop of this grass, tho' it can maintain no other sort; the more therefore of this, a certain indication of the greater poverty of the ground.—— I have at
this

this time, June the third (anno 1707) obferved, that this grafs has perfected it's feed, in it's feed-veffels, when other graffes were but flowering, and as it's feed-veffels cafily fall, fo they naturally propagate themfelves.

The way to deftroy the lob-grafs, or hooded-grafs, is to feed your grounds to prevent it's feeding, or elfe to enrich them by manure, fo that the tufted roots of better graffes may fo multiply as not to give room for the lob-grafs feed, which is a large feed, to take root ; the roots of that grafs feeming to be very weak, as having but few fibres, and fo may cafily be juftled out of the ground, as the innumerable fibres of other grafs-roots multiply by manure. —I fufpect the lob-grafs to be but an annual. The French fow it, and call it fromentel.

The teftuca avenacea hirfuta paniculis minus fparfis grows on walls, and hillocks, and on linchets or balks in fields, and on dry places. Ray's Synopfis, 261.—This is what we call lob-grafs.

§. 63. There are are feveral ranunculi common *Of the crow-foot or meadow ranunculus* in our meadows, which, when green, blifter and ulcerate the flefh ; thefe the cattle will not touch, but leave ftanding in the fields, and yet, as I am told, all forts of cattle will feed on them greedily, when dried and made into hay. Dr. Sloan, fol. 25. mentions this, to account for the caffavis-root, which, tho' ftrong poifon when green, being baked makes wholfome bread.

§. 64. My meads are very full of dandelion ; *Dandelion no fign of poverty.* but I conclude it no fign of poverty, Ray, vol. 1. fol. 244. faying, it grows in gardens, and areas, and paftures, and flourifhes through the whole fummer.—I fuppofe it is a grateful bitter to the cattle ; I do not find but they eat it very well either in grafs or in hay.

§. 65. The gramen minus duriufculum, or fmall *Small hard grafs—fign of poverty.* hard grafs, grows plentifully on my white chalky lands, at Crux-Eafton, not worth fix-pence per acre.

acre.—Gerard says, this grass is unpleasant to, and unwholsome for cattle, and that it grows in moist fresh marshes.—And Ray, vol. 2. fol. 1287. says, on walls and dry places: so that I find it is of the nature of moss, which grows equally either on walls or wet places, where the ground is out of heart, and wants strength; therefore such grounds want their cordials.

M E A D O W S.

§. 1.

Mush-rooms an indication of good meadow land.

FROM the observation I made of my own hill-country meads, I find, that an indication of the goodness of the soil may be seen in the mushroom season, by it's bearing (if it be a healthy pasture) plenty of mushrooms; for those meads of mine, the goodness whereof I full well know, by my soiling and feeding them do bear the greater plenty according as they are in heart, and the parts of the same mead proportionably to the goodness of the soil; whereas those meads, which are out of heart, bear no mushrooms.

Dwarf-flax in mea-dows, sign of poverty.

§. 2. Linum catharticum, or dwarf-flax, Mr. Ray says, abounds in the drier pastures, especially on the hills.—I have great plenty of it in those meads that are very poor, but in meads which are in very good heart, tho' only parted from the other by a hedge, none of it will grow: I take it to be a great indication of poverty, where-ever it grows, and indeed, dry and poor, and fat and rich, are reciprocal terms, when we speak of land; for dunging would moisten such dry lands, and alter their property, so that dwarf-flax would no longer take up an abode in them.

Of great and com-mon mea-dow grass.

§. 3. Mr. Bobart assured me, that the great or greatest of meadow-grass, gramen pratense paniculatum majus, is the best hay of the meads, as being most grassy or leafy, that is, the culms proceeding

†   ing

ing from the roots have the moſt gradus of leaves
on them, and are ſweet: the common meadow-
graſs, gramen pratenſe paniculatum minus, has no
leaves to it's culms, in compariſon with the other,
and only an herbage from it's roots that is low; yet
Ray, I find, ſays, it is greatly coveted by the cattle, but takes no notice of the former for that ex-
cellency. Vide alſo Ray's Synopſis, f. 257.——But
Gerard ſays, the [a] common meadow-graſs, gramen
pratenſe minus, grows on barren hills, and is only
fit for ſheep, and not great cattle.

§. 4. It ſeems to me, that the cauſe of moſs in
lands, or on trees, &c. is poverty: the Rei ruſticæ
ſcriptores ſay, that poor, dry, and hungry land is
ſubject to moſs, and it certainly is ſo; and we knew
alſo that a good ſtrong ſort of land lying wet, or a
hill-country land on a cold clay, or lying ſhelving
to the north, will be ſubject to moſs alſo, and yet
the land may be of a good ſort, and value, when
cured of the moſs.——Nevertheleſs the ſame reaſon
as above may be given for the moſs abounding in
the dry beggarly land as in the ſtronger ſort of land
mentioned after; for what difference is there between land according to the firſt inſtance poor and
dry, having no ſalts or vegetable ſpirits in it, and
the other ſort of land, wherein the ſpirits are bound
up, and chilled, and rendered unactive, by reaſon
of the coldneſs of the earth, it's wetneſs, or it's lying to the north, ſo that it's ſpirits cannot be rarified, nor ſet on wing in order to exert themſelves?
what ſignify ſtrong liquors, or juicy herbs, put into a ſtill or an alembick, if there be no fire ſet underneath to move them, and make their ſpirits riſe?——
Again, as to dry, poor, beggarly land, and as to
trees bearing moſs, we may compare their ſtate to
that of every dry ſtake or hurdle hedge, in which,

Moſs a ſign of poverty.

There is a middle ſort of meadow-graſs between theſe two.

as

as the sap and spirits of the wood are exhaled,
which will be at a year's end, a moss will grow on
the bark, and more and more the second and third
year it stands, as rottenness comes on ; so the moss
on the body of a tree, or it's branches, is an infallible sign of the poverty of the tree, or at least in
those places where it grows ; it shews that it's fibres
and fistular parts for conveying of juices, in those
arms or limbs, are decayed, or decaying, or by
some accident rendered useless.

§. 5. Columella is of opinion, that the older the
dung the less profitable it is for meadows. Fimum
pratis quo vetustius minus prosit, quia minus her-
barum progeneret, &c.—Columella, fo. 106.

The older the dung the worse for meadows.

§. 6. That hop-clover and wild broad-clover
come up in meads and pasture-ground, by strewing
ashes and lime, and in some measure by chalking,
seems to me to proceed from the heat of those manures, which render the principles of vegetation
more active, by attenuating them, and putting
them into a brisk motion, whereby they become
able to open and penetrate those seeds, which are
plentifully brought into the ground, by the feet of
both men and beasts ; but the principles of vegetation were too languid before for that purpose ;
yet dung will in some measure do the same thing ;
foot also, as I have experienced in my meads, has
the same effect. ——It is also to be observed, that
path-ways through meads and pasture grounds are
more subject to clover than other places, which proceeds from the same reason ; those paths by often
treading become better land ; feeding-meads
for the same reason produce clover. —— I question
much whether these manures laid on arable land
that is laid up to pasture would under a long time
produce the wild clovers, because the seeds are not
plenty on the surface but by long time.

Why lime and ashes useful to meadows.

§. 7. Mr

§. 7. Mr. Wise's farm at Newnham in Oxford-shire, lying much on the water-meadows, it happened that his meadows, and the neighbouring people's were, just before hay-making time, overflowed, and exceedingly stranded; the neighbouring people cut their grass in that condition, tho' hardly worth the cutting; Mr. Wise rolled his, which so lodged and fastened the knots of every spire of grass in the mud and strand, that from the knots there immediately sprung up a very rich aftermass, which he thought paid him the damage of losing his first crop of hay, and he mowed it to his great satisfaction. *Of rolling meadows after floods.*

§. 8. Columella recommends the sowing of grass-seeds in meadows that are thin of grass, the seed to be sown in a mild season, about February, and then to dung the mead, fo. 110. *When to sow grass seed in meadows.*

§. 9. It was a very burning summer (anno 1702), and we had no hay in the meads, but only bennets, and those not worth cutting : however the farmers and labourers all agreed, that it was for my profit to mow them, tho' it should not pay the charge of mowing; for, said they, the aftermass will prove away abundantly the better; whereas the grass will not grow afresh, unless the dying bennets be cut off, neither will horses, nor other cattle eat the bennets all the winter ; so the dead rowet will continue on the ground, and will prevent the growth of the grass next summer, and spoil the mowing of the meads the next year, and further, the bennets, if not mowed, would hurt the eyes of the sheep ;—and they all said, they knew this to be true by experience. *A meadow, tho' thin of grass, should be mowed.*

§. 10. Walking in the meadows on the 28th of May (anno 1714) I saw it was very manifest, that by feeding the meadows for two years last past, instead of mowing them, I had greatly increased the *Benefit from feeding meadows.*

broad-

broad-clover honeyſuckle, and deſtroyed the yellow rattle or coxcomb-graſs.

Of raking up hay after foddering on mea-dows.

§. 11. When meadows have been foddered on in winter, take care to rake up the hay before the worms have drawn the ends of it into their holes; for then it will not rake up, but will both hinder the mowing, and make the new hay fuſty.

Of hayning up mea-dows.

§. 12. I think meadows ought to be hayned from about the middle of Auguſt till the end of October, that, the ſown graſſes then going off, there may be rowet till the latter end of December for odd horſes; I think this will pay beſt, and if then hayn-ed, in caſe the meadows are in good plight, they will bring a head of graſs againſt lambing-time.

§. 13. What up-lands you deſign for mowing, in order to make hay, ſhut them up in the begin-ning of February. J. Mortimer, Eſq. F. R. S. fo. 25.[a]

PASTURES.

Paſtures in the hill-country fit-ter for ſheep than great cattle.

§. 1. HAVING, as I thought, greatly im-proved Crux-Eaſton, by laying down grounds to graſs, that were more natural for bear-ing graſs than corn; I conſidered thereon, that I might greatly increaſe the number of my great cat-tle, i. e. my cows, &c. and I purpoſed to keep oxen, knowing that I had a length of graſs for a bite for them; but I found myſelf miſtaken in this reſpect; for our hill-country ground, though it be a clay, and improved by manure and paſturing, yet it is of a cold and ſour nature; and though, by giving it time to grow, it may carry graſs to a length to anſwer the aforeſaid purpoſes, yet the tops of ſuch graſs will be coarſe and ſour, as running to a length beyond what the ſtaple of the ground can

a See the article Hay.

well

well carry, and so will do less service, in proportion
to the length of time it will require to arrive to so
great a growth as to maintain great ca. le, than it
would have done, by a less and shorter growth, in
maintaining sheep; for the grass, in such case, being kept short, and not of a length beyond what
the strength of the ground will carry it to, it is in
proportion so much the sweeter, and better for improving sheep than it would be, when run to a
greater length, for supporting great cattle; as the
common saying is, A lark is better than a kite.——
Again, the keeping of sheep upon such land will
make a much quicker return, inasmuch as the grass,
on hungry, or poorer pasture, will grow the faster
(when it is kept down, by keeping sheep on it, as
not to exceed an inch in growth) than it could have
done by keeping great cattle; in which case, tho'
you let it grow to a greater length, suppose three
times as long, it will require five times the time,
or perhaps more, in growing to the two inches beyond the first inch, than it was in growing that first
inch: if all this be true, it is apparent, that on such
ground you may maintain a much greater number
of sheep in proportion than you can of great cattle;
i. e. suppose the proportion of a sheep to a cow to
be five to one, you shall in this case be able to
maintain seven or eight sheep to one cow, and no
doubt, where the land is equally fit for either, but
that ewes and lambs will pay better than keeping
of cows. How little profit I can, in proportion,
make of a dairy, in comparison of what I can make
of sheep, I am fully convinced by the great turgid
udders of the cows at Gausuns, and the middling
udders of my cows at Pomeroy in Wiltshire, and
the lank udders of my cows at Crux-Easton; nay,
the cows at Holt carry much better udders than
mine, and those cows generally go with the sheep,
which shows the feed to be much sweeter than mine.

§. 2. The

§. 2. The proof of grafs, be it of the fame fort
with that in another ground, lies not in it's length,
but in it's fap and grofsnefs; for, if a ground be
poor in juices, the grafs will be fo long in growing,
and the fun will fo harden and confirm it's fibres,
that it will eat hard, and afford lefs nourifhment
than the fame fort of grafs, and of the fame height,
which grew in half the time, the fibres of which will
be tenderer than the other.

§. 3. This is a general rule that may be depended on in paftures; where graffes are, that naturally
grow in barren grounds, fuch lands want manuring,
and then the better fort of graffes, which carry
ftrong roots, will eafily overcome fuch poor graffes,
they having but weak roots, and fuch paftures are
to be looked upon to be in a better, or in a worfe
condition, according to the perfection and breadth
of the leaf, and the length of the culm or panicle,
which fuch poor graffes carry; again, if by manure
you fo alter the property of your pafture as to bring
up the clovers, you muft ftill obferve the breadth
of the leaf fuch clovers carry, and the largenefs of
the flower; for, if they arrive not to that growth
you fee them do in very good paftures, you may be
affured, your ground will ftill pay well for farther
dunging.

§. 4. Sir W. Raleigh, c. 3. fo. 31. fays, Quintus
Curtius makes this report; —that there are pafture
lands lying between the rivers Tigris and Euphra-
tes, which are of fo rich a nature, that they dare
not fuffer the fheep to lie long upon them for fear
they fhould be furfeited and killed,—which is incident to our rank graffes, as clover, and quick-
growing paftures of natural graffes, efpecially in the
fpring.

§. 5. I have obferved ferny grounds (which
have lain long to rowety grafs, and to a four impoverifhed grafs) fit almoft for nothing but to make
cattle

The good-
nefs of
grafs lies
not in it's
length, but
in it's fap.

Signs of
good and
bad pafture

Of the rich-
nefs of cer-
tain paf-
tures.

Of plough-
ing up fer-
ny rowety
pafture.

cattle loufy; I have feen thefe grounds ploughed up for two or three years, and laid down again without being fown to grafs, and have often obferved fuch grounds to have put on a frefh face, and to have born a more fappy and juicy grafs, and to have afforded a tolerable good pafture.—The reafon of this I conceive to be, that thefe rowety graffes (having for many years fhed their feeds, of which the ground was full, and the feeds alive) being by the ploughing killed root and branch, the feeds of thofe graffes take root, and bring forth a young tender herb, which continues fo for a few years, till the roots decay again, and then it is fit to be ploughed up again.

§. 6. As it is better to plough up lands at the latter end of July, or the beginning of Auguft, for a barley, or a peas-fallow, than to fat fo late in the year, as has been noted before, fo it is better to lay up a grafs-ground at the fame time of the year for a winter-rowet, fuch as will endure the frofts, which will in all likelihood pay better than late fummer-feeding: thofe who can only ufe the prefent minute, and go to that which is moft obvious, and for a prefent advantage, in a road with the crowd, muft expect but a vulgar advantage. *Of laying up paftures for winter-rowet.*

§. 7. I was at Pomeroy in Wilts in October (1699) viewing lands with farmer Stephens: it was a mighty year for aftermafs grafs, and he gave me to underftand, that he hayned the grafs-ground which he had fed all the fummer, for winter-feed, that the cattle might then have a good bite, and kept feeding the aftermafs-grafs after the hay was off, becaufe the grafs of the fed grounds is ftronger than the aftermafs-grafs, and will better endure the winter frofts, and fnows; whereas, were the aftermafs-grafs fuffered to grow to a good height, it would, if frofts came, be quickly cut off, or, being *Of hayning up paftures that have been fed.*

wafhy and weak, if fnows fell, it would be beaten down, and grow rotten [b].

DOWNS.

[b] Mr. Miller, to whom the world is greatly obliged for his excellent dictionary, under the articles of Barley and Trefoil complains of the ignorance, obstinacy, and covetousness of the farmers in fowing grafs-feeds with their corn, and he again repeats the fame complaint, when he gives rules for laying down land for pasture.—His argument against this practice is as follows.—If the corn, fays he, has fucceeded, the grafs has been very poor and weak, fo that if the land has not been very good, the grafs has been fcarcely worth faving; for the following year it has produced but very little hay, and the year after the crop is worth little, either to mow or feed. Nor can it be expected to be otherwise; for the ground cannot nourifh two crops; and, if there were no deficiency in the land, yet the corn being the firft, and moft vigorous of growth, will keep the grafs from making any confiderable progress. So that the plants will be extremely weak, and very thin, many of them, which came up in the fpring, being deftroyed by the corn, for where ever there are roots of corn it cannot be expected there fhould be any grafs; therefore the grafs muft be very thin, and if the land is not in good heart, to fupply the grafs with nourifhment, that the roots may branch out after the corn is gone, there cannot be any confiderable crop of clover.——In anfwer to this, the farmers argue from experience, and deny the fact; to wit,— " that, if the corn has fucceeded, the grafs has been poor and " weak nd fcarcely worth faving;" for they fay, it very rarely happens that a good crop of corn damages the crop of grafs that is fown with it, but, on the contrary, they acknowledge that the grafs has more frequently damaged the barley.——By neglecting to fow grafs with our corn, fay they, our ground lies idle, and we lofe a year's profit; for they will not allow September to be the proper feafon for fowing grafs immediately after a barley crop, for a reafon I shall hereafter mention, tho' it may fometimes fucceed.—They affert that the corn is a fhade and fafeguard to the grafs, and that the latter is very feldom deftroyed, but generally protected by it;—that the roots will branch out when the corn is gone, and the grafs get up after harveft, tho' it had been before kept down by the barley;— that the roots of the corn taking up part of the ground, appears to them to be of no real hindrance to the growth of the grafs after the crop is cut; for the roots of the corn dying away at the time the corn is cut, ceafe to rob the grafs of it's nourifh ment, and by their occupying part of the ground, the grafs is
thereby

D O W N S.

§. 1. I Think it very adviseable for gentlemen
who have great downs, to plough a furrow across them in some places, that they may turn
the best of such lands into arable ; and they may
have

thereby prevented from coming up too thick, and the plants
standing at greater distances from each other have more room to
tillow and spread; whereas, on the contrary, if clover were
sowed by itself, at least in the common way of sowing, it would
be in danger of coming up too close, and of running up into a
weak spire ;—that it is common, even on poor land, the first
year after corn, to cut a ton of clover from an acre, on good
land a ton and half, and sometimes two tons, which is supposed
to be as great a burthen, and perhaps a greater, for the reasons
before given, than the same land would produce if sown with
grass only. ——- As clover and rye grass however are but of a
short duration, they agree, that their crop is, generally speaking, not very considerable the second year, when they feed it
off and fallow the ground for wheat. It appears notwithstanding, from Mr. Lisle's account even of this second year's crop of
broad-clover, that it is not of that contemptible value that Mr.
Miller has represented it ; for in his observations on Grasses, he
reports, that twenty acres of broad-clover of the second year did
from the middle of April to the middle of May maintain twenty-three yearlings, and eight steers of four years growth, besides
a great many hogs, and yet the pasture grew on them, and run
more and more to a head every day, though early in the spring
the sheep had fed it down bare, so that the ground was not
hayned till the beginning of April, and the wind, as well as
drought, opposed the growth of the grass ; for no rain had fallen
for five weeks before, and the wind had been north and easterly
for six weeks, so that no grass of any other kind did wag : and
in another place, in comparing the profit of vetches with that
of broad clover, he says, the second year's crop of clover is a
very great profit beyond the rent of the ground.— The farmers
however, admitting their crop is of no great profit to them the
second year, wish Mr. Miller could make good his assertion,
and put them in a way of laying down land, which has been in
tillage, to grass, in such a manner as that the sword should be
as good, if not better, than any natural grass, and of as long

duration:

have many inclofures, that, by reafon of their poverty, may be fitter to be turned into rye-grafs downs than to be inclofed, and then not to be ploughed above once in five, fix, or feven years.

duration; but, in their opinion, the chief rules he lays down are not practicable, especially in large concerns, and among farmers in common hufbandry.—His firft rule is, that when ground is laid for grafs, there fhould no crop of any kind be fowed with the feeds. This has been already anfwered.—His fecond is, that the feafon to fow the grafs-feeds upon dry land, is about the middle of September, or fooner, if there is an appearance of rain.—To this they reply, that grafs-feed fown at that time of the year is generally killed by the froft; fo that, if you fow it at that feafon, you are in great danger of lofing your whole crop, and, if you defer it to the March following, you lofe a year's advantage; it is much fafer therefore to fow it with corn in the fpring, particularly on cold land, and grafs fo fown will be much forwarder the year following than that fown in September.——But Mr. Miller has taken notice of this objection, and to obviate it, advifes to well roll the ground in the end of October, or the beginning of November. This the farmers own might be of great ufe, but it muft be on ground that is naturally very dry indeed, or it is not eafy to be practifed; for the misfortune is, the weather is commonly fo moift during the months of October and November, that it is then exceeding difficult to roll the ground, which is wet and dawby at that feafon, and cleaves to the roller, and there hardly happens one year in twenty that you can roll it.——His third rule is, to lay the ground down to grafs by fowing the beft fort of upland hay feeds, and Dutch clover or white honeyfuckle.—None of the farmers I have had an opportunity of confulting have any great experience in this kind of clover; their objection therefore to this manner of laying down ground arifes from the difficulty of obtaining any great quantity of this fine fort of upland hay feeds; for grafs for hay is cut before the feed is ripened, and out of ten bufhels of hay-feed not three will be ripe enough to grow. and this laft is the number of bufhels Mr. Miller advifes to fow upon every acre of land: befides, fay they, in all paftures, be they never fo fine, there will be fpiry and benty grafs, which is what chiefly ripens, the finer grafs being kept down, and feldom producing much feed. They conclude therefore, that this may be a good rule for a gentleman, who has only walks in a wood or garden, or a fmall piece of land to lay down to grafs, but that it will not be of any advantage. to farmers, for it cannot be introduced into common practice.

BULLS

BULLS and OXEN.

§. 1. ᵃ COLUMELLA and Palladius agree in the character of a good bull, that he should be large in limb, gentle in temper, and of a middle age ; for the reſt they refer us to what they have ſaid of the ox, for the only difference between them, ſays Columella, is, that the bull has a ſterner countenance, a livelier look, ſhorter horns, a brawnier neck, and a ſtreighter belly.

§. 2. I find by farmer William ⸱artain of Wilts, that a light headed bull, with thin horns, not thick at the root, is preferable, cæteris paribus. And the farmers of Holt ſay, a bull will live very quiet with oxen, or young beaſts, all winter, till towards May-day, when he may grow a little rank. *Marks and age of a good bull.*

It is uſually ſaid, that a bull of two years old is the beſt to bull cows ; but I find by experience that if he be of the hill-country breed, he will, unleſs he be very well kept, be too ſmall to bull the cows of three and four years old.

§. 3. Mr. Raymond, who has better breeding paſture, and warmer ground than I have on the hills, ſays, that if you have yearling heifers, and a yearling bull of the Glouceſter-brown kind for a choice breed, one muſt often be renewing or keeping up the breed, by buying one of thoſe yearling bulls ; otherwiſe the breed will ſoon degenerate. *Of his breed's degenerating*

§. 4. I had, in November (anno 1711) an ox fell lame in the field, as he was ploughing, and I had, in the ſame field, my herd of kine, and a bull going with them ; the bull had never been yoked ; *Of a bull's killing oxen with his breath. See §. 7.*

ᵃ Membris ampliſſimis, moribus placidis, mediâ ætate ; cætera fere eadem omnia, quæ in bubus ; neque enim alio diſtat bonus taurus à caſtrato, niſi quod huic torva facies eſt. vegetior aſpectus, breviora cornua, toroſior cervix, ventre paulo ſubſtrictiore. Colum. lib. 6. cap. 20.

however

however the men ventured to take him, and yoked
him to an ox.—The bull bellowed as he went along,
for two three turns, but without making any re-
fiſtance; he ploughed quietly that day, and the
next; whereupon I was very well pleaſed, and
thought to have continued ploughing with him,
but my oxmen ſaid, if I did, he would kill the ox
he went againſt.—I thought they meant by horn-
ing him, or bearing on him, but they ſaid, the
bull would kill him with his breath.—I was ſurpriſ-
ed at the anſwer, and aſked how that could be;
they ſaid, by blowing on him with his breath,
which was very ſtrong, and that in Wiltſhire they,
for that reaſon, always ploughed with two bulls together in the ſame yoke. — But, ſaid they, the
ſtrength of their breath preſently ceaſes on their being gelt.

The better caſe a bull is in the better he bears cut-ting.

§. 5. In the beginning of December (anno 1711)
I ſent for the gelder of Kimbery to cut this bull,
and he came and cut him, and he ſaid, he thought
he would do well; but, as the bull ſeemed to be
out of caſe, I aſked the gelder, whether that was
better or worſe for him; he ſaid, they counted, that
the better condition the bull was in it was the ſafer,
and that he would bear it the better.

When good beef after cut-ting.
A bull kills an ox with his breath, &c.

§. 6. Mr. Biſſy ſays, if a bull be gelt, his bulliſh
nature will be ploughed out in three years time, and
he will make as good beef as any ox.

§. 7. It is agreed on all hands by the farmers
about Holt, viz. by farmer Sartain of Broughton,
farmer Stevens, farmer Loſcomb, &c. &c. that an
ox does not care to plough ſide by ſide, or under
the ſame yoke with a gale, or a bull, till his bulliſh
nature is ploughed off, i. e. till a year at leaſt be
ſpent in work; and the chief reaſon they aſſign for
it is, that the oxen cannot abide the ſtrong breath
of the gales; beſides, with their ſhort horns they
can eaſily hit the oxen in the face.-----They ſaid, it
was

was plain the strong breath of a bull will daunt an ox; for a bull of a year old was sufficient to keep the largest oxen in order, amongst an herd of cows, and to keep the oxen from riding them; for, as soon as the oxen once smell so small a bull's breath, they presently acknowledge his superiority without contesting it, and run away from him.—— Many farmers for this reason will by no means yoke an ox with a bull, because the bull's short horns, as well as his breath, are apt to beat the ox out of the furrow, and to tire him, by his endeavouring to use an equal strength to draw sideways from the bull as to press forward.

§. 8. The north-country beasts that are of the western parts, much exceed our's in bulk and weight; for, tho' we have as deep feeding in Somersetshire, and in the vale of Wiltshire, as they have in the North, yet because we work our bullocks, that stops their growth, whereas in the North they plough with horses, and keep their bullocks unwrought till they are fatted and killed. *Working young beasts hurts their growth.*

§. 9. Columella would have the oxen be provided with large hoofs, ungulis magnis, lib. 6. fol. 159. But the cows with small hoofs, or of a moderate size, ungulis modicis, ib. fol. 166. *Signs, small or large hoofs.*

§. 10. Being at Holt in Wiltshire in May (anno 1711) Mr. Smith, my tenant of Deadhouse, knowing that I had newly kept two teams of oxen, asked me how they held out in seed-time that spring; I told him, very well, for the spring had been so cold all the seed-season as not to make a trial how they would bear the heat; but, said I, tho' it has been very hot weather since I have been in Wiltshire, yet I did believe, that at my return I should be informed they had born the heat well in their fallowing for wheat.—Now they have been at grass near a month before the hot weather came, whereby their bodies are well cooled, there is no doubt, replied he, *Of oxen heating and scouring.*

but

but they will endure the heat much the better; but the time for their being overcome with heat was in the spring, their bodies during the winter having been dried up with dry meat, especially if any of the hay you gave them was mow-burnt or high-dried, which would dispose them to scour; the reason of which he thought to be, because it heats them so much as to make them catch at every mouthful of green grass, which sets them on scouring; for which reason, he said, his father used always in hay-making time to take particular care to dry a reek of hay thoroughly for his working oxen against spring, that it might not take any heat, but come out of the reek green, which colour it loses by heating, and that though such hay loses much of it's smell, yet it is thereby made much cooler for the bodies of the oxen, and they will eat the more greedily of it.—He said, he found, that in winter the oxen would eat heated hay without scouring as well as the horses, and if French-grass hay be well housed, and cut green, he cannot make his oxen eat of it beyond Candlemass, but if over-dry and ripe, they will not eat it after Christmass.—From hence it seems, the longer you can at first hand provide, and keep your oxen at aftermass, the better and cooler in their bodies will they be, when they come to their work in the heat of the spring; and so they will be, the less heated hay you fodder them with in winter.

Of breaking a young ox. §. 11. c In breaking the young ox, Columella says, you should not suffer him to stop midway in

---

c Sed nec in mediâ parte verfuræ confiftat, detque requiem in fummâ, ut fpe ceffandi totum fpatium bos agilius enitatur: fulcum autem ducere longiorem quam pedum centum viginti contrarium pecori eft; quandoquidem plus æquo fatigatur, ubi hunc modum exceffit, Colum. lib. 2. fol. 98. —— Jugerum vocabatur, quò uno jugo bovum in die exarari poffet: actus, in quo boves agerentur, cum aratur, uno impetu jufto; hic erat 120 pedum, duplicatufque in longitudinem jugerum faciebat. Plin. lib. 18. cap. 3

the

the furrow you are drawing, but always let him rest at the end, that the hopes of resting may incline him to go through with greater spirit. If your furrow be above 120 feet long it will fatigue him too much, and therefore it ought not to exceed that length. It may be observed here, that the measure of an acre of land was the ordinary quantity that a yoke of oxen could plough in a day, from whence it took the name of jugerum ; the furrow abovementioned to be ploughed at one heat, was called actus, and was of 120 feet, and this being doubled in length made the two sides of an acre, so that when Columella advises a furrow not to be carried above 120 feet at most, he intimates the customary manner of ploughing, and agrees with Pliny in ascertaining the measure of the Roman acre, which is said by the author last mentioned, to be 240 feet by 120 : this contains 28800 square feet ; our acre contains 43560 English feet square ; so ours is near double the Roman acre. Two oxen therefore might, in pretty light land, very well plough a Roman acre in a day.

My oxhind took three of my steers to break them, and to inure them to the yoke ; he yoked two of the steers, being two yearlings, together, and so suffered them to walk about the ground, where there were no pits, nor ditches, for them to receive hurt by ; he also tied the bushy parts of their tails together ; the reason of which was, because they should not be able to turn their heads to each other, so as to strike one another with their horns, or, by bending their necks too much, by endeavouring to face one another, and then striving, break their necks ; in this posture he let them go in the ground, if without holes or ditches, all night, or else turned them into an empty open barn so yoked, and thus used them two or three times before he worked them.

§. 21.

§. 12. If you turn off plough-oxen to lie by during the winter, in order to plough with them again in the spring, the young steers broken the summer before, which have not been housed in winter, my ploughman judges best for that purpose, because they'll best endure to lie abroad in winter: next to these the younger beasts will best endure it.

A broad
claw a sign
of a good
working
beast.

§. 13. Working makes oxen's claws grow larger and broader than otherwise they would do; therefore a broad full claw is a sign that an ox is, or at least has been, a good working beast, for hard working and free working will, either of them, make an ox's claw so to grow, because a hard working, especially a free working beast, puts his claws strong to the ground as he treads, and thrusts them hard against it, which will cause the aforesaid effect; whereas a false working beast will tread tenderly and lightly on the ground, and consequently never spread the horn of his claw.

§. 14. I always ordered my oxhind, the morning the oxen are to be * cued, to tie them where they may stand in some muck-hill, or moist place, in order to supple their claws; for as our nails, after washing our hands, pare the better, so will their claws do the same, and the nails drive the easier. After cuing the oxen are always tender in their feet, and therefore should be favoured for a day after, and not worked in hard or stony ground, and, if they are at stall in the winter, the dung from their hinder feet should be flung forwards under their fore feet to keep them supple; their hinder feet will be moist enough of course.

If you fling off plough-oxen for the winter, it is good to new cue them, or at least to turn them off with good cues on their feet; for, when they are not worked, their cues will last a long time, and in the mean while their claws will grow out well, and harden against spring.

It

It is not proper to let oxen go to carting in coppices within two or three days after being cued, till the cues are a little settled to their feet; otherwise they may be apt to tear them off amongst the stubs of the coppices.

§. 15. Cato, fol. 13. says, you should anoint the bottom and inside of your oxen's feet with liquid pitch before you drive them on the road, that they may not wear out their hoofs.—I do not perceive, tho' they used oxen so much, that they shoed them. *Of pitching their feet.*

§. 16. ᵈ Columella takes notice of the custom in many of the Roman provinces of drawing by, or, as he terms it, fixing the yoke to the horns, and says it is condemned by all the writers on husbandry, and not without cause, for oxen cannot draw with that force by their horns as by their necks and breasts. *Of drawing by the horns.*

§. 17. I am of opinion there is nothing saved by taking a boy to drive an ox-plough, though you plough with but six oxen; a man will keep so much the greater awe over them, and will make them go trig; nay, there is a considerable benefit, if two men go with the plough, for them to change hands in the middle of the day, and drive by turns; so much more notice will the oxen take of a different voice, that it will quicken them. *A man better than a boy to go with the ox-plough.*

§. 18. About half an hour, or somewhat more, after my oxen came home from their day's work of harrowing-in oats, I went into the ox-house, to see what order things were in there; my oxen were all laid down in their stalls, chewing the cud, but no meat in their racks, not a single stalk of hay; I thought this hard usage, unless my ploughmen had first fed them, before they went to their dinners, *Of feeding oxen after work.*

ᵈ Illud, quod in quibusdam provinciis usurpatur, ut cornibus illigetur jugum, fere repudiatum est ab omnibus, qui præcepta rusticis confcripserunt, neque immerito; plus enim queunt pecudes collo & pectore conari quam cornibus. Colum. lib. 2. fol. 98.

and

and the cattle had eaten that serving up; therefore I asked my head ox-herd concerning it; he said, they never served their oxen with fresh hay, at their first coming from work, but there was always some of the oughts or leavings of their breakfasts left in the racks for them; which was then, when they were hungry, welcome to them, and they required them first to clear the racks of that before they gave them fresh hay.——I note this, because some idle hinds might fling such oughts to the dunghil. The evening oughts or leavings, if the oxen will not eat them, ought to be lain by for horses, &c. because their bellies being well filled over-night, they are nicer in their food in the morning, and must have fresh meat.

Of keeping oxen's backs dry, and of foddering them with straw in winter.

§. 19. After many years using my ox-teams I was (anno 1719) almost inclinable to dispose of them, they being so chargeable to me in winter, in hay and vetches; but, whilst I had these thoughts, a Wiltshire farmer, of whose judgment I have a great opinion, told me, he should think I might at least keep one ox-team very advantageously, if it were only to help eat up my winter-straw, my cow-cattle not being sufficient for that purpose;—to which I replied, that to keep oxen all winter to eat up my straw would do me little service, when by vertue and strength of the straw I could not pretend, in winter, to do any work with them;—to which he answered, that was a mistake; for I might very well work them some time after they had eat up their fodder in a morning, viz. from nine o'clock till two, if I put them not to too hard work, and that such working every other day would rather do them good than harm, and would get them a stomach to their meat.—I made a scruple of working them so many hours, and said, I could contrive work for them of great use to me, and work them only from nine till twelve;—— but he insisted, that

I might

I might work them from nine till two, if I contrived it so as to give them the best of my straw, tho' he acknowledged that straw was not so good with me as with them in the vale. He said farther, that nothing in winter beat out cows or oxen more than their being wet on their backs or loins; it was therefore of great consequence to keep them dry over head, in order to hold them to their proof; for, if cattle carried their hides wet day by day, it was as bad to them as it would be to us to wear wet cloaths, and must make them sink or pitch.——From hence I resolved, that I would oblige my servants, during the winter, at least in wet weather, to tie up my cow-cattle in shed-houses, and to bring up my oxen from their straw abroad, in wet weather, to eat it in the ox-house;——and for the same reason it seems to me, that, if I work my oxen in winter, as above proposed, by vertue of straw, I ought not to work them in cold and wet weather; for working in one such day, will beat them out (as the farmer called it) and make them to pitch more than working three days in dry weather.——To this however I objected, that, tho' I tied up my cows and oxen in wet weather, yet I could not avoid letting them out to water in the wettest day, and though it rained never so hard;—to which he replied, that letting them out to water at such a time would do them no hurt; it was only their continuing in the wet for hours together that did them prejudice.——He said farther, that, if I put cows or oxen under skillins, or penthouses, though they lay open to the air on one side, that mattered not, provided their backs were dry.

The same farmer making me a visit, I told him what good success I had had in foddering my oxen with straw the last winter, and how well notwithstanding they did their work.----He told me, he did not doubt but they would do so, otherwise he would

Not beyond six or seven years old.

not

not have perfuaded me to it; but, faid he, I would not advife you to keep oxen, you propofe to work, with ftraw in winter to above fix, or however, not to above feven year old at fartheft; for, when oxen are paft that age, they fall off of their ftomachs more than younger cattle will, nor can they hold their flefh with fo coarfe meat, and work withal, as younger cattle can.

Chaff for oxen.

§. 20. Barley-chaff is not proper for oxen, but wheat, and oat-chaff they may eat: the barley-chaff is apt to ftick under the roots of their tongues.

Vetches for oxen.

§. 21. The plough-oxen may eat freely of the winter-vetches, and they will do them the moft good at the beginning of winter, before they are forced to be houfed, and whilft they have yet fome grafs left in the field to eat along with them; for the cold rowety grafs, and the dry and hot winter-vetches will qualify one another.

By all means, however, if, in the hill-country, you pretend to fat oxen, or to work oxen in the plough, take care to have a good reek of good old vetches in ftore againft fummer; for it will rarely happen but they will have great want of them, at leaft throughout the whole month of July; for the pafture-grafs in the hill-country, either burning up, or giving off growing by Midfummer, it is the

* or bent-ing.

oxen and cow-cattle's * bennetting-time, till a frefh fpring fhoots up by means of rain in Auguft, when the corn-fields begin to open to their pafture, tho' the fheep which bite clofe may fare well: at this time fuch a provifion of vetches to go on with the rowet, and the fmall pickings of grafs left, will be a vaft fupport to, and of great confequence with the oxen, nor is the want of old reeked vetches, in this cafe, to be fupplied by green vetches, which at this time of the year may be had in plenty; for, though at this feafon they are a good maintenance for horfes, yet they are unkind to the horned cattle,

and

and will be apt to scour them, and make them sick.

§. 22. It is agreed by the Wiltshire farmers, that from about the beginning of March to the beginning of May, i. e. till the ploughing oxen are put to grass, more especial care ought to be taken to give them hay in their rack, in little parcels, small pittances at a time, because, the hay then growing dry, and the oxen growing hot, their breath will be so much the more apt to blow their fodder, and then they will not eat it. *Of giving them hay in small parcels.*

§. 23. In inclosures in the hill-country, where there are dead hedges, especially if oxen are kept there, rugged posts set up in the fields, for them to scrub against, will be of great use to the oxen, as well as a safeguard to the hedges. *Of scrubbing posts for oxen, to save the dead hedges.*

§. 24. It was the 15th of November (anno 1713) when my oxhind proposed to me to take my plough-oxen into the house for the winter, it being then dry and mild frosty weather ; on the contrary, my bailiff was of opinion, that they might, for that reason, lie out a few days longer ; but the other said, the weather being dry was the reason that he proposed housing them at first when their backs were dry ; for it is a saying in Wiltshire amongst the plough-men, that, if in winter you staid till the rain came before you housed oxen, and then their backs were wet when you first housed them, their coats or hair would be apt to peel off in the winter.---e The ancients are very particular in their directions to keep the backs of oxen dry, and to rub them well when they come from work, and pull up their hides that they may sit loose and not cling to their flesh. *Of housing oxen when their backs are dry.*

e Boves, cum ab opere disjunxerit, substrictos confricet, manibus comprimat dorsum, et pellem revellat, nec patiatur corpori adhærere, quia id genus morbi maximè est armentis noxium. Columella, fol. 99.

           COWS

COWS and CALVES.

§. 1. [a] TO keep cows from being high in case before bulling, and the bull to be in high case, is Columella's rule, as well as Varro's. [b] It appears also by Columella, that in August and September they gave their cows leaves as a good part of their food. [c] He is likewise of Varro's opinion, that if the bull turns off to the right, it is a bull calf, and, if to the left, it is a cow-calf, but that only in case the cow takes not bull again, which rarely happens. [d] He and Palladius are generally agreed on the marks that distinguish a good cow, to wit, that she should be tall in stature, long in body, of a vast belly, broad forehead, black large eyes, neat light horns inclining to black, hairy ears, flat jaws, a dewlap and tail very large and long, hoofs and legs of a moderate size.

Choice of a cow.

§. 2. Markham in his Country Contentments, fo. 71. says, in the choice of a cow, she should ever have four teats, but no more ; her forehead broad and smooth ; her belly round and large : a young cow is the best for breed.

Marks of a good cow.

§. 3. A notable dairy-woman informs me, that in Leicestershire they observe, and she has observed

[a] Propter fæturam hæc servare soleo, ante admissuram, mensem unum, ne cibo et potione se impleant quòd existimantur facilius macræ concipere : sed tauri è contra impleantur duobus mensibus ante admissuram. Varro, lib. 2. fol. 58.

[b] A calendis Julii in calendas Novembris satientur fronde. Colum. lib. 6. c ap.3.

[c] Mas an fæmina sit concepta significat descensu taurus cum iniit; siquidem, si mas est, in dexteriorem : ad idem Aristoteles.

[d] Altissimæ formæ, longæque, maximi uteri, frontibus latissimis, oculis nigris et patentibus, cornibus venustis, et levibus, et nigrantibus, pilosis auribus, compressis malis, palearibus et caudis amplissimis, ungulis modicis, et modicis cruribus. Col. lib. 6. cap. 21.

2

the

the same herself, that a cow with thick horns, which do not lessen and thin in a taper manner, gives not so much milk as the cows with slender horns do.

§. 4. If you would choose a cow to feed, handle her navel, and, if that be big, round and soft, she is surely well-tallowed. Markham, lib. 1. fo. 62. *Mark of a fat cow.*

§. 5. When a cow has a calf, one may discover by the thriving of the calf, whether the cow gives very good and rich milk, or that which is but washy; but some, when they bring the cow and calf to market, will beforehand fill the calf's belly with two cows milk; but then the cow's udder, by it's fulness, will be apt to shew it. *A good cow known by the thriving of it's calf.*

§. 6. In discourse with a notable cow-keeper he said, that he counted not a cow old till she was eighteen or twenty years old, and that cows would very well live so long, though but few, as he believed, kept them beyond twelve, or thereabouts; they would not abate of their milk till they were very old. *Age of a cow.*

But another of the same profession replied, if a cow be kept above eight years old, though she might give good milk without abatement, yet she would be worth nothing for fatting, she would be tough; and that she must be helped up, when she was down, unless she were well fed; he also said, that many young cows would take a trick of not rising of themselves, but of lying, when down, till they were helped up.

Varro, lib. 2. de re rustica, c. 3. fo. 51. says, a cow is not good for breeding after she is ten year old.

The age of a cow, after she is three year old, may certainly be discovered; for every year after that age at the root of her horn she will put forth a rundle, like a curled ring: on examination I saw an instance of it in my own cows. *Known by the horns.*

An old cow also will lose her fore teeth in her lower jaw, and, if you should buy such a cow for the sake of a good calf by her side, and believing she may give good milk, if she has lost a tooth be- *And it's teeth.*

fore, you muſt not think of keeping her above a year or two at moſt, but muſt fat her off. If a cow be pot-bellied, it is a certain ſign ſhe is old.

Age, when a cow is in perfection.

§. 7. The farmers of the Iſle of Wight agree, that a cow is not in perfection for giving the moſt milk till ſhe is ſix year old, and that it is common in that country, where a perſon rents land of one landlord, and cows of another, to give ten ſhillings a year rent for a grown cow; but as for a heifer of the third year, which is the firſt year of her giving milk, you may have her milk for her keeping, and tho' ſhe may the next year let for ten ſhillings, yet ſhe will not give ſo much milk then as ſhe will do afterwards.

Caution— not to keep a cow beyond ſix years old in the hill-country.

§. 8. I was telling farmer William Sartain, and farmer Iſles, my tenants in Wiltſhire, the cold winters in the hill-country fell ſo hard on old cows with calf, they being long kept to ſtraw, which is with us ſourer than ordinary, that I was reſolved I would not keep a cow to the pail for the future beyond ſix year old;—they agreed, that I was much in the right of it.—Farmer Iſles ſaid, the keeping cows ſo long and hard to ſtraw, and having but little rowet for them, was the occaſion of their running out ſo much to be pot-bellied, as they uſually do.

And I am ſince confirmed by experience, that in cold hill-country air, where the ſtraw is alſo coarſe, by reaſon of the cold land it was produced from, cows ſhould not be kept till they are old, but be ſold off at ſix, or ſeven years old at fartheſt; becauſe ſuch cows, after that age, and in ſuch a place, will pitch much at the end of winter, eſpecially after calving time, nor will they pick up their fleſh again before ſummer is far gone, whereas young cows will bear the hardſhips of winter with ſour fodder better than old cows.

Signs of a free martin.

§. 9. Mr. Biſſy coming to ſee me, and looking out into the backſide, told me immediately, that I had a free martin.—I aſked him how he knew a free martin from a cow; he ſaid, very well, it being
ing

ing eafy to be feen ; for, faid he, the bearing of a
martin gathers up more like a purfe, and is not fo
firm and turgid as that of a cow ; her head alfo is
coarfer, and opener horned, like an ox, neither has
fhe fuch an udder as an heifer not with calf, but a
fmaller.——He faid, the meat of a free martin, if
well fatted, would yield an halfpenny in the pound
more than cow-beef would do.

Amongft the cows the Romans knew that there
were fuch as we call free martins, which they called
tauræ, and fuch they yoked with oxen. Columella,
lib. 5. fo. 166.

Free mar-
tin known
to the Ro-
mans.

A free martin is a fort of a barren cow, which
hardly carries any teats to be feen ; fhe will never
take bull ; fhe fats very kindly, and in fatting fhe'll
grow almoft as big as an ox ; fhe is counted efpe-
cial meat. When a cow brings two calves, a cow-
calf and a bull-calf, the cow-calf will be a free martin, and will never bear a calf ; but I believe the
bull-calf is not affected in the like manner, but will
propagate his fpecies as other bulls.

§. 10. Mr. Biffy, laying his hand on an heifer,
faid, fhe was barren ; I afked him how he knew
that ; he faid, very eafily ; for, faid he, when a cow
has not taken bull, or not gone through, her bearing
will be firm, and turgid, whereas, after fhe has
taken bull, and proves with calf, her bearing fhrinks,
and grows lank, and then again, about two months
before her calving, it grows turgid ; but this ful-
nefs of your heifer's bearing cannot proceed from
her being fo forward with calf, becaufe fhe looks
lank, nor can I feel any calf ; for he felt her ; and,
faid he, if we graziers knew not thefe things, we
fhould fuffer much.

Signs of a
barren hei-
fer.

§. 11. Captain Tate of — near Loughborough,
obferved to me (anno 1706) that, notwithftanding
the Leicefterfhire land was richer than that of Lancafhire, yet they could not keep up the Lancafhire
breed

Why the
Lancafhire
breed dege-
nerate in
Leicefter-
fhire.

breed of cows and calves they bought of them, but
they would degenerate so, that in the third descent
they had their Leicestershire breed again.——He could
not tell me the reason of it, but the next day meet-
ing with Mr. Clerk, he said, he conceived the reason to be, because they in Leicestershire were not so
choice in the breeding, and managing of them, as the
dairy men in Lancashire were ; for, said he, in Lancashire I have known them give eight, or ten pounds
for a bull-calf of a year old, which shall then be in
his prime, and large enough for bulling the cows,
but will decline and grow worse at two years old ;
then, to make their calves large, they wean them
with unskimmed cows-milk, whereas we in Leicestershire give them skimmed-milk and whey, after
their having had new-milk a month, and this regimen it is that so much improves the Lancashire
breed beyond ours.

I asked the abovesaid Mr. Clerk why the dairy-men
in Leicestershire did not prove as good husbands,
and order their cows as well as those in Lancashire
did ; he said, it would not pay, nor be worth while ;
for their land was better than that of Lancashire,
and turned to a better account in breeding coach-
horses and mares, and fatting of cattle, and they
kept but small dairies, and therefore it would not
be worth their while, where they milked but a few
cows, to go to such a price for a bull.——He said,
they observed farther, that their large breed of
coach-horses, if carried into Yorkshire, would degenerate and grow small, and if the pad, and saddle-
breed of Yorkshire, were brought into Leicestershire to breed, they degenerate into a fleshy heavy-
limbed sort of horses.

Our hill-country farmers and dames are of opinion, that weanling-calves, or yearlings, brought
out of the vale, do well in the hill-country ; for
they are no otherwise kept than they ought to have
been

been in the vale, that is, wintered with hay; but it is true, cows from the vale do not do well when they come to the hills.

§. 12. Being in company with farmer White of Catmore in Berkſhire, and farmer Crapp of Aſhmonſworth, Hants, I was ſaying, that I had winter-feed, eſpecially rowet, for more beaſts than I had, and did therefore intend, about Chriſtmaſs, to buy in beaſts of a year and an half old.— No, ſaid farmer White, I would adviſe you to buy heifers forward with calf, and, as you have rowet, you may keep them the better, and in all likelihood they'll fetch a good price in the ſpring; for laſt ſummer (anno 1701) was ſo dry, that abundance of calves either went through, or will come in late; therefore a forward heifer muſt yield a good price; —and you will not fail in having them that are forward with calf at Chriſtmaſs; if you go behind them, and draw their teats, and, if milk comes, they are for your purpoſe.

Of knowing and buying in heifers forward with calf.

§. 13. I aſked a notable Wiltſhire dairy-man, if it was not a frequent practice to fill the calf's belly with milk the morning they drove the cow and calf to a fair, to be ſold, in order to make the cow's udder appear full all day, and whether they had not a way, by drawing a ſtring through the calf's noſtrils, and tying it in the roof of the mouth, to keep the calf from ſucking; he ſaid, ſome did practiſe theſe things, but he never did; nor would he ever buy a cow in a fair, if her milk ſeemed to be pent up in her udder, nor where no ſign of the calf's having ſucked that day could be diſcovered; for in ſuch caſe he ſhould ſuſpect ſome cheat; nor did he ever ſerve a cow or calf as aboveſaid, and yet never found but they went off as well as other people's, who might uſe ſuch arts.—He ſaid, they had alſo a way of beſmearing the cow's teats with cow-dung, and then the calf would not ſuck, and in driving

Cheats uſed in fairs.

the

the cow to the fair her udder would be so dirty, and dusty, that it would not be seen.

Caution—
not to let
cows to
hire.

§. 14. I would never advise any man to let his cows ; for it never gives any content to either side, and the tenant will in all likelihood be negligent in letting the cow take bull that he may milk her the longer ; for if she be not with calf, she will have milk all the winter in good plenty, and, when spring comes, he cares not ; for he knows she must be changed off.

Of fatting
cows at
London.

§. 15. A person who lives in Moorfields, near to the cow-keepers and renters there, and says, he is acquainted amongst them, tells me, that the cows are fed with such foul and rank food, that it rots them in the space of two years, or two and an half at most, and the cow-keeper's practice is of course to put them away fat by such time, lest they should be found dead on a sudden. They are soon fatted, being good meat all the time they are milked ; the food they give them is grains, cabbage-leaves, and bean-shells, of which last their milk will taste strong during the season.

A cow or
calf well
summered
is half win-
tered.

§. 16. I was sensible this year (1718) that a cow well summered is, as the saying is, half wintered ; for this summer was two years I weaned twenty calves ; that summer being wet, there was consequently plenty of grass, and those calves were very lusty against winter and eat their straw, and throve very well all winter with straw, and the advantage of running in my wood; but, on the contrary, this last summer being very dry, and grass running short, my weaned calves, eleven in number, were pinched before winter, and so came but poor to their straw, the consequence of which was, they never eat their straw well, nor did they care to abide in the coppice to pick on the brier-leaves as the former calves used to do ; so five of the eleven dropped off in the winter by the wood-evil, and the other

six

fix I was forced to take to hay by the middle of
February, and could hardly preserve them, nor
could I thereby raise them but very little by the
middle of April.

§. 17. I asked farmer Chivers of Gausun in
Wilts, how much hay he consumed in a year; he
said, above sixty ton;——I thought that was a
great quantity for his stock; he replied, his was a
dairy of cows, and that, when they had calved,
they would eat a prodigious quantity of hay.——
Why, said I, have cows when they have calved
greater stomachs than before? Yes, said he, a cow
when she has a calf to maintain, and is also milked,
will eat as much as two other cows; a cow in that
case will eat as much as an ox.

A cow after calving eats much more than before.

Many other farmers agreed, that a milch-cow
would in winter eat as much hay as a fatting-ox;
for, said they, the drain from milking her is so great
that it keeps her up to a great stomach.

Id. a milch-cow in winter.

§. 18. The spring (anno 1714) proving so cold
and dry, that I could have no prospect of mowing
a good swarth in the French-grass, about the 24th
of May, I put in my working oxen, and milch-cows
to feed it down, it being, as I thought, a noble bite
for them; but we soon found, that the cows yielded less milk than when they went in the broad-
clover, nor did the oxen fill themselves so well as to
be able to go through with their work, and so my
oxhind feared.

French-grass in spring not equal to broad-clover for cows, &c.

§. 19. Being at Pomeroy in Wilts, and seeing
farmer Stephens had sowed vetches, I asked him,
why he had done so; he said, they were excellent
good to give his cows that calved in winter, or early
in the spring; for such cows would often be chilled
in their calving in cold weather, and such meat
would be a cordial to them; he had had, he said,
cows take such colds in their calving, that their

Vetches, a cordial to cows after calving.

bones

bones would be fore a great while after, fo that they would not be able to fet a leg forward; in fuch cafe he made a great toaft for them, and put it into two quarts of ftrong ale, and gave it them, repeating it two or three times, and found it did a great deal of good.

Id. rough barley.

The country-men generally agree, that to give a cow rough barley when fhe has calved, is very helpful to the bringing away the cleaning.—Quære, whether the reafon muft not be, becaufe it is a heartener, and a ftrengthener, and that the cleaning ftays behind by reafon of lownefs in the cow.

When cows calve, efpecially if they have had any hurt, or are in poverty, the cleaning often does not come away well, but will hang down, and if it be neglected, and the cow has not in a day or two a drench to bring it away, by heaving and ftraining to bring it away, fhe will fall into the running of the reins, which will come from her like the white of an egg; this will much daunt the cow, and fink her fo, that fhe will not foon get her flefh again. To prevent this, and to bring away the cleaning, I have known it a common practice to give her a handful or two of miflletoe; to which purpofe Mr. Ray alfo obferves, vol. 2. fol. 1584, Commanducatæ fruticis frondes, & depaftæ à jumentis & vaccis à rufticis ad fecundas remorantes ejiciendas utiles cenfentur.

In the hill-country let the cows go dry before you fodder them in winter.

§. 20. In the hill-country, where the winter provifion for the cows is but ordinary, it is certainly beft to let them go dry when they go to winter-fodder, or rather a little before that time, that they may be dry againft they go to fodder, and then you fhould alfo contrive as much as you can, to fodder them where they may have rowet: —this is the way to keep them in cafe all the winter, and to hold up your cows to a good body, and to bring them to

the

the pail in spring with good udders, and to support a good breed of calves : by being let to go thus early dry they will be better able to walk a field at some distance, where rowet may be had, or, if you have conveniency of foddering at a distance, they may abide where the rowet is to be had.

§. 21. The rule is not to give the short fodder in wet weather, because the cattle will be more apt to waste it and trample it under foot, than they will that which is longer.

Give cows long fodder in wet weather.

§. 22. Cows that are tied up in a cow-house never look so well, nor are in so good case as those that are foddered in a backside ; for they want the airings, nor will they prove ; tho' it is possibly they may require less meat, as all unhealthy creatures do.

A cow-house not equal to a backside for foddering.

§. 23. I asked farmer Lake, what was the reason that it harmed a fat beast to lick himself ; Mr. Bachelour of Ashmonsworth was then in company, and they both said, that where a fat cow licked, it would make a jelly in the place, under the skin.—— And, said farmer Lake, such cows do not begin to lick themselves till they begin to pitch, and sink by faring hard ; therefore the butchers care not to meddle with such cattle ; for where they have licked the tongue leaves a mark, and the butchers can easily see it.——I suppose when they begin to pitch they begin to itch, which is the reason of their licking.

Of cows licking themselves.

§. 24. It was May the 11th (anno 1702) when some farmers, good judges of cattle, were looking on my calves, which were then yearlings, and they being in a lusty condition, the farmers said, if I did not keep them from the bull, they would take bull by Midsummer, which would spoil their growth.

Of a cow's going to bull.

They said farther, that cows would take bull the sooner for a bull's going with them, meaning, that if cows were lusty, they would take bull in three or four days time, if a bull were put to them, though otherwise their desire would not come so soon.

One

One of them said; for the hill-country cows that
were small, a young bull of but a year old, and a
small one, was best.—He had, he assured us, a
lusty cow spoiled by a three-year old bull, which
flung the cow in the cow-barton amongst the dung,
and put out her hip.

In the beginning of October (anno 1703) I observed a cow, that had gone through her, riding my other cows; coming to Holt, and being
afraid she might prove troublesome to my cows
with calf in the foddering-yard, I asked Stephens
of Pomeroy, if she would be for bulling every three
weeks in winter, as well as in summer; he said, no;
she might not be for bulling above once or twice in
the winter, because it was winter.— But, said he, if
a cow goes thro' in the summer, and is apt not to
stand to her bull, if immediately after she is bulled
you take about a pint of blood from the rump-vein
of the tail, it will make her stand to her bulling :—
and further, said he, if you would have all your
cows come in well together, you must milk a cow
while she is bulling, and give each of the other cows
that you would have take bull a pint, or a quart of
the bulling cow's milk, and they will in two or
three days take bull.—Another said, that spatling-
poppy would do the same thing : I had a maid,
said he, lately used to the dairy-countries, who,
when I had a cow not apt to take bull, went into
the grounds, and gathered a large handful of spatling-poppy, and held it to the cow, and she eating
it readily went to bull in two days after, and this,
she said, in their country seldom failed.

Mr. Wiltshire of Road coming to Holt while I
was there, I had some discourse with him about
cows; it was in January (anno 1698); he said, he
had one that had gone through this year; —I asked
him, how that came to pass; he said, he suffered her
to take bull at a year and a quarter old, letting her
go

go on Road-common, where there were young bulls
of that age ; so she brought him a calf at two years
old, and when they calve so young, they usually go
through the year following [e]. —I wondered much
that a cow should calve so young ; ——upon which
he said, down in Somersetshire they used commonly
to let their young cows, where they were well maintained, take bull at a year and a quarter old. — The
same day farmer Pain shewed me two fine heifers
with calf, that took bull at a year and a quarter old,
but it was by accident and against his will, the bull
breaking loose to them.—He said, what Wiltshire
observed of such heifers going through the next year
might be very likely in their poor keeping, but
would not so likely fall out if they were well kept.

Farmer Stephens, and farmer Chivers say, unless the keeping be choice good, (such as Gausuns
near Bradford-Wilts) it is by no means proper to
aim to have calves to come at Candlemass, nor to
let yearlings take bull at Midsummer ; it utterly
spoils their growth ; —nor does Stephens like, that
his heifers at Pomeroy should take bull till two year
old. —Yet they say, that sometimes, if they are very well kept, though not often, heifers will take
bull at a year old, that is to say, at the beginning of
May, though regularly they will not take bull till
towards Midsummer ; but this is to be understood
of such as were calved about Candlemass, there being almost a year's advantage gained over them that
were not calved till May-day.

I was telling a great Somersetshire dairy-man of
a heifer I fatted, which from Midsummer to March
would never stand to her bulling, nor did she rise
in flesh, fit for killing, by March, though she had
corn with her hay most of the winter.— The farmer

[e] Sir Ambrose Phillipps's shepherd says the same with farmer
Wiltshire.

said,

said, he had had such heifers, and that they never would fat inwardly : as soon as one finds them take to that trick it is best to sell them off.

I was saying to Mr. Clerk of Ditchley in Leicestershire, that I had heard some farmers say, that, though a cow, which never had been with calf, would not fat kindly till she had been bulled, and was with calf, yet a cow that had once had a calf would take fat well enough, though neither bulled, nor with calf. ——To which he said, that the latter might prove better than the former, but nevertheless the latter would not come forward, nor prove any thing so well before as she would do after she had taken bull, and was with calf, but would every three weeks be on the fret, and run about chafing herself; and lose as much flesh in the day or two she was for bulling as she had got in three weeks before.—He says, if one buys in, what we call, barren beasts, to fat, they will require, and take bull as soon as they grow a little in proof.

Id. and of keeping a bull to go always with the cows.

§. 25. I have found by experience, that those who keep ploughing, and fatting-oxen, as I do, ought always to have a bull to go with the cows, to keep the oxen from riding them; for otherwise it is impossible to keep them separate; for the oxen will break over hedge and ditch after the bulling-cows.—The best way, in order for this end, is to buy a fine bull-calf from North-Wiltshire every year, and then you'll always have a bull of two years old, and a bull-calf, which will come up yearly for use, one year after the other; and the bull will be so master over the oxen, that the cows and oxen may go together without inconveniency; nay, it is a good way to have a bull go with cows, if it were on no other account than to prevent the other cows from riding those which were for going to bull.

§. 26.

§. 26. It seems to me, that in the spring of the year, and throughout the summer, till the barren cows have taken bull, the oxen ought to be separated from the cows, both at grass, and in distinct foddering-yards, because the oxen will be riding the heifers, and straining them, as well as beat out themselves.

There are often many damages and losses, which fall out in the way of husbandry, to rectify which, it may be, it is inconvenient at that present time, and so one bears with them; whereas it is ten to one but we shall be much more incommoded in consequence, for want of rectifying at first the first damage or loss.—An hundred instances of this nature might be given; a cow, for instance, wants to take bull, and it may be, at the first approach of the spring, you are not provided with a bull, and it being a busy time, it would very likely be a small inconveniency for you to spare a person to drive this cow to a neighbour's bull, perhaps a mile or two off; but this inconveniency of the two is generally the least; for, by not doing so, your oxen, if you keep any, will break out after this cow, and teach others to do the same, which they will hold to ever after, to a great inconveniency to your corn, &c. And it is almost incredible how even oxen in a distant ground will snuff up the effluvium of a cow going to bull, and break over hedges after her.

§. 27. As I was shewing a cow to a butcher, this cow, said he, is with calf.—I asked him how he knew; he said, very easily; when a cow is twenty weeks gone with calf, if one went to the right side of the cow, and pressed hard against the flank with one's hand, and did it with a swift motion, one might feel the calf knock against one's hand, of the bigness of a ball; till the calf be twenty weeks old, or thereabouts, it lies up high under the flank, but then, as it grows bigger, it falls down lower, and

then

then one muft feel lower for it; and where there is another perfon on the other fide of the cow, and he fhoves the flank on his fide towards you, it will help the perceiving it, when fhe is but very young; and fo the graziers, by the hardnefs and bignefs of the calf they fo feel, judge how far the cow is gone.

Id. and how far gone.

Two underftanding farmers were with me, viewing my beafts, and they obferved a heifer's uddēr to fpring much; whereupon my bailiff faid, fhe would calve in a day or two; ——but the farmers faid, it might be a week firft; for a heifer will fpring fuller in her udder, and for a longer time before calving than a cow.

William Sartain, an experienc'd farmer of Broughton in Wilts, affures me, a heifer will not, when fhe is half gone, fo eafily difcover herfelf to be with calf as an elderly cow will, becaufe the fides of an elderly cow fall in more; in judging of an heifer one may often be miftaken. ——He fays, when a cow is half gone, the graziers reckon that the calf preys on the cow, and that fhe waftes; not but that a cow may be fat in flefh, and very fit to kill, within three weeks or a month of her time; but in that cafe, withinfide, and in her fuet, fhe will be much impaired; ——and one in the company added, her flefh, though fat, would not in that cafe fpend fo well; to which William Sartain agreed, and faid, undoubtedly it would not eat fo juicy as the flefh of a cow but half gone.

Of cows overlaying themfelves.

§. 28. In January (anno 1700) I was difpleafed to fee the damage the farmer's hogs did me, in roading about, and told him, I would have them penned up in his foddering-yard. —— My dame replied, if fo fhe muft fell them; for they muft not come into the foddering-yard amongft the beafts; I afked her why; fhe faid, it would endanger the cows, being big with calf, overlaying themfelves; for, faid fhe, the hogs would nuzzel, and make holes

holes in the ftraw, and the cows lying down in fuch hollows might die before morning, becaufe they could not rife.——The farmer faid it was very true.——And I obferved, that tho' no pigs came there, they took care every night to lay the ftraw fmooth. I fpoke of it afterwards to Mr. Edwards, and he was well apprized of the truth of it.

If a cow be tied up in the houfe, great care ought to be taken, when her calving time draws near, to watch her by day and by night, left her calf fhould be drowned; for, the cow's head being tied to the rack, fhe cannot turn back to lick the calf; befides fhe may calve in her dung, and fo the calf may be fmoothered.

§. 29. If a young heifer be pretty forward with calf, that is, ready to come the beginning of July, and grafs fhould be like to be plenty that year, it may fometimes do well to let her go on, and calve; fhe may pay better to the dairy than to fell to the butcher; but, in cafe it fhould be like to be a fcarce fummer for grafs, fhe muft be heightened up in fat as faft as may be, and be fold to the butcher; otherwife fhe may lofe all her keeping; for fhe will fall away when fhe comes near calving, and, in cafe fhe calves, fhe may yield no more than what fhe coft when bought in. —— When a cow begins to come pretty forward with calf, her teats will be turgent, and fpring forth.

Management of a heifer with calf.

Mr. Cherry of Shotfbroke's bailiff informs me, that to let a cow keep company with other cows, after fhe has flunk her calf, will be apt to make fome of the others flink alfo.

Of a cow flinking.

§. 30. It is dangerous trufting to milk a cow all the year that has warped, for fhe will be in danger of warping again: fometimes one may venture to milk on a very good young heifer, but it is generally very unfafe. It is generally beft not to milk fuch a cow; for that will keep her very poor, and unfit

Not to milk a cow that has warped

to

to fell to the grazier; whereas, by letting her dry up, fhe will be in the better cafe, and fell the better, and pay more than fhe would by milking.

§. 31. Mr. Godwin of Glouceſterſhire told me in January, annο 1698, —— that he had had ill luck this year in his cows; for three had warped, and one gone through. The calves, he ſaid, were ſquatted, and one of their heads had a hole beaten into it, which he judged to have been done by his cow that went through; for it ſeems, it is the nature of a cow that goes through to deſire a bull once every three weeks after, and ſhe will then be riding the other cows, which another cow that has warped, or gone through, will like very well, but the cows with calf will ſlip away, and ſtep with their hinder quarters aſide from ſuch a cow's leaping them, and then it often happens, that ſuch a cow's knees fall againſt the ſide or flank of the cow with calf, and ſo ſquat the calf.

Stephens of Pomeroy being preſent agreed to the above; and ſaid, that he never had but one cow that warped in his life, and the reaſon why he had been ſo ſucceſsful, he believed, was, becauſe he never had a cow go through. —— It ſeems, the deſire in a cow that goes through for a bull every three weeks generally laſts about twenty-four hours, but ſometimes it holds three days, during which time. Mr. Godwin ſaid, if he obſerved it, he tied her up I aſked Stephens, if he knew what made a cow apt to go through; he ſaid, he was ſatisfied it was for the moſt part from hence; if a cow ſhould come too early with calf, that is, before the huſbandman would have her ſo to be, and conſequently ſhould be deſirous very early to be bulled again, the huſbandman will balk that deſire two or three times, that his cow may fall with calf at a more ſeaſonable time than otherwiſe ſhe would have done: after ſuch balks it is odds, ſaid he, but, when ſhe takes bull, ſhe

goes

goes through : and there is oftentimes a young heifer, that (in the year the farmer firſt deſires ſhe ſhould take bull, and the firſt time of the heifer's deſiring it in that year) when ſhe ſhall be brought to the bull, will be very ſkittiſh, and will not ſtand to be bulled ; in that caſe, ſaid he, for fear of the foreſaid danger, I have taken the heifer by the noſe, and held her till ſhe was ſerved — But, ſaid Godwin to Stephens, in caſe a cow be ſubject to go through, do you know how to prevent it ? Stephens ſaid, after ſuch a cow has taken bull, to bleed her well in the tail is the beſt thing I know of.

If a cow caſts her calf, you muſt let part of her bag that will hang down behind continue ſo till it rots off ; for if you pull it off, you will be apt, with it, to pull away what you ought not.— If you have a cow, that either warps her calf three months before her time (for if ſhe warps but a month before her time, ſhe may give milk never the worſe for it) or goes through on her bulling, never proving big with calf, diſcretion muſt be uſed, whether you may milk her on, or fat her ; and this ought to be, according as the cow is like to prove well for the pail or not.—The dairymen think the aforeſaid bag that hangs down, the other cows ſmelling to it, is apt to make them warp alſo, as well as the warped cows riding the others.

They count a cow's warping her calf a month before her time not to be ſo bad as an ewe's loſing her lamb ; for the calf when firſt weaned cannot be valued at above half a crown, and it robs afterwards more butter and cheeſe than quits coſts ; whereas, a lamb will yield a crown after it has ſucked milk that otherwiſe would never have turned to any account.

A neighbour of mine had three cows that ſlunk their calves, and yet he could find no hurt in the cows, nor could imagine the meaning of it ; a little

time after paying a visit to Mr. Dark of Becking-
ton in Wilts, and speaking of the accident, Mr.
Dark asked him, whether he had not rid some
ponds or ditches that year, and spread the soil of
them about ; he said, he had ; why then, said Mr.
Dark, I have often heard say, that will cause
the cows to slink. This seemed strange, but men-
tioning it afterwards to some of his workmen, they
agreed, that they had before heard such a saying.

I asked Mr. Hawkins, an experienced grazier, if
a three-year old heifer, that had warped early, as
suppose about January or February, would make
sound beef ; he said, not so good as one older would
do, but she would tallow the better for having
warped so early. — I suppose a barren beast, for
the same reason, will do so too.

§. 32. Mr. Bissy said, it was very common, at
this time of the year, about July, for a cow to die
in calving.—I asked, for what reason ; he said, at
this time of the year their calving over-heated them,
and, tho' they were like to do well, they must be
kept from cold water, of which at this time they
would be apt to drink a great quantity, and would
die thereon presently after ;— and, when they are
suffered to drink, they ought to have hay given
them before they drink. — I asked him, if drinking
when they calved was no dangerous in the spring ;
he replied, the cow was not then so thirsty as to
drink to harm herself ; however, he took great care
then to give them hay before he gave them water.

§. 33. June the 12th (anno 1718) I walked out
on Oxen-lease grounds in Wilts, with my tenants
Tomkins, and farmer William Sartain, to see Tomkins's cattle ; there was a cow that had not then
calved, but Tomkins expected her to calve every
day ; she was a fine large cow, and in mighty case,
for she was pretty good beef : farmer Sartain said
to Tomkins, he must have his eye to that cow when
she

Marginal notes:

Cows apt to die in calving in July—— Caution—— to keep them from much water.

Caution—— to give cows warm water, and but little at a time, when calving in June or July.

fhe calved, and not let her have water for twenty-four hours after fhe had calved, and when he did give her·fome, he muft fee that. fhe drank but a little, and that it was warmed.—I afked why that care muft· be taken ; he faid, when cows calve in fummer, or hot and warm weather, there muft be greater care taken of them than when they calve in the fpring; for their bodies in hot weather will in calving be heated, and in that cafe the cow will be very craving after cold water, on drinking of which fhe will take chill and die ; therefore in fuch cafe it is ufual to drive fuch a cow to the houfe as foon as fhe has calved, and not let her drink foon, and when fhe does, but fparingly, and of warm water, for about two days ; and this cow, faid he, being in high cafe, will have the more need of fuch regimen ; for fhe will in hot weather heat herfelf fo much the more in calving.—— I talked with farmer Chivers of Gaufuns about it next day,—— who faid all this was true, and that his next neighbour loft a cow a fortnight ago for want of fuch care.

§. 34. It is commonly faid, that a bull-calf, as well as a pur-lamb, comes a week earlier than the females. *Of a bull-calf.*

§. 35. Sir Ambrofe Phillipp's dairy·maid was advifing with the butcher what fhe fhould do with a cow that fell off of her milk, and her milk grew very falt : no hurt was vifible in the cow, nor had fhe got any cold. ——I afked him, if either of thofe things would have occafioned it ; he faid, yes ; he had known either to have been the caufe of it, and particularly, when the late cold (anno 1699) fo univerfally feized the horfes, the cows at Loughborough fhared in it, and they fell off of their milk, and it turned falt, and this was in June, and the farmers fuppofed the milk would not come well again till the cow had had a calf. *Of cow's milk turning falt.*

§. 36. A butcher of Whitchurch in Hampſhire, being with me, took notice of an old cow ſo forward with calf in June (anno 1702) as to be within a month, the cow being alſo in good caſe; he ſaid, it was a pity, and adviſed however to dry up her udder as ſoon after ſhe had calved as the calf was a fortnight old.—He ſaid, when we went about it, we ſhould anoint the udder with tar, but not the teats, and half milk her two or three times before we let her go dry; he aſſured me, this was the method of the Somerſetſhire graziers,---and tar is a cooler, and diſpeller of tumours.

In Derbyſhire, as ſome farmers of that country aſſured me, if a cow's milk does not dry up well after the cow is turned to fatting, by reaſon of the plenty of graſs, and puniſhes her, they give her a pint of verjuice at two or three days diſtance, which effectually does it.

§. 37. Being in company with Mr. Biſhop, and farmer Ryalls of Dorſetſhire, we fell into diſcourſe about milch-cattle, &c. Mr. Biſhop allowed me, that milk of cows was thicker in winter than in ſummer, but had not ſo much cream in it, but much of the ſubſtance of the milk cruddled on the top; that the milk, whilſt the cow was with calf, inclined towards bitterneſs and ſaltneſs.—He and Ryalls did agree, that, if cows were low in caſe, and eat only ſtraw, they would not give good milk, till they calved, but it would fall to raggedneſs ſix or eight weeks before their calving-time; but, if the cows were in good caſe, and had good hay, they might give tolerable good milk till they calved; however they thought it was not adviſeable, in either caſe, to milk them within two months or ten weeks of their calving; for that it did moſt certainly impoveriſh both cow and calf much more than the value of the milk came to, nor would the cow come in ſo early and forward in the ſpring for

her

her milk; they alfo agreed, that, whilft creatures were young, as lambs and calves, they fhould be well kept, and they would fhift the better for it ever after; for fuch a calf would, they faid, come in a year the fooner for the pail; and they agreed, that, though Mr. Bifhop fent his hog-lambs into Somer-fetfhire for rich pafture from Michaelmafs to Lady-day, and paid half a crown a-piece for keep-ing them, yet he was paid double fold for it.

In the months of May and June, fay Mr. Biffy and Mr. Pain of Wilts, a cow, in our good pa-ftures, ought to pay 3 s. per week in her milk, which rearing a calf till five or fix weeks old will not do, fo that about that time our butchers kill the calves at a fortnight old, mere carrion; for fuch calves will not pay us above 2 s. per week.

§. 38. Mr. Maferly was faying, it was agreed on all hands, that an heifer's calf was much better for rearing for breed than a cow's calf.—I replied it was fo, but I was at a lofs for what reafon it fhould be fo; – he faid, he fuppofed, the only reafon could be, becaufe the heifer could not be milked at the time fhe went with calf, which robbing the calf in the cow's belly muft needs do the calf a great prejudice. *An heifer's calf better for rearing than a cow's calf.*

§. 39. My ox-hind, who manages my ox-ploughs, and was for many years a farmer himfelf in the north-weft of Wiltfhire, says, according to his experience, and the experience of other farmers of his country, the latter fallen calves, as fuppofe in May and June, are never fo hardy afterwards when they are cows, nor will they bear the winter fo well when they are cows as thofe reared from calves which fell at the latter end of February, or the beginning of March.—It feems to me that the reafon for this muft be, becaufe the latter fallen calves muft confequently be weaned late, fuppofe, about Auguft, and calves always pitch, and fall away on their firft weaning, and then winter comes *Latter fall-en calves not fo hardy when cows as early fallen ones.*

H 3 on

on such late-weaned calves before they have recovered their strength; and again, such calves not being so well established in their vigor and stamina
vitæ, nor having had that share of the summer-sun
which early calves have, never do arrive to that
strength, in their cords, and ligatures, and solids,
as the early weaned calves do, and consequently,
being also when cows of a more tender nature, do
suffer more in winter, nor can they well bear the
hardships of it as the others can. —— He affirms farther, that such late weaned calves when they come
to be cows, will never shed their winter-coat so
soon, by a confiderable time, as the early weaned
calves will,—and indeed this is very true; for I
have now, being in the month of June (anno 1712)
a yearling calf, which, though he fell in June, and,
being a very fine one, I kept him, and let him run
with the cows all the winter, and he out-grew the
calves that fell in March, yet pretty much of his
rufiet winter-hairs are still on his back; whereas
the coats of the early weaned calves are sleek and
smooth. — He adds farther, that cows in a fair, in
May or June, that have not shed all their winter-
coats, are, in his country, as much concluded by
knowing farmers to have been late fallen calves, as
if they had seen them calved;—nevertheless I am
sensible the occasion of this may also often be from
the poverty, and hard winter's-keeping of the
cows. — I have now also three cows of my own breed,
which have not yet (though the latter end of June)
kindly and perfectly shed their winter-coats, and
yet are very well in flesh, which I believe to be from
the aforesaid reason; for though I do not certainly
know that they were late calved, yet, because of
the coldness of our situation, and the scarcity of
grass and hay in the spring, we are forced to contrive the bulling of our cows so, that the calves may
fall pretty late.— -It is certain, that the earliest bred

of

of the spring, of all kinds, are most valued, and the farmers find the above said account in them, as for instance, in colts, pigs, and lambs; the earliest are the most valuable, and to be endeavoured for, if the place will admit of it, and there be fit provisions for them.——School-boys, by experience taught, greatly prefer the singing birds hatched in March to those that come later, and it may be questioned, whether the early births of the spring may not have a special influence in regard to the vigor and strength of mankind, but that the soul of man, and the affections thereof, and the strange artful mixtures of food, under infinite noxious varieties interposing, exercise so vast and immediate dominion over health, and in the well or ill disposing the constituent parts of our bodies, that it is difficult to make the observation thereof; yet some little better judgment might be made in the wilder part of the Indies, where the savages conform themselves more to the methods of mere animal life : I should think the setting out on the race with the sun, even in the last case, cannot but give some advantage.——Note, from hence it seems to me reasonable, when we go to fairs early in the spring to buy barren beasts for fatting, to buy those that are sleekest, i. e. have nearest lost their winter-coats, because it seems they will thrive fastest.

I have taken notice, that calves late calved do not shed their coats so early in the spring, when they come to be cows, as those cows do that were reared from calves calved early in the spring, and being willing to know the opinion of some of the notable dairy-men about Holt, I found most of them had made the same observation.----Thomas Miles added, that such late-calved calves generally carried thick hides, and the reason he gave for it was, because the cows, which calve about May, are by that time got into good flesh and heart, and so nourish their calves the better ; for which reason their hides are thicker.—Farmer Chivers said, that, when such cattle were not forward in shedding their coats, it was a sign, that their strength of nature was backward, and their blood cold, for that cattle's blood in the winter, when they were out of proof, if they were let blood, was sensibly to the hand colder than in the spring, and colder in April than in May.

Note, there is, on the approaching spring, a certain degree of proof requisite to give activity to the blood to go to the extremities of the capillary vessels, in order to form new roots of young hairs, till which be done, the old ones still continue their roots, and are not expelled.

Of giving calves hay at their first weaning.

§. 40. Farmer William Sartain says, about them in Wiltshire the farmers geld the bull-calves at a month old, and then, in a week, or at farthest a fortnight's time, after they have recovered their being daunted by gelding, they wean them from the cows by giving them some locks of the sweetest hay they can get, in some convenient place, where there is an outlet to grass; and that the calves will delight to brouse on the hay more than the grass ; and this they make them to do for a fortnight before they turn them wholly to grass.--- I asked him for what reason they gave such calves hay at their first weaning ; he said, to dry up the water in them, and to harden their bodies ; otherwise, if they were at first turned wholly to grass, it would be apt to scour them too much at first, and make them pitch. —— But farmer Chivers said, on fat ground, such as Gausuns, they only wean the calves that fell about Candlemass at six weeks old, in order to their taking bull the next year, and then there is no grass, yet they do very well on hay alone.

Of weaning calves.

§. 41. An experienced dairy-man in Somersetshire tells me, if you rear a calf, he rather approves

of

of weaning him at fix or feven days old, which may be done by warming the fkimmed milk for him, into which if you dip your finger, and put it into his mouth, he will fuck, and then, if you put a little bundle of hay, and give it into his mouth, he will fuck that, and fo, if the hay be put into the pail, and his head thruft to it, he will fuck the bundle of hay in the milk, till he has drank it all up.—— He fays, he obferves the calves weaned thus early to grow better, and make larger cattle than thofe weaned at feven or eight weeks old; for then they will pitch very much upon their weaning: however this way is very good, when the cows are poor; for the milking of them will not draw them half fo low as the calves fucking will do.

Another, of great note in the fame country, agreed, it was beft to wean a calf early from the cow by giving him the milk out of the pail; for then he might run with the cows all fummer; whereas, if he was fuffered to fuck the cow till he was five or fix weeks old, he would be apt to fuck her again after being weaned, efpecially if the cow be any thing fond.

A new dairy-maid of mine (anno 1706) defired fhe might wean my calves at two or three days old, as foon as they could have drawn down the beeftings; for fhe faid, they would not be fo apt to fuck one another. ——— I note this the rather, becaufe we ufed before to keep them long with the cow, and they ufed to fuck one another.

Being in the Ifle of Wight (in Auguft, anno 1708) I afked my tenant farmer Farthing and his wife (that farm depending much on breeding cattle, and confequently in weaning calves) how they weaned calves; for fome years I had found ill fuccefs in trufting to the fervants weaning of calves; fome of them by ill and four diet, for want of their keeping their troughs fweet, grew loufy; others fell into
diſeaſes

diseases by being over-fed ; I found by them, that, amongst other things, they gave a rule to their servants, in the measure of feeding, in this manner, viz. they ordered every calf to be fed by it's self, in a bucket, by a prescribed quantity ; viz. they gave three pints to a calf on it's first weaning, and advanced it gradually, as the calf grew, to five pints, as the calf was able to take it, before being turned grazier for itself, and this was the largest quantity they ever gave one calf in a day.——They fed every calf at a separate bucket ; for they found many inconveniencies in feeding them together ; some calves having a greater stomach, or being quicker feeders than others, would eat too much, and the slower feeders would suffer, and have too little.

I had a mind to know dame Farthing's opinion of weaning the calves by letting them run with the cows rather than suckling them by hand : she said, if they took their weaning by running with the cows, they would not be so gentle, nor stand so well to the pail, as the others.

Farmer Stephens, farmer Box, and all the farmers at Holt agree, that it is a very good way to give weaned calves, when first turned out to grass, skimmed milk, morning and evening, in troughs, for some time, but say, in their country they cannot afford it, because of making cheese of the skimmed milk, and their hogs must have the whey.

Being at Holt the 23d of May (anno 1719) I went to Pomeroy, where farmer Stephens had a calf of but a month old, which he intended then to turn to grass.——I asked him, if he was not too young to eat grass, and live on it, he said, no ; they would take their weaning as early as that, but calves usually fell so early in the year, that there was no grass, but at this time of the year there is grass and leaves every where for them to pick on, upon which account they might now as well wean a calf at

a month

a month old, as in March at six or seven weeks old.

If in weaning calves the grass be apt to scour them, putting a little salt in their milk will be a means to put a stop to it.

§. 42. I saw two half-yearling calves of mine in December (anno 1701) sucking one another for a long time together ; two Gloucestershire yeomen being with me, they said, that tar must be put to their teats, to prevent it ; for otherwise in their country they look on it, that such calves will, when cows, get a trick of sucking themselves or each other. *Of calves sucking each other.*

§. 43. In taking a view of my lambs to see if they were meat for the butcher, my shepherd caught a fat lamb by the tail, for which a butcher of Whitchurch chid him ; but the prejudice thereby I knew not, till my butcher the market-day after told me I had spoiled a calf by halling him by the tail, whereby his kidneys were very red, and his loins strained, by which his thriving was spoiled ; he said it was the worst thing that could be done to a calf at his sucking-time to hall him about by the tail, or any other creature whatsoever, for the reasons abovesaid. *Damage from pulling a calf or lamb by the tail.*

§. 44. In Hertfordshire and Essex the calves coops are set so that the sun may come as little at them as can be. From J. Mortimer, Esq; F. R. S. fo. 169. *Of calves coops.*

§. 45. If calves and lambs cannot be well supported for the two first months in a kind way of fatting, it is hard to make them fat, but they being stunted at first will be pot-bellied. *Calves stunted.*

§. 46. Farmer Stephens of Pomeroy in Wilts tells me, (September 1712) it is now the practice of the butchers all over the country to buy the calves, or agree for them as soon as weaned, and to come when they are about nine days old, and bleed them *Of bleeding cows.*

in

in the neck, taking the quantity of about half a pint, and to come three or four days after, and bleed them again the same quantity, and a third time the butcher comes three or four days after that, and bleeds them a pint. Note, he is sure a pint is the least quantity they take from them the last bleeding; he rather believes it is a quart.

Mr. Perdue of Winchester has had good skill in fatting calves, and the butchers would prefer a calf of his beyond any others.—He says, he used, according as his calf was lusty, at about a fortnight old to take from him about a pint of blood, and about a fortnight after another pint; he used to bleed them in the neck-vein;—he says, he placed their pens so hollow from the ground that their piss might run through and off, but never used to remove their litter, but every day give them a sprinkling of fresh wheat-straw over their old bed; by this means, said he, the calf lies clean and dry, and much warmer than otherwise it would do, for, said he, a calf can't lie too warm, and the heat of the dung fermenting under the straw, will much contribute to warmth.

Of milk and bean-flour to fatten calves and whiten veal. §. 47. The method of the housewives in Leicestershire, if a cow gives but little milk, so that the calf is not well maintained, is to scald bean-flour and put it into the milk: giving them this milk very hot they think much contributes to the whitening the veal, as the bean-flour does to the fatting: you must give it them hotter and hotter by degrees, at first lukewarm, till at length they will be able to drink it as hot as you can endure your finger in it.

A cow-calf may be killed older than a bull-calf. §. 48. I was commending the goodness of my veal to a great dairy-man, and said it was of a calf two months old. Then, answered he, the calf must be a cow-calf, for otherwise it would eat strong at that age; the case is the same with a sucking-pig: a sow-pig will eat well at a month old, but a boar-pig at that age will eat strong.

§. 49.

§. 49. Sir Ambrose Phillips's keeper says, that veal cannot be white till after a calf be a month old; for till that time a calf does not begin to be white in his flesh.

§. 50. If yearlings or calves are so well provided in winter-time with rowet, which they can come at, that they need be foddered but once in the day, that time had best be early in the morning; because there is usually a hoar-rime on the grass, till the sun rises to melt it, whereas the rest of the day the feeding on the rowet is very good till evening.

No white veal of a calf less than a month old.

Time of foddering calves in the winter.

Diseases in COWS and CALVES.

§. 1. MR. Smith of Deadhouse in Wilts, walking with me at Gausuns, a poor woman came forth, and asked him, what he thought of a cow she believed was ill; he said, he thought the cow was not ill, because her nose was moist, and that, if a cow or a beast be ill, that moisture presently dries up; Mr. Bissy said, so it was observed also in the yellows, and red-water, which, it seems, are only a higher degree of the black water.

A moist nose a sign of cattle's being well.

§. 2. I asked Mr. Clerk of Leicestershire, whether he used to let his beasts blood that he bought in for grazing; he answered, it was not only a safe way, but they would also thereby thrive the better; he said, if oxen bought in had been hard worked, or cows hard drove, it was very proper to let out their corrupt blood, if it was only upon that account, after they had been a week or a fortnight settled to grass; besides, as to other cattle, it was very well to bleed them when they first came into proof, lest they should overflow with blood: it is, he said, the same also with horses.

Of bleeding cattle before grazing.

§. 3. I met Mr. Putchin, a great grazier, and a country-fellow, who lamented he had lost a cow of the

Of the murrain.

the murrain : we fell into discourse about the murrain, and they both agreed, that in such a case it was very necessary to bury the beast that died presently upon the spot, by digging a hole for it close thereto, and to drive beasts away out of the ground, and keep them from smelling to it, for, whilst it was above ground, they would be apt, if they could come at it, to smell to a dead beast; and, to prevent the rest from having the distemper, they rubbed their nostrils with tar, and daubed an egg over with tar and thrust it down their throats.— Sir Ambrose Phillipps's shepherd agreed to all this, only said, he blooded them also.

Of the joint murrain, or §. 4. In the month of November (anno 1707) I lost two calves by putting them into young fresh broad-clover that was grofs, and of this year's stubble.— They call the distemper the joint-murrain. — Farmer Munday, who lives by Aldern-Mead, Hants, says, it is common for calves to die so in the vale,— but it is not so on our hills.— The calves must be bled in the jugular vein, a pint of blood, and be drenched with it, with a handful of salt mixed with the blood.

Quarter-evil. The joint-murrain in calves, mentioned above in 1707, I find by others is called the quarter-evil; I find by farmer Stephens of Pomeroy, it falls on yearlings and two yearlings at spring, and autumn, that is, October, and it seems to me to be owing to the quick rising of grass at those seasons, especially where, through the goodness or the moisture of the ground, it grows faster than the sun can concoct it's juices, which chill and coagulate the blood in those cattle, and occasion a settled jelly in the neck, shoulder, or loins. The said farmer approves the medicine above prescribed, but says, he has found by experience, that an egg-shell filled with tar, and minced rue, and with a stick thrust down the throat

(with

(with blood-letting) is the best remedy; he says, to prevent this mischief, he has always found it best to let the yearlings and two-yearlings go with the cows, especially at such times of the year.—The reason for which I conceive to be, that the cows eat up the grosser grass, and thereby the calves feed the sweeter.---I find by him, that he never knew milch-kine to have the quarter-evil, for which this account, I think, may be given, viz. the morbifick matter is discharged by the cows with calf in the foulness of their urine.

§. 5. In discourse with my old shepherd, in July anno 1697, (who says, he has been a shepherd ever since he was ten years old) about the blain, he said, it fell on the cattle only in the spring of the year, and was over before the latter end of July; it comes from a little red worm that the cattle lick up, of which he has seen many; if it falls under the tongue, the beast may be cured, if it be taken in time, and the bladder occasioned by the bite be broken and rubbed with salt; but if the blain-worm be broken in the mouth of the cow, and be swallowed, and goes into her guts, he knows no cure for it; and yet, if the blain-worm be picked up by the cow, and swallowed whole, it will go through her, and do no harm.   Mr. Edwards's servant tells me, he has seen two blain-worms in the bladder under a cow's tongue; my shepherd says, he never knew it to fall under a sheep's tongue; if they have it, it is by breaking the blain-worm, which being so swallowed he knows no cure for it.

Of the blain. Vid. Diseases in sheep.

On the 23d of March (anno 1705) I went down to Gausuns, where I saw Chivers amongst his beasts; he was saying, he could never stir from them at this time of the year; for at the first spring of the grass their blood would suddenly rise, which is the blain, and a beast was soon lost; and then he shewed me one which was growing bad.   I asked him how he

knew

knew the rifing of the blood ; he faid, that a beaft's eyes would run with water, and, before he dies, as the diftemper rifes, his eyes will fwell, and his blood, when bled under the rump, will feel hot : in fuch cafe, faid he, we give them the following drench ; a pennyworth of Englifh liquorifh, of Englifh annifeed, of turmerick, of long pepper, of horfe-fpice or diapente * ana, ground all fmall, and juft boiled up in a quart of ftrong beer ;—but, if by the heat of the blood one finds the diftemper to proceed from a hot caufe, then the horfe-fpice is to be omitted.---He fays, though he has rented good lands, yet he never had land fubject to the rife of blood before ; for it muft be very quick growing ground, as indeed Gaufuns was.---Mr. Biffy fays, the bladder under the tongue in the blain will fome-times be as big as a pigeon's egg, and if they can-not find the bladder there to break it with their hand, they rake their bum-gut, and find it in their back.

* of each the fame quantity.

Difcourfing with a Devonfhire yeoman on the difeafes incident to cattle, and particularly the blain, he faid there is a diftemper that falls on a bullock in the fpring, between April and June, occafioned by the overflowing of the blood, which they in their country call the bladder ; the bullock will be taken with a fwelling of his lips, and running of his mouth, and fwelling of his eyes, and running of them ; if it be difcefned before he falls, he is cured by thrufting a pen-knife upwards, from the root of his ear, and bleeding him in that manner, and pull-ing out his tongue, and rubbing it with a little falt.

When I was at Mr. Cary's in Dorfetfhire, Mr. Bifhop told me for certain, and upon his own experi-ence, in talking on the blain in cattle, that, if one run a bullock fo diftempered through the ear, near the root, with a knife, it would cure him, and

was

was the certainest remedy he knew of; he seemed very ignorant of such a thing as the blain-worm, but knew well in such cases, that a bladder arose under their tongues, and that many for the cure would rub the bladder with water and salt, and break it.---He thought there was no cure for the red-water in sheep; but said he had often had the fancy to rip up the skins of their bellies, and let out the water, and sew them up again; he said the hog-sheep were most troubled with it.   Red-water

§. 6. They have in Wilts a disease on their cows, which they call a hask, or husky cough; the cow will cough huskily, and seem not to be able to bring up any thing, and loll out her tongue; this distemper seldom falls on them in the summer, but at the beginning of spring, and on the yearlings and calves more than on the cows: the remedy is, to take a pint of lukewarm milk from the cow, and put into it a quarter of a pound of the fat of rusty bacon minced small, and give it the beast to drink; you may, if you will, put into it a little sallad oil; it will do the better, and keep the beast fasting two hours before and after.   The hask.

§. 7. Notwithstanding the cow-kind chew the cud, yet they are subject to indigestion, as may appear from what I this day observed in some of mine (July 22) which having the night before broke out into some winter-vetches, which I was then cutting for winter-fodder for my sheep, eat plentifully of them, and the next night they scoured, and I observed in their dung the grain of the vetches whole, and in great quantity.   Of indigestion.

§. 8. There is a distemper in cows called maw-bound; their maws will be so bound, that what they eat will not digest, or pass, and will grow so hard, that what has been taken out, when the cow has been dead, would endure kicking about without breaking; at the same time the cow will have   The maw-bound.

a blackish watery looseness : the first symptom it generally discovers itself by is, the cow will be subject to coughing ; it is cured easily at the beginning by giving them a purge of cream of tartar, aloes, &c. [*] Columella has taken notice of this indigestion in the cow-kind, and tells us the signs of it are frequent belchings, and noise of wind in the belly, cramps, loathing of food, heavy eyes, &c. and adds that if it be neglected, it is followed by worse symptoms, such as swellings, gripings in the guts, groans, restlesness, and frequent agitations of the head and tail.

The distemper in cows called the maw-bound, Mr. Clerk says, comes from a surfeit by being overheated by driving, or when a new cow is worried by others ; he says, a cow will likewise sometimes be maw-bound by eating of sedges in the water. The cure is, to give her a quart of cream, just upon it's breaking, before it is turning to butter, viz. when it is oylish ; he says, the calves will also sometimes be taken with a cough; the cure is, to boil a pound of bacon, and give them a quart of the liquor in the way of a drench ; it will cure them after once taking.

§. 9. Farmer Way, and others said, that my tenant at Woodhouse would always sell a calf at a month old for twenty shillings, and his way was, as soon as the calf was calved, to boil a piece of the inside bark of oak as big as one's hand in milk, and give it to the calf to drink, and this at once taking would prevent the calf from scouring, though he

Of scouring. See Diseases in sheep, §. 12.

[*] In bove cruditatis signa sunt crebri ructus, ac ventris sonitus, fastidia cibi, nervorum intentio, hebetes oculi, propter quæ bos neque ruminat, neque linguâ se deterget. Si neglecta cruditas est, & inflatio ventris, & intestinorum major dolor insequitur, qui nec capere cibos sinit, gemitus exprimit, locoque stare non patitur, sæpe decumbere, & agitare caput, caudamque crebrius agere. Colum. lib. 6. fol. 161.

gave

gave it never so much milk after ; whereas the danger of filling a calf's belly is of making it scour ; then he would boil barley-meal and chalk in milk, and put it into a trough to stand knee high, and the calves would be frequently licking it.——Note, chalk is binding and drying; which I conceive to be the true reason why it is given to calves, the binding quality preventing the flux, consequently nourishing and making fat, as likewise making the flesh white.

For the scouring of a horse, cow or sheep, take wheat-flour ; tie it up in a cloth, and boil it in a pot of water five or six hours ; then bake it in an oven with a batch of bread ; then take it out of the cloth, and keep it in a pot ; when you use it, take a quarter of a pound of it, and as much bole-armoniac beaten very well together, and a handful of bramble-leaves choped small, and mix it with a pint and an half of cold spring-water, and so give it to a horse, and let him drink cold spring-water ; give it in milk to a cow.

A very good dairy-woman in Leicestershire assured me, she was positively confident on many and frequent trials, that if a calf has a lax or looseness, though never so great, giving it nine horse-beans to swallow morning and night, will certainly put a stop to it in once or twice taking ; she has tried other remedies without success, but never missed of success in this ; a mistress of her's who kept a great dairy, told her the secret, which at first she thought a jest.

§. 10. The following receipts for the red-water in cows and bullocks are frequently used amongst the dairy-men in Leicestershire. —— The best, —— bleed first either in neck or tail : then make a good strong posset with spice, and give it blood-warm ; then take a penny-worth of aqua vitæ and a hat-crown full of yarrow; pound and strain all the virtue out, and put it to the aqua vitæ ; take a red wil-

Red-water
See red-water in sheep, §. 13.

low-ftick and burn it to a coal: pound it fmall, and put it all together, and give it as foon as it can be got ready.——Another,—— take of fhepherds-purfe, red-fhank (that is, herb-robert) yarrow, knot-grafs, of each alike, and fhred them all together ; then put them into a quart of milk, and heat it with a red-hot iron, and give it blood-warm.

For the red-water in a beaft ; take moufe-ear and herb-robert, of each an handful, the inner bark of a barbery tree a pretty quantity, but not fo much as of either of the other two ; chop them very fmall, and put thereto a quart of new milk ; then make it as warm as milk from the cow, and give it with a drenching-horn to the beaft in the morning, and keep him fafting one hour after, and, if the blood turn not the next day, give him another drench of the fame, but no more ; for if the fecond draught does not cure him, you muft kill him, and eat the meat ; for it is never the worfe or unwholfomer for that difeafe, and the longer you let him live the leaner he will be, and at laft will die of himfelf.

Note, as to the red-water, and the above receipt, it is to be obferved, the ingredients are eafy to be had, and that moufe-ear is a great aftringent, and excellent againft the dyfentery and watery humours, unde, fays Mr. Ray, ovium gregibus noxia cenfetur. ——The barbery in all it's parts has likewife the fame virtues.

The we-ther in the reins.

§. 11. For the wether in the reins ; —— take two penny-worth of long pepper, and three fpoonfuls of henbane feeds ; beat them together, and mix therewith a pint of thin grounds of ale or beer ; heat it blood-warm, and drench the beaft, and then wind him up warm in hay.

Note, as to the wether in the reins in cattle, the henbane or the feed of it is excellent good againft the gonorrhæa or muliebria profluvia. Vid. Ray, fol. 711.

§. 12.

§. 12. For the wether that comes forth either before or after calving,—take anniseed and liquorish of each one ounce bruised, fennigrick a penny-worth bruised, the leaves of setwall, (i. e. valerian) and primrose-roots, of each an handful, picked, washed, shred, and then pounded ; boil all in three pints of strong ale, or beer, till it is half wasted ; then strain it, and divide it into two parts, and into one part of it put a piece of sweet butter, as big as an egg, and give it to the cow blood-warm, and keep her fasting an hour after, and the next day give her the other part of the drench blood-warm, with a piece of butter in it, as before; it is best to give it in the morning fasting, except there be need to do other-wise, and then the first part may be given at any time, as soon as it can be made ;---and if it be after calving, and that the cow should heave much, then the wether must be thrust in, and sewed up to sticks with a strong awl and shoe-thread, and the beast be kept warm, and drink warm water for five or six days after.——If the wether hang out much, some use to burn dry bean-stalks, and with fresh hog's lard make the ashes up into balls, as big as great wall-nuts, and thrust one of them into the beast, in the midst of the wether, and when she heaves it again, put in another ball, and so till she is well.

In the above receipt, setwall or valerian is good against burstings, primrose-root is very restringent, & cohibendo alvi profluvio magnopere confert, ven-triculum atque adeò universa intestina soluta roborat, & fœno-græcum, secundum veteres, fæminarum malis plurimum subvenit. Ray. Bole-armoniac is very astringent, good against the diarrhœa and dy-sentery, and menstrua profluvia.

§. 13. Sir Ambrose Phillipps's shepherd said, that their beasts were never troubled with the yellows, but that the beasts in some other places in the neigh-bourhood, where the feeding was very gross and

fat,

fat, were subject to it; so that he supposes rich feeding may be the chief cause of that distemper:--- he thought bleeding was the best way to prevent it.

A gentleman in Worcestershire told me, January 1696, that his cows had the last summer been very subject to the yellows; —— I asked him, if they were dangerous; he said, they often died of them.---I again inquired, how they appeared; he said, the whites of their eyes would look very yellow, their stomachs fail, nor would their food prove them; their udders will swell, and their milk fall away, and look yellowish; he said, if it fell on their back and loins, it was not easily cured, but if it fell on their udders, it might be cured by letting blood and drenching, and, if it were taken betimes, blood-letting only might do.---An hour after a farmer came in, and agreed to this, saving that he knew not what the yellows on the back and loins were.

A certain farmer said (in July anno 1701) that a cow of his had lately had the yellows, and the first coming of them to be known was by her milk being wheyish, and in rags, before such time as her udder looked yellow; he said farther, the remedy he uses, is, to bleed the cow presently, and then to take hot embers, and milk some of the cow's milk into them, and rub her udder therewith at evening milking-time for two or three evenings;--- he says, the cure by hot embers has been by experience very well approved of. In this distemper, if a cow has not a speedy remedy, she often loses a teat, and sometimes her udder.

The black-legs or wood-evil. §. 14. They have a distemper in Leicestershire frequent among the calves, which in that country they call the black-legs; but Mr. Glenn, who lives at Utoxcester in Staffordshire, calls it the wood-evil. It seems it is a white jelly, and sometimes a bloody jelly settling in their legs, from whence it

has

has it's name of black-legs, and often in the neck between the skin and flesh, which will make them carry their necks awry.—I find by Sir Ambrose Phillipps's shepherd, it is of the same nature with the wood-evil in sheep, which, he says, are also so affected, and so properly may be called the wood-evil; and, like the sheep, if it falls in the calves joints, they overcome it, but if in their bowels, they die, nor is there any cure.

V. Diseases in sheep.

§. 15. Farmer Stephens says, for the hassacks in calves he takes thin slices of the very * raftiest fat bacon he can get, and shreds it into small diamond-cuts, and then makes milk blood-warm, and puts as much of the shred rafty bacon into it as will answer the quantity of bread usually put into milk, and of this milk and rafty bacon he usually gives two horns to each calf, which cures them without fail, when they have been so bad as to loll out their tongues; he says, the quantity of milk you may give to each calf may be three quarters of a pint.---- Farmer Chivers says, for this distemper he gives two or three balls, as big as chesnuts, of an equal quantity of butter, tar, and rue choped small, and puts them down the calf's throat beyond the quilt.-- Farmer John Sartain says, it is looked on that hassacks often come on calves by their feeding on drier grass than ordinary, or by reason of their wanting water.---This might be the main occasion of it in the calves I brought out of Wiltshire, because my grass was drier than that, and, though they had plenty of water, yet it might be such they did not like so well as what they had been used to in the vale, calves being nice; and drought seems likely enough to be the cause of it, both in respect to food, or want of water, because it is generally agreed that the brousing on wood will give calves the hassack.

The hassacks.
* ruftiest.

Mr. Beach says, he has stood by and seen his father and his tenants give the following drench to

their

their calves for the haffaeks, viz. take about three quarters of a pint of milk, and heat it blood-warm, and put to it two fpoonfuls of fallad oil, when the milk is thus blood-warm, and give the faid quantity to each calf; it will be about two hornfuls.

The pipp.

§. 16. If a calf takes the teat into it's mouth, and refufes to fuck, fufpect the barbes under the tongue, almoft in the manner of the pipp, which you may take away gently, &c.---Maifon ruftique.

Oat-hulls in oxen's eyes.

§. 17. I faw an ox's eye almoft out, as I thought; three farmers ftanding by faid, it was only an oat-hull, which among the fodder would frequently get into their eyes; powder of fugar or ginger blown into their eyes would, they agreed, cure them.

Of greafe in the heels.

§. 18. I faw (in Auguft 1699) one of Sir Ambrofe Phillipps's cows with a bunch and fwelling in the outfide of either hind-leg, and I afked the caufe of it. His dairy-maid and the fhepherd faid, that the cow being in high cafe when fhe calved about Michaelmas was two years, heated herfelf in calving, and cold weather coming upon her, fhe took cold, and the greafe fell into her heels, but fhe was never the worfe; it was only an eye-fore.

The loore or fore between the claws.
V. the loore in fheep, §. 16.

§. 19. Farmer Elford of Upcern in Dorfetfhire tells me, cows will be fo fore between their claws that they cannot ftand, and will pine upon it; this he and others informed me, in that country was called the loore, and they agreed, that a hair-rope rubbed between their claws till the place bled would cure them; but Elford adds, that what will fpeed the cure is, to take verdigreafe and lard, and mix them together, and anoint the place: this he ufes to do, and had it as a great fecret from a cow-doctor.

Difcourfing with old Wilkins, a notable farmer of Hathern in Leicefterfhire, he and another creditable hufbandman agreed, that the fowle or loore in fheep's feet came from their going in wet ground,

and

and was increased by the long grass and rushes
which got between their claws, the pasture-sheep
being most troubled with it, but it seldom afflicted
the folded sheep : he said, bleeding a cow troubled
with it on each side the claws, would, at the beginning, before it was too far gone, cure it without doing more : but then it was, he said, a common saying, that you must cut up the turf she bled on, and
carry it, and hang it up in a hedge, and, as the turf
grows rotten, the claw will grow well : but, said he,
the meaning of cutting up the turf and carrying it
away, is, because, if the fresh blood of a cow lies on
the ground, the whole herd will come and smell to
it, and fly about the ground, and fall foul on, and
push one another, and spoil one another : for which
reason, if a cow be bled in the tail for the worm in
the tail, they always staunch and dry up the blood in
the wound perfectly well, before they turn her out
to the herd, otherwise they would smell at her, and
push her, and one another.

§. 20. Being in May (anno 1712) in company Tail-soak-
with Chivers, Stephens, &c. and having lately had a ed.
cow tail-soaked, or with a worm in her tail (as before noted) I was desirous to discourse on that subject with them, and I found they all well knew the
distemper, and had it amongst their cattle : they
agreed, that, though it sometimes fell on cattle in
good case, yet it more generally afflicted poor cattle.
—They did not seem to observe, as Mr. Hayes, a
gentleman farmer, whom I had before consulted on
this distemper, had done, that a cow which had once
had it, was more liable to it afterwards than another
cow.— I asked them, whether they had ever seen a
real live worm in the tail ; Chivers only in the company pretended to have seen such a thing, and said,
he once saw a long narrow fleshy string, like a thread,
cut out, it was of a red colour, and moved : they all
agreed that the cow could not rise up in such a case ;
and

and that the cure was to slit the tail where it was soft, and with a rag to bind in salt, rusty bacon, soot and garlick beaten together, and one of the company added rue ; but the tail must not be bound too hard, nor continue bound above a week, lest the cow should lose the brush of her tail : they say, in such a distemper a cow's teeth will be very loose : it seems, cows teeth are always in their best health somewhat loose, if you thrust them inwards with your thumb ; mens teeth will also be loose under ill habits of body.—Note, it seems to me, that both the medicine of oil of turpentine rubbed in, as mentioned in another place, and this medicine, act their cure by heating the marrow of the cow's back and loins, with which the spine of the cow's tail has a communication, for the disease seems to lie in the back, and that the tail indisposed alone could not in such manner affect a cow as to weaken her to the degree above related.

Speaking farther of this distemper to a Dorsetshire farmer, he told me, they call it the worm in the tail ; the joint of the tail near the rump will, as it were, rot away, and the teeth of the cow grow loose, and her stomach fall off, so that it will in a very little while sink the stoutest cow or bullock, tho' it seldom falls on a bullock in good case, but generally on cattle when they are poor.— The cure is, to cut a deep gash into the sore, at the rump, and rub a handful of salt into it, and so bind it up with a rag.—Again talking of it to farmer Ryalls, he agreed to what the other had said, only he added, they mixed soot and a clove of garlick with the salt, and that the tail must be well and carefully cut, or else the kine might be in danger of losing their tails ; he says, though they call it the worm in the tail, there is no worm there, but he takes it to arise from the blood, when the blood runs high.

The

The DAIRY.

§. 1. SO much cleanness in scalding relates to a dairy, that Chivers of Wiltshire averred (farmer Sartain being present, and consenting thereto) that the dairy-farms spent as much wood in fire, to that end, in summer, as they burned for other purposes in winter.

Of cleanliness in the dairy.

If the milk-vessels are not kept clean, they will be sour, and the cheese will be sour before it can come, and will eat sour and choaky.

§. 2. Chivers took notice how a cool dairy was a great means towards preserving the cream the longer from turning sour; said he, my milk-house is too small for so great a dairy as mine is, for the milk coming in hot, the steam of it heats the air of the room.

Of coolness.

§. 3. My next neighbour had a calf penned up, and the cow grazed in a ground by it, and the cow being kept from her calf, and yet able to come up near to the pen, grew unlucky to pigs that were routing in a dunghill near, and gored one of them in the eye, whereupon she and her calf were turned out together, but then the cow would not give down her milk to them that milked her. — I asked the farmer's wife, a notable dame, the reason of it. She said, when the calf was penned up, and the cow was brought to it, when they milked her, the calf was hungry, and would suck hard, and the cow would give down her milk to the calf, and then the maid also might milk her, but when the calf was turned abroad with the cow all day, when the maid came to milk her, the calf not being hungry, the cow would hold her milk up from the maid: and so, she said, other cows were apt to do.

Of cows not giving down their milk.

A gentleman farmer of Gloucestershire told me, (anno 1698) that he had a cow of six years old that

had

had ufually given good milk, but the laft year fhe would hold up her milk, and would not give any, and he knew not what fhould be the reafon of it.—— A farmer coming in, I afked him his opinion about it. It is odds, faid he, but fomebody has ill milked her; for if one milks fuch a cow by halves, that is, to ftep away, and come again, or to keep talking and milk her in a very flow manner, the cow's patience will be tired, and fo fhe will get that trick.

How many cows a woman may milk in an hour, &c. §. 4. I afked farmer Clerk of Holt in Wilts, how many cows a very good dairy-maid might be able to milk in an hour; he faid, and they prefent all agreed, that it was a good hour's work in their country, where the cows gave a great deal of milk, to milk fix in an hour; he faid, he thought his wife could milk as faft, and with as much ftrength as any body could, and fhe could once he believed have milked eight, but fhe was not able, though of but a middle age, to do fo now: farmer Chivers, and farmer Stephens agreed to this. ——They alfo faid, when cows began to give off their milk, they would, if not milked clean, foon grow dry. ——— I put the queftion, when it was that the cows began to give off the height of their milk; they agreed, that they began to abate about the time of the bloffoming of the wheat, and fo on, till a good aftermafs came, and then for a little while their milk would increafe again, but cold and rainy weather in the autumn will dafh the cows, and then their milk will abate again.—— I take the reafon why the cows milk abates about wheat-bloffoming time, to be, becaufe about that time the grafs of the field bloffoms alfo, and the flufh of the fap is come to it's height and maturity, and then abates; for the roots of the grafs at that time begin to harden and grow dry, nor do they take in the juices of the earth fo freely as they did before, and fo grow drier and drier till the feed is hardened; which feed being fo brought to maturity,

rity, the roots of the grafs for fome time, till the cold and winter checks them, ftrike frefh fap-roots or buds preparative to the enfuing fpring, and which will the next year be the fpring-roots and increafe; on thefe new efforts or eftays, as aforefaid; in autumn, after the feed of the grafs is perfected, depends the ftart of the autumn·grafs till the cold checks it, which we call the aftermafs, and from whence the cows milk fomewhat increafes.

§. 5. Good houfewives may know whether cows are well milked or not; for if the quantity of milk does not yield fo much cream as it fhould do, were the cows milked dry, then they may be affured that the cows ftroakings are not milked away, for, if the ftroakings are left behind, much the greater portion of cream in proportion is left in the udder; becaufe the waterifh part of the cream comes away firft, and the fatteft at laft; for they, being the laft of the cow's milking, lie up higher in the udder; and confequently are more digefted and concocted by the internal heat of the cow's belly.

How to know when cows have been well milked.

§. 6. Sir Ambrofe Phillipps had a cow which, when milked, gave blood with her hinder teat; and the dairy-maid endeavoured, as I obferved myfelf, with great pains to milk that teat; and after fqueezing with all the power fhe could, there would come forth a ftring of coagulated blood two or three inches long, which being removed, the like would follow three or four times together, and then there would come forth milk from that teat, as at other times, though much diftained with blood: the cow all the while would endure the milking, only when the maid ftroaked the upper part of the udder behind, to bring down the bloody matter, her hurt being conceived to be there, fhe would not endure it; this held for near three weeks.——And it feems they had known the like before: it was fuppofed another cow had run her horn againft the bag of the udder behind,

Of a cow's udder that has been bruifed.

hind,

hind, and bruifed it, and they anointed the udder behind only ; all the reft of the teats gave good milk.——It feems, if a lazy maid, who would not have taken fo much pains with the teat, had had the managing of the cow, the bloody milk having had no vent, would have fpoiled the udder.

§. 7. Sometimes a cow's udder will be hobbed after fhe has calved, that is, will be very hard like a board ; the cow will not give down her milk well, and her udder will afterwards quarne, that is, grow knotty ; in fuch cafe, till her udder is come into order, her calf ought not to be taken from her, becaufe fhe will not give down her milk fo kindly to the hand as fhe will to the calf, and thereby her udder will be apt to grow fore, and break as womens breafts do.

§. 8. Mr. Whiftler obferved, that the hill-country cows milk did not yield fo much cream to the fame quantity of milk as the vale-cows milk will do.—— But furely this muft proceed from the poverty of the hill-country cows, they being generally poor in cafe ; your thin necked and bodied cows, that are wafhy and flue, are obferved to give a great deal, though but thin milk : but feeing our beef and mutton, when fat, eats as fweet as any in the world, I cannot conceive why the milk of our cows, if they were in as high cafe as the vale-cows generally are, fhould not yield as much cream as their cows milk does.

I have heard it obferved by fome farmers and dairy-women, that cows with yellow horns, or with thick necks, give generally very good creamy milk, and that cows with thin necks are generally remark-ed to be flue cows, that is, cows that will not thrive with their meat ; and thefe will give a great quantity of milk, but it will be of a blue or grey colour, and will yield but little cream. A cow, they fay, fhould not be milked within about ten weeks of her calving,

Of a cow's udder growing hard after calving.

Of hill and vale-coun try cows. See §. 27. Of cheefe.

calving, for though she will give good milk to the very day of calving, yet the calf will be thereby starved. A cow should be milked very clean, or her milk will dry away.

§. 9. Farmer Moseley of the Isle of Wight, and his wife, being at Crux-Easton (anno 1698) they gave me the following account of a dairy; viz. that 45 s. per cow rent, was counted a good price in the island, that formerly it used not to yield so much, but upon the rise of butter and cheese, it now fetches as above : take one cow with another in the island, if they give two gallons of milk per day it is well; which will yield four pound of butter per week ; and from June to Michaelmass, if a cow yields 70 lb. of butter to be potted, which comes to 23 s. 4d.— and an hundred weight of skim-milk cheese at three half-pence per lb. that is 14 s. per hundred, it is what is commonly expected; besides which, there is the May-butter, for in the island they begin not to pot till June : then it is said, a cow's whey will maintain a pig ; but, said he, it will not ; the calf also may be valued at sixteen shillings. **Profit of a cow.**

§. 10. In case the first milk, which they call the beestings, be not taken away clean from the cow, upon her first calving, it will go near to make the cow's milk to dry away. **Of taking away the beestings.**

§. 11. The Roman writers on husbandry forbidding the colastra or beestings to be given to the calf, as if it was a poison, I asked farmer Stephens about it, he being in his way a notable observer, and milking a great part of his dairy-cows with his own hand : he said, at first he did let the calves suck the beestings, and found no inconveniency in it, but, said he, I have very often observed, when a cow has warped her calf, and we have put a calf of ten days or a fortnight old to draw down the udder (which is better done by a calf than by hand, because the cow is apt to hold up her milk when milked) that a calf of **Of giving the beestings to a calf.**

that

that age has been much purged by the beeftings, and received a great deal of harm thereby; and therefore he held that the beeftings might furfeit, and had better be drawn off; it ftands to reafon, if one faw what a curdled body they are of.

Of thunder breaking cream. §. 12. Thunder will fo break the cream, and turn the milk in the milk-pans, that no cream can be fkimmed up for butter; nor will the curd for cheefe hold together, but will break afunder.

Of a quart of cream making a pound of butter. §. 13. Though it be commonly faid, that a quart of cream will produce a pound of butter; this muft be underftood of a quart of cream that has fettled two or three days, for three pints of cream juft fkimmed from the milk will yield in three days little better than a quart. If you bring in the milk and ftrain it prefently into the pans, without letting it ftand to cool before you ftrain it, there will be much the lefs cream.

Beft butter and cheefe made after June. Vid. 149. Of cheefe. §. 14. Farmer Elford, of Chubbs, near Up cern, Dorfet, fays, he reckons the beft butter and cheefe to be made after June; and whatever may be faid of May-butter or cheefe, he thinks it not fo good by much as that made afterwards; and his reafon is, that though the grafs comes on thick in May, yet the cattle muft likewife get into heart before they can give abundance of milk, or that that is very good.

Of fcald cream for butter. §. 15. I am informed, that throughout Devon-fhire they make their butter in a different manner than elfewhere; for they fet the milk over the fire in many brafs pans to warm in, which makes the cream rife, and when a bladder rifes in the middle they take it off the fire, and take off the cream, and put it into a tub, and it then looks like a clouted cream; then a maid only by putting in her arm and ftirring it, brings it to butter prefently, which is very rich butter, but the cheefe that is

made

made of the skim-milk is very poor and has little goodness in it.

§. 16. It is agreed by the dairy men about Holt, that against peas and beans time grass-butter rises in it's price by reason of it's consumption on those legumens, therefore good houswives collect butter a month before that season, and salt and pot it.

Butter dearer about peas and beans time.

§. 17. I have heard that a young heifer's maw that has never been with calf makes better rennet, and is better for cheese than a calf's maw.

Of rennet.

§. 18. I find by the conversation of Chivers, John Sartain, and many other judicious dairy-men about Holt, that cheese made between hay and grass is apt to heave, (i. e. when the cattle eat of hay and grass, as in the beginning of the spring) and is a stronger sort of cheese than grass-cheese, and therefore is not fit to be sent to market under a year old, because till then it will not be mild: in a word, I find by all the information I can get, that the richer the ground is (as it is with the strongest beer) the cheese of it must be kept the longer before it is ripe, so as to eat mild and palatable, and then none will eat better.

The richer the pasture the longer the cheese must be kept.

§. 19. I am informed by farmer Stephens, my tenant at Pomeroy in Wilts, who is the most experienced man in all things relating to a dairy that ever I met with; first, that if milk be sour, the cheese thereof will always eat * chocky, and never eat fat, though there be never so much cream put into it, which is the reason why Chedder-cheese often eats so, being made so large, that they keep their milk collecting too long; such cheese in toasting will burn and bladder, a sure sign it is not fat.—Secondly, such cheese (to shew it is dry and not fat, notwithstanding a great deal of cream be put into it) will in it's coat on the milk-house shelves look white and dry, and never gather a blue coat: neither will cheese over-salted ever gather a blue coat,

Of cheese.

* Dry, chalky.

but in toafting burn at the fire, though never fo
much cream be put into it, and will look white and
dry in it's coat.

§. 20. Being with Stephens about Eaft-Lydford
near Somerton in Somerfetfhire, and having there
bufinefs with a great many farmers, I found by
Stephens and the confeffion of thofe farmers, that
notwithftanding their lands were much richer than
thofe of North-Wiltfhire, they could not pretend to
make fuch good cheefe as was made in North-Wiltfhire, and that the North-Wiltfhire cheefe of the
fame fort would out-fell the Somerfetfhire cheefe
by three fhillings or four fhillings in the hundred
weight. ——— It was allowed alfo, that the Somerfetfhire women could not make a cheefe with a yellow coat like thofe of North-Wiltfhire ; wherefore
the Somerfetfhire women, to difguife it, put faun-
ders into their milk, to give a yellow colour to the
coat of their cheefe, which giving alfo a yellow
colour to the infide, when people put in the tafter,
they find the art, and upon difcovery take excep-
tions, for the infide of the North-Wiltfhire cheefe
is white.——And it was confeffed by all, and agreed,
that down farther weftward, tho' the lands were
better, yet the cheefe was worfe than in thofe parts
of Somerfetfhire I fpeak of. ——— This allowed of
difference between the North-Wiltfhire and Somerfetfhire cheefe gave me many fpeculations into the
reafons for it, and I afked them prefent about it. ——
Stephens above-mentioned would have it, that in
Somerfetfhire they were not fo good houfwives as
in North-Wiltfhire, nor would he give any other
reafon, notwithftanding I had faid, if the difference confifted in art, intermarriages would foon
rectify that mifchief, and a farmer that is choice in
the breed of his bull and his cow, and goes far for
them, would alfo fend for the beft dairy-maid in
the country of North-Wiltfhire ; for the difference
he

he speaks of amounted to at least twenty pounds in two hundred pounds rent per annum, and it was not to be conceived a whole county would be so stupid as to suffer such a loss, when the North-Wiltshire parts, wherein he lived, were but twenty-four miles distant from those parts of Somersetshire I was then in.—They allowed also at Winchester fair, if the fair was dull, the Somersetshire men must stay a day the longer before they could sell.—I cannot give a reason for this, unless the following be one, viz. Somersetshire lying low and wet, though the grounds are very rich, the juices of the grass are from thence less spirituous, and less concocted and digested, more gross and gnash, and consequently the cheese wants the virtue of that from the North-Wiltshire grounds, where though the grass may grow slower, yet the watery juices are more rectified and qualified : therefore all this, if it be true, must depend on these suppositions ;—First, that dry grounds, by reason of poverty, afford no rich juices, and consequently no good cheese, for we must not say, because North-Wiltshire being drier than Somersetshire outdoes it in cheese, therefore the hill-country in Hampshire being drier than North-Wiltshire has better cheese, for the contrary is evident.—Secondly, that there is a medium in the watery temperature of the earth, either extream of which viliorates the juice, where there is not an equal heat of the sun or fatness in the earth to correct the juices of the superluxuriant grass.

§. 21. This spring (anno 1720) was throughout a cold and very wet spring, and the summer was wet and showery till July the 18th, and a great burden of hay and grass there was in North-Wiltshire, unless in the water-meads, where they were stranded ; however cheese bore a great price, viz. twenty-four shillings per hundred, for that first made in the spring ; and the tenants of Holt who were going

In North-Wiltshire the greater the plenty of cheese, the dearer it sells.

with their cheese to Maudlin fair at Winchester, which is on the 22d of July, expected a higher price : the reason of which was this; the last summer was so very dry, and the winter-meat, both hay and straw, fell so very short, that the generality of cows were much pinched, so that the cows about Holt gave but little more milk or cheese this wet summer than they did the summer before. Again, it is generally noted, that in North-Wiltshire when they make most cheese, they sell it dearest, and when the least, they sell it cheapest; the reason is, in wet springs and summers, the generality of North-Wiltshire not lying low and wet, as Somersetshire does, in those years they make most cheese there, whereas the land of Somersetshire, and Lincolnshire, and the deep lands of England, lie all the spring and summer under water, or so much in a poach, that the grass is chilled, and cannot grow ; but in the North-Wiltshire summers it is the direct contrary : then in cold wet summers the first cheese-fair of our parts, which is Maudlin-hill fair, carries the best price of all the later fairs, as falling before the Somersetshire cheese can come to a fair.

Of the blue coat or vinnow on a cheese.

§. 22. Stephens having before made it one of the characters of a good cheese to carry a blue coat on it, or a vinnow : I asked him whether it were good housewifery to wipe that off. He said, there were two sorts of vinnow on cheese, one in the nature of mouldiness, or long downy vinnow, not blue, which proceeded from the moisture of the air and weather, especially towards winter, and such vinnow cannot be too often wiped off ; and, if neglected, it will eat into the cheese, and give it a bitterish taste within the coat; whereas the blueish vinnow he spoke of proceeded from the inward sweat of the cheese, and would come on the cheese in dry weather as well as moist.

§. 23.

§. 23. Of the three forts of cheefe, viz. the hay cheefe made fome time after the cows calving, the fpring-grafs cheefe made in May and June, and the aftermafs cheefe, though the aftermafs cheefe be the heavieft, and but taftelefs, yet it is the fatteft of the three, and, if it be kept to a good age, is a fingular good cheefe; for then the cows milk has the moft cream: the hay cheefe, if the cattle feed on good hay, will caft as yellow a colour on the coat as any, and being made in the fpring, will have a very hard and fmooth coat, having the fpring to dry it in; it is a very good cheefe, and very profitable in a family, being very tart on the tongue, and will go very far in fpending.

§. 24. Being at Pomeroy in Wilts to tafte cheefe in the beginning of November, (anno 1714) Stephens, having fold his cheefe made in the fpring, had only the early aftermafs cheefe fit for fpending left; but he and his wife affured me, fuch cheefe was fatter and mellower than the cheefe made in April, May, and June, though the fpring-made cheefe was tarter. I afked them how the aftermafs cheefe could be termed the fatteft, when certainly the grafs in May and June was richer than in July, Auguft, and September.—They faid, they fuppofed the reafon to be, becaufe the cows about April having brought calves, which were not weaned from them till about the beginning of May, the cows were low in flefh and condition, having had little grafs to fupport them till then, and when the flufh of grafs comes in May, it is true they give a great deal of milk, but not fo much cream in proportion, nor fo fat milk as in the aftermafs feafon, when the cows being got into good heart, and flefh, they better concoct and digeft the juices of the grafs with thofe of their own bodies.—So from thence, faid I, it muft follow, that a poor cow muft always give thinner milk than a cow in good flefh. Again, I fuppofe on his reafon depends in fome meafure the tartnefs

K 3   of

of the cheese made in the spring, becaufe the cows
have not then good juices in their own bodies to
qualify and mellow the acrimony of the juices of
the grafs, nor has the fun had time to concoct the
juices of the grafs, which are therefore eager and
tart.

Broad clo-
ver will
not make
good
cheefe.

§. 25. Mrs. Biffy the elder of Holt affures me,
that broad-clover will not make good cheefe ; for
it will tafte ftrong and bitter, yet they have not
found it to heave : fhe alfo fays, that neither the
milk nor the butter tafte well.

A cheefe-
loft fhould
be high
and cool.

§. 26. It is agreed by the dairy-men in Wiltfhire, that the higher in the ceiling a milk-houfe is,
and the lefs heat underneath, as from cattle in a
ftable, &c. fo much the better for a cheefe-loft ; for
heat makes cheefe heave, efpecially if the land it be
made from be rich.

Where
cows give
the leaft
milk, the
milk has
more
cream in
proportion
to the
quantity.
* Vid. §. 8.

§. 27. When farmer Sartain and farmer Stephens
were making remarks how the cows of Gaufuns exceeded thofe of Pomeroy in milk, yet they agreed
that no cheefe exceeded that of Pomeroy, and that
thofe dairies, where the cows give fo much milk,
did not make the richeft cheefe ; for, faid they,
where the cows give the leaft milk, the milk has
more cream in proportion to the quantity.— * But
this feems to be contrary to a former obfervation :
and farmer Sartain faid, this I know by the farm at
Holt, for when I lived there, none made better
cheefe than I did, though I rented only the arable
and poor grounds —Upon which I objected foon
after to farmer Sartain and farmer Chivers, how
then it came to pafs, that poor ground would not
make rich butter ? to which Chivers replied, that
doubtlefs it would ; that is, faid he, if you fhould
have a fufficient large dairy, and milk enough to
make butter every day, or every other day at fartheft ; for then the cream being fweet, the butter
would be fweet and rich alfo ; whereas poor and
fmall dairies churn but twice a week, and then, the
cream

cream being turned, or upon turning, the butter cannot be good. And the cream of four and coarfe grafs, fuch as mine is at Crux-Eafton, will fooner turn four in proportion to the fourness of the grafs.

§. 28. September 5th (anno 1712) being at Holt in Wiltfhire, I encouraged my tenant Stephens of Pomeroy to come to Crux-Eafton in Hampfhire at Michaelmafs to fell his fpring cheefe; viz. that made in May: and he feemed inclinable to do fo.—Of which defign of his I acquainted farmer Chivers the next day.—Chivers fmiled and faid, he thought Stephens would be wifer than to go fo far at that time of the year to fell his beft fpring-cheefe; for, faid he, fuch cheefe does not likely meet with the beft price till towards Candlemafs, when the aftermafs cheefe is fpent, for in autumn and about Michaelmafs there is fuch abundance of foft aftermafs cheefe to be fold, and the poorer fort of dairy-men pour it fo faft into the market, as alfo their fpring cheefe (for then thefe dairy-men's harveft is over) that the fpring-cheefe will rife afterwards in it's value, like hard-keeping pippins, which yield double the price at Chriftmafs that they would in autumn, when the country was full of all forts of fummer-apples, the great plenty of which fummer-fruit depretiates for fome time the price of the hard-keeping fruit: and in like manner, when the corn-harveft is juft in, fo many farmers occafions for money being to be anfwered, the beft corn will not generally come to the beft market till the glut is over, and the barns grow empty. I grant, faid farmer Chivers, the latter made or aftermafs cheefe we muft all properly fell, whether poor or rich, becaufe though the aftermafs cheefe be in truth as fat as the fpring cheefe, yet it is a heavy deadifh cheefe, and will grow tough or glewifh by keeping,

Spring-cheefe rifes in price towards Candlemafs.

K 4 whereas

whereas there is no occasion for selling the spring-cheese, unless for want of money, because that will grow mellow and gain spirits by age.

§. 29. Mr. Raymond told me (in June anno 1709) it was always observed about them, at Puck-shipton in Wiltshire, about two miles from Patny, that when wheat was dear, cheese was dear also, which seemed strange to him; because, said he, it was a wet and cold spring that made wheat dear, and then we have always the greatest plenty of grass, which one would think should make plenty of cheese.—I replied according to a former observation, the reason was plain to me, because the country where he lived, and Pewsy in his neighbourhood, lay on warm sands, which land, and the hill-country of Wiltshire within two miles of him, bore great burdens of grass, as he said, in wet and cold springs; but, said I, the deep and low lands of England, such as Somersetshire, &c. &c. which sort of lands set the price to cheese as well as wheat, miserably fall short of a crop of grass in cold and wet springs, as I told him I was but then newly an eye-witness of, for I came then from East-Lydford in Somersetshire to him, being June 19th, and the grounds of that country had not then got a good bite of grass, by reason of the cold wet spring, nor had they been able to fat cattle in time.

§. 30. Our hill-country land is so much the more improper for a dairy, because our foddering season holds so very long, and is so tedious, by means of our rowet-grass falling off a month sooner than their's in the vale, and the spring grass coming a month later; so that the cows must needs be in a low condition at spring.

As I have taken notice that the clover is sour in cold lands, so doubtless the butter and cheese must partake of it's nature more or less, as the clover

may

In Wiltshire when wheat is dear, cheese is dear, and why.

Hill-country land improper for a dairy.

may be fourer or fweeter, which may reafonably be fuppofed to be the caufe of the butter and cheefe at Fatton being ftrong and rank.[a]

S H E E P and L A M B S.

§. 1. **I**T is very neceffary in inclofed farms, that, if the fhepherd be not required to hedge at fpare times, he fhould however be required to mend, for his bufinefs being much in walking about the grounds, he has the opportunity of feeing what is amifs.

The fhepherd to mend hedges.

§. 2. My fhepherd affures me, that by my fhepherd's cart I fhall fave the value of it this one year, (anno 1701); for, fays he, it is impoffible in this hill-country but broad clover hay efpecially muft be abundantly blowed away by the wind, when it is carried by bundles at the fhepherd's back; whereas the fides of the cart will preferve it from the wind.

Benefit of a foddering cart.

§. 3. Having made fome remarks on the fmall profit arifing from a flock of fheep, I imparted the fubftance of it to a gentleman in my neighbourhood of long practice in hufbandry; he faid, that I was in the right of it, who lived in inclofures, but if he, where there was intercommoning, muft buy new fheep yearly at fpring, that were not ufed to fhift for their living, in their bare commons they would be ftarved; they muft therefore keep up a flock accuftomed to the place.——Add to this, that the

Advantage of keeping up a flock of fheep in open common fields.

[a] Among other ufeful inventions with which the reverend and learned Dr. Hales has obliged the world, he has publifhed one to fweeten milk that has got an ill tafte from the cows eating of crow garlick, cabbage, turnips, autumnal leaves, &c. which he effects by volatilizing the rancid oil with heat, and, when heated, diffipating it by ventilation.—See his Account of the good effect of blowing fhowers of air up through milk, and alfo a plate of the inftrument for performing it, printed for Richard Manby, in the Old-Bailey, near Ludgate-Hill, 1756.

winter-

winter-fold, by reason of the grass not being so sweet, and the frosts falling on it, is not so good as the summer-fold.

§. 4. Mr. Bishop of Dorsetshire his shepherd says, they generally reckon an ewe's third lamb to be the best; and they reckon a sheep to be at full growth and prime at four years old; though, he knew not, he said, but, if an ewe had great keeping, she might belly some time after that; some sheep would grow broken-mouthed at five or six years old, and others not till nine or ten: when they find an ewe a good motherly one, and to bring a good lamb, they keep her till she is broken-mouthed.

Best age of an ewe and sheep.

§. 5. Sheep at two years old have but two teeth, at three years old they have four teeth, at four years old six teeth.

Of sheep's teeth.

Of BREEDING SHEEP.

§. 6. I bought about forty ewes out of Oxen-lease in Wilts (anno 1718) where the ground is coarse, and they also fared hard; I brought them to Crux-Easton in October, where they had plenty of hop-clover; they seemed to do very well till December came, and then they crouded up under shelter of hedges, and ran into the lanes, and their wool being thin, and short, and more knotty than ours, they could not bear the cold of Crux-Easton well, nor keep the open fields in winter, nor could we hold them with the best hay, but they would pitch.—From hence quære, whether it be so good husbandry as is imagined, to mend our flock of sheep or cows by a fine wool-sheep or Gloucester-brown; since the produce carry such thin fine-grained hides, as may not prove so well on our cold hills.

Sheep from a warm country do not thrive on the hills.

§. 7. Sheep

§. 7. Sheep without horns are counted the beſt ſort : becauſe ſo much of the nouriſhment doth not go into the horns. J. M. Eſq; F. R. S. fol. 177.

Sheep without horns the beſt.

§. 8. I carried farmer Miles of Wiltſhire to a field where I had ſome * couples fatting, I told him the ewes were leather-mouthed with thick lips. —— He ſaid, they were called with them hants-ſheep; they were a ſort of ſheep that never ſhelled their teeth, but always had their lambs-teeth without ſhedding them, and thruſting out two broader in their room every year.—Being the next day at Mr. Raymond's, I had an opportunity of diſcourſing his ſhepherd, who ſaid, he had been a ſhepherd thirty years ; he knew the ſheep by the ſame name, and ſaid, that now and then, in buying a parcel of ſheep two or three would creep into their flocks, but he never knew ſo many together as twenty, which at that time I had : he ſaid their teeth would not hold them ſo long as other ſheep,· but would wear down to a thickneſs by reaſon of their biting on them from lambs, ſo they ought to be fatted a year the ſooner. Mr. Raymond being by ſaid, there were ſuch a ſort of horſes called by the name of hants-horſes, that always ſhewed themſelves to be ſix years old.

Of leather-mouthed or hants-ſheep. *Ewes and lambs.

My ſhepherd bought me a ſcore of couples ; when he brought them home he ſaid, they muſt be fatted, for they would not live in our flock, but would be ſtarved : they were a ſmall ſort of ſheep, and out of caſe. I wondered at it, and aſked him how that could be. He ſaid, they were thick lea‧ ther-mouthed cattle, of which ſort there were many in Wiltſhire and Berkſhire, and therefore they could not bite ſo cloſe as our ſheep, if they went in the flock with them.

§. 9. Mr. Oxenbridge of Wilts ſays, he grew weary of ſending his † hog-ſheep from Michaelmaſs to Lady-day into Somerſetſhire ; for, though by that means he brought them home in high caſe,

† Young ſheep ſhould be well kept.

and

and could maintain them so all the summer, yet he found they expected as good keeping the next winter, and for want of it would pitch, and not hold their flesh so well as those which had always continued on the farm.— I told farmer Ryalls, and Mr. Bishop's shepherd of this; they said, they were against sending hog-sheep abroad, if there was land to maintain them in the winter without pinching the flock; for, if the winter proved hard, they would often be cheated of their meat, and be neglected abroad: but a hog-sheep ought to be kept up well the first winter, to be brought into good bone and limb; for, if a * thief be not kept up well, and should pitch in yeaning-time, unless you take her lamb from her, and put it to an ewe, it is odds but you lose both thief and lamb; for it will bring the skenting or scouring upon her and kill her; and it is a very good way to put a thief's lamb to an ewe that has lost her lamb; for the ewe will maintain it well, and she is past improving, but the thief will thrive much the better for having the lamb taken from her.

* Young ewe of the 2d year, called also a two-teeth.

A free-martin sheep.

§. 10. Mr. Bissy says, an ewe-sheep that is a free-martin, besides the pissed stinking tail she carries, has a lesser and lanker bearing than other sheep.

Farmer Collins of the Isle of Wight assures me, there are free-martins in sheep both male and female; he has for a fancy sometimes kept one of each four or five years; he says, they will stink like a goat if you come near them, so that one can hardly bear the smell; and the female does not piss as other ewes do, but her piss comes dribbling from her, and the piss of the male runs dribbling down along his yard.

Of ewes not taking ram.

§. 11. Being at the fold with my shepherd, he pointed at an ewe, saying, what a fine ewe there is! her tail is apt to be so rough, and loaded with wool, that next ramming I will clip her; for, said he, I

believe

that laſt year the ram could not ram her for that reaſon.—I obſerved indeed her buttocks to be wadded with wool. —— That year (anno 1702) I had about thirty of my beſt ewes that went through and proved barren, which might be for the aboveſaid reaſon ; for I keeping my ſheep very well, they might by ramming-time carry too much wool on their buttocks : the year before I alſo had about twenty proved barren.

§. 12. Diſcourſing with a farmer in the Iſle of Wight about ſheep, I ſaid, now (in November 1718) ſheep being dear, an ewe-fold would pay better than a weather-fold becauſe of their increaſe. —To which he replied, it was undoubtedly ſo, in caſe the ſheep went in incloſures, where one could give them their bellies full ; but in caſe they go on common downs or fields, then of neceſſity one muſt keep weathers, becauſe they can fare hardier than ewes, or elſe your neighbour's flock will ſtarve your ewes.

In incloſures, when ſheep are dear, an ewe-fold pays better than a weather-fold.

§. 13. The ewes muſt be well kept all the winter, and better than the weathers : a weather's wool is of much leſs value than the wool of an ewe, and will ſcarce pay for his winter's keeping, but his tail in folding on the barley in ſpring, when the ewes muſt not be folded, will turn to better account. — Weathers among a flock of ewes will thrive better than by themſelves, becauſe they will beat off the ewes, and have the top of the graſs in ſummer, and the beſt of the hay in winter.

Of ewes and weathers.

§. 14. In buying ſheep for fatting at the firſt hand of the year in ſpring, one may be pretty ſecure of buying in thoſe that will thrive, inaſmuch as ſheep, which ſeem forward in caſe early in the ſpring, muſt be of a thriving ſort, otherwiſe they could not be forward in fleſh ſo early : but for the ſecond fatting it is not ſo certain, foraſmuch as ſheep may be in good caſe at Midſummer, and yet

Of buying ſheep for fatting.

have

have been a tedious while in arriving to that condition, and consequently will be so in their progression.

Of rubbing sheep's eyes with salt.
§. 15. My neighbour's shepherd asked me, if I knew how to make rotten sheep sound; on which I inquired of him, if he knew how to do it; he said, to rub their eyes with salt would deceive the buyer, and make the whites of their eyes look curious and red; that practice, said he, is common among the sheep-jobbers.——Afterwards I asked farmer Elton about it; he said, he had heard that the sheep-jobbers did use it.

Of making sheep to appear like folded sheep.
§. 16. Sir Ambrose Phillipps's shearers said, it was a common cheat about them, to get reddish clay, and dissolve it in water, and colour the sheep with it, and two or three hours after, when it was dry, to card their wool on their backs, to make the buyers believe they had been folded-sheep, and not pasture sheep; for folding the sheep on the fallows gives their wool that reddish colour; and in case the sheep were forest, or pasture-sheep, many would not buy them, because being not used to a fold, nor fallows, they would not be able to keep them in either, but they would break away.

Of lean sheep being dear in June 1707.
§. 17. Lean sheep sell well at this time (June 8, 1707) though the spring and summer-part of the year to the 22d of May (when rain fell) has been the driest in the memory of man; I was at a loss for the reason of this whilst in Hampshire, which is a breeding country of sheep; but when I came into Wiltshire, a grazing and fatting country, I soon saw the cause of the dearness of lean sheep: for it seems, a greater demand had been for their fat lambs for three years last past than ever was known, and greater droves of them carried to London, and when the ewe-lambs were fatted, the ewes were consequently fatted too, and this extraordinary consumption has wasted the breed of sheep, and consequently raised the price of lean weathers, but especially

cially of ewes.— In difcourfe afterwards with Mr.
Biffy on this fubject, he allowed there had been
greater drifts of lambs fent to London for thefe three
years laft paft than ufual, the reafon of which was
the breed of fheep greatly increafing, becaufe there
had been no rot, which moved farmers to fat lambs,
becaufe fheep were like to be cheap; but, faid he,
the aforefaid reafon is not the only one, why lean
fheep are dear, but the drought is the chief reafon,
for no rain falling till the 22d of May, and dry
weather following, graziers bought fheep, fearing
they fhould not be able to fat greater cattle, grafs
being fo fhort, and the feafon of the year fo late.

Being at the fold with my fhepherd, I afked him, Marks of a
what ram-lamb he would fave for a ram; he point- proper or
ed at one, which he faid was deep-woolled behind, improper
and had broad buttocks.——That is true, faid I, ram-lamb.
but yet I do not approve of him, becaufe he is fo
wide-headed, that is, his horns ftand fo wide, which
may endanger the ewes in yeaning by bringing fuch
lambs of the breed, as I have often heard it obferved by old experienced fhepherds.—— He admitted
this to be a proper objection.

§. 18. At Loughborough Capt. Tate was fay- A large
ing, that he would buy him a Lincolnfhire tupp to Lincoln-
improve his flock.—Major Hartop was there, and ʃhire tupp
bid him have a care that he was but of the leffer for ʃmall
fize, otherwife his ewes might die in yeaning, unlefs ewes.
they were large fheep. The next day I met Mr.
Clerk with captain Tate, and he faid the fame thing.
We fee it happens to little lap-bitches often, if lined
with a great dog.

§. 19. ᵃ Palladius, Columella, and Pliny, fpeak- Of the
ing of the choice of a ram, direct us, not only to choice of a
                                             have ram-from
                                                  the antient
                                                  writers.

ᵃ Cujus coloris fub linguâ habuere venas, ejus & lanicium eft
in fœtu, variumque, fi plures fuere. Plin. lib. 8. cap. 47.—Non
ʃolum ea ratio eligendi arietis, fi vellere candido veftitur, fed
                                                         etiam

have a regard to the whiteneſs of his wool, but to his palate, and the veins under his tongue, ſor, if theſe are black or ſpotted, according to their notion, the lambs that proceed from him will have black or ſpotted fleeces.

ᵇ Other qualities required in a ram, as delivered by the antient writers, are theſe. His figure ſhould be ſtately and tall, his belly big, ſwagging, and woolly, his forehead broad and well frizzled, his eyes of a haſel-grey, encircled thick with wool, his breaſt, ſhoulders, and buttocks broad, his tail very long and fleecy, his teſticles huge, the ringlets of his horns circling inward. Not·that a ram, ſays Columella, is more uſeful for having horns, for the beſt are thoſe that have none, but becauſe one of this *Probably kind is leſs * hurtful than thoſe, whoſe horns are to the ewes more open and extended : in climates however that in yeaning. are cold, wet, and ſubject to ſtorms, we rather recommend the largeſt headed rams ; for the greater and more ſpreading the horns, the more will their heads be covered and protected from the weather.

Of a ram, §. 20. Mr. Biſhop's ſhepherd ſaid, that they and the reckoned a ram would ſerve thirty ewes, though proportion they uſually kept two or three rams over and above of males to to their flock : they kept their rams well againſt females. ramming·time, but afterwards turned them out to

etiam palatum atque lingua concolor lanæ eſt ; nam cum hæ corporis partes nigræ aut maculoſæ ſunt, pulla, vel etiam varia naſcitur proles. Colum. lib. 7. cap. 3. Pallad fol. 161.

ᵇ Sint fronte lanâ veſtiti bene, ravis oculis lanâ opertis, auribus amplis, pectore & ſcapulis & clunibus latis. Varro, lib. 2. cap. 1.

Habitus autem maximè probatur, cum eſt altus atque proce‑ rus, ventre promiſſo atque lanato, caudâ longiſſimâ, denſique velleris, fronte latâ, teſtibus amplis, intorti‑ cornibus ; non quia magis hic ſit utilis (nam eſt melior mutilus aries) ſed quia mini‑ mè nocent. Quibuſdam tamen regionibus ubi cœli ſtatus uvidus, ventoſuſque eſt, arietes optaverimus vel ampliſſimis cornibus, quod ea porrecta altaque maximam partem capitis à tempeſtate defendant. Colum. lib 7. cap. 3.

the

the hardest fare ; and if the ewes warped, they turned them out to the rams again, and they would bring lambs again about St. James's-tide. The above is a large proportion of rams to ewes, for a good ram will very well serve no less than sixty ewes.

Mr. Bishop said, he knew how not to be deceived in a fair by a ram that had his stones in his back, for a weather : for he had a thicker nose, and was ram-headed.

Jacob presented to his brother Esau 200 she-goats and 20 he-goats, 200 ewes and 20 rams, 40 kine and 10 bulls, Genesis, cap. xxxii. ver. 14 and 15.—Quære, whether that might not be the proportion of males allotted to females in those countries.

§. 21. Mr. Bachelour of Ashmonsworth is much for keeping the ram from the hog-sheep till they are two years old ; for, says he, they make the only sheep for our hill-country, but hog-sheep in our hill-country make very ill mothers, unless extraordinarily kept. Columella recommends an ewe of two years old. Elige ovem bimam.

Ewes in the hill country not to be put to the ram till two years old.

The farmers are apt to give their ewes they sell at St. Leonard's the ram at Bartholomew-tide, and early, that they may thrive on it before they come to the market.

§. 22. I was saying to farmer Lake of Faccomb, Hants, that I wondered how my rams could break out, and get to my ewes, and ram them, because we coupled them together, and kept them in close inclosures, and they must get out to the ewes, because twenty of them had lambed a little after Christmass.—The farmer said, I suspect some of your forward ram-lambs might ram them, they not being kept separated from the ewes, for such ram-lambs will ram the ewes ; I myself, said he, had forty so rammed : and those ram-lambs of yours,

Of ewes being rammed by ram lambs.

which

which were lambed at Chriſtmaſs, will ram your ewes again, if nct ſeparated as ſoon as the rams are.

Colour of the lamb mark of the ewe's health.

§. 23. Farmer Ryalls of Dorſetſhire walking with me in Mr. Biſhop's ewe leaſe, he went up to a lamb not long lambed, that was of a yellowiſh hue, ſo coloured I ſuppoſe from the ewe : he ſaid ſuch a colour argued, that the ewe was in good heart and caſe, but if the lamb when lambed was of a greeniſh or blackiſh caſt, or of a pale white, it was otherwiſe.

Mark of the good caſe of ſheep.

§. 24. In walking he turned up ſome of the ſheep's-dung, which was of an intire clot, with only one or two foldings in it : he ſaid, and ſo did Mr. Biſhop's ſhepherd who was with us, that it was a ſign ſuch ſheep were in good caſe, and had their bellies full, whereas, if their dung came away in pellets it was otherwiſe.

Sign of an ewe's being near lambing.

§. 25. Cows and ſheep will fall away, and look hollow in the flank, a day or two before they calve or lamb, as if they had done ſo : and cows will always pitch upon their rump, that is, have more hollowneſs there than any where elſe.

Of tailing the ewes.

§. 26. Tailing the ewes in the ſpring-time, that is, cutting away the wool from under their tails, and their udders, is very proper, eſpecially in deep and fatting countries, where they fat their lambs, and do not fold : it keeps their udders ſweet and free from chopping by the heat of their urine, ſo that the ewe may the better bear the lamb ſucking her, for her udder being ſore, ſhe will not let the lamb ſuck, but will wean it ; and the ſweeter her udder is, the better will the lamb like to ſuck it ; whereas otherwiſe the lamb will be apt to take to graſs, and wean itſelf, whereby a lamb intended for fatting will be prejudiced.

Of the care of ewes, and lambs.

§. 27. In lambing-ſeaſon the hill-country ſhepherds have a hard time of it, being obliged to watch the ewes ſometimes for a month together, every

every night of the week, left they fhould be frozen
to the ground : it is fometimes very troublefome to
make the young ewes of a year old to take notice of
their lambs : if ewes are not wintered well, they
will never have good lambs, but rafcally ones ; it is
all in all to feed the ewes fo, that they may bring
good lambs.—— Oftentimes they are forced to give
the lambs milk, which if not boiled, will carry them
off by a loofenefs.—The warmer part of the downy
hill-country allow three tod and an half of hay to
the wintering of one fheep, and fuppofe the half tod
to anfwer the accidents of a feverer winter than ordinary, but at Crux-Eafton it is neceffary five tod
fhould be allowed to every fheep ; for the winter is
longer at Crux-Eafton than on moft part of the
downs, it lying under fnow fometimes a fortnight,
or a month together, when the other downs are
free from it.

About lambing time when they hurdle up the
lambs new fallen in the mead at night, it is cuftomary
for them to go forth at midnight, and to ftir up the
ewes ; for fome ewes will be fo lazy as not to rife
all night, and then their lambs will be almoft ftarved by morning, whereas when they are thus raifed,
their lambs will have opportunity to fuck.—By that
means alfo a lamb may be faved, which the ewe
could not lamb without help ; and fometimes a
lamb will be faved, which was in danger of being
loft, by getting out of the fold between the hurdles.
ᶜ The antients laid a great ftrefs on the attendance
and care of the fhepherds at yeaning time, and Palladius advifes to put the lamb to the teat as foon as

ᶜ Paftor partus pecoris non fecus ac obftetricum more cufto-
dire debet ; neque enim aliter hoc animal quam muliebris fexus
enititur, fæpiufque laborat in partu.——Columella, lib. 7. c. 3.
——Agnus ftatim natus uberibus maternis admovendus eft :
manu prius tamen exiguum lactis, in quo fpiffior eft natura, mul-
gendum, quod paftores coloftram vocant ; namque hoc agnis,
nifi auferatur, nocebit.   Pallad. in calendar. Novem.

it is fallen, but to take the beeftihgs from the ewe firft, left they fhould be hurtful to the lamb.

Of ewes taking ram

§. 28. My ewes not lambing fo faft after they had begun in March (anno 1702) as ufually, I was fpeaking of it to my fhepherd : he faid, he believed it was, becaufe we folded them late in the year, on the cold wheat-land, after it was fowed, which made them not take ram fo faft.

Knotted fheep often breed from horned, &c.

§. 29. Mr. Bifhop fays, he fees no difference between the horned and knotted fheep : if he fees a fine lamb of the knotted fheep he keeps him, though his flock be horned : he fays, he has often a knotted lamb from the horned fheep, and a horned lamb is often bred from a knotted ewe ; — and fometimes a black lamb from a white ewe and ram.

The firft lamb generally pot-bellied

§. 30. It is to be obferved, that the firft lamb an ewe brings is generally potted, that is, pot-bellied, fhort, and thick, which is not fo good a lamb as the long ftraight-limbed lamb is ; [d] the antients feparated thefe from the reft of their flock, as being of a weak nature, and not fo long-lived as thofe that came from older ewes.

Of cows milk for lambs.

§. 31. It is advifeable to be provided with a cow with calf in winter, that the weak and fickly lambs may have milk in the fpring; and the offall hay the fheep make will fodder her ; but, if ewes are kind to their lambs, and have milk enough for them, it is better not to give them cows milk ; for it does not agree with lambs fo well as ewes milk, but is apt to fcour them, for which reafon they ufually boil it.

Of recovering chilled lambs.

§. 32. If a lamb, when firft lambed, is overcome by the hardfhip of the weather, wrap it in a wifp of ftraw, and bring it to a hay-reek, and it is ftill better if it be in a fheep-barn, where the fheep may go

---

[d] Oviculas ex primiparis natas abalienare oportet, ceùminimè diuturnas.—— Didymus in Geoponicis, fol. 430. Primiparis minores fœtus. Plin. lib. 8. c. 47,

round

round it ; thruft the lamb into a warm hole of the
reek, and in a day's time, if any thing will, it will
recover the lamb, and then you muft bring the ewe
to it, that it may fuck : the reek is much more fuitable to the nature of the lamb than the fire-fide.

§. 33. The main care to preferve lambs at yeaning time, if fnow fhould fall, is to bed them with
ftraw. A young ewe will be fhy of her lamb by
reafon of the tendernefs of her udder : the young
ewe, being forward, muft be kept hurdled up for a
day and a night, till fhe takes to her lamb, in the
fame manner as when a ftrange lamb is put to an
old ewe.

Of the care of lambs.

When Mr. Bifhop's fhepherd had tamed an ewe
that he had tied up to a ftrange lamb, he ufed, when
he let her out, to tie her hinder and her fore leg together with a ftring, that fhe might not run away
from her lamb.

If an ewe warps her lamb before her time, or
the lamb comes at it's full time, but in an ill condition, or dead, it feems improper, to me, to put a
twin-lamb, or a thief's lamb to fuch an ewe ; for
fuch an ewe's milk will not be kindly, nor will the
lamb thrive ; but, if the lamb comes at full time
and found, though dead, or is afterwards killed by
an accident, then fuch ufage is very good, and I
have done accordingly.

If any good ewe lofe her lamb by a fox, or wea-
fel, or other accident, the fhepherd ought to fet a
thief's lamb or twin-lamb to her : the lamb's head
to be wiped with the fheep's green tail, till brought
to it's nature ; and

If there be no lamb in that flock to fpare, a lamb
ought to be fought in a neighbouring flock.

In lambing-time always put thofe ewes that
brought twins apart by themfelves ; becaufe, if you
let them go with the other ewes and lambs, they

are apt to lose one of their lambs, till they are a little
settled with them.

^c Palladius speaking of the ewes that have newly
lambed, says, the lamb should be shut up with the
ewe for two days.

Of wean-
ing lambs.
§. 34. As to weaning of lambs, in some places
they never sever the lambs from the dams, especially in the best pastures, where the ram goes constantly with the ewes; because, when the ewe goes
to ram again she will go dry, and wean her lamb
herself; and in unsound pasture they reckon it best
for lambs to run with their ewes, because they seldom rot while they suck, unless the ewe's milk
fails. J. Mortimer, Esq; F. R. S. fo. 179.

Of care in
catching a
lamb.
§. 35. The butcher coming to kill me a lamb,
which I helped to catch, I held it up by the back to
weigh it ; and, when he had killed it, I observed
the blood, where I had griped the lamb on the back,
was already settled in a bruised manner, though
killed immediately upon it.——He says, it neither
hurts calf nor lamb to catch it by the hinder leg.

Of cutting
lambs.
§. 36. They used at Crux-Easton formerly to
cut their tup-lambs early, within six weeks old ;
but of late (anno 1697) they have put it off to St.
James's-tide, because they find the lambs, when so
old before they are cut, carry a better head for it. —
In Wiltshire they cut them at six weeks old. — The
Wiltshire farmers judge it is hard to keep the wound
from the flies, when cut so far on in the summer.

Id. and of
spots on
lambs
thighs.
Farmer Farthing of Appleford in the Isle of
Wight, who had in April (anno 1700) newly cut
his lambs, assured me, that several of the lambs
would have under their legs, on their thighs, red
spots in the flesh or skin, as big as the top of one's
finger, and if they cut such lambs they would most
certainly die in less than twelve hours ; nay, said he,

^c Per biduum natus cum matre claudatur. Palladius, fol. 118.

if

if such lambs be but slit in the ear or ear-marked, so as blood be drawn whilst they have those spots, they look on it that they will die: but three or four days after those spots appear they will go away, and then they may be cut : ——he had half a score that he forbore cutting at that time for that reason.——He says, in the island they cut the lambs in the beginning of April at farthest, that they may cut them before these spots come forth, for they observe the spots to come forth when the hawthorn bushes begin to bud.--To all these points farmer Glyde did agree, and says farther, that, if they had no spots under their thighs, yet, if they were in their bodies, which was not to be seen, it was the same thing ; for he had lost lambs, and when he had flead them, he saw the spots.——Farmer Farthing's shepherd caught me a lamb or two to shew me the spots, which were like a bloody scurvy-spot.

In the island they approve of cutting lambs and not of girding ; because girding makes them not limb so well in their thighs, nor be fat there, when they come to be fatted.

When I discoursed my shepherd, and farmer Elton about the red spots under lambs thighs, and told them, in the island they all looked on it to be mortal to cut a lamb at that time, I asked whether they did not observe the same about them. I found they had heard something of it, but said, the method in their country was to sear, and if it be dexterously done, no blood will be drawn, nor do they regard whether they do it when the spots are on the lambs or not.

Sir Ambrose Phillipps's shepherd knew nothing of the red spots under lambs thighs, and yet cuts them about the beginning or middle of April ; he observes not the sign, nor thinks it ought to be regarded, only he takes care not to cut them when the weather is too hot, nor in wet weather; for the wet

falling

falling on their loins at that time, is apt to give them cold. — He says, it is a common opinion amongst them, that if a man cuts lambs who has a stinking breath, or that takes tobacco at the time, either of these will poison the place, and make it apt to gangrene.——An Irishman, coming to Sir Ambrose's to buy mares and rams in that country for breed, wondered to see the shepherd cut his lambs on a day when the wind was northerly, and said, they should in Ireland look on it to be certain death to the lamb, if cut on such a day.

Formerly the butchers used not to like searing, but would have the lambs be drawn because it hurt the leg of mutton, it never being full there, which was true as they then managed it; but of late we find searing to be the safer way, and to put the lamb to less pain than drawing, and we now prevent that mischief by searing as little of the cod away as possible.

The butchers assure me, that a pur or ram-lamb will never be so fat for the butcher as an ewe-lamb : they say, the pur-lambs I intend to fat should be drawn as soon as they are a fortnight old; they would fat much the better for it ; and if I should keep them to be weathers, though they will not run so much to a head as those that are cut or drawn later, yet they make better mutton

June 3d (anno 1702) I cut my pur-lambs, the weather being very hot, and they seemed to my shepherd to do very well that night and all the next day, not being able to come to the pond to wet themselves ; the third day they had the liberty of the pond, when he observed they would take the water, and even swim, they went in so deep: that week I lost six of them, which died of the rankling of the cutting : I had at the same time ten lambs cut, which went by themselves from the flock, being twin-lambs, but they could come at no water,
and

and thefe did very well.— Therefore it may be
fhrewdly fufpected that the other lambs rankled
from their running up fo deep in the water, and
that they fhould be kept from water, efpecially in
hot weather, for three or four days after their being
cut.—Mr. Edwards affures me, he has often heard
that going into the water was very dangerous for
new-cut lambs ;—but farmer Bond fays, he keeps
not his from water, nor has he found that it hurts
them.

Mr. Biffy draws the ftones both of his calves and
his lambs himfelf with his teeth. I wondered at it,
becaufe it feemed at firft, as if he thought touching
the ftones with the hand or an inftrument might
not fucceed fo well; but he faid, the only reafon he
knew of was, becaufe by the help of his teeth one
man could do two men's work ; for whilft he draws
the ftones with his teeth, he has his two hands at
liberty to hold back the ftrings of the ftones that
they are not drawn away ; for the ftrings run up into the loins and back-bone, and if care be not taken
to keep them back with both hands, the ftones
would draw the very cawl after them, and then the
lambs muft die ; therefore the way is to draw the
ftones leifurely with the teeth, that you may be fure
to hold the ftrings from drawing after.

Mr. Bifhop fays, in Dorfetfhire they cut not their
lambs till the latter end of May. I afked him the
reafon of it. He faid, they kept them the longer
from cutting, that they may be able to fold on the
barley-grounds, which they would not be, if they
were cut in March : their great fair for pur-lambs
at Sherbourn is in July.—They have three ways in
Dorfetfhire for cutting lambs ; by cutting and fearing ; by fwigging, which is girding them hard
round the cods, and cutting the cod away clofe to
the ftring ; they know whether it be well done or
not by it's not bleeding afterwards ; and thirdly,

drawing,

drawing, which is done by making a flit in the cod as wide as an half crown, and drawing out the ftones, which will bring away with them a back ftring, and ftuns the poor lamb for the time : if this way kills them it is in two or three days time, but in fwigging they will die fometimes a month after : Mr. Bifhop ufes drawing, and fays it is the beft way : and fo faid another farmer.

About Holt they cut their lambs at a fortnight or three weeks old, though they fhould fall at Chrift-mafs : and then, fays Ifles and William Sartain, they will eat as fweet as the ewe-lambs : they take care to cut them in dry or frofty weather, and not in wet, and to keep them walking after it, and to raife them up three or four times, and keep them ftirring that day they are cut.——Note, they all draw their lambs-ftones with their teeth, which is the on-ly way if you intend to fat them.—— They fay, it is fo eafy to do, that any one may do it.

They advife me to put my ewes to ram, in cafe I would fat my lambs, fo as to come the latter end of January, or, confidering the coldnefs of our coun-try, in the middle of February.—— William Sartain faid at another time, that he fcrupled not to draw the ftones of his lambs at four or five days old, if they were come down, fo as to take hold of them, and had commonly done it, but never loft any.

The north country, as Lincolnfhire, and thofe counties that fend their knot-headed lambs (i. e. not horned ones) to Smithfield market, (they being great lambs of large-fized fheep) do not fend their lambs to London till about Midfummer, and hold on fending till about Bartholomew-tide; thofe lambs are coarfe, efpecially the males, becaufe they do not geld them, though they fat them, which makes them the larger ; for they agree, that gelding them makes them of lefs growth, though the meat is the fweeter for it.

§. 57. Mr.

§. 37. Mr. Clerk was telling me how they ma- Of fatting lambs in Essex.naged their lambs in Essex to sell them so fat in the London markets, as they do before Christmass ; he says, they keep their ewes as high as ever they can, and house their lambs, and bring in the ewes to them at six in the evening for all night, and turn them out at six in the morning till nine, and then take them in again for some time, and turn them out till six.—But as soon as an ewe's lamb is fatted off, and sold, they keep such ewes to serve the lambs that are left ; the ewes that feed all night are taken in in the morning about nine, and then the mother-ewes are not called in in the day-time : the foster-mothers are held whilst the lambs suck : all the time of fatting the lamb has it's bed of straw changed once or twice in twenty-four hours, and a chalk-stone to lick on.

§. 38. Virgil seems to be wraped up in his poe- Of ewes bringing lambs twice a year.tical spirit when he triumphs on the fruitfulness of Italy, and says,—" that the lands bear two crops in " a year, and the ewes lamb twice." By which he must mean, that the ewes so lamb twice in a year, as to bring up their lambs to a marketable condition, within the compass of the year, that is, so as to have taken their weaning, or be fit for the butcher ; otherwise if he means, that their ewes bring lambs twice within the compass of the year without rearing them, he says no more than what is common throughout the world.— The Rei rusticæ scriptores say, " that when the ewe takes ram again, she will " wean her lamb." But it seems this expression of the Rei rusticæ scriptores is generally to be understood ; and doubtless, according to the common condition of flocks, the ewes are not in so good case as to suckle one lamb and breed another, and therefore will, if with lamb again, wean the sucking lamb. —But it happened otherwise with farmer Stephens, my tenant, for he had three ewes that went in good pasture, which brought him lambs at Christmass,

which

which he fold fat to the butcher at Lady-day laft (anno 1707) and at the beginning of June thinking his ewes to be mutton, for they looked big, he went to fell them to the butcher, who handled them, and found their udders fpring with milk, and that they were near lambing, and accordingly did lamb the firft week in June : and this his neighbours know to be true.——Thefe ewes being well kept, did in this cafe, it is evident, take ram three months before they weaned their firft lambs : and thefe ewes had always been ufed to bring twin-lambs, and fo of a more fruitful fort, though in this cafe they brought but fingle ones.

I am informed from Dr. Sloan, that in Jamaica ewes bring forth twice in fifteen months, without any regard to the time of the year, but cows as in Europe.

Time when lambs, &c. are eatable. §. 39. When God demands the firft-born of cattle for himfelf (Exod. xxii. 30.) he fays, " feven " days it fhall be with it's dam, on the eighth day " thou fhalt give it to me." On which Dr. Patrick remarks, " that till then the young were not " of a maturity, nor accounted wholfome."——To which I muft add, that they are not fo by that time in our cold-country in England, where a fortnight is the fooneft we think well of fuch creatures for eatables : but it is very reafonable to believe they were maturer in half that time in Judea ; for it is apparent to me, on experience, that fucking-pigs, and lambs, and calves, thrive much fafter in England in the hot months of the fummer, than they do in winter.

OF SHEARING SHEEP.

To let fheep cool before they are wafhed. §. 40. Being on the 4th of June (anno 1701) to wafh our fheep on the morrow, I afked my fhepherd, what time in the morning he would drive them to the wafh-mills ; he faid, they fhould not

begin

begin washing perhaps till ten, but he would begin to drive them by five in the morning, or earlier, that the sheep might have time to cool after they came there, before they were washed, otherwise it might make them ill.

§. 41. Going along with my sheep to washing, my shepherd asked me, if I should in a week's time want to kill a fat sheep, because if I did, said he, I will not wash him; for the tumbling and rubbing the sheep damages the mutton, if killed so soon after, but it is never the worse for it in a fortnight's time. *Not to wash a fat sheep you intend to kill in a week after.*

§. 42. In Kent, near Hiam-kill-marsh-priest, about ten miles beyond Gravesend, they wash their sheep in the following manner; —— there being creeks, that are muddy, when the tide is down, but, when the sea flows, are deep in water, they tie ropes to three or four sheep of the flock, and hall them over, the rest willingly following, and then the said sheep are drawn over again in the same manner, and by the time they have swam over seven or eight times, which is as often as they well can do in a tide, they will be well washed : — and this washing, they say, is preferable to our scouring and rubbing them : — from hence it appears the salt water is not pernicious to their wool. *Manner of washing sheep near Gravesend.*

§. 43. I asked Sir Ambrose Phillipps's shearers, if they did not reckon a slow-running water better to wash the sheep in than a quick-running stream, because it scoured better. — The shepherd said, he had heard it so reckoned, but he rather liked a sharp stream, for if it did not scour so well, yet it left not that oily smell behind it that the other was apt to do, which would invite flies to blow the wool between washing and shearing. —— The shearers said, —they believed they could not wash their sheep so clean as we could at Crux-Easton, because their sheep went much *Washing sheep in Leicestershire.*

much on a fandy foil, and the grit of that would
not wafh out fo well as the clay.

Of fhearing
fheep's tails
in the Ifle
of Wight
and Hert-
fordfhire.
§. 44. Coming over Appleford-common in the
Ifle of Wight, I obferved the tails of the weathers
fheared clofe all along down from the rump, fo that
their tails hung down like rats-tails : I inquired the
meaning of it, and was anfwered, that they always
did fo in the Ifle of Wight both to weathers and
ewes, and particularly to the latter, becaufe they
fo bepiffed their tails, that it burned and fcorched
up their dugs.—They fometimes began to do it in
the beginning of April, fometimes not till May,
according as the feafon proved.—My bailiff fays,
they have the fame cuftom in Hertfordfhire.

Of care in
fhearing
ewe-lambs.
§. 45. Shearers ought to go very foberly and
carefully to work, left they cut off the ewe-lamb's
teat, and yet, be they never fo careful, that may
fometimes be done ; and in fuch cafe they ought to
take care to mark fuch a lamb, that it may be fatted.

Of care,
that fheep
may not
fcour be-
tween
wafhing
and fhear-
ing.
§. 46. I was talking of driving my fheep into a
lay-ground of frefh grafs after wafhing, and before
fhearing : but many that were prefent faid, by no
means ; for that would fcour them, and foul their
wool ; and alfo, when drove into the barn, they
would be trampling in their dung and daub themfelves ; therefore, faid they, we take care to give
them the fhorteft pafture, after wafhing till fhearing,
we can get, that their dung may be pellets.

Of prick-
ing fheep
in fhearing
§. 47. In fhearing the danger is, left any of the
fheep fhould be pricked with the fhears, which if
done, and not taken notice of, fo as to cut it out
with the fhears, it will be apt to rankle, and kill the
fheep in twenty-four hours time ; but cutting does
Of fheep
being fmo-
thered in
the fhear-
ing-barn.
little or no prejudice if tarred.

§. 48. The night before fhearing we drove the
fheep into the barn, left rain fhould come : my
shepherd,

shepherd, and those who helped him, were in fear lest any of them should be smothered, and therefore they ought to be looked to, to see they keep their faces in the air. — My next neighbour lost seven or eight in one shearing-time, and divers others have had the like misfortune happen.

§. 49. Mr. Weedon, and Mr. Cowslade of Wood-hay, usually shear and wash their fatting-sheep by May-day: the reason they give for it is, because their inclosures are very small, and consequently too hot, and therefore their fatting-sheep need to have their coats off so much the earlier, and they thrive the better for it. *Fatting-sheep in inclosures to be sheared early.*

§. 50. ᶠ It was an ancient custom (as the Rei rusticæ scriptores tell us) to pluck the wool from the sheep's backs, instead of shearing it, and this custom lasted in some places even to Pliny's time, and Varro derives the word vellus, a fleece, from vello, to pluck. *Of plucking sheep.*

§. 51. I never used to shear till the Monday before Midsummer-day, but I now (anno 1714) find I was in an error in so doing, and that, as my keeping is very good, by which means the wool grows the larger, and heats the sheep the more, and their fleshiness being such as to bear the cold the earlier in parting with their fleeces, I ought to begin to shear the first week in June; and the sheep would not only thrive much the better, when the load of their wool was gone, but their new wool would also have more time to grow against Weyhill fair, which would make the sheep look more burly. Sheep when shorn have better stomachs, for the heat of the wool takes away their appetites. *Sheep well kept may be sheared the earlier.*

ᶠ Oves non ubique tondentur; durat quibusdam in locis vellendi mos. Plin. lib. 8. c. 48. Et Varro de re rustica, lib. fol. 64. ait, Ex vocabulo—vellera, animadverti licet, prius lanæ vulsuram quam tonsuram inventam.

What

What in scripture is tranflated the fhearing-houfe, fignifies in the original, the houfe of the fhepherd's binding; for they bound the feet of the fheep when they fheared them. Vid. notes on 2 Kings x. 12.

To avoid houfing fheep if the weather will permit, before fhearing.

§. 52. Two or three days before my fheep-fhearing, I was confulting with my fhepherd how to provide barn-room enough to houfe my fheep the evening before fhear-day, in cafe it fhould be likely to rain that evening.—He was very defirous to have more barn-room than former fhepherds, to keep his fheep cool; but had great hopes the weather would be fo very fair, that they need not be houfed till the morning of the fhear-day; for, faid he, the houfing them over-night before fhear-day, when they are loaded with wool, heats them fo, that when they are fheared they catch cold, and will be glandered, and fnivel very much.

A great advantage to poor fheep to have moderate weather after fhearing.

§. 53. The fhearers agreed, that, if fheep were poor, it was a great advantage to them to have two or three good feafonable and moderate days of weather after fhearing, for, if the fheep were poor when fheared, and two or three hot days came prefently upon them before they were fettled, it was wonderful to fee what alterations it would make on them: their fkins would turn fcurfy and ftarky, and their wool grow thin: and, if the weather fhould prove cold, and exceeding wet, it would quite chill fuch fheep; about fix weeks ago, it being about Midfummer (anno 1699) a mighty cold and wet day and night falling on fuch fheep the next day after their fhearing, they were fetched home dead in dung-pots; but neither of thofe forts of weather had much effect on fat fheep, or thofe in very good cafe.

Why they fhear lambs in Hamp-fhire and not in Wiltfhire.

§. 54. I afked farmer Biggs, Mr. Edwards being prefent, why they fheared their lambs in this country, and not in our part of Wiltfhire. They faid, they judged we folded not fo much as they: and that lambs being folded and kept hot thereby, it

would

would increase their tick which breeds in them; and they observed the wool, if let alone, would quite eat out the flesh of the lamb, and bring it to be out of case.

§. 55 Many farmers in Hampshire always let alone shearing their sheep till a week or ten days after the washing; it is held that the sheep's sweating so long in their wool does it good, and makes it weigh the heavier.

Not to shear till a week after washing.

Farmer Biggs and I discoursing on sheep-shearing, the farmer said, it was a great damage to wool to have the moth, which was chiefly got, especially if the wool was kept above a year, by laying it against a south, south-west, or other damp wall, or by shearing the sheep before the wool was dry after washing.—But, said I, how can one help it? if shearing-day be set, and it should so fall out that much rain should fall between washing and shearing-time. — Said he, the rule of the country is, that farmers that use the same shearers, and are to come after, must put back their shearing-days, that you may stay till your wool be dry: but, added he, such hindrance seldom happens, for, lest rain should fall the night before shearing-time, they that have barn-room use to drive their sheep in there the night before, or, if rain should fall on them the day before, they will drive them close up into a barn, where their wool will heat, and the wet soon be dried up: others will not drive them up into a barn the night before shearing, if not likely to rain, but will watch them, lest rain unexpected should come.—And they that have dry downs for their sheep to go in, will keep them a week or ten days after washing, before they will shear them, that the sheep may sweat in their wool, which is a very good way; for by the oily goodness the wool gets, it will grow till that be spent after shearing.

Id. and of the moth in wool.

On the contrary, Mr. Raymond and his shepherd were discoursing on washing, and proposed washing to be on a Monday, and shearing the Wednesday after.—I asked if that was not too soon ; they said, no, the heat of their bodies and the sun would dry their wool in one day and a night, and that many farmers would shear the next day. — The shepherd seemed to be desirous of having it done the sooner, lest the fly should damage the wool by blowing it : all however agree the wool should be dry before it is sheared.

Of not marking sheep till two or three days after shearing.

§. 56. In shearing the sheep at Sir Ambrose Phillipps's, the shepherd gave them the ruddle-stroke, but not Sir Ambrose Phillipps's-mark. — I asked him, how that came to pass ; he said, he thought it was better to let them alone two or three days first, for while they were so bare of wool they were apt to be burnt with the iron, which would make the place sore and subject to the flies.

OF FOLDING SHEEP.

Of the sheep-folds of the eastern countries.

§. 57. Numb. xxxii. 16. " And we will build sheep-folds here for our cattle." Which looks as if such husbandry was in use then as is now-a-days. But quære the original, and see the 14th verse, which being compared with this, it seems their sheep were kept in immoveable houses, not in moveable folds as now-a-days.

Columella says, " Quæ circa Parmam & Mutinam macris stabulantur campis." lib. 7. fo. 173.— Therefore it seems they had some way like our sheep-folds, and did not trust altogether in sheepcoats.

It further appears, that the sheep-folds of the eastern countries were not such as our's, but houses, to which

said he, two hundred ewes and their lambs will do as much, if not more, good by folding on an acre of land, as four hundred weathers: I have, said he, folded apart on the same land at the same time two hundred ewes and their lambs, and in another fold of equal dimension five hundred weathers, and I have always found, that the folding of the ewes did me the best service, and brought me the best corn.

§. 63. My shepherd is of opinion, that ewes ought not to be folded on the barley-fallows, or any other fallows in lambing-time, but weathers only ; for the lambs being wet when lambed would be dirtied with the fallows, and the ewes would presently forsake them ; therefore the ewes ought in lambing-time to be folded in the meadows, where it is clean, and the folds removed as often as the cold wind should change from corner to corner. – And afterwards, he said, they ought to fold weathers on the barley till a fortnight after May, but the ewes never after Candlemass. *Of folding on barley, &c.*

It is plain that the early folding an ewe-flock and lambs in April, on wheat-fallows, pinches the lambs, and so does folding them at that time on the barley-grounds, both which are too cold for them, especially in our hill-country ; care ought therefore to be taken, that those lands do not of necessity want folding on in those months, but that they may be otherwise provided for, and that during that time the ewe-fold may be on grass-grounds, or lay-grounds designed for fallows.

We must be more cautious in April and May of folding an ewe-fold on the barley-land, they being wettish, than of folding them on the wheat sown in August or September ; because the lambs in April and May make the ewes rise often and move, whereby the ground becomes much more trodden at that time of the year by the ewe-fold, than it

M 3   would

would be by a weather fold, or an * hog-fold, as may apparently be seen, if the folds be divided.

§. 64. Telling Mr. Gerrish the grazier, and farmer Isles, how dear Mr. Eyres our minister sold fat lambs to the number of fifteen, May 18th, viz. for ten shillings and six-pence each, and that they had been folded all along to the very day he sold them. —— They replied, that folding the lambs did very little hurt them with respect to their fat, provided they were drove pretty late to fold, and let out early in the morning.

§. 65. Sunt qui optime stercorari putent sub dio retibus inclusa pecorum mansione. Plin. f. 299. So it seems this was a folding as we do, unless by sub dio, be meant, by day.

§. 66. Walking with Mr. Raymond into his arable-common-fields October 25th (anno 1708) we met his shepherd pitching the fold on the new-sowed wheat. —— I asked him, whether he did not find that pitching the fold on the wheat at this time of the year, and a fortnight later, turned to a much better account than folding for the barley-crop for the year following. Mr. Raymond and his shepherd readily replied, undoubtedly it turned to the best account to fold after this time on wheat. —— I said, for my part, I had observed the fold carried on the land designed for barley so early in the winter had little effect, it's strength being spent and washed away by spring, so that it will make but little shew in the crop of barley next summer, and that therefore I chose to preserve four, five, or six acres of wheat-fallow that lies warm, and will bear sowing late, to carry my fold over to the latter end of October, rather than finish my wheat-fold by the end of September, and then carry it on my barley; for though the latter part of October might, in our cold country, be too late to sow wheat, yet it was

better

better than to be so soon folding barley, which would be no better for it.—— To which they replied, I was much in the right.——And as I have before observed how insignificant the fold is in the winter, especiaily in hard frosts, I imparted it to Mr. Raymond, who concurred with me, and said, he had folded on arable land in snow, and found not the least benefit : whereupon he resolved in such cases to fold on meadow and pasture, in mighty expectations of grass, but it made no return, wherefore in snows, he now lets his sheep ramble.

§. 67. Whereas I have said, that in cold clay-ground, and in a cold high hill-country, a winter-fold does little good, yet I have by experience found the contrary in such parts of the hill-country, where the land is dry and light, and that it does great service to the barley crop.—— This difference may be reconciled thus, i. e. where the land, though called hill-country land, does not lie very high, for the height much tends to the chilling of the ground : again, the explanatory reason of this difference, though hardly accountable for, yet seems to me chiefly to lie in the chilling quality of the ground which at first receives the dung and piss, and that deadens the ferment ; whereas in warmer ground it's progression toward that end is supported by a sufficient benign warmth, since in both sorts of earth the urine does undeniably sink into the earth and mix with it.

Of winter-folding in the hill-country.

§. 68. My ground being cold and feeding, I should in the spring of the year, when I come either to pitch my fold on the barley-fallows, or on the sown barley, set it very wide, in order to avoid the usual inconveniencies of penning at that time, viz. the rankness and lodging of the barley, and the consequences, thinness and coarseness.

To fold wide in spring on cold feeding ground

§. 69. It was the 10th of October (anno 1720) when my fold was going to be set on the wheat-fallows

Caution against folding on wheat in wet land soon after sowing.

M 4 lows

lows of a field, which was heavy land, and the fallows, where the fold was to go, were to be ploughed up the next day; I was afraid the land would be too wet to fold on after the wheat was sown, and spoke to the shepherd about it.   He said, he believed I might be in the right, especially since the rams had been some days put to ramming the ewes, because the rams would keep moving and stirring the ewes all night in the fold, whereby the ground would be battered and trod, and so squatted that the wheat might not get through.

§. 70. That the Greeks did pen up their sheep that they might piss through hurdles, as in Herefordshire, you may see in Palladius's calendar, November, to avoid dirtying and damaging their fleeces.

Of penning sheep on hurdles.

§. 71. Farmer Miles, whom I have often mentioned with approbation, advised me, if I would turn arable into meadow, and lay it up to grass, to fling straw upon it that is less than half rotten, and then fold upon it the same night, and it will bring the ground on very fast.

Of turning arable to meadow.

§. 72. Pursuant to what has been before said, that folding in winter for barley is not profitable, because, by waiting for the fold's running over the land, we lose the principal season of fallowing; yet however it may be proper to fold till Christmass, and then go on the wheat-lay; because we can lose no fallowing season by that; we cannot well have finished our fallowing any year before Christmass.

Of winter-folding for barley.

I find by Mr. Antill and Mr. Clerk, and others, that in Leieestershire they have no winter-folding for barley; they leave off by Michaelmass at farthest, and sometimes cannot fold again till May; the reason is, their lands are so wet they would be always in a poach, and the coldness of the lands would kill the sheep: to help which defect, they

Id. in Leicestershire.

muck

*muck their barley-lands, and from thence begin   *Dung.
their hufbandry, and fow wheat the year after, often
under furrow, on their barley-ftubble, for they fay,
if they fhould dung their wheat-ground it would rot
their wheat, and they fow peas or beans after the
wheat, and then lay the ground to fummer-fallow
again, to be mucked in May for barley, or to fold
for wheat; fo that they carry out their dung before
it is half rotten, or the feeds of the weeds killed:
but in their inclofures they fow four crops of corn
all on one earth, without dung, for the moft part
beginning with oats, and laying down to grafs with
wheat.

§. 73. I am told, that in Dorfetfhire the aim of Folding in
the farmers is, to fold on their fheep-leafes in the Dorfetfhire.
middle of July, and fo till Michaelmafs, that in the
winter there may be a good head of grafs for the
milch-ewes.

§. 74. It feems to be inconvenient to grafp at fo Of folding
large a wheat or barley-crop, as hardly to be able to unfeafon-
compafs it without folding late on the wheat after it ably.
is fowed, or on the barley-land after it is fowed; for
by being under the above neceffity, in order to compafs what one has engroffed, one may often be obliged to fold unfeafonably on each fort of corn, nor
will the fold in that cafe make good the damage
done to the flock by the latenefs of the feafon: and
an ewe-fold is often damaged by folding on the cold
land at the latter end of October; whereas it is better to come early with your fold off of the wheat-
lands on to the barley lay-grounds, and from the
fowed barley on to the wheat-fallows; for thereby you will fold the fame quantity of ground of
the refpective grains without the refpective inconveniencies.

Between wafhing and fhearing-time fheep ought
not to be folded, becaufe of dirtying their wool, nor
from the cutting of the lambs till a fortnight after,
                         nor

nor in sheep-leases or arable in wet weather, for it will tread the grass into dung.

Of folding in frosty weather.

§. 75. A servant of mine, a man of very good understanding, tells me, he has been many years a shepherd, but could never observe that the fold ever did any good in frosty weather : particularly he remembers a very sharp frosty winter, in which a whole flock used daily to gather to a hay-reek, in a ground where they were foddered, yet he could not observe there was any better corn there than elsewhere.—I asked him the reason of it ; he said, the frost wasted and preyed on the dung ; and I the rather approve this observation of his, because of the great prejudice strong beer and spirits receive by being frozen, even so as to become mere caput mortuums.

If frost has the same effect on dung, by impoverishing it, that it is said to have on the sheep-fold, and on strong beer : quære, whether it be proper or not, to leave horse or cow-dung spread on land without ploughing it in.

Mr. Raymond is also of opinion, that the winter-frosts do very much deaden the folding of the sheep, and rob it of it's virtue.

What land to fold first.

§. 76. Farmer Elton said, the method he best approved of in folding, was always to fold that land first that was first designed to be ploughed, such as white or whitish land, they not being apt to bear weeds, nor will the fold be apt to cause weeds to come, and such land he would sow first, viz. at St. James's-tide.——I said, I should think, though such land should be sowed ever so wet, yet, if the month of August should prove dry and scorching, it would burn, and suffer by such early sowing.—He replied, if sowed wet, yet so as it came up, he never knew the drought to hurt it.

Of folding on barley in a dry season.

§. 77. It was a very dry season from the first of March to the sixth of May (anno 1701) during which

which time I set my fold on my barley.—Several of
the farmers in my neighbourhood said, it would be
apt to do the barley more harm than good, for the
sheep would scratch up the seed; whereas if rain
had come, so that the ground had not been in a dust,
their scratching would have done no harm.——But
I rolled before I set my fold, and so I presume the
ground was so fast as to receive the less damage, it
being also stony, and therefore the sheep could not
search it so much as otherwise perhaps they might
have done : the event was, the fold did no harm, but
good.

§. 78. Mr. Gilbert of Madington was telling
me, the way of husbandry about him, near Salisbury, was, to fold on their wheat after it was sowed
till St. Luke's-tide, which is in the middle of October; then to draw off their flock for a month to
fold their sheep-leases, and then on the barley-fallows.——I asked some North-Wiltshire farmers, if
about them they ever folded on the wheat-land after
it was sowed; they said, no, they never knew it to
be done in any parts thereabouts, yet folding after
the corn was sown did it more good than before;
but the reason why they did not do it about Holt,
&c. they believed was, because they were forced to
lay up the wheat-lands in high ridges by reason of
the deepness of the earth, and it's wetness, and the
sheep if folded on such land, would do nothing but
lie between the furrows, which would do the land
but little service : besides, they said, in the hill-
country the land was rather of the lightest, and
the treading of the sheep, after it was sowed
pressed it closer than it was before, and so did it
service.

Of folding about Salisbury and Holt in Wilts.

§. 79. Mr. Raymond assured me, that sheep folded
on sandy lands would thereby be sensibly more impoverished than those folded on clay-lands, and this, said
he, the shepherds agree to, who live where there are
    such

Of folding on clay and sandy land.

such different sorts of land. — The reason seems to be, because the sandy lands draw forth and drink up the moisture of the sheep, to fill up which emptiness of the outward vessels, a fresh juice must succeed, and so on ; or else that the sandy lands being hot, make the sheep perspire more than clay-lands do, whereas the cold clay rather repels perspiration.

If sandy or light ground, as has been before hinted, draws the fat and moisture of the sheep-fold off, so as to impoverish a flock more than if they had been folded on cold clay-lands, it must be allowed on the other hand, that light ground may be better enriched by a fold than heavy land, because the light ground imbibes more of the moisture and fat of the flock ; and this gives some account why it is said, poor lands often pay better for their folding than strong lands : for the same reason winter-folding, when the ground is wet and cold, holds no proportion to summer-folding.

§. 80. Discoursing with farmer Biggs on husbandry, he said, he folded on the fallows all winter long, though never so wet ; yet, said he again, sometimes the fold does harm : let it be never so wet, said he, early in the year, folding on the fallows does no harm ; for, in the first, there is heat enough in the ground at the first hand of the year to keep off the chill, and then the ground is not so settled, but that the rain soon runs through it, but at the latter end of the year the ground is settled ; then treading it with the fold in wet weather makes it hold water, by which it may be chilled, and kneads the very wet into it, whereby there will be the less corn.

§. 81. Before I came from Crux-Easton in February (anno 1698) in order to go into the Isle of Wight, I had a discourse with an old experienced shepherd about folding the flock on fallows : he said,

Of folding on fallows in winter.

Of folding on barley.

said, as to wheat, it was excellently good, but they rarely folded on barley-land after it was sowed, for if it was a whitish land, and a hot summer came, it would be burnt up: besides, the sheep would be scraping at that time of the year on the barley-land, and would take the corn out of the ground; but the wheat, said he, lay too deep for them to do so.——But when I came into the Isle of Wight, farmer Collins was of a different opinion, and said, he had always folded with good success on hot dry sandy ground after it was sown with barley, and was earnest with me to try it; for, said he, you will quickly see the benefit, and though the sheep should scrape, you will find the barley come thickest there.——There is land however about Husborne and Stoke in Hants that will burn by folding on in the spring, and get more harm than good, if hot weather come, it being a hungry sharp gravel.

§. 82. As it seems to me, the double folding on the early wheat-fallows, to be sown on one earth, cannot occasion the roots of the grass ploughed-in to shoot up afresh, but rather prevents it, by treading the earth down into a hard plaister, so that they cannot rise ; it is true, it may bring up a fresh new grass, which, having weak roots, will easily be torn up by the draggs. *Of folding the early wheat fallows.*

§. 83. [g] Columella, speaking of feeding sheep, says, there is no sort of land, or food, but what (by the continual use of that only) sheep will be tired of, unless you give them some salt now and then to lick, from whence they may procure a new appetite to *Manner of feeding sheep among the antients.*

[g] Nec tamen ulla sunt tam blanda pabula, aut etiam pascua, quorum gratia non exolescat usu continuo, nisi pecudum fastidio pastor occurrerit præbito sale, quod, velut ad pabuli condimentum, per æstatem canalibus ligneis impositum, cum è pastu redierint, oves lambunt, atque eo sapore cupidinem bibendi pascendique concipiunt. Colum. lib. 7. fol. 175.

their

their meat and water. ʰ All the summer time during the hot feafon they muft be let out to feed as
early as may be, while the dew is on the grafs ; and
when the fun is about four hours high, they muft
be led to water and under fhade, and again to feed
towards fun-fet.   In the dog-days the flock fhould
be fo led as to feed with their heads towards the
Weft in the forenoon, and towards the Eaft in the
afternoon ; for it is of great confequence, fays he,
that the fheep's heads fhould be turned from the fun,
which would be hurtful to them.   And Varro gives
the fame directions, becaufe, fays he, the fheep's
heads are extremely foft.— -Perhaps this may be
the chief reafon of the rams and ewes in companies
turning face to face, in hot fun-fhiny days. During
the winter and early in the fpring they fhould be
kept in their fold, till the fun has melted the hoar-
froft from the grafs, which would occafion rheums
in their heads, and would alfo fcour them : for this
reafon in the cold wet feafons of the year they fhould
be watered but once a day.   ⁱ They let their ewes,
as Varro affures us, go out to feed with the reft of
the flock, but kept back the lambs, which were
fuckled by the ewes at their return, and then again

ʰ Dum mane novum, dum gramina canent, et ros in tenera
pecori gratiffimus herba : inde ubi quarta fitim cœli collegerit
hora, ad puteos et umbras ; rurfus ad pafcua producendum folis
ad occafum, &c.——Et in caniculis, ante meridiem grex in oc-
cidentem fpectans agatur, et poft meridiem progrediatur in orien-
tem ; fiquidem plurimum refert, ut pafcentium capita fint obverfa
foli, quia plerumque nocet animalibus.   Hyeme et vere intra
fepta contineantur, dum dies arvis gelicidia detrahat ; nam
pruinofa iis diebus herba pecudi gravedinem creat, ventremque
perluit, quare et frigidis humidifque temporibus anni femel tan-
tum ei poteftas aquæ facienda eft.—Ita pafcere pecus oportet, ut
averfo fole agat, caput enim ovis molle maximè eft. Varro, f. 53.
ⁱ Matres cum grege paftum prodeunt, retinent agnos qui, cum
reductæ ad vefperum, aluntur lacte, et rurfus difcernuntur. Varro, fol. 54.

separated

separated from them. [k] They also tethered their lambs at ten days old, lest they should dislocate or hurt their tender limbs by playing together.

Of FEEDING and FATTING SHEEP.

§. 84. When I was giving Mr. Lawrence of Dorsetshire a description of Crux-Easton, and the farmers management of their sheep there : he said, he knew how the farmers managed there, and that they were to blame ; for they might manage their sheep better, and have full as good there as at Upcern, if they would feed them well in the winter, and at the latter part of the year send them abroad for a month, as the Dorsetshire farmers do, into the vale-lands to refresh their own grass, and would fold on their sheep-slates : but, said he, they in Hampshire follow the plough so much, that they neglect their sheep ; and suffering their hog-sheep to run in the woods all the winter was a foolish thing ; for they lost their wool by it, and it stunts them in their growth, by keeping them so poor : and it is the greater folly, as they are to come into the places of their old ewes, whereby the flock is spoiled : besides, said he, when they become ewes, they will always afterwards be losing their wool in the hedges : and if they in Dorsetshire find but one ewe in a flock apt by that means to be bare, they will sell her off at the next Weyhill fair.

Management of sheep at Crux-Easton blamed.

Mr. Bishop of the same county said, he always takes care to keep his sheep up in high case in very cold weather, or in deep snow : and the better hay, and the more of it, you give your sheep, the better

[k] Circiter decem dies cum præterierunt, palos affigunt, et ad eos alligant librâ, aut quâ aliâ re levi distantes, ne toto die currantes inter se delibent teneri aliquot membrorum. Varro, fol. 54.

will

will their wool and their foil pay for it, and over-
pay too.———— He faid, a weather would grow fat
with hay fooner than with grafs: and, if the fnow
be but moderately deep, viz. not above a foot, the
fheep will fcrape for the grafs: but then in fevere
weather care ought to be taken to put them in a
ground out of bleak winds, and where the grafs is
longeft, as having been firft hayned.—— He approved
not of the Hampfhire way of fitting up with their
folds in lambing-time; for their walking up and
down with their lanthorns greatly difturbs the fold,
and makes the ewes apt to be frightened, and to run
away from their ftands in the fold, by which means
the lamb is either over-laid, or feparated from the
ewe; whereas otherwife the ewe and the fheep folded would keep in the fame place.—— He likewife
fays, the beft thing that can be done in lambing-
time is in hard weather to fling five, fix, or feven
truffes of hay into the fold amongft the fheep, for
them to trample down, to fave the lambs from being frozen, and to keep them dry: the hay, fays he,
is of an infignificant value to the fervice it does to
the lambs.—He adds, if it be a wet feafon in lambing-time, the folds ought to be made the larger:
if a hard frofty time, the clofer the better, nor need
one be afraid of the lambs being over-laid, if the
fold is not difturbed.——He fays, in lambing-time,
the fold ought to be vifited in the morning, and the
firft thing to be done ought to be to walk round it,
and fee what outermoft ewes have lambed, and then
flip a hurdle and draw the ewe and lamb out carefully, that the ewe may go away with her lamb to
graze, and keep together; for, if the flock be let
out with them at the fame time, it is the nature of
the ewe to go away to graze, and amidft the whole
flock the ewe and lamb will foon lofe each other:
then you fhould go inward, ftill drawing out the
outermoft ewe and lamb.

§. 85. That

§. 85. That there is an idiosyncrasy in cattle of the same sort, or species, has been already hinted; to which may be added, that farmer Isles my tenant assures me, that if they about Holt, i. e. in the vale, buy sheep against the winter out of the hill-country, such sheep will, as usually, expect a great deal of hay, though they have never so much plenty of grass.

—— And probably they may in a great measure expect it, through their constitution of juices; for otherwise it cannot be supposed how giving the younger sheep hay in the hill-country, but perhaps for one year, should entail a necessity of continuing it for the next, where the juices of the grasses so much exceed those of the hills.--To exemplify which, having bought sows with pig out of the vale, for the sake of a large breed, where they had been used to be fed only on whey; these sows, when they were brought into my yard in the hill-country, where there was plenty of shattered corn, sufficient to keep my own country hogs, which thrived well on it, grew lean, and made but a poor livelihood; and what more surprized me, the pigs of these sows which were littered with me, took after grazing, and, when they came to be great hogs, they would not stay in the stubble-fields to get their bellies full, but would soon beat out into the grass grounds, and so would the breed of the breed last mentioned do. —— Thus says Horace, " Fortes creantur fortibus, nec feroces aquilæ pavidas generant columbas."—— And this idiosyncrasy seems more visible in beasts and men that live on the simplest food than in those that live on varieties.

§. 86. 't ought to be contrived in hill-country-farms, which usually have but a few acres of meadow and pasture, and the rest in arable, that there be a few acres of arable (according to the bigness of the farm) laid down on different parts of the farm,

N therein

Side notes:
An idiosyncrasy in cattle of the same sort.

To provide grass ground to receive the sheep occasionally.

therein commodiously to receive the flock of sheep
after harvest, as often as the stubble-grounds may be
dirty ; for in wet weather, if the flock should go in
such stubble, they would spoil more than they eat.
———— But yet, if grounds are laid down yearly to
clover-grasses, as is usual in the hill-country, then
it is to be noted, that grounds of the second year's
clover are very fit to receive the flock of sheep in
such wet weather ; for ground of the second year's
clover is well settled and covered with grass, nor will
it be like to be trampled to dirt, it being firm, nor
is it gnash and luscious, as the stubble-clover is, and
so is very fit for the sheep, and will not put their
mouths out of taste for other coarser grasses, as the
stubble-clover will do.——Nevertheless fatting sheep
may be suffered to feed freely on the stubble-clover ;
for they must be supported with other grasses, as
good as that, had they not that, and sweet pasture of
natural grass must be found for them when that is
fed out.

§. 87. Having in November (anno 1707) a
good crop of turnips for the winter-feeding my flock
of sheep, I had a desire, before I entered on the doing
it, to consult a farmer's shepherd, who had for many
years used his sheep to turnips : I understood from
him, as also from others, that turnip-feeding was
apt to breed wind in the sheep and gripings, for
which, while they were under the distemper, they
knew no remedy, but to cut their throats, if they
were fatting : you may perceive the distemper by
their stretching out their limbs, and spreading them :
but, to prevent this evil, they agree it is necessary to
give the sheep some dry meat in the evening,
though coarse.

It is farther agreed, that an ewe-flock is not so
subject to the abovesaid distemper by feeding on
turnips, as a weather flock would be, the lamb in
the

Turnips apt to breed wind in sheep.

the ewe carrying off the water, that, in such case, the ewes are overcharged with from the turnips; for the ewes, when with lamb, piss and dung much more easily and plentifully than the weathers do; which is but reasonable to believe, all creatures with young being apt to make water often, and dung, nor are they so able to retain it as when not so: and particularly physicians look on child-bearing women to be more secure from cholick, gout, &c. than when child-bearing is over, for the abovesaid reason.

§. 88. It is a thing commonly known, that after harvest sheep must be kept out of the barley-stubble till the hogs have eat up the scattered barley, lest by swelling in the maws of the sheep it should kill them. ——But I also find by my shepherd and others, that sheep ought to be kept out of all sorts of stubble till the corn is well eaten up by the hogs; because the wheat and oats they lease will be apt to make the sheep scour, as this year (anno 1719) wheat made many of my sheep scour. *Sheep to be kept out of new stubble.*

§. 89. Tills are excellent good for ewes, to breed milk for their lambs, being given them instead of hay, and is the true use of that grain: they will grow very well in strong clay-land, but are rather reckoned an impoverisher than an improver of the ground, contrary to what other kidded grains are. *Tills good for ewes.*

§. 90. The reason why sheep are in less danger of being hurt by broad-clover than cows are, may be, because the sheep feed only on the very finest and tenderest part of it, nor can they easily be brought to taste of the grossest part of it: this I plainly saw when I fatted sheep in the broad-clover this year (anno 1702). It is however a luscious food, and apt to throw sheep into a scouring. *Why broad-clover more hurtful to cows than sheep.*

Broad-clover will not fat sheep so fast, nor so well as hop-clover will do.

§. 91. Farmer

Of putting sheep into woods after shearing.

§. 91. Farmer Elton advised me by all means, if the season proved dry after my sheep were sheared, to put them into my woods of four or five years growth, for a week or a fortnight : he assured me, if it were a dry time, they would do the woods no harm ; for in that case the rowety grass in the woods would be sweet, and the sheep would not be tempted to crop the shoots ; but in wet weather the rowet turns sour.—— This, he said, would do them a great kindness in sheltering their coats from burning, and their bodies from damage thereby : and at the shepherd's whistle they would all come out of the woods to folding.— It may be serviceable to the sheep, but I doubt of the former part of his assertion, viz. that they will eat the rowet, and not crop the shoots.   See my observations on woods.

I had a few teg or hog-sheep of my own, and at Michaelmass I bought in some more, and put them then into the meadows, the hedge-rows of which being cut the year before, put them upon browzing at that time of the year.—— About the latter end of November, I put them into my young coppices, where they soon fell to browzing : we wondered at it, and were at a loss for the cause ; till my shepherd remembered me what we had done, having enticed them into the fault at the first hand of the year.

Of leaves for sheep.

§. 92. Cato dicit, fol. 2. Autumnitate frondem populeam, ulmeam, querneamque cædito per tempus ; eam condito non peraridam, pabulum ovibus. So that they were not the dead worthless leaves they collected, but they stripped the branches of their leaves whilst growing, and made a kind of hay of them.

Swine's-grass bad for sheep.

§. 93. [1] Poligona, knot-grass, swine's-grass, or blood-

[1] Est etiam ovibus gravis pernicies herbæ sanguinariæ, quam si pasta est ovis, toto ventre distenditur, contrahiturque, & spumam

blood-wort, according to Columella is very pernicious to sheep, occasioning violent distentions and
contractions in their bellies, by which they bring
up a thin, frothy, stinking matter. —— The cure is
to bleed them under the tail, close to the buttocks,
and also in the upper lip.

§. 94. The Maison rustique speaking of sheep, *Sheep not to be drove to the fie'd too early in frosty weather.*
says, in winter, autumn, and spring, you should
keep them close in the morning, and not carry them
to the fields until the day has taken away the frost
from off the ground : for at these times the frozen
grass begets a rheum and heaviness in their heads,
and looseneth their bellies. fol. 157. The same
observation has been made by the antients, as I have
noted before.

Some say, that, in the open moist weather in the
winter, the sheep have more need of hay than in the
cold frosty weather, and it does them more good ;
for it dries up the water, the grass then making
them flue.

§. 95. In deep fat lands farmers may be in the *Of foddering sheep in winter.*
right to hope for, and to endeavour to preserve their
sheep without hay in winter, or as long as they can,
because their lands may be able to do it ; yet,
quære, in case they should buy in sheep to winter,
which have been used to hay, whether such sheep
will not only expect it, but will not also pay for it,
if it be given them. But for hill-country farmers,
whose winter-grass cannot be supposed to maintain
their flocks, I say, they ought to fodder in good
time ; otherwise their flocks will soon eat up all
their grass, and then they must, as they draw near
to lambing-time, eat all hay, which is not so well as

mam quandam tenuem tetri odoris expuit, celeriter sanguinem mitti
oportet sub cauda, in ea parte quæ proxima est clunibus, nec minus
in labro superiore vena solvenda est. Colum. lib. 7. fol. 178.

hay and grass earlier in the winter would have been; and then the grass would have held out.

Racks for foddering sheep commended.

§. 96. Farmer Biggs commending racks to fodder sheep in, said, it was a very wasteful, slovenly way to fling the hay loose about the fold, as some would do; for whatever hay the sheep sat down on, neither they nor any other cattle will touch after, for which reason no cattle care for feeding after sheep, their dung and piss being a great nuisance; but cows, said he, had rather pick the dungy straw and litter on the dung hills, which comes from the horses, than to have the sweet clean straw that comes out of the barn.

On my asking several good shepherds, why they set the hay-reeks open to the sheep in each ground; they assured me, that, in that country, Dorset, they had tried all ways of giving fodder to the sheep, and did find, that to let them go to the racks when they had a mind to it, was best; for many sheep liked grass, and would thrive better on it than on hay; and others would eat hay better than grass, and if the hay was very good, they would give as good milk for it; and many sheep would eat it best, if you let them have their own time of eating it.

Of cribs.

A very good shepherd near me, approves very much of cribs for foddering sheep in: he says, in wet weather they they save littering of the fodder, and trampling it under foot: — but he says, sometimes a cow or a sheep has hung it's horns in the bow, and broke it's neck, but this rarely happens: that the gentleman whom he serves had only lost one heifer by such accident in twenty years time, and a sheep or two. — Another told me, his master never lost any cattle that way; but one morning, said he I came in good time, and saved two that were hanging.

I told my shepherd what sort of racks I designed
for

for my sheep to be foddered in, which were according to the Dorsetshire fashion, as the shepherds there had advised me to make them; and he approved very well of it for the saving of hay: but, said he, the cow-cribs with bow partitions are very serviceable on one account; for when an ewe, by reason of a lusty lamb, has had a hard labour, whereby the lamb is stunned, or much weakened, such lamb will be able to get up and suck, by strengthening itself with leaning against such cribs as they lie in the fold.

§. 97. Farmer Biggs said, that he was confident, if it was a hard winter, 300 sheep would eat 25 if not 30 tons of hay.—Farmer Crapp said, he had often given above 25 tons to that number of sheep. *What hay sheep will eat in a hard winter.*

Mr. Slade of Tilshade tells me, that they allow a ton of hay for every score of sheep they winter on their downs, and provide for the winter accordingly.

I asked my shepherd, what quantity of hay would maintain a sheep at Easton in a hard winter. He gave me no ready answer; I told him, I looked on five todd and an half to be a noble provision: he could not rightly fall into a consideration of that proportion, but said, if it was a hard winter a score of sheep would eat a ton of hay.——Whereupon we computed the difference of our estimates, and found that mine held a fourth part greater than his: however he said, he thought his a great allowance.

§. 98. Farmer Elton told me, that his father and he had lost many a pound by not buying coarse or under-hill hay at the first hand of the year for their ewes; for, when a hard winter has come, they have been forced to give them a coarse hay at last, which has impoverished them, and made them pitch, and in the breed made them spoil the whole flock. *Of providing coarse hay early for wintering sheep.*

§. 99. About Tilshade in Wiltshire there is little hay, and the chief support of the sheep during winter *Vetches for sheep.*

ter is vetches : Mr. Slade affures me, if vetches cut
greenifh for fheep fhould take a month's rain at firft,
if they can at laft be housed dry, the fheep will eat
them ftalks and all better than the beft hay.

Houfing
fheep bene-
ficial to
their wool. §. 100. I have heard, that in Spain they houfe
their fheep on nights, which I doubt not but contributes to the finenefs of their wool.—And the warm
fold, made warmer by the fheep than of itfelf it
would be, is better for the wool of the fheep than
for them to lie abroad.

What
fheep to be
firft fatted. §. 101. In fatting fheep, the barren ewes, and
thofe which have loft their lambs, come firft in
order, and then old fheep that are to be fatted with
grafs.

Whether
ewes
fhould be
rammed
before fat-
ting. §. 102. Sir Ambrofe Phillipps's fhepherd being
in difcourfe with me, I afked him, fuppofing one
fhould fat fheep, whether the cafe was not the fame
with the ewes, as with cows to be fatted ; that is,
whether or not the ewes might not be firft rammed;
and whether they would not then fat the kindlier for
it.   He replied, the cafe was not the fame with
ewes as with cows ; for the ewes would take ram but
at one time of the year only, fome earlier, others
later : but befides, the ewes going but twenty weeks
with lamb, they contrived they fhould not be with
lamb, becaufe they would be too forward with lamb
before they could be fat. —— I then afked him, if he
ever knew a ewe bring a lamb twice in the fame year.
He faid, never ; but an ewe that had warped her
lamb very early might fometimes have another within
the year, though very rarely.   He fays, the graziers contrive their cows fhould be bulled at fuch a
time, as that they might be fat for the market by
the time they are half gone with calf, for then they
tallow beft, and their meat is a great deal the firm-
er for it.

Of fatting
a ewe that
warps. §. 103. The farmers in the Ifle of Wight reckon
                                                      an

an ewe that warps any time by or before the middle of February, so that she may make early mutton, while it yields a good price, is as good as * couples.

*An ewe and lamb.

§. 104. It was the 25th of December (anno 1707) when I had at autumn fatted twenty weathers, which I designed to kill after Christmass : at this time my shepherd came to me, and said, he could not hold up the sheep in their fat, unless I could find them some grass to go with their hay : he told me they would waste the best hay he could give them, and eat but little of it.—Till now I thought one might have fatted sheep with hay alone, if it were very good : but on enquiring I have found, that such sheep as abovesaid, must have a little grass with their hay.—Therefore, if you would have fat sheep to kill from Christmass till spring, you ought to contrive to keep a reserve of grass for that purpose, or to sow turnips in autumn for the feed of their leaves.

Weathers will not be fat in winter on hay only.

§. 105. Mr. Slade of Tilshade, and Mr. Bissy of Holt in Wilts, made me a visit : and having often before complained to Mr. Bissy, that I could not fat lambs at Easton, Mr. Bissy said, he was sure I might fat lambs at Easton ; only I must take this special care, to put the ewes and their lambs, within a fortnight after the falling of the lambs, into clover, and must keep them well, and not let them sink ; for both Mr. Bissy and Mr. Slade said, if once I let them sink, there would be no raising them again : and Mr. Bissy said, I must take care not to let the clover be too high.

Of fatting lambs in the hill-country.

§. 106. I find by farmer Isles of Holt, that they can in that country fat lambs exceeding well on broad-clover ; but, says he, we cannot afterwards fat the ewes so well, for they will rise but slowly in

Of fatting lambs in the vale on broad-clover.

flesh:

flesh : the reason that he gave for it was, because the
lambs were fatted in the spring, while the broad-
clover was young and sweet , for it will hold sweet
and good, till towards Midsummer, but then falls
off, which is about the time the latter lambs are fatted, and then the ewes will not thrive so well with
it as the lambs will do.   He sold his lambs fat this
year, 1716, by the 20th of May, and then by Midsummer the ewes were well in flesh, that is, half fat
with the broad-clover ; but then they got no farther
by the broad-clover, only held their own till harvest, when they throve apace, and soon got fat in
the stubble.

The same farmer, having been two or three times
at Crux-Easton, and seen our broad-clover, admits,
that we cannot pretend to fat lambs with it near so
well as they can at Holt ; for the clover at Easton
must be sourer and bitterer than theirs at Holt, both
from the coldness of the ground, and the coldness of
the air : for, said he, we at Holt, though we lie on
a warm stone-brash, cannot pretend to fat lambs in
a cold spring as we can in a warm one, for the said
reason ; and particularly this dry and cold spring,
1719, I observed, added he, when I brought my
couples home from where I had wintered them, the
ewes would keep walking much about the ground,
and continue bleating, whereby I knew they disliked
their clover, and said I, I shall have no good fat
lambs this year, and so it proved. —— I like not,
said he, when the ends of the wool on the backs of
the sheep twirl, and stand spriggy, as they were apt
to do this year.

§. 107. If an ewe's milk after she has lambed,
dries away by reason of bad hay, or scarceness and
poverty of grass, so that the lamb pitches, it will
never be recovered, and lambs so pinched will never
                                                    fetch

If a lamb
once pit-
ches; for
want of
milk, it
never reck-
vers it.

fetch it forward again, so as to be so well grown or
so fat, or so soon fit for the market as otherwise they
would have been; in all which respects there will
be great loss, and this holds in some degree in other
cattle.

§. 108. On telling Mr. Biffy what encouragement I found for fatting lambs at Crux-Easton,
I also added the difficulties I should meet with in
that affair.—He said, if i thought my broad-clover would prove too sour, and be apt to scour my
lambs, I must sow half broad-clover and half hop-
clover seed mixed together; and he said, that he
and several others had of late (anno 1720) done so,
and found it very effectual.----And I am apt to fancy, if a sprinkling of rye-seed, it yielding a sweet
grass, was mixed with the clovers, the variety would
be grateful to the lambs, and make them fat the
faster.-----But it is my opinion, that if you reserve
the fattest of your arable-land clovers, the land being in good heart, such clovers will be fat, juicy,
sweet, and nourishing; for I have observed, that,
when ground has been ploughed out of heart, though
it was in it's own nature strong ground, yet the clovers it has produced have in their nature been weak,
and their leaves thin and not sappy, nor of a deep
verdure, but of a pale colour, and speckled on the
back of the leaves as if fly-shitten, and consequently
has no good nourishment in it; nor would hogs or
other cattle abide in such clover any longer than
they were forced to it; and the leaf of such clover
has to my taste been an ungrateful bitter, whereas
the fat sappy-leaved clover has been agreeable.

Of fatting lambs in the hill-country.

§. 109. When sheep are thriving, their wool is
of a bright white colour.

§. 110. I find by Mr. Gerrish of Broughton in
Wilts, the great grazier, that the rising up of the fat
on the back of a sheep in a bladderiness, or sort of
froth

A mark of a sheep's having been fatted kindly.

froth and foam, is a very good sign of the kindly
fatness of that sheep; which, says he, the turnip-fat-
ted sheep will do even in the winter time, whereas
the fat of our sheep, fed in winter on hay and good
grass, will lie close and flat on their backs, and not
rise in bladders when they are flead. —— He assures
me, that thirty acres of very good turnips will fat
four hundred weathers.

I went to Sir Ambrose Phillipps's sheep-pen with
the shepherd : in handling the sheep he shewed me
the piece of fat by the brisket, before the shoulder,
which is called the mouse-piece, which I handled
in many of them, it being bigger or less according
to the degree of fatness the sheep is in : the dent also
on the rump I felt in many, which is occasioned
from the rising pieces of fat on each side, where the
sheep are fat.

I asked the shearers of Garenton, where a sheep
was to be handled to know whether it was fat or not;
they said, if a weather-sheep or an ewe that never
had a lamb, it was to be handled at the dug, and
at the rump of the tail, for those that are very fat
will sometimes be as big there as one's wrist, and
the same on the brisket and shoulders : an old ewe is
to be judged of in the same manner, except in the
first mentioned place.

An experienced butcher who is to draw out a
number of sheep at a certain price, will always
choose for the fattest, though there are larger sheep
in the flock, and in good case too ; because the fatter the beast or sheep, the more juicy will his flesh
be, and consequently weigh the heavier, which will
make it most profitable to the butcher. —— And a
beast fatted by grass will weigh heavier than a beast
fatted by hay, because the flesh will be more juicy.

Of fatted
sheep, viz.
on turnips
and broad-
clover, and
of driving
them to
London.

§. 111. In discourse with several butchers, they
agreed, especially if the winter proved wet, that
turnip-

turnip-mutton would be waterish, and not answer
it's weight when killed, so well as other mutton, for
perfect water would run out between the skin and
the flesh, it being withinside : and, said they, your
mutton fed with broad-clover does not give that satisfaction that other mutton does; for the fat will
be apt to look yellowish ; yet in truth no mutton
eats so sweet as that, the fat whereof has a yellowish
cast, though people do not generally like it.—They
said further, that a sheep or lamb fatted would drive
from Crux-Easton to London, with losing but a very
little of it's weight; this they said, because I told
them that in driving from Holt in Wiltshire to London, a weather of about seventeen shillings price
would lose eight pounds of flesh; to which they replied, though cattle will not lose much flesh
in driving fifty miles, yet if you drive them fifty
more they will lose their flesh very considerably.—
And, said they, a sheep barely mutton, such as we
buy of you, will not bear driving to London,
though it may be but fifty miles, because they would
lose that little flesh they had got.——The hinder
quarter of an ewe, that has had a lamb, is not profitable to us, nor acceptable, because the udder
will waste, &c.—— they owned, however, it was
otherwise with a barren ewe, but, said they, there
are few of those in this country.———— If an ewe be
going to ram when she is killed, the mutton will eat
rank.

§. 112. I find by conversing with our Wiltshire
graziers, that fat lambs come not to Smithfield
from the North till after Whitsuntide, and then,
though they are huge lambs, in comparison of the
southerly and western, even as big again, yet they
are very lean compared with our's of the southerly
counties.—I find, one reason, why not only lamb,
but mutton and beef also, out of Wiltshire and the
southerly

Of the nor-
thern and
southern
lambs, and
why the
Wiltshire
lambs, &c.
fell dear in
a wet
spring.

foutherly countries, fells dear in wet fprings, is, becaufe the roads from the North and Somerfetfhire,
&c. are bad to travel on, and the cattle cannot go
into thofe deep leafes, they being under water, or
fo trodden and poached, that, by reafon of the cold,
grafs does not thrive for a bite for the beafts, nor
improve them till towards the middle of fummer.

Difeafes in S H E E P and L A M B S.

Of young
fheep that
have their
gums
grown over
their teeth.

§. 1. MY fhepherd was talking in June (anno
1703) of drawing out my old ewes
for the market; and faid, in all likelihood there
would be three or four of the younger fort drawn
out with them; and for the moft part it happened fo every year; for now and then a young fheep,
even one of two teeth, will have it's mouth hang
over, that is it's gums will be grown out fo long as
to fhut over it's teeth; and fuch fheep muft as
much be difpofed of as broken-mouthed fheep, for
they cannot well get their living, but will always
be out of cafe.

Of a fheep
fpewing up
it's grafs.

§. 2. Being at my fold, I faw my fhepherd turn
out a young fheep to be fold with the ewes. —— I
afked him why he did fo; he faid, becaufe it fpew-
ed up it's grafs; and then he fhewed me the outfide
of it's mouth and nofe bedaubed with the green
juice; fuch fheep, he faid, would never thrive.

Of lambs
drowned in
the ewe's
belly.

§. 3. My fhepherd fays, that the caufe of a lamb's
being drowned in the ewe's belly, (the ewe's being under a fcarcity of water, and having dry mow-
burnt hay) is, that by the greedinefs of the ewe's
drinking when fhe gets to water, fhe gluts the lamb
with the abundance of water fhe drinks. —— Farmer
Bachelour alfo believes it is fo, yet fays, that he has
feen lambs with a watery humour, as if they had a
dropfy.

§. 4. A

§. 4. A sheep which is cored, after is has been *Of a cored* so a year, or thereabouts, (for which time it may *sheep.* very well live, if chiefly fed with hay) will have a water-bladder, as big as an egg, under it's throat, it's eyes likewise will be white, and so will it's mouth and gums.

If any sheep in a flock core in the winter, it will be easily seen at shearing-time ; for such sheep will be poorer than the rest, and shew it that way by that time ; and their wool will run into threads, that is, their wool will twist together at the ends, and look somewhat like teats : yet I have known shepherds say, that sometimes the wool of very sound sheep will be apt to run together into threads, and the finer the wool the apter so to do.

Mr. Bishop's shepherd caught a sheep that was cored the last year, and shewed me how it might be seen by the eyes of the sheep, they being in the valves and veiny parts, (and the eye lids when turned up) milk-white ; whereas the other healthy sheep, he shewed me, had eyes as red as a cherry. —— He told me, some would say, thinness of wool on the breast was a sign of core ; but he had had no regard to that saying ;—that sheep that were so cored, being in a healthy country, and taking to eat hay, might live a year or two the longer for those reasons, but would never recover. —— Note, this milkiness of the eyes shews that such sheep are far gone ; they may be cored before they have that to shew : these cored sheep have the fluck, or plaice-worm in their livers, with which their gall is also full before they die : they call these worms [a] plaice-worms from their figure, which is like a plaice. —— When they

[a] I am assured Dr. Nichols has lately communicated to the Royal Society several curious observations on the form and the nature of this animal, which will be publish'd in the next volume of their Transactions.

look

look on a sheep's eye to see whether the sheep be cored or not, their term is, they will see how the sheep tests.

Of the rot.   §. 5. Mr. Cheſtlin of Leiceſterſhire ſays, that ſheep when firſt touched with the rot will thrive mightily in fatting for ten weeks, but, if they are not diſpoſed of when they are come up to a pitch, they will in ſeven or eight days time fall away to nothing but ſkin and bone ; he has often had them die in the height of their pitch in half an hour's time with twenty-ſeven pound of tallow in their bellies.

Mr. Raymond, Mr. Biſſy and I being together, Mr. Raymond ſaid, that if the ſummer did not rot the ſheep, it was generally agreed that the winter would not.— Mr. Biſſy replied, that he had often heard the ſame; and ſo they agreed, that there was no danger of the extreme wet winter this year (anno 1702) rotting the ſheep, ſeeing the foregoing ſummer had been ſo hot and dry as it had been — I aſked Mr. Raymond, what he thought might be the reaſon of ſuch a ſaying ; he ſaid, that a gloomy wet ſummer gave an undigeſted quick growth to the graſs of cold land, which occaſioned a rot among the ſheep : and the ſaid graſs was in danger of continuing on in that unwholſome way of growing all the following winter, till the month of March, and the next ſpring came to give it a check, and the ſpring brought forth a new graſs ; whereas the power of the winter alone was not ſtrong enough to begin a rot.

Marſh-tre-   [b] Mr Ray ſpeaking of marſh-trefoil, ſays, Sir
foil good   Tancred Robinſon commends it for dropſical caſes,
for the rot.

[b] Dominus Tancredus Robinſon trifolium paludoſum in hydropicis affectibus commendat, ſeque ſæpius obſervaſſe, ait, oves tabidas in paludes hâc herbâ abundantes compulſas, ejus eſu reſtitutas ſanitati. Ray, fol. 1099.

and

and says, he has known sheep, that have had the rot, drove into marshes where this herb has grown plentifully, and cured by it.

Mr. Boyle says, on the beginning of a rot among sheep, where it appeared, by the killing a sheep or two, that the whole flock were touched, a friend of his cured the rot by giving each sheep a handful of Spanish salt for five or six mornings together. *Id. Spanish salt.*

Mr. Raymond of Peck-Shipton in Wiltshire, says, that, when the meadows are slabby and full of water, they are then safest, and less subject to bane than they are in a dry winter.

John Earle, of Parks in Wiltshire, shewed me how the sheep had cropt and fed mightily on the broom : they will eat it heartily all the year, but especially in the spring, when it is in blossom : it stains their teeth as black as soot ; we caught one, that I might be an eye-witness of it. ——— He says, he believes it will preserve sheep from the rot, and he shewed me twenty, that he had bought five or six months before, which, he said, were so rotten, that they would hardly drive home, but they were now recovered and grown fat, though the ground he had kept them in had hardly any pickings in it but what the broom afforded : he had another ground where the broom had been suffered to run to seed, and the sheep had not been in it above three weeks, before they had eaten all the kids up. —— Broom, says Mortimer, in his book of husbandry, is one of the best preservatives against the rot in sheep : I have known sheep, when not too far gone in the rot, cured of it, only by being put into broom lands. *Id. broom.*

In Somersetshire they keep no flocks of sheep, for fear of a rot, it being a deep country ; but are very glad of the opportunity of having the tails of the hill-country flocks : again, the hill-country farmers are glad to send their flocks thither for a month, after their corn is cut, to feed on the stubble-grass, there not being there any danger of a rot.

The wood-evil. See Diseases in cows and calves.

§. 6. As to the wood-evil in sheep, I find Leicestershire is very subject to it : it is agreed that it is occasioned in May, and about Michaelmass, by bleak cold easterly winds ; it falls chiefly on the lambs : if an ewe be in good heart, she will overcome it very well ; but when it falls into their bowels, it is held incurable, nor could I find they had any medicine for it when in the limbs, but only time would wear it off. —— One may perceive the distemper in them by their going lame, their necks, or some of their limbs will be drawn up altogether by it.

The staggers.

§. 7. The sheep-land at Appleford, in the Isle of Wight, is subject to the staggers : the chief remedy they find is, to drive the sheep to change of grounds often, to keep the grounds from tainting.

I observe lambs that die of the staggers, do not die of them so very young, as whilst they merely suck, suppose within the fortnight, but after they begin to eat grass, and of those the hopefulest and lustiest ; by which I do conclude, that it is not the cold weather alone that brings the staggers, for then it would fall more on the lambs of a week and a fortnight old than on others, they being most unable to bear it : it arises therefore from their feeding on the cold watery grass in the months of March and April, which makes them abound with watery humours in their bodies, which the cold winds seize on and chill, and bring those cramps and aches into their limbs. It is observed this disease is much prevented by early folding of the lambs, and with good reason, for thereby in the cold nights the lambs are kept warm, and also prevented from eating so much grass as otherwise they would, whereby such watery humours are fed. —— Quære, whether our cold country may be be proper for fatting of lambs till towards May, when the sun has got a full power.

§. 8. In opening the sheep's skull for the giddiness, it may be discovered where the bag of water lies, by the thinness and softness of the skull, and so to know in what place to open it, for it will bend under one's finger. ——A farmer at Upcern told me, if the bladder lay under the horn, there was no coming at it.

The gid, or giddiness.

I am informed also, that the bladder under the horn or skull, which makes beasts giddy, never falls upon any sheep above the age of a hog or a thief nor upon any bullock after two years old.

§. 9. Some years the sheep will be apt to be taken with a disease they call the shaking; some farms are more subject to it than others: it is a weakness which seizes their hinder quarters, so that they cannot rise up when they are down: I know no cure for it.

Of the shaking

This-shaking, as I observed, is incident to some farms, insomuch as some years an hundred of a flock have died of it : neither Mr. Oxenbridge, Nat. Ryalls, nor Mr. Bishop's shepherd knew of any cure for it.—— But they said that horses going with sheep are apt to cause it, and so are briery hedgerows growing out in the ground ; but that milchkine and goats going with the sheep were good against it.—— Farmer Bartlet who rents 800 l. per annum of Mr. Freek, whose farm was subject to it, would pick out a sheep presently that had it.

§. 10. Mr. Lewis of Broughton informs me, the sheep of that side of Wiltshire are not subject to the shaking, nor to the white scouring: as for the green scouring, either in sheep or bullocks, he says. verjuice is beyond the oak-bark, and a more certain cure ; a wine-glass full is enough for a sheep, and a pint for a bullock.——He says, that about his part

Of blindness, and of the green scouring.

of

of Wiltshire, the sheep are troubled with a blindness, their cure is anointing their eyes with goose-dung.

The over-flowing of the blood.

§. 11. Mr. Bishop's shepherd says, he can presently see if any of his sheep are sick by the dulness of their countenances, and their looking still forwards: but he knows of nothing to give them in such case, unless when they are sick with the over-flowing of the blood, which is about Michaelmass; it comes from high feeding, and a quick shoot of the grass, and then he bleeds them either in the eye-vein or tail-vein, and takes more or less blood from them, as they seem to be more or less infected. ——— When he bleeds them in the tail-vein, he lets it bleed till the blood stanches of itself: but when he has a mind to stop the eye-vein, it is only holding his thumb on it a little while. ——— He says, he approves of bleeding them in the eye-vein, but he never knew any body to do it but himself.

I asked him again about his bleeding his sheep in the eye-vein and the tail-vein for the overflowing of the blood about Michaelmass; for another shepherd had said, he only knew the hog-sheep to be subject to it: but the shepherd says, it is true, the hogs are most subject to it, and apt many times about Michaelmass to die of it; but yet he says, the ewes and weathers will sometimes have it.

Of scouring.

§. 12. The sheep in this country about Crux-Easton are little troubled with scourings.——— I asked my shepherd how that distemper came; he, said, by a quick shoot of the grass in the first hand of the spring; but it was easily cured; for, when they found it, they brought them to their hay again, and that stopped it: but he said, in the vallies, and some places where the weed grunsel grows, the sheep are much troubled with it.

I shewed an experienced farmer a lamb which scoured, having had no vent but what the shepherd cut,

cut.—He said, by all means, if it can live, fat it off; for he never knew such a lamb live to be a sheep; it would always need fresh cutting and opening.

Mr. Smith, of Deadhouse, says, that broad-clover is more apt to scour sheep or other cattle than hop-clover is, and that they are both more apt to scour than natural grass, and consequently not so proper as other grass to raise a beast or a sheep in fat; that a beast, cow, or sheep, if they scour but one day, will lose more flesh than they can get again in a fortnight; that, when sheep or lambs scour, if you cut off the ends of their tails, it will stop the scouring, so that they will scour no more that season.

I told Mr. Bishop of Dorsetshire, of the rind of the oak that lay under the bark, to cure the scouring of sheep · he knew nothing of it, but said, the distemper came from a quick growing of the grass in the spring, and that they looked on it that their sheep would not thrive in the fore hand of the year till they had had it; but that scouring at other times of the year was mortal, and that he knew of no cure for it; and that their scourings then would be of a nasty white sort of matter. vide Diseases in cows and calves, §. 9.

His shepherd says, all sheep will have the skenting in the spring; if they have it in the winter they look on it as unseasonable: the white skenting or scouring is very rare in sheep: it happens oftener to the lambs, and very seldom are they recovered of it: he knew a lamb of their flock, he says, recover of it last year, (anno 1696) but when they do, they will afterwards peel all over.

When I told Sir Ambrose Phillipps's shepherd, that verjuice was good to give beasts for the scouring: he said, he did not think so well of that way, either for sheep or cows, as to give a purge: in such

cas:,

cafe, he fays, he gives one groat's-worth of cream of tartar, two penny-worth of aloes, a penny-worth of fennigreek-feed, a penny-worth of turmerick, or a farthing or half-penny-worth of long pepper in a quart of warm ale, for a cow; but of thefe ingredients, mixt together, and put into fuch a quantity of ale, he would not give a fheep above two fpoonfuls.

§. 13. One of the chief diftempers in fheep is the red-water, of which not one in a hundred ever recovers: it is thought to come by feeding on four grafs; if it feizes on a fat fheep it will be worth nothing but the fkin, for, if you boil the flefh for the tallow, it will ftink all over the houfe in a ftrange manner: this diftemper is apteft to feize on thofe fheep and lambs that are beft in proof.

I afked a farmer in my neighbourhood, who keeps a very large flock of fheep, and has had long experience in them, what he thought to be the occafion of the red-water; he anfwered, a quick growing of the grafs in the fpring, and a too quick thriving of the fheep upon it, but he admitted it not to be curable. An old and very underftanding fhepherd afterwards affured me, that it came only on the fheep when they were out of condition, and weak, and fell firft on the fpring-grafs, efpecially if it were four.—— He faid, before it is long gone they are eafily cured by giving them the infide rind of the bark of oak, but as for hay, when they are in that weak condition, they will not eat it.——Three or four little pieces will do, if one makes them chew and fwallow it: he fays, the chewing it has often ftopped a loofenefs with him.

I had much difcourfe with an Irifhman (anno 1700) who feemed very fenfible in hufbandry, and talking with him about the difeafes in fheep, he afked me, if I knew any cure for the red-water; I faid, no, I thought it incurable.——He faid, in

Ireland

Of the red-water. Vide red-water in cows and calves, §. 10.

Ireland they had of late found out a remedy, which cured many though not all ; it is as follows ; when you find the sheep's breath to stink, which will shew itself in the red-water, take two quarts of brandy, and two gallons of tanner's owze, that is, the liquor out of the tan-pit, with the lime-bark, and the wash-ings of the skins in it, and mix the brandy and this liquor together ; then take an hen's egg and blow it, and take off the top of the shell, and fill it with the liquor, and put it into the horn ; this is the quantity to be given to each sheep, but if a sheep be very weak, then lessen the quantity ; though the medicine be not infallible, he has cured, he says, many in his flock with it.

With us they usually give the sheep the following drench for the red-water, or rather to prevent it. If it be for a score of hog-sheep, then about this proportion, a spoonful of bole-armoniac, a spoonful of the powder of ginger, a handful of rue, a hand-ful of red sage, and about a quart of water to be boiled to a pint, give three spoonfuls to each sheep.

Sir Ambrose Phillipps's shepherd says, to prevent the red-water in sheep, he always bleeds them twice a year in the tail-vein, at Michaelmass, and in the the spring, and two or three times in each season, bleeding them as he sees occasion, that is, as they seem more or less to rise in proof : he takes four or five spoonfuls of blood at a time, from his whole flock round : he prefers bleeding in the tail to the eye-vain, both for the red-water, and the shaking, which his sheep are subject to. —— But he confesses, for the red-water, when it has seized on the sheep, he knows no cure. —— He says, garlick steeped in new milk is said to be extreme good to prevent the red-water, given twice or thrice, a spoonful at a time. —— Sir Ambrose's sheep, he tells me, are

Id. and of blindness.

troubled

troubled much with blindneſs, which begins after
the ſhearing-time; they have a white film over their
eyes; he cures them, he ſays, with eye-water made
of allum and vinegar.

**Of the
ſtone.**

§. 14. Common dog-graſs, quick-graſs, or couch-
graſs, 'Mr. Ray ſays, is a cure for ſheep and black
cattle when they are afflicted with the ſtone, which
they are apt to be in the winter and ſpring. He
quotes Fran. de la Boe, and Gliſſon for his autho-
rity; but I muſt enquire farther of this, for neither
the Rei ruſticæ ſcriptores, nor Worlidge, nor Markham, do obſerve in oxen or ſheep ſuch a diſtemper
as the ſtone.——My ſhepherd ſays, he has known a
white round ſtone in the neck of a ſheep's bladder,
of which it died.

**Of blind-
neſs.**

§. 15. My ſhepherd came to me in July (anno
1701) and told me, I muſt get better graſs for my
ſheep, for a great many of the lambs were blind or
going to be ſo: he ſaid, a ſcum grew over their
eyes, which, as he had obſerved, uſually happened
at this time of the year, in caſe they pitched, or
ſunk in fleſh by ſhort commons; and that my wea-
ther-lambs were moſt ſubject to it. — I told him that
might be becauſe they were but lately cut, ſo they
muſt be ſubject to ſink on that account.——He ſaid,
that might be ſomething, but when the grief of that
was over, it was the ſame as before; but ewe-lambs
and ewe-hog-lambs, and ewe-hog-ſheep, and old
ewes, were hardier than the weather-ſort, and would
bear the winter better. I aſked him, if there was
not ſome other cauſe of their growing blind, for I
had heard of others; he ſaid, yes, he knew of one
more, and that was all; in wet and growing years,

ᵉ Oves & boves calculis vexati in hyeme & verno tempore liberantur a recenti gramine canino. Ex Obſerv. Fran. de la Boe,
p. 300.————— Idem jampridem obſervavit dominus Gliſſonius.
Ray, lib. 2. fol. 1255.

when

when the sheep fared so well that they could not keep the bennets down, they would be apt to get into their eyes, and blind them for some time. —— Note, if the ewes be the stronger and hardier constitutioned creatures than the weather-kind, this gives some account why the ewe-fold should be better than the weather-fold, that is, manure the land better.

Sheep's eyes will often run with water, and be blind by feeding too much in the wheat-stubble: the cause is, the wheat-stubble runs into their eyes.—— This I have heard shepherds say before, and my shepherd assures me it is true.

Sir Ambrose Phillipps's shepherd agrees that goose-dung is good for blindness in sheep.

In the isle of Harries, the natives pulverize the * sepiæ, which is found on the sand in great quantities, with which they take off the film on the eyes of sheep. Martin of the Western Isles, fol. 38.

> * Cuttle-bone.

A quantity of wild sage being chewed between one's teeth, and put into the ears of cows or sheep that are blind, they are thereby cured, and their sight perfectly restored; of which there are many fresh instances, both in Skie, and Harries islands, by persons of great integrity. Martin, fo. 181.—Wild sage chopped small, and given to horses with their oats, kills worms. ib. 182.

§. 16. The sheep near Loughborough are mightily troubled with the loore or soreness of the claws, and so are the cows; sometimes an hundred sheep in a flock shall be down together, and so troubled with it that they will be forced to feed on their knees; and many times the cows, for want of good management, never recover it, but continue always lame, and grow club-footed: verdigrease and hog's lard is a good medicine for it; and some use aquafortis for it.

> The loore. Vid. the loore in cows and calves, &c. §. 19.

For the fowle or loore in cattle, the best method

is

is to take two penny-worth of allum, two penny-worth of arfenic, one pint of wine-vinegar, and two quarts of fpring-water; boil the water till it is half gone, then pound the powders fmall, and boil all together. ——This diftemper breaks out between the claws of a beaft or a fheep, with rottennefs and ftink: before you drefs the fore, you muft pare the claw fo far as it is hollow, then put fo much of the liquor as will run all over the fore; the foot muft be dry when it is drefled, and kept fo an hour: in once or twice drefling you need not doubt of a cure.

The fcab.

§. 17. I faw Sir Ambrofe Phillipps's fhepherd drefs the fcabs in his fheep, and he fhewed me how to know where the fcab was not killed after drefling; for where the fcab was alive, there in the drefling and rubbing it would itch, which would make the fheep mump and nibble with their lips: he faid, it was not good to let the fheep-water be too ftrong, it was better to have it of a moderate ftrength, and to drefs the fame fheep twice, than to think to kill the fcab at once, efpecially if the fheep be pretty far gone with it; for it will make them grievous fore: the fheep, he faid, had the fcab very much when he came firft to Sir Ambrofe's, and he thought to cure them the fooner by making the water ftrong, but he harmed them by it; for it made fome of them fo fore, that for three days and nights together they would lie down, and only feed round about them without rifing. His fheep-water is made of tobacco, and the liquor of falt-beef, and fometimes he puts foap-fuds to it.

I told a Leicefterfhire farmer, I obferved two or three of his fheep to break out, and grow fcabby on the back.——He faid, it was true; but he dared not to meddle with them then, it being in January (anno 1698) becaufe they were big with lamb, for fear of fquatting their lambs.

An

I

An old shepherd of Derbyshire told me in September 1697, there was lately discovered a better medicine for the scab in sheep, than tobacco, and salt, and the murrain-berry root, viz. [d] a quart of spring-water with about half an ounce of quick-silver in it, boiled to a pint : and once anointing of the scab with it would cure it.

The gundy or foulness of the tail, shoulder, or breast in a sheep, is a sort of itch that comes with over-heating by over-driving, or double folding them, and to rams, by heating themselves with the ewes : it is cured by dressing with sheep-water, made of tobacco, salt, and murrain-berry root, boiled in human urine, or water, three or four hours : half a peck of salt, and three pounds of tobacco, and a hatfull of roots, to a barrel of water or urine.——If it runs on after Michaelmass, when wet weather comes, it is hardly to be cured all the year, nor is it to be washed in wet weather.——The good quality of a shepherd is, to discover this distemper ere the wool be broke by it.

Mr. Bishop's shepherd says, when the gundy or scab in sheep first appears, it is a boyl no bigger than the top of one's finger, and may be discovered in a sheep by it's standing still, and wriggling, as if feeling after the itch.

When my shepherd uses the sheep-water, to kill the scab, he shears off the loose wool they have raised with rubbing, by clipping it as short as the other wool, that by the breaking of it again, he may know whether the scab be cured or not.

He says, nothing will sooner give the sheep the

[d] A gentleman of Hertfordshire communicated to me the following remedy for the scab, which, he says, has been used with good success in that country. An ounce of white mercury, and two ounces of stone-vitriol; dissolve these in three quarts of water boiled in a glazed earthen pot, and wash the part affected with this liquor.

scab,

scab, or breaking out, than hunting them on nights, and heating them before they are folded; whereas, on the other hand, before the ewes are half gone with lamb, or when they are not with lamb, nothing is better, when they are turned out of the fold in the morning than to drive them a little; it will set them which have any stoppage on coughing, whereby they will force the phlegm through their nostrils.

The maggot.

§. 18. Sir Ambrose Phillipps's shepherd, for the maggot, lays the juice of elder, and the juice of arse-smart to the sore.

In discoursing with an old shepherd about the maggots in sheep, it being in July (anno 1697) he said, if they fell upon the back, or woolly part of the sheep, a good shepherd would be careful of the wool, and not cut it off, but take the maggot out, and rub bruised hemlock, or bruised elder upon it, and all over the body upon the wool, which would keep off the flies.———— An hour after discoursing farmer Elton's shepherd, he said the same, and farther, that, if the maggot was in the tail, he would cut it out, and rub hemlock and elder upon it, but not tar the tail.——I told him, I had seen the tail tarred: he said, then it was by a young shepherd that understood not his business; for it would not come out, but spoiled the sale of the wool.—— He said, the plains were little troubled with the maggot, the flies seldom coming there.——Afterwards discoursing with a third shepherd, he said, at this time of the year, and after shearing-time, he used tar to the tails, for the maggot, but not before shearing time, for, said he, it would now wash out again by the weather.

If a sheep has the maggot, it will be sick and pine, and creep into the hedges: the cure is sallad-oil, or fresh butter mixed with tar, and made into an ointment.

My

My fhepherd was faying, that an ewe-fold re-quired more trouble and care to look after it than a weather-fold did.—I afked him why; he faid, ewes and lambs were much more fubject to the flies and worms than weathers were; becaufe ewes could not be fheared fo clofe as weathers, on acconnt of their teats; and ewes and lambs were much more fubject to fcour than weathers.

§. 19. Mr. Bifhop's fhepherd told me, that it was Of lice. natural to fome fheep to be loufy, let them be never fo well kept, but poverty would greatly increafe the lice: if a fheep was fubject to be loufy, they ufually put fuch away, though otherwife never fuch good fheep; for it was odds but their lambs would be fub-ject to it too.

He added, it was eafy to fee whether fheep were either fcabbed, or loufy, or not; for the fcab, when it firft appears, pitches in one fingle patch, from which the fheep will rub, or bite off the wool: but when they have lice, fheep will be raifing and thin-ning their wool, by rubbing their horns on it, and biting it off in many places: the beft thing he knows of to kill the lice, he fays, is goofe-greafe; and to cure one fheep will take a quarter of a pound.

In fhearing-time, I obferved many lice in the fheep; and I was told, that, if thofe fheep were fheared, fo that the crows and magpyes could come at the lice, the fheep would in a week's time be rid of them.

It being an extreme wet winter (anno 1707) wherein we had fcarce any froft; I obferved to my fhepherd, that the wool of my fheep ftared very much.——He faid, that was occafioned by their fucking their wool, by reafon of their lice, with which this winter had filled them full; for, faid he, it is wet that breeds lice, and makes them increafe, nor is it to any purpofe to fearch their fleeces, or to
medicine

medicine them, to kill the lice, till dry weather comes, becauſe the rains will continually waſh away the medicine; whereas, when ſpring and dry weather comes, it will put a ſtop to the progreſs of the growth of the lice, and then the medicines will eaſily exert their virtue.——So that I perceive the winter months are the great breeders of lice in ſheep.

Of adders biting ſheep.

§. 20. Riding in a furzy and ferny ground of farmer Stephens's, with him and farmer Sartain, I told farmer Stephens the ground was only fit for ſheep.——He ſaid, the graſs was fit, but the ground did breed ſo many adders, that he did not care to venture ſheep there in ſummer time, for one ſummer he loſt a ſcore out of threeſcore, by the adders biting them: he ſaid, it was the udder-flank, or throat, that they uſually bit the ſheep in, and that the place would look black, but they could not recover them by any ointments.——Farmer Sartain ſaid, they had ſuch a ground by Broughton, which would do the ſame; they agreed that cow-cattle and horſes were not ſo liable to this miſchief as ſheep were, becauſe in hot weather it is the nature of ſheep to riſe up often, and then run a few yards and lie down again, as alſo to run with their noſes low to the ground: it is probable the hides of the great cattle being thicker than the hides of the ſheep, the teeth of theſe venomous creatures have ſeldom force enough to enter. [g]

Of ſheep lark-ſpurred.

§. 21. I had an ewe in June (anno 1701) that broke out moſt miſerably about her eyes, and had a watery running, with a ſwelling, with which ſhe was blind, and continued ſo for ſix weeks: we could not imagine what was the matter with her.——My ſhepherd ſaid, he believed ſhe was lark-ſpurred.—— I aſked, what that was; he ſaid, at this time of the

[g] Note,——to bathe the part with warm ſallad oil is now a known cure for the bite of an adder.

year,

year, when the larks build their nests, if a sheep
should come so near to a lark's nest as to tread on it,
the lark will fly out, and spur at the sheep, and, if the
spur made a scratch any where on the eye or nose, it
was perfect poison, and would rankle in such manner as this ewe's eye did : this, said he, is certainly
true, and other shepherds would tell me the same.

Of H O R S E S.

§. 1. THE Latin writers have given us some
few rules concerning the breeding and
choice of horses, but, the greater part of them relating to those that were designed for the war, or
chariot-race, such observations can afford but small
instruction to the farmer, and I might, it will be
said, have spared myself the trouble of translating or
transcribing them. It may however be agreeable
to many of my readers to be acquainted with what
little they have told us of their method of treating
these creatures, and with what were esteemed perfections among them ; add, that some of these perfections may be required even in the draught-horse,
and perhaps the more he partakes of them it may
render him the more valuable. ———Columella, in
his rules for breeding horses, directs, that the stallion
be pampered, and kept high with food ; that he
cover not less than fifteen, nor more than twenty
mares in a season (but this, says Palladius, must be
regulated by judgment, according to the strength
of the stallion, who will last the longer in proportion as he is less drained :) a young stallion should
not cover above twelve or fifteen mares at farthest :
that he be not suffered to cover before he is three
years old (not till he be compleat four, says Palla-

h See the author's Observations on wool.

dius).

dius) and he will laſt very well to his twentieth year.
—If the mare caſt her foal, or ſhould foal with difficulty, he preſcribes a drench of polypodium, bruiſ-
ed, and mixed with warm water ; but, if ſhe brings
forth eaſily, he particularly cautions us by no means
to aſſiſt the birth with our hands (nor handle the
young for ſome time after they are brought forth,
ſays Palladius) as the leaſt touch may be an injury
to the foal.

The mare ſhould not take horſe till ſhe is two
years old, nor after ſhe is ten ; for when paſt that
age ſhe will bring a weak and unprofitable breed :
in this ſhe agrees with Varro. She ſhould not be
ſuffered to breed oftener than every other year, that
ſhe may keep her milk the longer to bring up her
foal, which ſhould ſuck two years.—— Colts ought
not to be broke till they are two years old, according to Palladius (but Varro ſays, till they are turned
of three ; if for domeſtick uſes, ſays Columella, at
two years old, for the race, &c. not till after three.)
He orders horſes to be cut in the month of March,
which he alſo ſays is the proper month for covering,
but Varro ſpeaking of the latter, ſays, any time between the vernal equinox and the ſummer ſolſtice.
[a] According to theſe writers, if you intend your
horſe

[a] Equos ad admiſſuram quos velis habere, legere oportet am-
plo corpore, formoſos, nullâ parte corporis inter ſe non con-
gruenti. Varro.—Cùm vero natus eſt pullus, confeſtim licet
indolem æſtimare, ſi hilaris, ſi intrepidus, ſi neque conſpectu,
novæque rei auditu terretur, ſi ante gregem procurrit, ſi laſciviâ
& alacritate, interdum & curſu certans æquales exſuperat ; ſi
foſſam ſine cunctatione tranſiliit, pontem flumenque tranſcendit :
hæc erunt honeſti animi documenta.—In formâ hoc ſequemur ;
ut ſit exiguum caput & ſiccum. pelle propemodum ſolis oſſibus
adhærente. Palladius ;—— brevibus auriculis, argutis, arrectis,
applicatis. Var. Columella, Pallad.—- nigris oculis, Col. &
magnis, Pal. naribus apertis ; cervice latâ nec longâ ; denſâ
jubâ, (&.fuſcâ, Var.) & per dextram partem profuſâ, (latè pa-
tenti, Pal.) & muſculorum toris numeroſo pectore ; grandibus
armis

horse for a stallion, you should endeavour to procure one that is full sized, and beautiful, and well
proportioned. His nature and disposition, even
when a foal, may be soon discovered, by his live-
liness and intrepidity; by his betraying no fear at the
sight or sound of things he is unaccustomed to; by
his being the leader of his company, more wanton
and playful than the rest, and sometimes making
trial of his speed with them, and excelling them in
the race; by his leaping the ditch, passing the
bridge, or plunging into the stream without hesita-
tion: all these are presages of a generous and noble
spirit. —His make and shape should be as follows;
——his head of the smaller size, and lean; the skin
just covering the bone; his ears little, picked, upright, and close to his head; his eyes black and
large; his nostrils wide; his neck deep, and not
over-long, with a thick dark-coloured mane flowing
on the right side; his bosom deeply spreading, and
very muscular; his shoulders large and strait; his
sides rounding inward; his back-bone broad, and,
as it were, double, but at least not prominent; his
belly of a moderate size; his loins broad, and sloping downward; his buttocks round; the muscles of
his thighs visibly numerous and protuberant; his
legs strait and equal; his knees round, not big, nor
turning towards each other; his foot neat and firm,

armis & rectis; lateribus inflexis; spinâ duplici, (sin minus non
extanti; ventre modico, Var.) latis lumbis & subsidentibus,
(deorsum versum pressis, Var.) rotundis clunibus: feminibus torosis ac numerosis, Col. cruribus rectis & æqualibus; genibus
rotundis, ne magnis, nec introrsus spectantibus, Var. pede sicco,
& solido, & cornu concavo altius calceato, Pal. cui corona me-
diocris superposita sit; caudâ longâ & setosâ crispâque, Col.
vastum corpus & solidum; robori conveniens altitudo; mores,
ut vel ex summâ quiete facilè concitetur, vel ex incitatâ festina-
tione non difficile teneatur, Pal. de stirpe magni interest quâ
sit, Var.

hollow

hollow hoofed, and not low heeled, with a small coronet on the top of it ; his tail long, full, and wavy, his whole body large and compact ; his height proportioned to his strength ; of so manageable a temper, as to start forth at once on the least encouragement, and be stopped without much difficulty when at full speed.—— Great regard must be had to the race he comes of.——— Palladius has added also a list of the colours they most approved ; but we choose, says he, a stallion of one true colour, and reject the rest, except a multitude of other perfections atone for this defect. [b] I have only one observation to add before I close this section, which is, that the characters of a fine horse given us by Virgil and Columella are in so many particulars the same, that the latter undoubtedly copied from the former.

§. 2. The tenth commandment forbids us, to covet

---

1 Primus & ire viam, 2 & fluvios tentare minaces
Audet, 3 & ignoto sese committere ponti ;
4 Nec vanos horret strepitus.——Illi ardua cervix,
5 Argutumque caput, 6 brevis alvus, 7 obesaque terga ;
8 Luxuriatque toris animosum pectus.
9 Densa juba, 10 & dextro jactata recumbit in armo ;
1 At duplex agitur per lumbos spina.—— Virg. Georg. lib. 3.

1 Ante gregem procurrit, 2 pontem 3 flumenque transcendit,
4 neque conspectu novæque rei auditu terretur — 5 Exiguum caput, 6 substrictus venter, lati lumbi, 8 musculorum toris numerosum pectus, 9 densa juba, 10 & per dextram partem profusa, 11 spina duplex. Columella.

1 The first to lead the way, 2 to tempt the flood,
3 To pass the bridge unknown.
4 Dauntless at empty noises ; lofty-neck'd,
5 Sharp-headed, 6 barrel-bellied, 7 broadly-back'd ;
8 Brawny his chest, and deep.
9 On his right shoulder his 10 thick mane reclin'd,
Ruffles at speed, and dances in the wind.
11 His chin is double. ———
Mr. Dryden's Translation of the third Geor.

vet our neighbour's ox or his afs : it is probable the horfe is not mentioned, becaufe there were but few horfes among the Ifraelites till Solomon's time.——So alfo, Exod. xiii. ver. 8. it is appointed for every firftling of an afs to be redeemed ; Bifhop Patrick fays, there was the fame reafon for horfes and camels, but an afs is mentioned. becaufe there were plenty of them, though but few of the others.

§. 3. Mr. Clerk of Leicefterfhire affures me, *Of buying colts for the plough.* that if I buy colts of two years old, 1 may begin to work them gently in the plough, and at harrowing time :, and that, if I laid out twelve pounds, which he would advife me to do, rather than but ten pounds on a colt, by the time he came three years old, he would very well earn his meat.——This, he

The above characters given us by Varro, Columella, Palladius, and Virgil, according to our author's remark, feem principally to relate to thofe horfes that were defigned either for the manage or the chariot-race; obferving however that thefe characters are not fufficiently diftinguifhed but too much blended with each other, he has taken from all of them together what he thought made a proper and uniform portrait of a fine horfe, in which, it appears to me, he has an eye to the war-horfe only.—The like want of precifenefs in diftinguifhing one kind from another, was perhaps a fault not uncommon among the antient writers on hufbandry, and may particularly be feen in Varro, who, under the article——de Bubus & Vaccis——has given us a defcription that, taken in the whole, is fuitable to neither ox. bull, nor cow, but has fomewhat that relates feparately to every one of them, at leaft in the judgment of our prefent graziers, and dairy men. I know no one that has diftinctly characterized the various forts of horfes, excepting it be our countryman Mr. Dodfley, who, in his Poem on agriculture, having firft fpoken of thofe that are proper for the draught, and the road, has fo well defcribed the hunter, and the war-horfe, that, if Mr. Lifle's book were not intended merely for inftruction, I fhould have been tempted to have inferted fome lines of it in this note, for the reader's entertainment ; I take the occafion however of recommending it to him, as, I think, it has been lefs taken notice of than it deferves, and as I wifh the author may find encouragement to purfue his plan, and oblige the public with the two remaining books he at firft propofed.

P 2   faid,

said, was the practice of all Northamptonshire, viz.
to buy their colts at that age, and by the time they
came four, to sell them off for the coach.—— He
assured me, they would be presently gentle, by being
wrought two or three times with other horses; and
that their food should be oats in the straw, and barley in the straw.

He says, that colts of two years old will very
well do two, or three days work in the week at the
plough, and at harrowing; but in Leicestershire
they do not plough so hard as with us in Hampshire.

Of keep-
ing mares
for breed.

§. 4. Being at Appleford in the Isle of Wight
(anno 1711) farmer Farthing was speaking of his
mares, that he chose rather, for sake of breed, to
keep them than geldings, and that he had a stallion
for that purpose, which went in his team.—— I asked him, how he could manage that matter so as to
keep his stone-horse quiet, and free from unlucki-
ness, and within inclosures; he said, he kept no geldings; for whenever a gelding came into the field
or the stable with the mares, the stone-horse would
immediately be biting the mares, and kicking the
geldings, but would go as gentle as possible with
the mares by themselves: then, said he, that he may
not break over hedges, we always fetter him with a
mare, and so he will be easy.—— I replied, if he went
with the mares, he would be apt to spoil the mare
he went with, by leaping the other mares, which
would endanger the putting out the shoulder of the
mare with which he was fettered.—— He said, he
made the links so long that there was no danger of
that; for the stallion often leaped other mares in
the field, whilst he was fettered to a mare, without
any inconveniency.

It is profitable to keep mares for foaling: the only inconveniency in them is, that their foals must
come in March or April, or be worth but little;

and

and then such mares can do but little service in barley-seed-time: but afterwards you may work them
as much as the other horses.

§. 5. I bought colts of two and three years old, Of keep-
ing colts
in woods.
and put them into the woods, from whence they
broke out and strayed: the farmer said, I should
have kept them in the meadows till they had been
acquainted, before I had turned them into the woods.
—I replied, it being then the beginning of December
(anno 1700) that the meadows would have made them
so sweet-mouthed, they would not have endured the
woods. —— The farmer said the meadows at that
time of the year would not make them fine-mouth-
ed, but he granted the hop-clover grounds would.

§. 6. I was saying to farmer Parsons of North- Of keeping
mares for
breed:
amptonshire, that I intended to keep mares, and to breed:
breed: this was anno :701. —— He cautioned me and of
colts.
not to do as many did, viz. keep up the foals from
the mares, and only let them suck morning and
night, before the mares go to, and when they come
from work: this will spoil both the mare and the
foal; for the mare will fret, and her milk being
pent up will over-heat, and that will surfeit her foal:
whereas a mare should do very little work, but go
with her foal at grass, till the foal is fit to go after
the mare, and then it is best for the foal to follow
the mare at work, and to suck a little at times.—
Columella in part lays down the same rule.

§. 7. If your grounds are bounded with good Of keep-
ing colts.
hedges and ditches, it may be convenient to keep a
few colts to eat up the offal hay, the waste and offal
of the sheep.

ᶜ Columella speaking of sucking colts, says, cum firmior erit, in
eadem pascuâ, in quibus mater est, dimittendus, ne desiderio partus sui laboret equa; nam id præcipuè genus pecudis amore na-
torum, nisi fiat potestas, noxam trahit.—— Therefore it seems
farmers allow the sucking colts to follow the mares by their sides
in carting.

§.- 8. It would be no paradox to affert, that, whereas a brace of faddle-geldings at London, cannot be kept for lefs than 50 l. per annum, yet the fame geldings, in the country, may, by a gentleman, who keeps land in his own hands, be kept in a manner for nothing : or in other words, every horfe in the country is worthy of his meat. Two geldings will give twenty-four load of dung in the year, which will nobly dung an acre of ground ; this acre, modeftly fpeaking, will bring four crops, equivalent to four quarters of oats per acre per annum, and a new acre is to be dunged yearly, fo there will foon be the produce of four acres yearly, to be accounted for in the fame proportion, for the maintenance of thefe two horfes ; and will alfo pay for the rent of the ground, feed, and ploughing, for three bufhels per week will maintain them. And the like computation for the yearly produce of four acres of clover, enriched by the manure, fhall nobly maintain your two horfes in hay and grafs.——— In the fame manner may the bread-corn for a family be provided for almoft nothing ; for, in my family, that fpends a bufhel and an half of wheat in a day, and burns ten chaldron of coals per annum, befides wood, I have from thence at leaft twelve dung-pot loads of afhes in the year ; and from garbage and duft, and wafhing of the kitchen, brew-houfe, and milk-houfe, at leaft twelve loads more, which is yearly noble manure for one acre, each of which acres will, modeftly computed, produce equivalent, for four years, to fixteen bufhels of wheat per acre, and four times fixteen is fixty-four bufhels. — Your grains alfo, and your pot-liquor devoured by the pigs, produce fome loads of dung, nor ought the pigeon-dung to be flighted.———And the fown-graffes in each acre holding two years, eight acres of grafs are yearly to be accounted for on the fcore of

the

the manure arifing from the two horfes, and eight acres on the fcore of the houfe-manure, in all fix-teen acres, four of which will provide hay for the two horfes, another four acres will fat forty-eight fheep, that is, fix fheep per acre, twice in the year, and the other eight acres will fat twelve cows for the houfe.

§. 9. In our hill-country we ought always to have a confideration to the pafture-grounds we referve for our cart-horfes in fummer, fo as to be able at leaft to allot pafturage for them under good fhelter, in cold, windy, or rainy nights; for warmth at fuch times is of as much regard as their food. *Of pafture for cart-horfes.*

§. 10. Speaking of the great expence of keeping ftone-horfes in the houfe, my bailiff affured me, that ftone-horfes kept in the houfe in barley-feed-time would not be kept up in flefh by oats, without peas or barley.——I replied, that I thought barley might give them the fret.——He faid, if it did heat them, as it would be apt to do, the carters would, unknown to their mafters, clap barley in an old fack into the pond for a night, and take it out early in the morning, and would give them of this half malted, and it would cool them again : he faid in feed-time, when the carters would be giving them barley, it would, as I faid, heat them, and, when they had been heat-ed, one might perceive it, by their gnawing and eating the earth when they could come at it. *Of barley for ftone-horfes.*

§. 11. I have heard many carters fay, that when a horfe is out of condition, and hard worked, no quantity of oats will make him thrive ; for his work will lie fo hard upon him, being out of cafe, that it will keep him low, give him what meat you will : but a horfe in cafe may eafily be kept up with lefs meat, notwithftanding he is worked. *A lean horfe hard worked cannot thrive by corn.*

§. 12. Farmer Ifles of Holt, Wilts, affures me, that peas-ftraw, or peas-halm, if well houfed, is the *Peas-halm for horfes in Wilt-fhire.*

P 4

the beſt and heartieſt fodder for cart-horſes, beyond barley-ſtraw, or middling hay, and the horſes will eat it better, nor does it ſcour them, nor give them the fret.——I was ſurprized-at this account, becauſe in our hill-country we ſeldom give peas-halm to horſes, nor do the cow-cattle much care for it, for they will but pick on it a little ; which makes me ſuſpect, that, as in other caſes, ſo in this, the peas-halm in our cold hill-country is not ſo ſweet as in the vale, but of a ſour juice, and the cattle will pick but little of it, be it never ſo well houſed.— ── William Sartain ſays the ſame, but adds, it will be apt to make horſes, if they be held to it, piſs high-coloured water.

In Leiceſ-terſhire. I find the uſual method in Leiceſterſhire is to give their horſes peas-ſtraw, and they care not how little barley or oat-ſtraw they give them : they think the peas-ſtraw to be more cooling, and more heartning, and leſs binding than barley-ſtraw.── They ſeldom give oats in provender, but peas or beans mixt with wheat-chaff, or barley-chaff.

In Hants. I was telling ſome of our Hampſhire farmers, that in Leiceſterſhire they gave their horſes peas-ſtraw, and thought there was more ſtrength in it than in any ſtraw-fodder, and valued it the moſt : whereas I obſerved, they in Hampſhire made little eſteem of it, and flung it to the dung-heap. ──They replied, that they looked on it too as a very hearty ſtraw, but it was likely that, when I obſerved they flung it away, the year muſt have been bad, and it had been ill houſed ; but, ſaid they, the ſtraw as well as the peas, if not well * hinted and dried, are dangerous to give to a horſe, which is the reaſon we the ſeldomer give it them in this country.

* Well put up toge-ther.

Winter-vetches for horſes. §. 13. Take care to have a good ſtore of winter-vetches between the latter end of Auguſt and the beginning of November; for the old ſtraw being

then

then gone, and the new not ready, and the grass almost at an end, they will be a great support to your horses.

I observed in the Isle of Wight in May (anno 1699) that, after seed-time, the farmers baited their horses sometimes with grass; for it seems, the fodder by that time has but little goodness in it —— In our part of Hampshire, against that time, the farmers use to lay up some winter-vetches and peas for their horses, to help out with the dryness of the straw, and to give them a bundle after watering-time, morning and evening: but peas and vetches in the straw are by no means counted wholsome till after Candlemass, when they have sweated in the mow; for if they be given sooner, they often give the horses the fret; the drier the peas and vetches are in the straw it is counted the better. —— They generally reserve the greatest part of the peas in the straw till seed-time, and then they give them the horses, to cool their bodies after hard working.

To have winter-vetches in reek against barley-seed-time, is as good husbandry as to have them gainst the beginning of winter, when there is no straw, and the grass is pretty near gone; for before barley-seed-time the straw is too dry for horses.

§. 14 This year, 1704, was a mighty dry year, Of goar-and consequently goar-vetches the safer to be given vetches. to horses: our carters gave our horses of them very freely, they being very dry and good, and I had six acres of them: but they filled my horses very full of blood, and one of my coach horses fell down dead in his harness; his blood being a little heated by driving, and too thick to circulate, burst the vessels: therefore to drive them leisurely, if full of blood, is best, and, let the goar-vetches be never so good, give the horses dry meat every third week.

§. 15. I

Winter-vetches.

§. 15. I afked Mr. Bachelour of Afhmonfworth, how it came to pafs, that winter-vetches were not thought proper in the halm, unlefs the weather were very dry; feeing, if they were well hinted, as mine this year (1700) were, without taking wet, and had well fweated, I faw not how a wet day could affect them; he replied, that their halm was loofe and fpungy, and would give in damp weather, though in reek, which would be apt to give horfes the fret.

Of hay and chaff mixed.

§. 16. Farmer Knap of Burclear gave his horfes hay and chaff, but no ftraw, and does affure me, that he allowed his horfes winter and fummer but one bufhel of oats a piece per week, and one bufhel of beans per week amongft fix of them. In the eight winter and fpring months he faved fix bufhels of oats per week, which comes to twenty-four quarters, and at 14 s. per quarter, makes 17 l. —— but then for the four quarters of beans to be difcounted for at 20 s. per quarter, the oats faved will be but 13 l. ——The hay the fix horfes will eat in the eight months will be twelve loads, which cannot be valued at lefs than 18 l. —— So that this way of farmer Knap's is worfe by 5 l. per annum, than the common allowance of oats with ftraw, only he has faved all his ftraw, which cannot be worth much more than 5 l. —— Therefore this way of farmer Knap's feems to be a proper fort of hufbandry in the vale, where hay is plenty, and their land too good for oats; for farmers are very unwilling to buy oats, though they come cheaper than hay, but always make the product of their own farm ferve all occafions; thus few farmers will buy beans for their horfes at the fame price they may fell oats: it is alfo a good way, where, in the hill-country, a farm grows more French-grafs hay than the farmer can get chapmen for.

§. 17. Oats

§. 17. Oats being very dry in April (anno 1707) *Of feeding* I thought it would be cheaper to feed my-horses *horses with* with barley ; so I proposed it to my carters : but *barley.* they were all against it, and said, the time of the year for that was over ; for, if I gave them it during the summer, it would heat them too much ; the season for that was in the winter. ———— But quære why they give horses barley in the hot countries.

§. 18. In discourse a out feeding of plough-horses, *Of feeding* several farmers allowed dry peas or vetches to be *horses* very hearty and wholsome for them, provided they *with dry* had sweat well in the mow, otherwise very impro- *peas and* per. ———And one of them asserted, that four bushels *vetches.* of peas, mixt with oats, would go as far as a quarter of oats.

§. 19. In Leicestershire they hold it very impro- *With chaff* per to give horses chaff and oats together ; for with *and oats* the chaff they will be apt to swallow the oats whole. *mixed.*

§. 20. The Loughborough carrier gives his horses *With* no oats, and but very little hay : he gives them, *beans and* when at Loughborough, oat-hulls and beans ; viz. *oat-hulls.* after the proportion of a peck of beans to a bushel of hulls : a quarter of a peck of beans to a peck of hulls he thinks enough for one horse at a time : he says, with this feed, when at Loughborough, seven or eight horses, from Friday-noon to Tuesday-noon will eat him up but three, or four hundred pound weight of hay, which is at most but sixteen todd : his oat hulls cost him 2d per bushel : so then, if a plough-horse has two baits in the day, he will eat half a peck -of beans, which at 6 s. per bushel, will come to 9d.—and the hulls a penny.

§. 21. At London the said carrier gives his *With* horses only beans and bran ; viz. a bushel of beans to *beans and* two bushels of bran : but there he gives them hay, *bran.* because he must pay for it, whether they eat any or not.

§. 22. In

New peas
give
horses the
fret.
Id. peas-
chaff.

§. 22. In carting of peas in harvest, horses should be kept from eating them; they are apt to give them the fret.

I gave my horses peas-chaff in October, and it gave two of them the fret the second day. Note, this was too early in the year to give them peas-chaff, which, when given ought to be the chaff of peas well housed.

Of clean-
ing chaff.

§. 23. Mr. Bayly of Wick advises me by all means, to prevent surfeiting my horses, and breeding distempers in them, to see my chaff well cleansed from the dust in the barn before it is brought into my chaff-bin in the stable; for, when the chaff is carried foul to the bin, the carters are many times careless, and in haste, so that they give it not proper, nor indeed any cleansing, which is very pernicious to a horse, and the dust and dirt binds up his body.

What chaff
best, — also
what al-
lowance
for a horse.

§. 24. Mr. Edwards says, barley-chaff is accounted better than wheat-chaff, the common price of which is 2s. 6d. per quarter, and a bushel of oats per week to a cart-horse with this chaff is accounted a full allowance in the height of work.—— But the farmers say, they allow eight bushels to six horses, and it scarcely does.—— Chaff is accounted fouler feed than oats, and so not so good for saddle-horses as for cart-horses.—Now, supposing oats at 20 s. per quarter, the above allowance comes but to 6 l. 10s. per annum for oats.—Note, the farmers say, barley-chaff is too hot and binding for horses not used to it, and oat-chaff is little worth.

Farmer Lavington and Thomas Miles of Wiltshire say, that wheat and barley-chaff mingled together are best for horses.

Coming into my stable (and suspecting I had not the best chaff for my money, for I bought my chaff that year of the farmer) I found, as I thought, too much oat-chaff with the barley-chaff, and was angry: but

but my carter answered me, there was not oat-chaff enough; if there were more, he said, the horses would eat it better: one part oat-chaff and two parts barley-chaff was the best proportion; for the barley-chaff, though the more heartning, yet was rough in the mouth, and very troublesome and unpleasant on that account, but the oat-chaff softened it: especially after watering, barley-chaff alone was very improper, but before the water washed it down. —— Then, said I, wheat-chaff mixt with the barley-chaff seems to me to be best, because that is soft, and answers all the ends of oat-chaff, and is more heartning.—This he agreed to.

§. 25. Conformable to the opinion of the antients, viz. that those sorts of chaff were most nourishing which were smallest, as has been before hinted, is our practice amongst the farmers: for, when fodder-straw is dear, we cut it, finding it thereby to be most nourishing; it seeming, that of the smaller parts any thing consists, it the more enables the juices of the stomach to digest it, and the juices of that thing are the easier extracted from it: thus we grind corn for poultry, hogs, &c. whereby we suppose it more nourishing than whole corn.

The smaller the chaff the more nourishing.

§. 26. I thought my barley-hulls this year (anno 1718) would be very good, because my barley had taken no rain in harvest, and, the summer having been very hot and dry, they were the pure oils of the barley, without any mixture of leaves of weeds, &c. with them.—— But my thresher told me, that my hulls, for that reason, were never worse; for they were so rough and coarse, and so harsh to the horses mouths and throats, that my carters complained of them, and said, their horses care not to eat my barley-hulls as usual: whereas, said he, in wet years, when the broad and hop-clover grow to a height in the corn, as also other weeds, their leaves soften the asperity of the barley-hulls.

Of barley-chaff.

I threshed

I threshed hop-clover for seed (anno 1701) and saved the leaves, which we beat out, and gave to the horses, and they liked them much better than chaff.

§. 27. It is good to save barley-straw and peas

To save barley-straw and peas-halm for litter.

halm, in the spring after threshing is over, for litter for horses throughout the summer; to save wheat-straw, for which there is always in the hill-country, where there are many barns, and wheat-reeks, and less wheat sowed than in the vale, a greater occasion than for barley-straw, for thatching.

ASSES and MULES.

§. 1. WITHIN five days of a she-ass's foaling, she should be horsed again: a she-ass was horsed two seasons with a jack of her own foaling, and she went through both times.

Asses of great price in Spain.

§. 2. I asked Mr. Garret, if he had not seen a jack-ass sell for 30 l. —— he assured me, he had seen two in the king of Spain's stables at Madrid, which cost him 60 l. each; they were fourteen hands high, but were strange rough, dull looking creatures, especially about the head; the king had them to get mules.

Of mules.

§. 3. He said, there was one thing very remarkable, when a mare takes a stone-ass, and has a mule-foal by him, such a mare will ever after go through, if leaped by a stone-horse, and will never bring a horse-foal after.

The mule begot between an he-ass and a mare is commonly livelier, and more like the nature of the mare, than a mule begot between a stone-horse and a she-ass. Partus sequitur ventrem, says Mr. Mortimer.

Of slitting asses noses.

§. 4. In the island of Malta, Ray first noted the custom of slitting up the nostrils of asses, because they being naturally streight and small, are not sufficient to admit air enough to serve them, when they
travel

travel or labour hard in the hot countries: and thence he philosophically reasons, that the hotter the country is, the more air is necessary for respiration.

W O O D.

§. 1. IF your acorns, mast, and other seed be to *Of acorns,* be sowed in a place too cold for an autum- *mast, &c.* nal semination, your seeds may be prepared for the vernal semination, by being barrelled or potted up in moist sand or earth, stratum super stratum, during the winter, at the expiration whereof you will find them sprouted, and they will be apter to take then than if they had been sown in the winter, and will not be so much concerned at the heat of the season, as those which are crude and unfermented would, when newly sown in the spring, especially in hot and loose grounds. Evelyn's Sylva, fo. 7.

§. 2. I know it is a tradition, that the elm and sal- *Of the elm* low have no seeds: but I have raised several of them *and sallow.* from seeds. Cook, fo. 5.

§. 3. Mr. Raymond put me very much upon *Of ash-* sowing ash-keys up and down in my woods; and *keys,* setting plants in all vacancies. ——— I have known great improvements made in coppices by sowing ash-keys

§. 4. The withy, sallow, ozier, and willow, may *and withy,* be raised from seeds, but, as they seldom come to *&c.* be ripe in England, the other ways of raising them are more practicable. Mortimer, fo. 364.

§. 5. The ash is one of the worst trees to take root *Of laying* by laying:-but yet it will take. Cook, c. 1. fo. 1. *ash, oak,* ——— The oak will grow of laying, and so will *and elm.* the elm very frequently. ib. Cook.

Those sorts of trees which will grow by cuttings, are the easiest to raise by layings. Cook, fo. 9

§. 6. Touching the best way for laying your *Of laying* layers of trees, observe, if they be trees that hold *trees.*

their

their leaf all winter, as firs, pines, holly, yews, box bayes, laurel, ilix, &c. let them be laid about the latter end of August. ib. Cook.

But if they be such as shed their leaves in winter, as oak, elm, lime, sycamore, apple-trees, pear-trees, mulberry, &c. let such be laid about the middle of October See the reasons, Cook, ib.

I know in small plants the spring or summer doth very well for laying them, for they, being short-lived, are the quicker in drawing roots. ib. fo. 10. The same rule holds for cuttings, as to the season. ib. fo. 12.

In laying, if you will, you may twist the end you lay in the ground like a with. ib. —— As to laying, the harder the wood is, then the young wood will take best, laid in the ground, but, if a soft wood, then elder bows will take root best. Cook, fo. 11.

I think Mr. Ray says, that the elder stick will put forth roots, if it be set in the ground, at any place between the knots, though there be no joint: however, if Mr. Ray has not said it, I am sure it is true.

Of raising trees by the roots. §. 7. In raising trees by the roots of a tree, let the tree be a thriving tree, neither too young nor too old; for, if it be too young, then the roots will be too small for this purpose, if too old, it is possible the roots may be decaying, and then not fit for this purpose. Cook, fo. 13, and 14.

Of raising suckers. §. 8. You may raise suckers from such trees as may be propagated by suckers, by digging about the roots early in the spring, and finding such as with a little cutting may be bent upwards; raise them above ground three or four inches, and in a short time they will send forth suckers fit for transplantation: or you may split some of the roots with wedges, or break them, covering them with fresh mold; they will quickly sprout out. Mortimer, fo. 323.

§. 9. Monsieur

§. 9. Monſieur Quinteny, part 2d. fo. 180. ſaith, I affect to plant preſently after Martinmaſs, in dry and light grounds, but care not to plant till the end of February in cold and moiſt places, becauſe the trees in this laſt can do nothing all the winter, but may more likely be ſpoiled than be able to preſerve themſelves; whereas in light grounds they may begin even that very ſame autumn to ſhoot out ſome ſmall roots, which will be a great advance to them, and put them in the way of doing wonders in the following ſpring.——I recite my author, becauſe I think it applicable to planting quick-ſet hedges; having in the year 1702 planted quick-ſet hedges in November, in very good, but ſtrong cold clay-land, and the winter proved wet, whereby ſuch land muſt be ſo much the colder; but the ſummer proved a very dry hot ſummer, which one might have thought more beneficial to ſuch earth, but (according to Monſieur Quinteny's obſervation) the ground being chilled, the plants came not away all the ſummer following, making very poor ſhoots, and but juſt ſaved themſelves from dying; and I believe their condition was ſo much the worſe, becauſe I ploughed up the trench wherein the ſets were planted, before it was dug, whereby the earth laid ſome time a ſodding: on the other hand, I planted a mead of cold clay-land the latter end of February, but the land was very good; and the plants made extraordinary ſhoots.

Legendre, the Frenchman, ſays, in ſuch ſoils as are moiſt and backward, it is beſt to ſtay till the end of February before you plant; becauſe too much moiſture corrupts and rots during winter, but the hot and early grounds muſt be planted in November, that the roots beginning before winter, whilſt the warm weather laſts, to put forth ſome ſmall filaments, may ſo unite themſelves with the earth, that

the trees at spring may grow and flourish so much
the faster, fo. 19.—Trees are not fit to be replanted,
till their sap be wholly spent, for if there be any
sap in them, when they are taken up, having now
no more nourishment, they fade, and their bark
which is yet tender, will grow rivelled and dry, and
so it is the less capable of receiving the new sap when
it begins to ascend in the spring, fo. 93.—We see
that, if trees grow yellow, and sick, having but
a small store of sap, they presently cast their leaves,
ib. ——— Now seeing the sap falls sooner in dry
grounds than in those which are moist, it is certain
that in such grounds trees may be both taken up,
and also replanted earlier, ib.—The small branches
and buds of a tree new planted must be taken off,
which open a passage in the bark, and come out of
the body of the tree, for they always grow up with
the greatest vigour, fo. 96.—In pruning, and stop-
ping the growth of the boughs, care must be taken
to cut one short one between two long ones, that
being unequal when they come to spring, the middle
of the tree may be the better furnished. In the same
manner must the dwarf-standards be cut, because
that each branch, which is cut, puts forth many
more, and therefore being cut all of the same height,
they cause confusion of branches in the top of the
tree, and the midst of it in the mean while remains
unfurnished, because the sap designs always to ascend,
and runs more willingly into the high boughs than
into those that are lower, fo. 124.

Lord Pembroke tells me, it was a common saying, that all trees were to be planted when their leaves
were falling : and he looked upon it to be a good
rule for such trees as were naturally of the growth of
the same country where they were transplanted, or
of a cold country, as the northern fir, which naturally grows in the north ; if any of them are transplanted

planted hither, or raised from seeds, they may be
transplanted at the first fall of the leaf before winter:
but it is otherwise with the southern fir, for you
must stay till the warmth of the spring for the transplanting of that; and this distinction, said he, it
was reasonable to think held good in all cases between
northern and southern plants.

I observe fir and holly-leaves do not fall so often
on our cold hills, as in the vale, nor do the spruce-
fir in particular litter our walks so much as in warmer places: the reason why these ever greens keep
their leaves some years, is from the viscidity of their
juice, which is more so in our cold country, but in
a warmer soil or clime is so attenuated, that the
leaves must fall oftener.

Langford of planting says, that when the seedlings are grown up to a foot high fit to be removed
into the nursery for inoculating, &c.—the tap or
heart-root ought to be cut off, that it may not run
directly downward beyond the good soil, but may
spread it's roots abroad in breadth.

Strong and well-grown trees may prosper as well
or better than small ones, especially in uncultivated
or stiff land by nature, where young trees cannot so
well put forth roots. And if you should have a tree
between ten and thirty years old that you have a
mind to remove, you must about November, the year
before you transplant it, dig a trench as narrow as you
please, but so deep as to meet with most of the
spreading roots, at such a distance round about the
body of the tree as you would cut the roots off at
when you remove it; about half a yard distance
from the body of the tree may do very well, except
the tree be very large, but, if you have not far to
carry it, leave the roots the longer; as you make
the trench, cut the roots you meet with clear off,
and smooth without splitting them, or bruising the
bark; then fill up the trench again, and by the next

Q 2 October,

October, when you take up the tree, you will find those great roots will have put forth many fibrous roots, and made preparation for more, which fresh and tender roots upon removal will enable the tree to draw more nourishment than otherwise it would be able to do. Langford, fol. 18.

Of cutting off the tap-root.

§. 10. Before I had read Quinteny, and found by him, how necessary it was to spread the uppermost range of roots flat down, so as to run between two earths, I knew not the reason for cutting off the tap-root; but now it is plain the uppermost range of roots could not be so spread unless the tap-root were cut off. —— There is also a farther reason for cutting off the tap-root, because being a stronger root than the rest, it draws the nourishment from them, and shooting downwards, after some time dies in the poor clay, and the other spreading roots being cramped and stunted at first, never after make good roots, or recover it.

Rules for planting.

§. 11. [a] Columella advises, to set trees removed towards the same aspect they grew in before. lib. 5. fol. 150.

In transplanting omit not your placing trees towards their accustomed aspect, ib. and, if you have leisure, make the holes the autumn before. — Plant deeper in light, than in strong ground, and shallowest in the clay: five inches is sufficient for the driest, and two for the moist land, provided you establish your plants against the wind. Evelyn, fol. 224.

[b] On a rocky, chalky, or gravelly soil, if you can-

[a] Mr. Miller concludes this rule to be of no consequence, from several trials he has made.

[b] Mr. Miller advises, if the trees have been long out of the ground, so that their fibres are dried, to place their roots in water eight or ten hours before they are planted; observing to place them in such manner, that their heads may remain erect, and their roots only immersed therein; which will swell the dried vessels of their roots, and prep re them to imbibe nourishment from the earth.

not

not conveniently raise a hillock, and plant on the surface, dig the holes shelving inward, that the roots may find their way upwards, and run between the turf and the rock.

Plant forth in warm and moist seasons, the air serene, the wind westward ; but never while it actually freezes or rains, nor in misty weather, for it moulds and infects the root. Evelyn.

ᶜ I was discoursing with Lord Pembroke on his plantation of elms at Wilton, which were of the largest magnitude any had been known to be planted : he said, of those, the heads of which he had lopped when he had planted them, not one in twenty lived, but those he had planted with their heads unlopped, not one in twenty died.

Trees produced from seeds must have the taproots abated, the walnut-tree, and some others excepted ; and yet if planted merely for the fruit, some affirm it may be adventured on with good success : you must spare the fibrous parts of the root, those who cleanse them too much are punished for their mistake. Evelyn, fol. 224.

§. 12. If you are to plant a coppice, it is a good way to set your plants in trenches. as one raises quick-set hedges, and not to sow seeds, for they are

Of planting a coppice.

ᶜ Mr. Miller greatly disapproves the modern practice of removing large trees. If planters, says he, instead of removing these trees, would begin by making a nursery, and raising their trees from seeds, they would set out in a right method, and save a great expence, and much time ; and they would have the constant pleasure of seeing their trees annually advance in their growth, instead of their growing worse, as will always be the case where old trees are removed.—For of all the plantations which I have yet seen, let the trees be of any sort, there is not one which has ever succeeded.——New planted trees, says he, should be watered with great moderation, and he proves, from an experiment made by the reverend Dr Hales, that it is impossible such trees can thrive, where the moisture is too great about their roots.

tedious

tedious in coming forward, and will tire one's patience in weeding them.—I would not set above four plants in twelve feet square, and at regular distances, so that the benefit of ploughing might not be lost, and then at six or seven years growth I would plash, by laying the whole shoot end and all under the earth in the trenches, which would not therefore be choaked, but shoot forth innumerable issues: this, by great experience, oak, ash, hazle, and withy, will do

In our parts we never set less than an hundred plants in a double chased lugg; and, if the earth turned up such rubbish and stony stuff that the edge of earth on which they are to plant, is too narrow for a double chase, then they always set eighty plants on a single chase in a lugg.

§. 13. Young ashes taken out of the wood to be planted, will neither be well rooted nor taper, but top-heavy; therefore you will be obliged to take off the heads before you replant them; and then at best, expect but a good pollard, and it is possible you may wait long before you can get it to thrive; for the head being taken off leaves such a wound as will be long in curing, and yet you were obliged to do it, or else the roots could not have maintained that head: it is the same with a walnut, therefore be sparing of taking off the topmost of them. Cook, fol. 2.

Of young ashes taken from woods.

If you move a little ash-shoot of about one foot in stature, you must not by any means take off it's top, which being young, is pithy, nor by any means cut the fibrous parts of the roots, only that downright or tap-root is totally to be abated: this work ought to be done in the latter end of October or the beginning of November, and not in the spring, Evelyn's Sylva, fol. 41. The side branches of such a shoot may be cut off, ib. Being once well fixed, you may cut it close to the ground, as you please, it will

Id. and of walnuts.

cause

cause it to shoot prodigiously, ib.—Never let your
walnut-tree, when transplanted, be above four years
old, and then by no means touch the head with your
knife, nor cut away so much as the tap-root, if you
can conveniently dispose of it, since being of a pithy
and hollow substance, the least dimunition or bruise
will greatly danger the killing it. Ev. ib.

Walnut, ash, and pithy trees are safer pruned in
summer than in winter, in the warm weather than
in spring, whatever the vulgar may fancy. [d] Ev.
fol. 223.

§. 14. The feedingest ground makes the toughest Of timber.
timber, for where an oak grows most in a year, that
oak will make the toughest timber ; but in dry
grounds oaks grow slow, and the annual circles
being close together, the timber must then be the
finer grained. Cook, fol. 37.

The inside rings, says Evelyn, are more large Growth of
and gross, and distinct in trees, which grow to a timber.
great bulk in a short time, as fir, ash, &c. smaller
or less distinct in those that either not at all, or in
a longer time grow great, as quince, holly, box,
lignum vitæ, ebony ; so that by the largeness and
smallness of the rings the quickness or slowness of
the growth of any tree may perhaps at certainty be
estimated. These spaces are manifestly broader on
the one side than on the other, especially the more
outer, to a double proportion or more, the inner
being near to an equality. It is asserted, that the
larger parts of these rings are on the south and sunny side of the tree, which is very rational and probable ; and this seems to be the reason for setting a

---

[i] Mr. Miller advises by no means to cut off the main leading
shoots when you transplant, for, by several experiments he has
made, he has found, that the shortening of the branches is a
great injury to all new-planted trees. —— See his Dictionary—
article—Planting.

tree, you remove, in the same position, because of maintaining the same parts in as good a manner as before. Wafer, in his book of the isthmus of Darien, says, the Indians know not, when the sun is obscured by clouds, how the points of the heavens lie, but by cutting round the bark of a tree, and on that side the bark is thickest they know to be south. — It must be much more so in our northern climates than under or near the tropic.

Of the circulation of sap.

§. 15. There is dispute among the learned inquirers whether there is a uniform circulation of sap in plants, or not. ᵉ The author of the Burgundian philosophy assures us, that, if some of the roots of a plant be put into water, and other roots of the same plant be kept out of water, yet these latter will increase, and shoot forth fibres as well as the former; again, if a plant, that has two branches, be taken up by the roots, and the extreme part of one of these branches be put in water, this whole plant shall remain a long time without any decay, and even sometimes put forth leaves on the other branch, when another plant of the same kind, taken up in the same manner, and none of the roots or branches put in water, shall soon wither and die. From these two experiments lie infers, there is a reciprocal circulation of sap from the trunk to the roots. —— We are told by Ray, fol. 18. (Malpigius and others concurring) that one of the main uses of the leaves in trees and plants is to prepare and concoct the nourishment of the fruit,

---

ᵉ Si ejusdem plantæ quædam radices aquâ sunt immersæ, reliquæ extra aquam extarent, eæ tamen, ut radices intra aquam demersæ, increscere visæ sunt, & novas fibras emittere; quod demonstrat quod reciproca circulatio est à trunco in radices. Phil. Burgund fol. 1149 Eadem est ratio plantæ à terra cum radicibus avulsæ, & in duos ramos divisæ; nam si unius rami extremum aquâ immersum fuerit, planta diu integra & viridis permanet, & interdum folia in ramo altero germinat, cum alia planta ejusdem generis tunc avulsa statim marcescat.

and the whole plant, not only that which afcends from the root, but what they take in from without, from the dew, moift air, and rain. As a proof of this, it is afferted, that if many forts of trees be defpoiled of their leaves, they will die, as it happens in mulberry trees, when the leaves are plucked off to feed filk-worms ; and if in the fummer feafon you denude a vine branch of it's leaves, the grapes will never come to maturity, becaufe the juice returns from the leaves that ferved to nourifh the fruit : hence alfo they infer a circulation of the juice in plants. —— That there is a regrefs of the juice in plants from above downwards, and that this defcendant juice is what principally nourifhes both fruit and plant, is well proved from the experiments Mr. Brotherton has made. Phil. Tranfact. No. 187.

Mr. Bobart affures me, that in a nurfery, he has bent the top of a young grafted plum-tree to a plum-ftock, and grafted it; and that, when the graft took, he cut off the young tree from the root ; which tree notwithftanding flourifhed, and bore fruit by the retrograde fap, which fhews the fap defcends as well as afcends.[f]

§. 16. My woodward affures me, that windy weather makes the fap rife much fooner in trees than

Wind makes the fap rife.

[f] In oppofition to the notion of the circulation of the fap in trees, fays Mr. Miller, the reverend Dr. Hales has prefented us with many experiments, and thinks upon the whole, from thefe experiments and obfervations, we have fufficient ground to believe, that there is no circulation of the fap in vegetables; notwithftanding many ingenious perfons have been induced to think there was, from feveral curious obfervations and experiments, which evidently prove, that the fap does, in fome meafure, recede from the top toward the lower parts of the plant ; whence they were, with good probability of reafon, induced to think, that the fap circulated. —— Vid. thefe experiments in Miller's Dictionary, article, Sap, or in Dr. Hales's Treatife on vegetable ftatics.

it

it otherwise would do, though not attended with rain, especially if the wind be southerly or westerly.

A branch that blights one year apt to blight the next, and why.

§ 17. It is very generally to be observed, that where a whole tree, or arm of a tree, is much blighted one year, it is very apt in such case, to blight again in following years, especially if the season of the year shall not be kindly : for which this reason may be given ; there are particular roots which for the most part feed particular branches, though there may be also a considerable nutriment from the general circulation of sap ; now, if any such root fails, as by many causes it may, no wonder if the branch so depending on it should yearly blight, and yet it may at spring put forth leaves, &c. by reason of the great redundancy of sap, by participating of the supposed circulation ; but when the sap grows less vigorous, then the failure will appear. Again, in all blights you must suppose a shrinking, and contraction of the fibres, and vessels of the branch that blights : no wonder then, if on such withering, contraction, and closure they never receive the sap so kindly as before, especially after the run of the spring-sap is over, which may for a time produce leaves and blossoms, but will by Midsummer, when that plenty abates, be deserted.

Not to put cattle into woods to eat up the sedgy grass.

§. 18. I observe the sedgy grass comes not up in felled coppices the first summer ; consequently the young shoots have a year's start of that grass ; the next summer the sedgy grass comes up, and grows ancle-high, equal with the two-years shoots ; but what harm can it then do to the wood ? The third year the sedgy grass dies, and you see no more of it. I speak this, in answer to the country-man's objection, who pleads for putting some sort of cattle into coppices to keep down the sedge, which he pretends otherwise will choak and damage the plants. —— I have experienced this to my cost.

§. 19. It

§. 19. It was May the 6th (anno 1701) that I Oak-buds bought some yearlings; and I asked the farmer, if poison to I might not put them in the coppice till Midsummer; the farmer said, not yet, by any means; for fear they should be oakered, that is, lest they should bite off the oak-bud before it came into leaf, which might bake in their maws and kill them, but after the oak-bud was in leaf it would be safe enough.—— The higher coppices are fit for yearlings, and the coppices of the last year's growth for hog-sheep in winter.——My shepherd said, what the farmer observed as to the oak-bud was true; but he thought that the year was so backward that they were not yet come out, and so there could be no danger at present.———Farmer Elton said, his father had lost abundance of yearlings by the oak-bud, by putting them into the coppices while that was out.——I have since experienced the same, and have remarked it, when I treated of black cattle. See Grazing, §. 17.

§. 20. It is a common saying, that calves will Of calves not crop in woods: but I put six calves into my cropping woods, in November, which very much cropped the yearling-shoots. All husbandmen I told of it very much wondered at it; but the reason to me was clear, viz. on first putting them in there came three or four days hard frost, with a shallow snow, and a rime that laid on the bennetty grass, so that they could not come at the ground, but only meet with brier-leaves, of which, though I had plenty, they were but thin diet to depend on altogether, yet together with other pickings would have been a noble maintenance for them, if they could have come at the rowet: this streightness of commons brought them to the necessity of cropping the young shoots, which they afterwards continued to do, having got the habit of it, and finding, when the open weather came,

came, the fhoots to be toothfome, though the row-et in the coppices would have been fufficient.

For a general rule, newly weaned calves are lefs hurtful to newly cut fpring-woods than any other cattle, efpecially if there be abundance of grafs ; and fome fay, colts of a year will do no harm ; but the calves muft be permitted to ftay awhile longer, and furely the later you admit beafts to graze the better. Evelyn, fol. 147.

Of wood hurt by cattle.

§. 21. I was at my coppice where my labourers were felling, and obferved to them with fome wonder, that, though the coppice then felling was of my own preferving, ever fince it was laft felled, yet the growth feemed not more than it was, when in the farmer's hands, who abufed it with cattle, nor did I fell it for more than when I lafted felled it. —— The reafon they judged, was, becaufe the biting it in the farmer's time had brought it to a fmall ftem, and, faid they, wood of a fmall ftem or ftock will not bring a large fhoot : for it requires two or three fellings to pafs, though preferved, before wood abufed can recover to a ftem, fo as to fend forth a good ftrong fhoot. —— Note, from hence arifes a corollary, as a farther inducement to let coppice-wood grow to fourteen years growth, if the land will fo long maintain it, becaufe the circle of the annual growth is not only thereby much increafed, but alfo from a larger ftock or trunk ftronger fhoots will put forth, and carry a proportionable annual increafe to the fourteen years end.

I carried two experienced woodmen into my woods, they having bought fome lops of me, and fhewing them the damage the farmer had done me, they obferved it, and faid, it was much to be lamented ; becaufe thofe fhoots, which were cropped, would grow forked, and never be fit for rods. I afked my woodman what price my rods yielded ; he

faid,

said, the laſt year 12d. per hundred, but this year, 1699, wood being dearer, 14d. per hundred, and, in caſe they were not bit by cattle, they would fetch 15d. or 16d. per hundred. —— The above two men adviſed me to cut this coppice at ſeven or eight years growth; for, ſaid they, the roots are ſo much damaged by the feeding of cattle, that they will be apt to die away, and not maintain their burden to ten years growth.

I was ſeeing my woodman make his fold-hurdles, he was very uneaſy about the ſplitting them and working them; he ſhewed me two or three knots in moſt of the rods where they had been bit in the growing by the cattle; where the rods had been ſo browſed that they would hardly ſplit through thoſe knots, at leaſt not by an equal diviſion without ſnapping off, and many of them did ſnap off, and ſuch ſplit rods, if they would ſplit, and the whole rods, when they come to work and-wind, would in twiſting often break at thoſe knots.— From all which I do conclude, that it is of a very ill conſequence to put cattle into coppices, for which the treading down the briers and ſedge is but a ſmall equivalent. —And if hog-ſheep are put in, and at ſeaſonable times, it is endleſs watching them; for when they begin to fall on the wood, they will all fall on together, and bite every ſtem in two days time. —— And it may be concluded from that brittle knottineſs, which the working thoſe rods diſcover, how ill the ſap can paſs upwards, to feed the top-ſhoots, through the whole compaſs of years they have to grow, to the growth of which the obſtruction the ſedge gives for one year can be but little: admitting which, I would then adviſe the ſhepherd, at a proper time, to go with his whole flock, and tread down, and eat up ſuch rowet in one day's time, taking ſuch a time or times for it as may be moſt ſeaſonable,

able, as suppose frosty weather, the rowet being then the sweetest.

The 17th of January (anno 1702) I ordered my hog-sheep to be turned into the coppice, intending they should eat up the rowet for some time.———— My shepherd immediately drove them thither, but, as he observed, the sheep instead of eating the rowet, fell on the young shoots, and eat them with that greediness, that he called the labourer who was felling in a neighbouring coppice, to observe it also: and he told me of it afterwards, and said, he stood by and saw them bite off shoots at half a foot in length. The reason of this, said he, must be from their sweet feed on your clover, for which cause they will not, like other sheep, touch your sour rowet.

The reason why shoots bit off by the cattle perish farther downwards than the same branch would do, if cut with a knife, is, because the top of the shoot being bit, is rugged, whereby the water runs not off, but keeps soaking down; whereas, had it been cut with a tool, it's smooth and sloped edge, like a hind's foot, would cast the water off.

It is generally said, that sheep going in woods, and rubbing against the trees, or the young shoots, do by their wool poison the very bark, so that it shall in that place canker, or at least the tree in that place shall visibly grow hide-bound, and bend in, and grow gouty above such rubbing place. ——This I suppose must arise from the abundance of oil in the wool, which, the sun and wind drying it in, enters the bark, and choaks up the pores, where the passage of the sap is: in the same manner ointments laid on swellings are repellers, inasmuch as they stop the pores of perspiration; and linseed-oil laid on bricks keeps out weather.

Damage from hogs in woods. §. 22. Farmer Rutty told me, he had once heard say, that hogs would do as much harm in a young

coppice

coppice as any other cattle ; but he did not believe it, till fetching away some wool he had bought of me in July (anno 1701) he found a farmer's pigs broke into my coppices, and he observed them to fall on the shoots, and eat them up as fast as other cattle. [g] I wonder the antients, who preferred wood to pasture, should not consider the damage that cattle did them.

§. 23. My woodward assures me, that if I would let my coppices run to fourteen years growth, instead of ten, which I might do by dividing them accordingly, they would yield a fourth part more profit, because a coppice at fourteen years growth will yield double the value of a coppice at ten, the increase of wood when it comes to be eight or nine years old does so much advance.——But here it is to be noted, that there are some parts of my coppices which grow on very barren land, that is out of proof, and the wood will be scrubbed and grow rotten, and dead on the tops before it is ten years old ; it cannot be profitable to let such wood grow to fourteen years of age.—He also assures me, that my hazle at fourteen years age, which runs up without knots, is as fit for hurdles, being split, as any other.

Of letting coppices grow to fourteen years.

I was speaking to my labourers of the advantages of letting my coppice-woods run to fourteen or fifteen years growth, where the land was in condition good enough to support the wood to that growth. They added to what I had said, that, by letting the coppices stand so long, the wood would be run to so large a stature as to over-shadow the grass, whereby the roots of the sedge-grass, which so much over-run the young coppices, to the prejudice of the young wood, would thereby in a great measure be killed.

Letting coppice-wood grow to sixteen or seven-

[g] Páscuntur armenta commodissimè in nemoribus, ubi virgulta & frons multa. Varro, fol. 56.

teen years growth is of great service to young heirs, because by so many years growth their barks are case-hardened, and able to withstand the cold, when the coppice is cut, and they must stand naked, whereas, when coppices are cut at ten and eleven years growth, the barks of the young heirs are so tender, that they are starved with the cold air and winds. Ivy itself, says Evelyn, (the destruction of many a fair tree) if very old, and taken off, does frequently kill the trees by a too sudden exposure to the unaccustomed cold.

When coppice-wood is of fourteen or fifteen years growth, it will fetch a better price in proportion than younger wood, because it will be applicable to more uses, and particularly in the cooper's business; for he will use the withy and some of the ash for hoops and wine-hogsheads; another part of the ash may serve for prong-staves, rake-staves, and rath-pins for waggons, and the rest may be parcelled out for hurdle and flake-rods.

Oaken stems of fourteen years growth are (in my woods, which in a great measure consist of them) as high as the ash or withy, and measure more in the diameter; for oaken stems are stronger at root, and will hold growing longer than ash, withy, or hazle. When hazle grows spriggy in the body, and shoots forth from the sides of the bark, it is a sign that it has given out, and done growing at the top.

Of the time of cutting coppices.

§. 24. Coppice-wood, in hedging and hurdling, wears much better and longer, if cut between Michaelmass and Christmass, but sells best in faggots, if cut between Christmass and Lady-day, because it shrinks less, and is most swelled, and looks best to the buyer; the method at Crux-Easton, and the hill-country thereabouts, is only to oblige the buyers to rid the coppice by Midsummer; they think the coppices are not harmed, if rid by the time

the

WOOD.

the Midfummer-fhoots fpring up : they had not rid
this year (anno 1697) by the latter end of July.

It was the firft of May (anno 1701) and I propofed to cut coppice-wood for the fire : my woodward
faid, it would not hurt the ftools to cut it fo late,
but it never would wear well in hedging, nor burn
well ; for, after the blaze was out, the coals would
burn as dead as if water had been flung on them.

I had a doubt how I fhould fence-in my corn
and hay-reek I was going to make, Auguft the
27th, (anno 1701) having no wood cut fit for the
purpofe, and fuppofing it too early then to cut for
it. ———— But my woodward affured me, it was very
fafe to cut coppice-wood at Bartholomew-tide, and
it did the mores no damage ; and, faid he, all the
farmers in the country, in the laft year of their leafe
make a felling between Bartholomew-tide and Michaelmafs, of all the underwood their leafe will jufti-
fy them in.

It is obferved, that coppice-wood, cut for hedging
at the latter end of winter, will not endure fo long
by a year as that which is cut at the beginning of
winter : which, as I believe, may not only be, becaufe the wood late cut, is cut after the fap is rifen,
or attenuated by the fun, but alfo oftentimes becaufe
it is not cut long enough before fuch rarefaction is
made ; for, if a tree, or a cyon cut to be grafted,
as Quinteny affirms, will endure many weeks of the
winter out of the ground, or without being grafted,
and, when fpring fhall come, it will by vertue of the
fap inherent in it, when attenuated, put forth buds
for fome time, till it dries away ; fo it follows, that
the fap inherent always in the ftem of the wood, if
not cut fo early as to have long time to dry, may be
put into motion at fpring, fo as to effect the above-
mentioned inconvenience ; therefore I hold hedging-
wood and fire-faggots fhould be cut in October.

My woodward says, he thinks it is best for coppice-woods to be felled the latter part of the year, about February or March; for, says he, if they be felled early in the winter, the frosts fall on their stools, and dries, parches, and shrinks them at the top, and obliges the bud at spring to shoot forth three or four inches lower than else it would do; whereas, if they be cut late, the bud will break forth at the top. ——A short time after, I asked Harding of Holt the wood-merchant about it, and he agreed to the same.

It is a common practice of husbandmen to fell their hedge-rows, and small brakes within the grounds, those years they sow the grounds with wheat; but such persons ought well to consider, first, whether such land, after the wheat is off, will not bear a rowet too long for sheep to eat, and, if so, great cattle must be put in to eat up the long rowet, and the sooner the better for their tooth, and then attendance must be given by a cow-keeper by day, before the harvest is in, and consequently the wages the dearer, and when you may have many other offices to employ such a person in: therefore, in such case, my advice is to let the hedge-rows stand till after the wheat-crop be got in, when great cattle may be suffered to feed down the rowet without prejudice to the hedge-rows, and at that time of the year such grass is wanted by night, and, during the future three crops, it is to be supposed the rowet will not be so large, but sheep may overcome it, nor will they very much prejudice the young wood.

Of the manner of cutting coppices.

§. 23. In your coppices, says Evelyn, cut not above half a foot from the ground; nay the closer the better, but slope-wise to the south, fo. 149.

Of pollarding oak, elm, and beech.

§. 26. The oak will suffer itself to be made a pollard, that is, to have it's head quite cut off; but the elm so treated will perish to the foot, and certainly

tainly

tainly become hollow at laft, if it efcape with life.
Evelyn, fo. 151.

The beech is very tender of lofing it's head. Ev.
fo. 151.

§. 27. [h] The bark in the hill-country will not ftrip ^{Of ftrip-ping off the bark.} so foon by a month as in the vale : again, in the same wood on the hill, there will be a fortnight or longer difference between the ftripping of a tree, that is in proof, and one that is not : the fap runs fasteft up a tree in proof.

After ftripping, when the bark is dry, it is high time to rid the wood of it, for, if a quantity of rain should come it would do it much hurt, and take off it's ftrength, and then it would grow * finnowy : ^{* Mouldy.} therefore the tanners, when they buy bark, hurry it away with all the carriages they can get, as they would to fave corn from damage.

The fap after open winters never runs well in barking-time at fpring ; for it fpends itfelf gradually before-hand, and forwards fome part of the branches of a tree when other parts ftir not, and fo all the branches will not bark equally alike : again, a hard frost at the entrance of the fpring, as this year (anno 1708) fo as to check the rifing fap, and difturb it while it is rifing and fpending itfelf, is a great hinderance to the kindly barking for that feafon, and makes the fap do it's bufinefs by halves ; but a

[h] Mr. Miller obferves, that the time for felling timber is from November to February, at which time the fap in the trees is hardened ; for when the fap is flowing in the trees, if they are cut down, the worm will take the timber, and caufe it to decay very foon, rendering it unfit for building either fhips or houfes. He thinks therefore it would be more for the publick benefit, if (inftead of the ftatute now in force for felling trees during the fpring feafon, when the bark will eafily ftrip) a law were enacted to oblige every perfon to ftrip off the bark of fuch trees, as were defigned to be cut down in the fpring, leaving the trees with their branches ftanding till the following winter ; which will be found to anfwer both purpofes well.

froft

froſt ſome time before the ſpring does a kindneſs : in ſhort, the greater the fluſh of ſap (coming all at once) it makes the better bark, and is better both for the tanner and the ſtripper.

As I have obſerved before, the ſap in oaks riſes ſlower at ſpring, and the bark ſtrips worſe, and the tree that year makes worſe ſhoots, when in a linger-ing manner lucid days too early in the ſpring have often invited forth the ſap from the roots, which has as often received ſudden checks by the cold, than when the beginning of the ſpring of the year con-tinues cold, whereby the ſap in the roots continues filling and is kept from ſpending itſelf in the trunk and branches, till the uninterrupted heat breaks forth, and the fluſh of the ſap aſcends with continual ſoli-citations by the heat : in like manner it is, I ſup-poſe, with leſs and tender plants ; their ſhoots are ſtronger, the graſſy part more tender and groſs, when the backward ſpring carries afterwards an uninter-rupted heat, than when the buds and ſhoots are earli-er invited forth, and then ſtopped by the cold. We find all garden-herbs in like manner, which have ſlowly kept growing on all the winter, not ſo tooth-ſome to the inſects as thoſe, the ſeeds whereof are not committed to the ground till ſpring.

Of trees living when barked.

§. 28. Between the annual circles doth ſome ſap ariſe, as is plain in a tree barked round, which yet will live ; and the more porous this tree is between theſe annual circles, the longer that tree will live ; as I have experienced in walnut, and aſh, but holly and box died in leſs than a year ; for trees that hold their leaves, their wood is cloſe and compact between the annual circles, and that is the reaſon they die ſoon after being barked round. Cook, fo. 48.

Time of faggot-ing.

§. 29. I aſked my woodward the 13th of March (anno 1702) if it was not time to faggot ; he replied, the wood-chapmen did not care to have their wood

faggotted

faggotted so early, till it had shrunk, else, after it was faggotted, it would be apt to shrink and fall to pieces: therefore, said he, we faggot that wood first which was first cut.

§. 30. In loading wood one man on the cart can stow to two men that pitch it up : therefore, where you cart wood by change of waggons, you do not find your horses full employ, where but one man pitches. *Of pitching and stowing wood on the cart.*

§. 31. I cut down green timber in August (anno 1707) to set my lath-maker to work to make laths for immediate use : he desired me to let him set them out sunning for four or five days before he bundled them up, or that I used them, that they might be dry ; for, said he, the timber being green the nails will rust, and so rot, and then break off, unless the laths were first dried.—And so said the carpenter. *Of drying laths before using.*

§. 32. Oak-underwood and white-thorn are the worst of any to grub ; because they both shoot their roots more downwards than any other. *Of grubbing.*

It was the beginning of March (anno 1701) I agreed with two labourers to grub a hedge-row : they desired they might go upon it presently, before the sap was got plentifully into the roots ; for such roots, if they were full of sap, as well as their branches, would, they assured me, if cut then, though never so dry afterwards, burn dead, and make but a sorry fire.

FENCES.

§. 1. MAPLE, if it grows in hedges, will destroy the wood under it ; for it receives a clammy honey-dew on it's leaves, and, when it is washed off by rain, and falls upon the buds of those trees under it, it's clamminess keeps those buds from opening, and so by degrees kills all the wood under it. Cook, p. 72. *Maple bad for hedges.*

§. 2. I would advise the country-gentleman to
sow many haws, &c in his nursery, that, where
they grow thin in his hedges, and there are vacancies, he may dig up those plants, earth and all, and
carry them to fill up such empty spaces. It will be
good however to sow those haws in poor ground, for,
if transplanted from a rich soil to a poor one, they
will not thrive well.

§. 3. The flow, or hedge-peak-bush is apt to die
in the hill-country, where the land is poor, and they
are let to grow in the hedges till seventeen or eighteen
years growth, before they are cut : therefore the best
way of preserving such hedges is to cut them at eight
or nine years growth. The stones of these also
should be sown in nurseries.——Mr. Evelyn excepts
against black-thorn being mixed with the white, because of their unequal progress. [a]

§. 4. By

---

[a] Mr. Miller gives the following directions for raising quick-
hedges.————The sets ought to be about the bigness of one's
little finger, and cut within about four or five inches of the
ground ; they ought to be fresh taken up, strait, smooth, and
well rooted. Those plants which are raised in a nursery are to
be preferred.

Secondly, If the hedge has a ditch, it should be made six feet
wide at top and one and an half at bottom, and three feet deep,
that each may have a slope ; but, if the ditch be but four feet
wide, it ought to be only two feet and an half deep ; and, if
it be five feet wide, it should be three feet ; and so in proportion.

Thirdly, If the bank be without a ditch, the sets should be
set in two rows, almost perpendicular, at the distance of a foot
from each other.

Fourthly, the turf is to be laid with the grass-side downwards,
on that side of the ditch the bank is designed to be made ; and
some of the best mold be laid upon it to bed the quick ; then
the quick is to be laid upon it, a foot asunder ; so that the end
of it may be inclining upwards.

Fifthly, When the first row of quick is laid, it must be covered with mold, and the turf laid upon it as before, and some mold
upon it ; so that when the bank is a foot high, you may lay another

§. 4. By all means set your dead hedges at a good distance from your quick-set plants, not only on account of preserving your plants, but your dead hedges also: for, if great cattle have any likelihood of reaching your plants, in reaching after them, and pressing

ther row of sets against the spaces of the lower quick, and cover them as the former was done; and the bank is to be topped with the bottom of the ditch, and a dry or dead hedge laid to shade and defend the under plantation.

Sixthly, There should be stakes driven into the loose earth, at about two feet and an half distance, so low as to reach the firm ground. Oak stakes are accounted the best, and black-thorn and sallow the next: let the small bushes be laid low, but not too thick, only a little to cover the quick from being bit by cattle, when it springs, and also lay long bushes at the top to bind the stakes in with, by interweaving them. And, in order to render the hedge yet stronger, you may edder it, as is called, i. e. bind the top of the stakes in with some small long poles or sticks on each side; and, when the eddering is finished, drive the stakes anew; because the weaving of the hedge and eddering is apt to loosen the stakes.— The quick must be kept constantly weeded, and secured from being cropped by cattle; and in February it will be proper to cut it within an inch of the ground, which will cause it to strike root afresh, and help it much in the growth.

The following is Mr. Franklin's method of planting quick-hedges, as given us by Mr. Miller.

He first set out the ground for ditches and quick ten feet in breadth; he sub-divided that by marking out two feet and an half on each side (more or less at pleasure) for the ditches, leaving five in the middle between them: then, digging up two feet in the midst of those five feet, he planted the sets in; which, although it required more labour and charge, he says, he found it repay the cost. This done, he began to dig the ditches, and to set up one row of turfs on the outside of the said five feet; namely, one row on each side thereof, the green side outmost, a little reclining, so as the grass might grow.

After this, returning to the place he began at, he ordered one of the men to dig a pit of the under-turf mold; and lay it between the turfs placed edgewise, as before described, upon the two feet, which was purposely dug in the middle, and prepared for the sets, which the planter set with two quicks upon the surface of the earth, almost upright, whilst another workman

laid

preffing upon the dead hedge, they will break it down a year fooner than ordinary, and learning fuch a habit, and finding the fuccefs, they will not afterwards be broke of it.

For the two firft years, fays Mr. Evelyn, to diligently

laid the mold forwards about twelve inches, and then fet two more, and fo continued.

Thus being finifhed, he ordered another row of turfs to be placed on each fide upon the top of the former, and filled the vacancy between the fets and turfs as high as their tops, always leaving the middle, when the fets were planted, hollow and fomewhat lower than the fides of the banks by eight or ten inches, that the rain might defcend to their roots; which is of great advantage to their growth, and by far better than by the old ways, where the banks are too much floping, and the roots of the fet are feldom wetted, even in a moift feafon, the fummer following; but if it prove dry, many of the fets, efpecially the late planted, will perifh, and even few of thofe that had been planted in the latter end of April (the fummer happening to be fomewhat dry) efcaped.

The planting being thus advanced, the next care is fencing, by fetting an hedge of about twenty inches high upon the top of the bank on each fide thereof, leaning a little outward from the fets, which will protect them as well, if not better, than an hedge of three feet, or more, ftanding on the furface of the ground; for, as thefe are raifed with the turfs and fods about twenty inches, and the hedge about twenty inches more, it will make three feet four inches; fo as no cattle can approach the hedge to prejudice it, unlefs they fet their feet in the ditch itfelf, which will be at leaft a foot deep; and from the bottom of the ditch to the top of the hedge about four feet and an half, which they can hardly reach over to crop the quick, as they might in the old way; and befides, fuch an hedge will endure a year longer. ——Where the ground is but indifferent, it is better to take twelve feet, for both ditches and banks, than nine or ten; for this will allow of a bank at leaft fix feet broad, and gives more fcope to place the dead hedges farther from the fets; and the ditches, being fhallow, will in two years time, graze.

As to the objection, that taking twelve feet waftes too much ground, he affirms, that, if twelve feet in breadth be taken for a ditch and bank, there will be no more ground be wafted than by the common way; for in that a quick is rarely fet, but there are nine feet between the dead hedges, which is entirely loft all

the

gently weed is as neceſſary as fencing and guarding from cattle.

§. 5. To ſteep cow-dung and lime in water, and to ſprinkle young hedges with it, is ſuppoſed to prevent cows and ſheep from browſing them; and it is good to ſerve hedges the ſame with horſe-dung, where horſes feed, and when it is waſhed off by the rain, to renew it.——The end of mingling lime ſeems to be, to make the liquid ſtick, and to bind it. *Of ſprinkling young hedges with cow-dung and lime water.*

§. 6. If a hedge by ill uſage, or by age, be grown thin, the beſt way is to cut it cloſe to the ground the year you ſow it with wheat, and to fling earth to it, to refreſh it, and to make a dead hedge without it; by this means the old ſtems will tillow afreſh and thicken; whereas by plaſhing, unleſs a hedge be thick enough to afford the loſs of young ſhoots, by dropping on them, they will be killed. But in doing this you muſt not cover the ſtems with the earth you fling up, leſt you choke and kill them; if you intend therefore to lay a great quantity of earth to the roots, you muſt leave the ſtems ſomewhat the longer. *Of thickening a hedge.*

The digging a trench or ditch by flinging freſh mold to the ſtools of an old hedge is of ſpecial uſe, foraſmuch as the trench, laying many of the roots of the old hedge bare, makes them ſend forth ſhoots, whereby the hedge is thickened; for roots turn to branches when expoſed to the air.

Take a well-rooted ſet of holly, of a yard long, and ſtrip off the leaves and branches, and cover

the time of fencing; whereas, with double ditches, there remain at leaſt eighteen inches on each ſide where the turfs were ſet on edge, that bear more graſs than when it lay on the flat; but admitting three feet of ground were waſted, he ſhews the damage to be inconſiderable. He then compares the charges, and aſſerts, that forty poles planted in the old way will coſt ſeven pounds, and the ſame meaſure in the new way but three pounds.

them

them with a competent depth of earth, and they will
send forth innumerable quantities of suckers, and
quickly make a hedge. — Mortimer, fol. 4. — A
holly or other ever-green, if striped or blanched in
the middle of the leaf, will in time lose it's stripes,
and the natural green will overcome ; but, if the
edges of the leaves are white, they will always so
continue ; therefore the latter is three times more
valuable than the former, and this is the difference
the gardeners make.

**Of plash-
ing a
hedge.**

" §. 7. [b] In plashing a hedge, round a hedge-row
or coppice, leave the plashers of the hedge withinside
the coppice, and turn the brushy part to the close,
that it may not injure the young shoots by dropping
on them, and that the cattle may not come at the
shoots of the plashers, and browse them, and kill
them.——Take care also to set the stakes outwardly,
and off the shoots, whereas the hedgers for riddance,
and for sake of making stakes of the live standards,
work the plashed hedge strait on, most likely
through the middle-most part of the hedge, which
must drop over your young shoots arising from the
stools, and leaves many without, exposed to the
ground, to be fed ; though by this means you make
the more luggs of hedge, yet the good husbandry of
it will repay you.——Plashing work for the most part
ought to be ended early in April ; because, as soon
as the bark loosens by the sap, when the plash is
bent back in the cut, it hollows, and gapes from the

[b] In plashing quicks, says Mr. Miller, there are two extremes
to be avoided ; the first is laying it too low, and too thick : because it makes the sap run all into the shoots, and leaves the
plashes without nourishment ; which, with the thickness of the
hedge, kills them.———Secondly, it must not be laid too high ;
because this draws all the sap into the plashes, and so causes but
small shoots at the bottom, and makes the hedge so thin, that it
will neither hinder the cattle from going through, nor from cropping it.

wood,

wood, and so is apt to die, because the sap cannot be conveyed to it. Withy and ash will first take damage by late plashing, because the sap first rises in those kinds of wood. But as to the cutting down a quick-hedge, if it be the latter end of April, it will shoot as soon, if not sooner, than that cut in the winter. It is too common to see withy and ash-plashes dead in hedges, which comes from their being plashed too late.

It being frosty weather in November (anno 1700) yet my woodward was for going on with a dead hedge I was making: I said, surely it would be very improper, and that the wood would not work, but would snap by means of the frost.—— But he answered, no, that was a mistake, it was plashing that was improper in hard frosts.

The white-thorn in hard frosts will be so brittle as in bending to break like a rotten stick; but the black thorn, withy, and crab-tree will endure bending in the hardest of weather.

As I was riding with Stephens, he went to pull up a large brier, which by it's length had bent downwards to the ground, and had at the end struck forth plenty of new roots; from whence it may be observed how apt they are to propagate: I also conclude any other part of a brier that touches the earth will be apt to strike new roots, and so it may be useful in some vacant places by plashing to encourage them. — In wet summers, when the ground is open and moist, as this year (anno 1703) they propagate abundantly; but in dry summers they are not so plentiful.

§. 8. If an hedge has been in ill hands, and often bit, and abused by cattle, and is an old hedge; if you cut down this hedge, that it may thicken, and grow better, remember not to cut it down too low, not so low as the old stem, but leave some little length, about three or four inches of the thriving

Of cutting an old hedge to thicken it.

and

and younger wood standing on the old stem, for, if
you cut below that, the old stem often happens to
be near rotten, and the tubes that convey it's juices
to the young roots are but few, and their springs are
easily lost, if you divert them from their common
current, and channel, and the coat and bark of the
stem is commonly so case-hardened, that no bud can
break through ; whereas by leaving a little part of
the young wood on the old stem you preserve the
old channels of the tree, and they carry a bark with
them sappy and easily perforable by a bud. — N. B.
I once lost a hedge by cutting it down too low.

Of stakes
for fences.

§. 9. Oak-lops and hollow pollards cleaved
make excellent stakes for fences, and, considering
their lastingness are the best husbandry, or if two of
these stakes are placed in each lugg, they will greatly preserve the rest of the hedge. Withy will rot
the soonest of all wood, and a small hazle-stake will
last longer in a hedge than a great withy : but an
ash-stake, next to oak. will last longest.

Of making
a dead
hedge too
thick.

§. 10. I was walking between the coppices with
my woodward, and he bid me take notice of a hedge
on one side of the way, and said, he had advised the
making it so thin as it was, and it was now five
years since it was made, and yet it stood well ;
whereas, said he, by and by you will come to a
fence-hedge of the coppice, not made longer ago,
which is rotten and down ; for your labourer would
make it too thick, and cram in abundance of wood,
whereby the wet lodged in it, and made it rot much
the sooner.

Hedges
not to be
made in
frosty wea-
ther.

§. 11. Hedging ought not to be done in frosty
weather, for with the bar they cannot make holes
for the stakes to go into, but what stakes must be
less than the bar, nor can they be drove farther than
the pick of the bar ; and upon the first thaw the
hedge will sink away and fall.

Of spliting
rods for
hedging.

§. 12. When you make a hedge, it is adviseable
to

to split the rods, for you may observe the unsplit rods in a hedge grow speckled by the sap oozing through in spots, which opens and loosens the pores of the wood, and prevents it from clinging, and binding, as it does when split ; for then the sun dries it up with all it's sap, and is next of kin to burning the posts-ends of gates ; which dries the inmost sap out of the posts, that would rot them, and gives a cole of that depth to the outside, through which the moisture of the earth does not soak.

§. 13. In the spring, during March and good part of April, I find it very useful to view carefully all over those sort of hedges which may need repair, and not only mend where there is an immediate necessity, but wheresoever also they may decay before harvest ; as also all such hedges, where though you can receive no trespass till harvest, by reason they border on other corn, or mowing-ground, yet are liable to it in harvest, when grounds must lie open ; these you ought to mend, for men cannot be then spared, nor can you then get wood.

Time of mending hedges.

§. 14. It is a common practice in the hill-country to cart hedging-wood, and fling it down in great heaps, perhaps half a load in a heap, and to suffer it to lie, perhaps a month or two, before it is hedged up, to the great detriment of the wood ; which by so lying on the ground and receiving the rain and rime, which commonly fall there, and being imperviable to the wind and sun to dry it, soon rots, and suffers more by so lying in such thick wads a month or two in the field, than it would have done in three times the time in the coppice, where it lies on the roots, and is thereby kept hollow from the ground, and lies thinner, whereby the wind can soon dry it after rain.

Caution— not to let hedging-wood lie long in heaps on the ground

§. 15. Farmer Farthing of the Isle of Wight exceedingly commends the cleft timber-hurdles for a fold, and that they are beyond rod-hurdles ; he says,

Rod hurdles not so good as those of cleft timber.

4

he has had the experience of them both, and the former go much beyond the latter in cheapnefs, though
at the firft hand they are dearer : befides, he fays,
with the rod-hurdles he has had a fheep fpoiled and
ftaked by leaping over the fold, and this he has
known pretty often.

Of rods.　　§. 16. The goodnefs of rods depends greatly on
their ftraitnefs without knots ; fuch will laft half a
year the longer for being fo, befides, the more knotty rods are, the more will the fheep rub off their
wool againft them.

My labourers were twifting fome hazle-rods,
which were apt to break, of which they complained :
they were red-hazle, not white ; I afked them the
difference, they replied, it was very great ; for the
white hazle might be feen by the white bark, and
the red by the red bark : the white hazle will twift
ten times better than the red, being tougher, and
confequently abundantly better for all forts of hurdling work, and for the winding of a hedge, and for
fpars for thatching ; nay, faid they, the white will
laft near a year longer in hedging. To this my
woodman feemed to agree, and fo did another experienced woodman, whom I talked with the next
day ; only the latter faid, he did not know that the
white had any advantage of the red in hedging, but
only in hurdling, where the rods were to be twifted.

Of hedges.　　§. 17. Where great cattle pafture never truft to a
patched, or a half-made hedge, you will continually be making good the trefpaffes, and the cattle will
get a vicious habit, of which you will never after
break them.

If a hedge needs patching, and is to be a fence
againft hogs or great cattle, efpecially where water
and fhade are wanting, it is much the beft hufbandry to make it all new, though the reft may be tolerable, and fome of it feemingly fufficient for another
year, for a declining hedge will decay more in a year
　　　　　　　　　　　　　　　　　　　than

than one can eafily imagine : and if fuch cattle find any one place of it weak enough to be forced, the ftrongeft part will never ftand againft them ; fo that you will be daily patching fuch a hedge, and at times when you can ill fpare a fervant, fuppofe in hay-making or harveft-time ; and at laft you fhall have a continual patched hedge from year to year, wherein there will be fome parts you will think too good to pull down, and yet no part of it good ; whereas in mendings wood cannot be fo well joined as when it is worked into an intire hedge at once.

Dividing open fields into inclofures by quick-fet fences, where ten acres of ftrong land is divided from thirty acres of light land, and the like, is a real improvement, in refpect that a tenant will give much more for the lands fo divided : whereas before the good land was fwallowed up by the poor land ; nor could the light and poor land be ploughed as often as the ftrong land, nor the ftrong land fo feldom as the poor land, without reciprocal inconveniency.

If your corn-grounds, that lie contiguous, are well fenced againft each other, you will have thereby the advantage, as foon as the corn of one field is rid away, to put in cattle, or hogs, to eat up both the grafs and loofe corn ; whereas otherwife your cattle may be kept out a great while, when they need it, till other ground be rid.

ORCHARD or FRUIT-GARDEN.

§. 1. DO not fteep feeds of trees in water, as fome may advife you ; for it is not good to fteep any fort of feed, unlefs fome annuals, and to fteep them is good, efpecially if late fown ; but to fteep ftones, nuts, or feeds, that are not of quick growth, in water may kill them, by making the kirnel fwell too haftily, and fo crack it before the

Not to fteep feeds except fome annuals.

fpear

spear ean do it, or it may mould or stupify the spear. Cook, fol. 63.

§. 2. The antients always preferred orchards to pastures, and pastures to arable.   See Varro, fo. 32.

Of planting apple-trees in the hill-country.

§. 3. In our hill-country, where we are on cold clays, or else the earth is so poor that it's vegetable particles are not copious, nor very active, it has been observed that apple-trees are very hard to be raised, unless the crab-stocks be planted where they must remain two years before they are grafted, or rather unless the crab-kirnels be sowed where they are to continue unremoved, and so grafted. —— Probably the reason for this may be, because there is a considerable knot of transverse fibres where the graft is jointed, through which the juices and vegetable particles find it a very hard task to pass, where the juices of the ground are cold, as in clay-lands, or the particles of vegetation less copious and active, as in poor lands, especially when the stock itself being planted after it's being grafted, must be supposed to receive a check, and it's tubes some streightness by closure, and therefore cannot admit a free passage of juices upwards to the graft : whereas when the stock has been planted two years, and it's roots settled, the juices may have a vigorous passage, and so can easily force their way through the fibres where the graft knits : yet where there is a mellow ground, or a rich fat sand, there the vegetable corpuscles rise so strongly and plentifully, and the juices of the earth are so thin, that they can easily pass upward to the graft through the knot, and in such a happy soil a tree planted after being grafted may do well.

Of transplanting crab-stocks.

§. 4. I by no means think well of removing crab-stocks out of the woods and transplanting them ; because such stocks, when they come to be exposed to the open air, and taken out of their shelter in the

warm

warm woods, do not bear the cold winters well, nor
even the summer suns.

§. 5. Your cuttings for planting should be from
half an inch to a whole inch diameter; for, if they
be less than half an inch, they will be weak and have
a great pith, which will take wet and be likely to kill
your cuttings; and besides, when your cuttings are
too small, they are not prepared with those pores,
that is, little black specks on the bark, where the
roots break out, if set in the ground; a sign that
those that have that mark on them will grow, as elder, alder, sallow, water-poplar, &c. and if they be
too young they will not have that burry knot which
is very apt to take root: and if they are above an
inch diameter the tops of your cuttings will be long
in covering over, and so may decay by the wet.
Cook, fo. 12.

Of cuttings for planting.

§. 6. The French gardener translated by Evelyn,
fo. 54. says, the best grafts are those which grow on
the strongest and master-branch of a tree, and which
are wont to be good bearers, and such as promise a
plentiful burden that year, being thick of buds; for
hence it is that your young grafted trees bear fruit
from the second or third year, and sometimes from
the very first; whereas, on the contrary, if you take
a graft from a young tree, which has not as yet born
fruit, that, which you shall propagate from such, a
cyon, will not come to perfection a long time after.

Of grafts.

I went with my gardener into my crab-stock nursery, to choose some stocks for grafting on: I had
some that came from another nursery, and others
that I had raised from crab-kirnels, but had never
been removed; these seemed to be the most flourishing, and on these I would have had him grafted;
but he refused, saying, that they had only a tap, but
no fibrous or bushy roots, and therefore, when removed, would not be able to feed their stock and

graft.—— Note, such stocks removed may be well able to maintain themselves, but it is a different thing to maintain their grafts, and forcibly transmit juices enough thro' the knot of the graft, where the fibres run transverse.

Cyons grafted upon suckers are more disposed to produce suckers than grafts on the main stocks do. Ev. 140.

In January or February, as you find the weather grow warm, the wind neither being north nor north-east, you may graft cherries or plums, but not apples till the bark of the stock will rise or peel from the wood, which is seldom before the middle of March, and often not till April : this is the best way of grafting them, but if you will graft apples in the cleft, you may do it sooner. Langford, fo. 46.

The great use of grafting by approach is, where trees (such as the vine, or ever-greens) run so much to juice, that the graft cannot easily consolidate to the stock by reason of the great fluidity of sap ; there by length of time and patience it will consolidate by approach.

Of budding. § 7. I gathered withy-shoots over which the cart-wheel had run, and pressed them flat, in which shape they continued to grow, and the sap swelled through their fibres, and rising higher there than in other places of the bark, plainly shewed, that the sap is conveyed by those fibres, to each of which in their progress broke forth a bud sooner or later, and it was to be observed that the fibre lessened extreamly as it passed on, after it's having sent out it's bud, not being able farther in it's whole progress to send out another ; for all buds that appeared above being well observed, could be perceived to be collateral, and to belong to some parallel fibre, though sometimes the bud above might seem to turn athwart the fibre of the lower bud, and hang

perpendicularly

perpendicularly over it.— From, hence may appear
the reason why an inoculated bud may not take,
viz. because it is not placed on a fibre ; therefore
care is to be taken to place the inoculated bud perpendicularly under another bud, that it may be fed,
and not over, left the under bud weaken the fibre
that passes from it, and it should not be able to feed
the inoculated bud.

Mr. Bobart of Oxford tells me, he once inoculated a blossom-bud of an apricock, and the blossom
grew to be a ripe apricock.

To bud a walnut-tree, when five or six feet high,
doth not alter the property of the wild kind, but
makes the tree more naturally bear fruit, both sooner and better too. Cook, fol. 61.

I know Lord Bacon tells you, that peaches come
best of stones unbudded ; but I advise you to bud
all you raise of stones, seeds, &c. though it be to
take a bud off from the same stock, and to bud it on
that, as I have often done. Cook, fol. 61.

Currants and gooseberries may be inoculated on
their own kind. Mortimer, fol. 455.

§. 8. As good pruning helps the growth of Of prun-
trees, so also doth it prolong their lives : for it is ing.
well known that the pruning some annual plants will
make them last more than one year. Cook, fol. 1.

Le Gendre says, a gardener ought not to prune
the large shoots of some trees, such where the sap is
very plentiful by being in good ground : for, if the
sap be stopped ever so little, it will cast itself into
the buds, which would have born fruit, and make
them grow into wood ; therefore he ought to manage
it so as to leave neither the foot nor body of the trees
too much unfurnished ; for this reason he must rather cut the tall-shooting branches, unless in the case
above, too short, than leave them too long, taking
most from the highest branches, and such as are to-

S 2   wards

wards the top of the wall, becaufe thefe draw all th fap to themfelves, and leave the bottom of the tree unfurnifhed : this is the caufe that peach-trees are fo difficult to be kept, experience teaching us, that, if the gardener does not perfectly underftand the way of cutting them, and taking their fprouts away as they ought to be, they will be ruined in fix or feven years. fo. 127.——— Trees, to be well pruned, muft have their boughs every year refrefhed more or lefs, according to their force, by cutting away the wood that fprings in the month of Auguft, which being the fhoot of the latter fap, cannot be ripened, unlefs it be neceffary to preferve it for want of better, or that it be found to be ftrong and well nourifhed. fol. 127.———Thofe boughs alfo that fhoot too faft muft be ftopped and kept fhorter than the others, for they draw all the fap to them and wrong the reft that are weaker : but the mafter bough muft always be preferved, being that which grows ftrait upwards, fo ftopping it from year to year that it may always be the ftrongeft, and maintain the fhape of the tree : thofe boughs alfo, which are weak and fmall, muft be fhortened, and thofe, which are difpofed to bear fruit the following year, to the end that they may grow ftrong, and that their buds may be well nourifhed. ib.——— It is farther neceffary to prune thofe branches that are full of fruit-buds, for too great a quantity of bloffoms confumes the tree, befides that from thence the fruit comes lefs fair ; but in the pruning of thefe it muft be obferved to cut them above a leaf-bud, and as near to it as may be, for two reafons, the firft is, becaufe by that means the fruit will profit moft, for, when it is not covered with leaves, it dries, and feldom arrives at it's natural perfection : the fecond reafon is, becaufe fo the branch will recover itfelf that very year ; whereas, if it be cut higher, and far from a leaf-bud, there will

remain

remain a little ftub at the end of the twig, which dries up, and cannot recover itfelf in two or three years: as for fuch boughs as are taken wholly off, they muft be cut as near the ftem as may be, for fo they will recover the fooner, and that without making any knot. fo. 129. —— The pruning of peachtrees muft be the laft of all, and then, when they begin to fpring, and are ready to flower ; becaufe their young wood is fo tender, that, if it be cut, it will be dried and fpoiled upon the leaft froft, from whence a great many of the fmaller twigs die, and muft oftentimes be cut again. ib. ——Plum-trees and cherry-trees muft not be cut, or ftopped on the fap, but only cleared and difcharged of their ufelefs wood within the tree : and for this reafon they are not proper to be kept as bufhes or dwarfs. fol. 131.

Some trees are fo apt to run to bearing, that thereby they will ruin themfelves in a very few years ; to diminifh this, their heads muft be cut off, or their boughs fhortened to the half, and for two or three years all their buds taken off, for by this means, provided their roots be lively, they will grow much into wood. Le Gendre, fol. 149.

§. 9. It will be neceffary every year to prune and nail wall-fruit to the wall twice or thrice, according as they grow more or lefs, in doing which you muft obferve, to bend down the ftrongeft fhoots that would grow upwards, towards the fides, otherwife they will be apt to run ftraight upwards, and not cover the fpace you defign for them, and by their luxurious growth will extreamly rob the fide-branches of their nourifhment ; there will branches enough fpring out frefh to run upwards out of them when they are fo bowed. Langford, fol. 54. *Of nailing.*

§. 10. A tree, fays Le Gendre, draws it's nourifhment only from the fmall roots. fol. 136. —— When it is neceffary to dung apple-trees, peach- *Of dunging apple, peach, and apricock trees.*

trees or apricock-trees inoculated on a plum stock, or pear-trees grafted on a quince-stock, it is enough to spread the dung upon the ground six feet about the stem, and so to dig and work the earth and it well together, for these spreading near the surface of the earth are easily sensible of the amendment. fol. 138.

Many farmers in the Isle of Wight thresh winter-vetches for their breeding-pigs, and give them to them in the winter ; and one that I know in particu-lar gives them the vetches round about his apple-trees, and says, their soiling, or nusling, and keep-ing the grass and weeds down, or digging and hol-lowing the ground, is the reason why his orchard brings apples every year when others fail.

§. 11. In cold countries both the bark of trees, and the rind of fruit is thickest : so it is plain of lat-ter peaches, &c.

Eaves ser-
viceable in
blossom-
ing time.

§. 12. ᵃ This spring (anno 1708) was very wet and cold, with frosty mornings, especially at apri-cock

---

ᵃ This observation is agreeable to the instructions given by Mr. Miller, under the article Blight.—" There is a sort of blight, says he, against which it is very difficult to guard our fruit-trees ; this is sharp pinching frosty mornings, which often happen at the time when the trees are in flower, or while the fruit is very young, and occasion the blossoms or fruit to drop off ; and some-times the tender parts of the shoots and leaves are greatly injured thereby. The only method yet found out to prevent this mis-chief, is, by carefully covering the walls, either with mats, can-vas, reeds, &c. which being fastened so as not to be disturbed by the wind, and suffered to remain on during the night, by taking them off every day, if the weather permits, is the best and surest method that hath yet been used in this case ; which, although it has been slighted and thought of little service by some, yet the reason of their being not so serviceable as has been expected, was because they have not been rightly used, by suf-fering the trees to remain too long covered ; by which means the younger branches and leaves have been rendered too weak to endure the open air, when they are exposed to it ; which has often been of worse consequence to trees than if they had re-mained cock and peach-bloſſoming time, infomuch that rain would fall in the night and freeze in the morning ; the confequence of which was, that apricocks were ſix and eight ſhillings a dozen : but an ordinary neighbouring man to me, who had an apricock-tree next his houſe, being watchful of moſt contrary ſeaſons, and finding the benefit of nurſing his tree under difficulties, did by night cover it with rugs and blankets from the rain, the confequence whereof was, he had thirty dozen of apricocks on his tree : his name was Timothy Skrine, of Broughton near me in Wiltſhire. — I alſo obſerved that year in ſome few places ſome thatched eaves, which hung a fóot and an half over ſome garden-mud-walls, where were good ſtore of apricocks and peaches ; and I judged they owed their fruitfulneſs to theſe cauſes, for they were thus ſhaded from the rain, which falling at night into the bloſſoms of others, and congealing,

mained intirely uncovered. Whereas, when the covering before mentioned has been performed as it ought to be, it has proved very ferviceable to fruits ; and many times, when there has been almoſt a general deſtruction of fruits in the neighbouring gardens, there has been a plenty of them in ſuch places, where they have been covered : and though the trouble to ſome may ſeem to be very great, yet, if theſe coverings are fixed near the upper part of the wall, and are faſtened to pullies, ſo as to be drawn up or let down, it will be ſoon and eaſily done : and the fucceſs will ſufficiently repay the trouble.

The latter part of Mr. Liſle's obſervation may ſeem favourable to horizontal ſhelters, but, if rightly confidered, it implies no more than Mr. Miller has allowed ; for it is far from concluding that they ought to be fixed and conſtant, or that walls ſhould be built in that manner, nor does it aſſert any thing of the goodneſs of the fruit, but only of the quantity. He brings theſe inſtances of the projecting eaves to confirm the opinion he had delivered before, viz. that the plenty of fruit that year on ſome trees was owing to their having been protected from cold winds, rain, and froſts, in the time of their bloſſoming ; but, notwithſtanding this, fixed horizontal ſhelters may, at other times, and in other reſpects, be very prejudicial both to the fruit and the trees, as Mr. Miller has ſhewn both from reaſon and experience.

burned

burned them up and mortified them; and how they piecemeal mortified, the morning after was very visible. -- The 17th of August I was at Oxford in Mr. Bobart's physic-garden; I related the matter to him with my reflections on it. -- He was pleased with the relation, and said he would carry me to an object which should confirm my opinion: he shewed me the house he lives in, planted on the walls of the physic-garden, on which walls, as far as his house goes, is a large eaving to his house, which saved his peaches from the north wind and the rain, so far as his house went, and so far he had good stock of peaches on several trees, but no farther; and the end of his house reaching to the middle of a tree, the fruit ended there.

§. 13. This year (anno 1720) the spring and summer to August the 13th (when this was wrote) was often very rainy, and the days for the season of the year very cold, it was observable, that in my kitchen-garden, where the land was very good, the plums which were standards, and did cleave from the stone, such as the Orleans, the Damascenes, the the Queen-mother, &c. did all chop in several places, not, as I believe, one plum on a tree excepted, and gum issued out of the chops; but a violet-plum, a standard there, which is a plum that does not cleave from the stone, did not in the least chop: it was farther observable, that such plums as grew against the walls, and did cleave from the stone, though they grew against a north-west wall, did none of them chop.---- And the same observation I have made other years, in cold and wet summers: it may also be added, that the soil in my kitchen-garden was full as good, and as well maintained as the borders of my plum-trees against the north-west walls: from this experiment I draw the two following conclusions, viz. that the reason why the plum that did cleave from the stone in my kitchen-garden did

Plums that come from the stone chop in cold wet weather, others do not, and why.

chop,

chop, was, becaufe fuch plums, which cleave from
the ftone, are of a drier pulp, and do not overflow
fo much in juice as the violet-plums do, and thofe
which do not cleave from the ftone ; and therefore,
through the wet and cold feafons of the year, the fpi-
rituous juices, which can only ftrain through the
ftalk of the plum, being not rarified, through
want of heat, could not afcend, and fo thofe plums,
dry in their nature, being now made more fo, for
want of moifture chopped : but moifture enough
afcended the violet-plum, though lefs than in other
years, which by nature overflowed with juice, to preferve that from chopping.

The fecond conclufion is, that the much rainy
and cold weather, to both which the ftandard-trees
were expofed, was the only reafon and caufe of this
circumftance of the chop in the aforefaid plums, and
made the difference between the ftandard-plums,
and the plums againft the north-weft wall ; for
though the fituation againft fuch expofition one may
think very cold, as not having fo much benefit of
the fun from all quarters, efpecially from the eaft
and fouth afpect, as the garden-ftandards had, by
which means the garden-ftandards were on as good,
if not better footing in hot and dry fummers, yet
in fuch a cold and wet fummer as this was, the
cloudy weather which intercepted the fun, and the
cold windy and rainy weather, from which the plums
under the north-weft wall were very much defended,
fo chilled the juices, as to produce the ill effects
above-mentioned.

I have feen fruit-trees ftanding in hedges pallifade-
wife, in fome particular part of which hedges, poffibly for a lug or two, the trees every year blighted :
I have known new earth to be laid to the roots, and
the old to be removed, without effect : then I have
known new trees to be planted in their room, yet
ftill

still the evil has continued. In such cases I have always observed the position of the place to be the disease, either that there has been a repercussion of an easterly wind from a piece of wall on the place, or some angle which has turned the strength of a malignant wind on it, which cause being removed the effect ceased.——I was speaking to Mr. Bobart of this, and he said, that London the king's gardener had told him, that he was at Versailles, and observed that the king of France for this reason could have no fruit. [b]

G A R D E N.

Of the rose. §. 1. THE common damask-rose is the ancient inhabitant of England. Mortimer, fol. 477.

I was telling my gardener how much fruit depended on the leaves of the tree, &c.—he added, that in the monthly rose he could stop the progress of it's blossom a month by pulling off the leaves of the tree ; for it would not blow again till it had put forth fresh leaves.

Of wood-
bines.
§. 2. The woodbines or honey-suckles in my borders have not thriven, but for the most part died yearly, and I have been forced to renew them ; I first thought our country was too cold for them, but at length I was rather inclined to think our soil was too dry and too hot, our garden being much exposed to the south sun ; so I laid heaps of grass to the roots, and quickly found it to have success.——Agreeable to this seems Mr. Ray, Historia plantarum, vol. 2. fol. 1490. Hæc species in septentrionalibus regionibus, Germaniâ, Angliâ, Belgio, &c. in sepibus frequens.

[b] See the article, Water and Watering, from §. 5. to the end.

§. 3. I

§. 3. I would have those that lay salt on their gravel-walks, to kill the weeds, to observe, if in a few years they do not produce more weeds than those gravel walks that had had no salt laid on them did. For the salt at first stupifies the roots, as being more than they can digest, till washed in by the rain and qualified. Cook, fol. 18.

Of salt laid on gravel walks.

KITCHEN-GARDEN.

§. 4. Worlidge, fol. 257. says, removing of plants, and alteration of the soil is a good way to improve them ; several esculents grow the fairer for it, as cabbages will not leaf well in case the young plants be not three or four times removed before the spring, the same is observed in lettice, onions, and several others, if they are removed into improved earth every time, they will eat the tenderer and finer.

Of improving plants by removing them.

§. 5. Columella recommends ashes to be laid on artichoke beds, which he says is extreamly beneficial to that plant[a]. But Mr. Powel the gardener was a stranger to the agreeableness of that manure to them.

Ashes good manure for artichokes.

§. 6. The latter artichokes will keep till autumn, if you cut them before they are ripe or going to blow, but it must be in a dry season, and when they are very dry, and hang them up in a cellar; for they will keep growing on, and blow, and seed: I have known them kept so two months ; or you may cut the spring-artichokes when half ripe, and then they will bear again at autumn.

Of keeping artichokes.

§. 7. Carrots and parsnips are said to delight in different soils ; viz. carrots, in sandy and the lightest ground, parsnips, in the strongest land.—Mr. Ray agrees to this, for he says, the carrot delights

Of carrots and parsnips.

[a] Cinara multo cinere stercorandum, id enim stercoris huic oleri videri aptissimum. Columella.

in

in gracili folo, but the wild parfnip in folo pingui & opulento. It is a good property in a carrot to be thick and fhort.

If carrots and parfnips are not gathered as foon as they come to their perfection in growing, which is to be known by the withering of their leaves, the worm will eat them, which will caufe a canker.

Of cab-bages.

§. 8. One of my labourers put me in mind of earthing up my cabbage-plants; I knew they would thrive the better for it; but he faid, it would make them take frefh roots, whereby they would better in their ftem fupport their cabbage-heads, which otherwife would be flung by the wind.

Of tranf-planting herbs.

§. 9. Markham in his book of hufbandry, and fkill in cookery, p. 51. fays, that herbs growing of feeds may be tranfplanted at all times, except chervil, orage, fpinage, and parfley, which are not good after being tranfplanted; but obferve to tranf-plant them in moift and rainy weather.

Of liquo-rice.

§. 10. Glycirriza, or liquorice, Mr. Ray fays, rarius autem in Germaniâ aut Angliâ floret, ideoque fterilis a nonnullis fed temerè credita. Now Eng-lifh liquorice being the beft, fhews plainly the per-fection of the root has no affinity with the perfec-tion of it's tafte; for no doubt but the root of liquo-rice grows more perfect, that is, larger, in thofe countries where the plants flower and bear fruit, though there it may eat more fticky and ftringy, and be lefs pleafant in tafte: fo that the perfection in the tafte of the root may be a defect in it.

Of onions.

§. 11. Sharrock in his book of vegetation fays, that Englifh feed of onions brings but fcallions or fmall onions. I find this to be true, and that they will not keep long, but grow foft, and rot in three weeks time after they are taken up.

WEEDS.

WEEDS.

§. 1. FARMER Chivers of Gaufuns in Wilts fays, the thiftles came at firft there, as in other rich paftures, from the ill hufbandry of the farmers, who in hard winters foddered with thiftly ftraw, or thiftly coarfe hay, and from thenceforward they have increafed to a great degree. —— I remember that by foddering in my meads, in a very dry fummer, with goar-vetches, I filled my meads with morgan and other trumpery.

Of foddering with weedy ftraw.

§. 2. Poppy or red-weed feldom grows in the deep and wet lands of Hants, nor in the deep lands in Leicefterfhire, nor indeed do the plants which come up from the fmalleft feeds, fuch as rue, whitlow-grafs, &c. grow in ftrong lands, but in the lighteft lands, which are confequently the barreneft; becaufe thofe fmall feeds are eafily oppreffed in ftrong or wet lands, nor are the vegetative particles heated, and thereby refined enough to penetrate the pores of their feeds.

Of poppy or red-weed.

§. 3. The farmers do not in the laft crops lay down their lands to clover in the ftrong and deep foils of Northamptonfhire, becaufe they would then be prevented (if they made any benefit of their clover the next fummer) of taking fo effectual a remedy by an early fummer-fallow, and after that of giving their lands a fecond tillage, perhaps to deftroy the withwind (which I have often obferved to trouble them) and other fuch ill weeds as are apt to grow up with their wheat, if not fubdued by an early fummer-fallow. After all it muft be confeffed, that nothing is better hufbandry in our ftrong clay-grounds in the hill-country than to keep them in tillage, and not to fuffer them to run to a fword of natural grafs, which is prevented by ploughing

Of killing weeds.

up

up the firſt ſummer's clover to a wheat-crop, about the beginning or middle of Auguſt, after you have in a manner had the benefit of the ſummer-crop; and yet this practice is ſubject to the inconveniency of cultivating the weeds ſuch ſort of land is ſubject to, eſpecially when it ſhall be folded or dunged, as wheat-land ought to be. Therefore it ſeems a medium ought to be taken in this caſe, and you ought to obſerve carefully what ſort of ground is ſubject to what ſort of weeds; for ſome of my clay-grounds are not ſubject to withwind, and ſome of my light and white grounds are not ſubject to morgan or red-weed as others are, and yet I can ſee little difference in the grain of the land; accordingly you may ſuit your huſbandry, in humouring your grounds, and venturing the aforeſaid method in one ground, which for the foregoing reaſons you ought not to riſque in another: again, it often happens in our hill-country-land, we have ſeveral ſorts of earth in the ſame field, as ſtrong red clay, ſome mixed earth, and ſome white; in ſuch caſe, when in the courſe of huſbandry you ſhould lay down your laſt crop of corn to clover, you may forbear ſowing that part of the field which is of ſtrong clay to clover, that you may not be hindered from doing that which perhaps may be moſt for your benefit; viz. of giving it an early ſummer-fallow in order for a wheat-crop. Again you muſt be nicely careful of giving ſuch lands as are ſubject to weeds the firſt froſty fallows of the winter ploughings every year that they are ſown to barley, oats, or peas, in caſe you fallow for peas: by this method you will in time gain in a great meaſure a dominion over thoſe ſorts of weeds, which otherwiſe would eat out and overtop your corn.

Sowing clean ſeed, and laying grounds down to graſs-ſeed, will at length overcome all manner of weeds,

I

weeds, whereby the heart of the ground is eaten out, and the more in heart you accustom to lay down your grounds to grass-feed, the thicker the grass or clover will grow, and the better effect it will have.

Mr. Ray speaking of ludweed (with which the fields at Crux-Easton are very much troubled) says, it grows chiefly on dry, barren, and gravelly ground. —— If so, it seems it may be extirpated by improving the land by good husbandry : and it seems to be the same with all other plants that affect barren and poor ground ; the juices being poor and sour that they feed on, they go off of course by making the land generous : and indeed good healthy land seems much easier to be cured of the weeds incident to it than poor land, without altering the condition and property of each sort, because colt's-foot, docks, wild carrot, parsnip, &c. excepting the thistle and knapweed, may easily be destroyed by being prevented from seeding; whereas the plants of barren grounds being both small and infinite, the labour of destroying them would be also infinite without altering the property of the ground. Therefore the consequence of ploughing lands hard is very discernable, as also of how great consequence it is sometimes to feed meadow-lands for a year or two, thereby to destroy those weeds which are annual by preventing them from seeding.

Sharrock however in his book of vegetation, fo. 141. says, that the plants which annually die, if they are disappointed of running to seed, will continue and survive many years, even till they are permitted to run to seed. —— If so, the feeding of meads, and cutting thistles, &c. in order to destroy annual weeds, may not be so effectual as above proposed.

The measures to be taken in the three seasons of the summer for cutting of weeds seems best to be

taken

taken when they are fulleſt of ſap, which we may
judge of by the ſtripping of oak, which is moſt in
ſap in the breaking out of the bud into a leaf, before
the leaf be full grown : and ſuch half-grown leaves,
by reaſon of their fulneſs of ſap, the froſt ſeizes
ſooner than the others : ſo that the weeds ought to
be cut down when the ſap is moſt in the root, viz.
at ſpring, Midſummer, and Michaelmaſs ſhoot,
which is on the full ſwelling of the bud.

Our farmers ſay, one need not regard what weeds
come up in the ſummer-fallows, or when one ſows
wheat ; for thoſe weeds and May weed will all be
killed by the winter, but it is the weeds that come
up in the ſpring that do the harm.

Why wet brings up weeds and not corn. §. 4. If much wet brings up weeds, how comes
not the corn alſo to thrive in wet weather ? The rea-
ſon is, becauſe many weeds are natural to wet
ground, ſuch as colt's-foot, docks, thiſtles, &c.
and to cold clay ; the wetter therefore the year
proves the more ſuch plants will grow to the maſtery
of the corn: but wet ſeaſons agree with no ſort of
corn : God having ordered that man ſhould live by
the ſweat of his brow, has given that general defect
to land, as to ſtand in need of being laid dry by art
and tillage.——According to what has been ſaid,
lands lying aſlope to the north from the ſun, will
be the more ſubject to weeds.

Why wheat ſown dry becomes weedy. §. 5. It is the obſervation of country-farmers,
that, if the ſeaſon of ſowing wheat be dry, it brings
many weeds into the corn: ——becauſe the ſeeds of
weeds have a moiſture in them by lying ſo long in
the ground as eaſily makes them grow when the
ground is made fine for them ; whereas the corn,
being put into the ground as dry as may be, cannot
by that little moiſture of the ground grow, and ſo
the weeds firſt ſet out ahead of the corn : beſides the
ſeeds of many weeds by much wet may burſt, as it
is in many garden ſeeds.

§. 6. It

§. 6. It is commonly said, by those who forbear Caution not to weed corn when near in ear. See §. 10, 12. to weed their wheat till it is quite, or almost in ear, that what is trod down or bent will rise again : but I weeded my wheat in the beginning of May, at least three weeks before it was in ear, and on the 23d of May I walked by the sides of the corn, and saw many of the bent and trodden down blades, which it was impossible should rise : I found in the bending of all of them, where they had been broken down, the juices in that bending turned black, and became an iron-mould, which in all probability before harvest might rot them off : I found all such blades mounted upwards from the first joint above the bending, making directly upwards towards the sun, as the young shoots of trees fallen down will do, and the bended head of a pea, as it shoots out of the ground, which rises upright in the blade, making a right angle in the joint ; and so it is to be observed that barley blighted by being * more-loose * Loose at root. does, which falling down at the root, the blade in like manner bends inwards at the first joint above the root : undoubtedly therefore such weeding corn when so high does it harm ; it would be worth the observing at harvest what ears such corn produce, as also whether the blades trod down to the north and facing the south do not rise more upright to meet the sun, than those trod down towards the south do in rising towards the north, and so from other points of the compass : as we tread down onion, turnip and carrot-tops to strengthen the roots, and to weaken the heads, think you not it does the same to wheat ? and consequently the bruising and treading it down must be prejudicial to the corn.

§. 7. There is not always the same reason for Some corn does not want weeding like other corn. weeding corn, though the weeds may be as full set at one time as at another : for sometimes one is sure the ground is in very good heart, and the weeds, by coming up late, are not so ; it often happens that the corn starves the weeds and overcomes them; but, if the land is poor, so that the corn shall be in danger of falling off, the danger will be of the weeds starving that.

What corn chiefly to be weeded.

§. 8. Special regard ought to be had to the weeding of such corn, which ought not to lie long abroad in the field after it is cut, such as white oats, barley, and wheat; because they will not bear to lie out so long, as that the weeds cut with them may dry without damage; whereas black oats and peas, the first may lie out without damage till the weeds are dry, and peas must, to be dry themselves, lie out so long that the weeds may be dry also: however, it is best to weed oats.

Of weeding a second time.

§. 9. If you know a ground in it's own nature subject to poppies, thistles, morgan, &c. it is good, if the summer prove cold and wet, to look over it a second time, though you had weeded the wheat in the spring; for it is incredible how a second crop of those weeds will flourish in such years, (though they were out of proof at the first early weeding) and keep on growing till harvest, so as to burn the corn and eat out the heart of it.

Not to weed wheat near in ear. See §6. 12.

§. 10. My wheat was putting out into ear when I sent weeders to weed it, but found at the day's end, that their stooping to pull up the may-weed and red-weed had bent many of the reeds under the ear, for the wheat was tall, and not likely to look up again, it being thick; therefore much of it was trodden down, or rather broke off near the root, the reed being grown stiff: I sent my bailiff and others to view it, and they reported, that the weeders had done a great deal of injury to the corn.—So for the future I hope I shall be wiser, and see my wheat weeded earlier: but, had my wheat been shorter and thinner, and a poor crop, it is probable to such wheat very little damage might have been done: certainly it is best to weed wheat as early in the

I

spring

spring as the weeds are all come up, and, if it muſt
be weeded a ſecond time, ten acres will be weeded in
the time of one. I ſee quick-ſet plants and garden-
ſtuff thrive ſo exceedingly the more for being weeded, that I cannot believe but that early weeding the
corn will have the ſame good effect.

§. 11. I aſked my bailiff, it having rained the
day before, why he did not go to thiſtling my barley ; he ſaid, by no means, he ſhould do more harm
than good, whilſt the top of the earth was clammy ;
for it would clod to their ſhoes, and in treading on
ſuch barley as was ſhallow-mored it would ſtick to
their ſhoes, and they ſhould pull it up after them,
as well as tread other ears into the ground which
would never riſe again.

Not to weed im- mediately after rain.

§. 12. I began weeding my barley early this
year (anno 1703) and my oats ſooner by a fortnight
than others thought of it : I had about ten weeders
in my corn, and yet found by the latter end of the
weeding-ſeaſon, by the damage they began to do in
treading down the corn, that I had great reaſon to
rejoice for ſo doing: I had my weeders all ready
againſt hay-making-time, which was then at hand :
but when I had done weeding, the farmers had ſcarce
begun, rain coming and preventing them, as they
had miſſed making uſe of the ſeaſon when they
might : he that thinks he ſhall have a good crop of
any ſort of corn, had beſt weed it early, becauſe his
corn, running thick and groſs, will receive the more
damage by late weeding.

Of weed- ing early. See §. 6. 10.

Weeds cut late, when groſs, and the barley groſs,
it is likely the corn muſt have been much kept down
by the weeds falling on it, ſo that it can never riſe
again.

§. 13. ª Mr. Ray ſpeaks of wild oats as a weed
difficult

Of wild oats.

ª Inter ſegetes nimis frequens eſt, nec agri, qui ea ſemel in-
fecti ſunt, facilè hâc peſte liberantur ; etenim ante meſſem ma-
tureſcens,

difficult to be got rid of ; for ripening before harvest and shedding it's seed in the ground, it will remain there till the ground be ploughed up again, though it be for a whole year, and then come up with the corn.

The Isle of Wight is extremely apt to run to wild oats, which major Urry says, will lie four or five years in the ground, and come up when it is ploughed ; his way to kill them is, to lay the ground down to clover, and to mow the oats and clover together before the oats are ripe, and their roots will never grow again.

Of furze. §. 14. Mr. Cary's woodman walking with me upon Winterhay's farm in Dorsetshire, I observed the grounds to be much over-run with furze ; he said, they were the worst sort of furze, they were French furze, which run up higher than the English furze does, but would not be so easily killed with chalk, nor were they tender enough for the cattle to eat them : they begin to blow in the middle of January, and last all the summer ; the English furze begin to blow the latter part of the spring, and hold it all the summer. —— I could see little difference between them, only the English was of a closer thicker prickle, and the smaller prickles tenderer.

Of fern. §. 15. Mr. Ray, speaking of the fern, says, it is killed by cutting it two years together.

The destruction and killing of fern by cutting it seems to me to depend on the judicious time of doing it, viz. at the three proper seasons, the spring, Midsummer, and Michaelmass, when and just after the respective buds are shot forth, to which nature has designed the current of the sap, which having no vent, must cause a plethory at the root and body

turescens, semen in terram effundit, quod per hyemem ibidem reptans, aut per integrum annum, si satio intermittatur, cum segete denuo succrescit, fo. 125,

of

of the plant, and turn to corruption ; for the fap
muft break all the capillaries, of which there are a
multitude.

§. 16. Taking a view of my corn about three
weeks after it had been thiftled, I could not find
that any of the ftems of the thiftles, which had been
cut off, fhot upwards fince the thiftling-hook had
taken hold of them, nor did they anywife tillow out
or fhoot up fuckers ; but I found three or four of
the ferpentine leaves to every thiftle (which crept fo
low it was impoffible the hook fhould take hold of
them) to have fpread themfelves out pretty largely,
yet not fo confiderably as might have been expected,
the fap feeding them plentifully ; nor could I find
the roots of thofe thiftles, which had been cut off,
thrive beyond their fellows afterwards : it may be
worth the enquiry whether thofe lower creeping
leaves would not rife much higher, if one had patience to ftay, fo as the hook might cut below them ;
but the beft way of all, both for difpatch and profit,
I conclude to be, to draw the thiftle before it be
grown to that bignefs that they ufually cut them,
and when the ground is reafonably moift : when
they are pretty big they will eafily draw by the
thumb and two fingers, but falfe fingers of hard
leather may eafily be had.

About a month after I had thiftled oats and barley, I obferved the barley-ground to be full of thiftles again, whereof many ftood fo near to the old
ftems, viz. within fix inches, that I fuppofed they
had tillowed from them ; therefore I dug down carefully half a foot in the ground, but could not find
the roots of the young thiftles inclined towards the
old ftem : I tore up the young thiftles with roots of
nine inches long, broken off and very taper and flender
at bottom, with fmall fibres belonging to them, as
other maiden-thiftles had : nor is it to be conceived
that nature, which is ordered to go the neareft way,

T 3   fhould

should from the slenderest and lowest part of the old root send forth it's sucker, but from the upper part and strongest of the whole root, nearest to the surface; so I observed some small tillows or issues from the old stem, which did not advance to any great height; they issued out between earth and air, and, as if maintained by the old stem, they carried a shrivelled dwarfish look with them: they issued out more freely and longer here than in the white soil though thistled a fortnight before this ground; for either the stems here carried no suckers, or very dwindling ones: therefore there is less danger of the thistles growing again by tillowing in thistling white land early than stiff clay; nor did the under-leaves of the old stems shoot out to any length in the white ground in comparison to what they did in the clay: the wet year was the occasion of these tillows.

August 24th (anno 1711) I dragged a nine-acre piece of wheat, sowed on one earth, which was very thick, and full of thistles that had tillowed out from old stems, which I had cut about a month or six weeks before, lest they should run to seed; I was a little apprehensive, though I knew the thistle to be but an annual plant; whether the tillowing thistles from the old roots might not strike fresh roots to the great prejudice of my wheat; there were also many thistles which were seedlings.—— November 17th I visited my wheat, and though the forehand of the winter-season had been very mild, yet I found all the thistles dead and rotten in the roots: it may be the drags battering them might hasten the effect, but I believe they had been dead some time before.

If wheat be not well thistled, the reapers take up the grips so tenderly, lest they should prick their hands, that by their loose handling them many ears are left behind, and such foul work is made, that the wheat left behind might sow the ground.

Though

Though barley and oats should both be thistled, yet, if it is impracticable to accomplish both, the oats should be left unthistled rather than the barley, not only because the oat-straw is generally less proper for fodder than the barley-straw, but also because oats may lie longer in swarth and in cock than the barley, and so the thistles may have a reasonable time for drying: it is further also to be noted in thistling spring-corn, that, if the thistles be once grown tall, strong, and prickly, as they commonly are before the barley be out in ear, and about five weeks before it is cut, then I think, though the barley be not so high, nor thick, as to take harm in thistling by treading, yet the thistling in such case does more harm than good; first, because the thistles being grown so sticky will not thoroughly wither, nor shrink and waste away, as it were to nothing, by harvest, but will be raked up with the corn; secondly, by harvest such great thistles will turn black, and spoil the fodder (being raked up with the swarths) a great deal more than if they had stood till harvest; for then, being cut green with the corn, they will hold a good colour, and drying they will eat tolerably well, nor will the cattle refuse them in the straw. Chalking land is an excellent way to destroy the thistles.

It need not be wondered at, that in borders, alleys, grass-plots, gravel-walks, &c. weeds, grasses, and trumpery should so increase as they do, if we observe that such weeds and grasses, however low they seem to be kept, run to seed when they are so small as to escape our observation, and before they seem to be worth weeding up.

I was weeding my barley (anno 1701) so long before it was in ear that one could not know it from oats; the thistles were then pretty high and strong: but a farmer in my neighbourhood said, he never

weeded

weeded so early, because the thistles would grow up again.— Upon which, I talked with all the weeders, and with other husbandmen, and I found by them plainly, that, notwithstandtng what the farmer had said, it was good husbandry to thistle as I did; for otherwise the thistles would grow so big as to eat up the heart of the corn, which it would not recover; and though the thistles might grow again, yet they would not seed nor be rank, but still be over-topt and kept under by the corn; whereas by going into corn when in ear damage was done, and then the thistles were so big, that being cut down they would fall on the barley, and sink it down, so that it might some of it never rise again, and that more especially, if they cut down the thistles in rainy weather; for thereby they would be gross and heavy, and not apt to wither so soon as otherwise it would do, and so the corn might be in danger of being ever held under: but when the corn was as young as mine, thistling when wet did it no harm: and, if by thistling so early you were forced to thistle again, it was no more than the best husbandmen often do.

This day, being June 25th, (anno 1703) I conceived a fancy for reasons before hinted at, that a better method might be found out for destroying of thistles than cutting them; so I went into a ground with a pair of tongs (which also might be improved) and with them I took hold of the lower stem of the thistle, and drew it up with all it's roots nine inches in length, the stems of the thistles being nine inches or a foot long, and that with greater expedition by much than the labourer could cut them, as he, being eye-witness of it, was satisfied. This instrument may not, it is possible, do so well in wheat, because the ground may be too hard to draw the root; the practice must only be in barley, where the ground is loose: if the ground be somewhat moist, it will be the better.

It

It is good to thistle broad-clover, and to cut out the docks, and scabius's, &c. as well as corn, for thereby the broad-clover (I know it by experience) may be made a day the sooner.

§. 17. All this spring (anno 1708) being wet, and lands being generally obliged to be sowed wet, it was observed there was an infinite quantity of charlock in cold red clays, both peas and barley-land; but in white or lighter land the charlock did not so much over-run it: therefore it seems one should avoid ploughing and sowing cold clays wet, if only on the account of charlock; the reason for this seems to be, because charlock-seed is very oily and hot in taste, as has been before noted, and therefore resists putrefaction, and consequently the fibres of the seed are not easily opened, and loosened, nor penetrated by a great deal of moisture; whereas white and light earth is soon dry after rain, and so the water does not continue long enough on it to set such seed on growing: therefore cold wet lands are always more subject to charlock than white land. —— In this the turnip-seed is of a direct contrary nature to charlock-seed, which latter to the taste conveys in a very apparent manner a much tarter, stronger oil; for though the turnip-seed requires a speedy shower of rain to bring it up, yet much rain, when it is first sown, makes it drunk, and it's parts being loose and uncompact imbibe the rain so freely, that if they continue in it they are converted to mucilage: I have often sowed charlock-seed and turnip-seed in flower-pots at the same time, and watered them, and found that whereas turnip-seed will shew itself in three days, charlock would not appear under ten days; the seed-leaves and roots of the last are much hotter and more peppery than the plant of turnip; therefore none who sow turnip-seed need be at a loss on the first appearance of the plant, to know whether

it

it be turnip or charlock ; for, if the seed-leaves appear within a week's time, it cannot be charlock ;
again, if leaf or root tastes hot, it cannot be turnip,
which tastes mild ; the advantage of knowing which
is, that one may lose no opportunity to sow turnip-
seed again in a very few days, and consequently lose
not the season, if it comes not up, which by the
aforesaid signs one may know ; whereas, if one must
learn the difference from the leaves they put out
after the seed-leaves, that must take up at least
three weeks, and thereby the season of sowing again
may be lost ; for if we have not showers or moisture for the sowing of turnips, it will be to little
purpose.

On observation past on my corn of all sorts June
8th (anno 1715) my wheat, which was sown on one
earth, worked very fine and pretty dry, i. e. a little
drier than we commonly desire it to do for wheat,
and which was sown pretty early, ran very much to
charlock : I also observed that my blue peas which
were sowed in March, and the ground ploughed fine
and dry, brought up abundance of charlock : whereas the wheat-ground which ploughed up as heavy,
and wet, and as cold as we commonly desire it, and
the grey partridge-peas, which were sown from the
beginning of February to the 20th, when the ground
and weather were colder, produced very little or no
charlock : all this seems to depend on one and the
same reason in relation to the sowing, whether at
spring or autumn ; viz. the charlock-seed being
close in it's tubes and vessels, and full of oily parts,
which resist putrefaction, as aforesaid, the juices of
the earth (whilst cold and wet, and the season so
also) could not insinuate into the charlock-seed, it
not being attenuated enough by heat : whereas, when
the season of the autumn and spring, and the ground
was warmer, and turned up very fine, the juices easily

ly penetrated the veſſels of the charlock-ſeed, and ſet them on growing ; that afterwards, when both the weather, and the ground grew warmer, the char-lock-ſeed did grow up, is not to be wondered at, ſince the good diſpoſition of the bed ſeeds are at firſt committed to is of the greateſt moment, and the earth ſoon ſettles, and hardens, and falls cloſe, and becomes unfit to make the ſeeds grow.

This ſpring (anno 1701) I ſowed goar-vetches on a ſtale fallow of a head-land, and ſowed another piece of goar-vetches the ſame year on a ſecond ſtale earth of a month turned up; at the ſame time we gave a ſecond earth for barley; and I had nothing but charlock on the latter, and nothing but thiſtles came up in the for-mer; from whence I collect, that harrowing on a ſtale ſpring-fallow tends to nothing but producing ſuch weeds the ground is inclined to : therefore I had better have given another earth upon the ſowing of my vet-ches, which would have buried the charlock that had took root, which the harrows alone could not do.

I winter-fallowed two grounds (anno 1702) when in very good temper and dry : the latter end of Fe-bruary or beginning of March I ploughed one again and ſowed it with peas, the ground working dry : I likewiſe ploughed the other again, and ſowed it to peas and goar-vetches at the ſame time ; in both theſe grounds, and all over them, came up abun-dance of charlock, ſo that they were perfect yellow with it ; only about two acres of the latter was re-ſerved till the latter end of April, and then had a ſecond earth, and was ſown to more goar-vetches ; but then rain had fallen and the ground worked pretty lumpiſh, and therein I had not a ſtem of char-lock came up.

We had a very ſhowery wet ſpring all March, Id. and of April, and May, and the firſt week of June, and thiſtles. my lands being in very good tillage, worked exceed-

ing

ing fine at fowing-time for peas, oats and barley,
as alfo had my wheat-land and vetches, and I never
knew fewer thiftles in all forts of my corn, but there
was abundance of charlock, which I have often obferved to be the confequence of land's working fine
and dry.   Charlock therefore is more the produce
of poor ground; becaufe that generally works finer
and drier than that which is ftrong; but thiftles are
more commonly the produce of ftrong land, becaufe that generally works colder, wetter, and
rougher, which properties bring thiftles; confequently in thofe years, wherein the ground works
worft, the thiftles come up thickeft.   Perhaps the
reafon of this may be, becaufe the feed of the thiftle
may have taken root before the fpring-corn is fown,
and, when the ground works rough, it may not be
torn from many clods of earth, and fo dies not, but
abundance of the roots, having a faftening to the
earth, ftill live; whereas, when the ground works
fine, the roots of the young tender thiftles may be
torn away from the earth, and fo wither and die;
and that this may be the reafon I am apter to believe,
becaufe, when ground works rough, a crop of thiftles
foon appears, and tops the corn which could not
be, except the thiftles had had fome rooting before
the ploughing for fowing; for where the ground
ploughs fine, as the thiftles are few, the corn tops
them, till it leans down it's head before the harveft,
and then the thiftles, which were not weeded up,
may fhew their heads above the corn; and in this
cafe the thiftles are generally weak, as having no
root but what might grow from the feed after the
corn was fown; for, as was faid before, where the
ground works fine, what tender young thiftles had
taken root, which are the thiftles fuppofed moft to
annoy corn, are, by the fine working of the ground,
conceived to be torn up by the roots; thus the fine
                                                    tillage

illage of the ground prepares a bed for the seeds of
weeds, but tears up root and branch those weeds,
which had before taken root, which generally speak-
ng, are the most hurtful weeds; fine tillage of the
ground therefore, in the general, is a quality of
good husbandry.

What may be the cause of producing charlock I
cannot tell, but it seems, it must be either the sowing ground early, or dry; for that part sown late
and wet had none: nor did my barley that year
sowed late and almost in the dust, produce but very
little charlock : but after sowing the barley in April
and May, there was no rain for a long time, yet the
barley came up well, but the charlock came up very
thin. —— From hence I cannot but conclude, that,
though a dry summer, and a dry winter-fallowing
tends much to the killing of the weeds, which arise
from roots or fibres, as also from seeds, by laying
open the ground to the frosts in winter, and to the
scorching heat of the sun in summer; yet that,
when such earth comes to be sown either to winter
or summer-corn, the finer and drier it works, and
the better for bringing up the corn, the better and
kindlier in proportion for the seed of weeds, by reason the seeds of weeds are of less pith than the corn,
consequently more apt to be choaked when the
ground works stiff : but when it works well for
the corn, it does so also to bring up the weeds,
which arise from seeds, or for the bringing up such
weeds as arise naturally from the ground, the body
of the ground being more opened to the sun and
rain's visiting all it's pores and impregnating it :
for I cannot see why earth best prepared to bring up
the seed-corn, is not also best prepared to bring up
the seeds of weeds, and such weeds as are natural to
the ground. But the seasonable winter and summer-
fallowing, as before hinted, may reasonably prevent
and cut off such weeds as arise from roots or fibres.

And

———And to such weeds as arise by roots or fibres of roots, the drier and dustier corn is laid into the ground, the more must such roots be separated from the earth, and be exposed to wither by the heat of the sun : but, as was said before, I think it holds quite contrary in weeds arising from seed, and that the good disposition and mellowness of the ground is fittest to produce weeds either from seed or naturally ; the garden-mold being so fine, is for the same reason so subject to weeds. I see quick-set plants and garden-stuff thrive so exceedingly the more for being weeded, that I cannot but believe early weeding the corn will do the same good to the ground ; and this may appear from mellow earth flung up in digging a pond or other hole, which earth is generally of a mellow, hollow sort, whereon thistles, and other weeds will grow abundantly, whether they come up naturally or by seeds sown; this seems to shew how much fitter the better tempered mold is for weeds as well as for seed-corn : but when a mere and perfect strong clay is flung out in a heap in digging such a pond or hole as aforesaid, then, as I have observed, such mere clay has produced no weeds, the earth wanting that hollowness and fit mellowness, till by lying two or three years the upper crust is hollowed by the sun, or by the treading both of men and cattle.

Of couch-grass. §. 18. Mr. Raymond says, the most destructive grass to corn is the knot or couch-grass, it being of that increasing nature, that, if but a piece of a root were left, it would in one season spread over a patch of ground as big as a small casting-net.

Of great and small bind-weed or with-wind. §. 19. Mr. Ray speaking of great bindweed, says, it is frequent in hedges in watery places, it's root is perennial, but it's stalk annual; I suppose the small bindweed is of the same nature, as to the soil it desires, and the perennial root it carries ; it grows

grows in my clay-land, to the corn's great prejudice: therefore land may be presumed cold that runs to it, and must be treated accordingly; I am apt to believe it propagates itself by seeding in pasture-ground, for it seems to flower too late, in corn, to seed before the corn is cut.

In both barley and wheat, in the deep rich land, near Ilsley, in Oxfordshire, I observed, withwind with mighty grossness climbed up most of the halm to the top, no doubt, but to the prejudice of the corn in many respects, which must be eat up before harvest.

I have known withwind or bindweed multiplied and propagated both in barley and wheat, where the land has been strong, and therefore more subject to that weed ; for, when such ground has been ploughed for some crops, to peas, barley, or oats, for which corn the land is only ploughed in the winter months, or for winter-vetches, for which end it is not tilled till about September, there is no killing thereby the roots or seeds of weeds as by the summer-fallows for wheat, but the weeds, which multiply from the off-sets or joints of roots, or from seeds, do increase thereby; in such case I have known clay-land folded for barley (and particularly that part of the ground, which waiting for the folds going over at last was latest fallowed) bring up a great increase of withwind, though the spring and summer has been very dry, insomuch that every blade of barley had a withwind round it ; that, as the fold has brought up a crop of barley, it has, with it, to every blade of corn brought up it's enemy to eat it out, and pull it down before it is ripe, and prevent the filling of the grain, whereby the crop of barley is greatly hazarded after it is cut also, by the danger it must run by laying in swarth till that weed is withered, before it can be carted.——Again, near

the

the end of the firſt ſummer, after the firſt year of a
hop-clover-crop, which I fed, that is, about the beginning of Auguſt, I fallowed a ground for wheat,
and then dunged the fallows, and ſowed my wheat
before Michaelmaſs : I had a very good crop of
wheat, but a withwind came up to every blade, ſo
that, had it been a wet and cold ſummer (whereas it
was a hot and dry one) my wheat had been pulled
down and lodgrd while green in the ear, and in the
milk, and then could not have filled in body and
flour, and ſo had been of the nature of blighted corn:
the increaſe of this withwind was, without doubt, occaſioned by the laying down this ground only to one
ſummer-feed after the hop-clover was ſown, when
the ground had born three or four crops of ſummer-
corn after it's wheat crop, whereby, by the winter
ploughings, as I intimated before, the off-ſets of the
roots of weeds, and their ſeeds were propagated ; and
I could not properly by a ſeaſonable ſummer-fallow
deſtroy theſe roots or ſeeds, by giving the ground a
ſummer-fallow the beginning of June; for then I had
loſt the fruits of my hop-clover crop by ploughing it
in at the beginning of the firſt ſummer, which would
have contributed much to the killing of the withwind ; and by delaying the fallowing three months
longer, viz. to the beginning of Auguſt, the ſun had
both ſo loſt it's ſtrength to burn up the roots, and
malt the ſeed, and the ground the opportunity of lying long to a fallow, that the dung laid on the fallows gave new life to the roots and ſeeds, which was
very apparent by this one experiment : there had
been a great deal of hop-clover ſeed ſhed that year,
becauſe I could not feed the hop-clover down low
enough (I had ſo great a burthen on the ground) and
this ſhattered ſeed being on the beginning of Auguſt
fallowed in, laid under the fallows alive till about
the 1 cth of September, when I turned up the ground
again

again for fowing wheat; then the hop-clover feed was turned up again, and grew mightily by virtue of the dung, and at harveft produced, with my wheat, fo fine a crop of clover, that I thought it would better pay the feeding it a year, than to proceed on in the ufual courfe of hufbandry, viz. to winter-fallow after wheat, for peas, oats, &c.

§. 20. Every one agrees the lighter one makes ground fubject to red-weed, and may-weed, by giving it more earths, the more of thofe weeds it will bring, and thofe are fome of the worft weeds in corn, for I have known as good a crop of wheat as one would defire all the winter-time, and by thofe two weeds coming up in the fpring and fummer, it has been eaten out fo, that there has not been the feed. *Poppy or red-weed, and may-weed.*

I find all agree, that in weeding the morgan or may-weed, and the red-weed, they fhould be drawn up by the root rather than cut up with the hook; becaufe they have a flender tap-root, which draws eafily, without loofening the ground, and mores of the corn, whereas, if they be cut, they will tillow and come again; but the thiftle has too great a root to be drawn, and when cut comes not again.

Seeing poppy requires a winter and fummer for growing, to make it's feeds grow, in order to fallow them up the fummer after, and deftroy them, it feems the fummer-fallowing the year before, or the October before, is much conducing towards a wheaten crop.

The poppy is a winter and not a fummer weed the feed requiring to have root very early in the fpring; therefore I never could obferve it grow in barley or oats, unlefs it was barley and oats fowed on one earth, which is very early fown: the rooted feed, poffibly, in fuch cafe, being not pulled up by the harrows, grows, tho' in very little quantity.

It is ufually obferved, that the white land in our hill-country is very fubject to poppy, if ploughed with two or three earths, and made thereby light, but clay-lands are not so subject to be reduced : — the reason of which seems to be this ; because the poppy-seed is a most small seed (for Mr. Ray computes many thousands to lie in a pod) which seed, by reason of it's smallness, is easily buried in clay-land, and less able to shoot it's seed-leaves through, because it sooner settles and binds than light land, through which it's seed-leaves easily pass : it is very likely therefore, the evil of red-weed being so great, it may be better to sow white land on one earth.

The poppy is much hardier than the wheat, for that blossomed exceeding thick in the grounds where the wheat was almost all killed, exposed to the cold winds of this winter 1709.

It is very plain that braishier shallower ground in the hill-country is very subject to red-weed or poppy, and the strong clay-ground not so ; therefore, wherever in a clayey piece of ground there is a sinking or fall, or the grete runs shallower (as in some places of most of my clay-fields it does) as also in the lighter fields, there I ought to give the weeders stricter orders to be cautious and circumspect to pull the poppy-weed up : ——but, as to the strong deep clay-land, even the poppy, though it does appear there thick, need not be much regarded ; for it will there every day dwindle, and the cold clay will starve it ; whereas, on the contrary, what poppy appears in spring in the light shallow stone-braishey land, though the root and stalk seems poor, will spring forward, and thrive apace all the summer till it blows and seeds.

When the farmer says, red-weed, morgan, &c. burns up corn, it is only meant that, when that gets ahead, it sucks up the moisture from the corn, and then indeed it's lamentable effects are as if the corn was scorched up.

§. 21. Being

§. 21. Being with farmer Lake of Faccomb, we Cockle.
fell into difcourfe on hufbandry, and I told him I
was gathering the cockle in the field out of the winter-vetches, left I fhould bring them into the dung
of the back-fide : he faid, he faw not how that pro-
fited much, unlefs I defigned them for feed, and then
it might be inconvenient, but, if they were for
horfes meat, if the cockle with the vetch s came into
the dung, it would be heated thereby, and never
grow again ; the fame he faid of charlock : I afked
him then if he never thought abundance of trumpery was carried into the field with the dung, which
grew again ; he faid it was fo in cafe green new
dung was carried forth, but in cafe the dung was
firft flung up in heaps to rot, the feeds in it of weeds
did not grow : he faid, if his feed-wheat was clean,
he never obferved he had cockle.

§. 22. Mr. Ray fays of the corn-marygold, it Corn ma-
has a woody root, and ftrikes deep, therefore muft rygold.
eat out the heart of the ground, and muft be a great
harm to corn ; if it's feed ploughed-in will grow,
as the garden-marygold will being dug in, it is
hard to overcome the increafe of it.

§. 23. Farmer Biggs told me, that a field of his Colts-foot.
was all over-run with colts-foot, and that he fowed
it to vetches, and that thofe vetches britted or fcattered, fo that he put in his pigs to fatten in it, which
nufsled about as much as they thought good,
whereby, as he thinks, they trod and nufsled in many
of the vetches, for they came up very thick, and he
preferved them, and had a very good fecond crop;
which two years crop of vetches killed almoft all the
colts foot, fo that there has been but little there fince.

Colts-foot is feldom known to grow in the common arable fields, for the fheep fare fo hard there,
that they eat up all the roots on the fallows, but, unlefs one was to bring fuch fheep on our fallows, they
will

will not be eaten, for our sheep will not destroy
them.

The reason why laying a ground down long to
grass is said to kill the colts-foot and other perennial weeds, is, I suppose, because the roots of the natural grass matting more and more every year, do in
four or five years time so fill the ground and fasten
it, that the colts-foot cannot come through at spring,
they may also happily so bind the surface of the earth
together, as to hinder the root from that communication with the air at other times as all plants may
require ; to hasten therefore the destruction of colts-
foot, I apprehend that plat of the ground, where it
abounds, should be laid down to rye-grass, to continue so till it is destroyed ; though the other part of
the ground be sowed to clover, and ploughed up
again, yet the colts-foot should continue lay, and be
dunged well, and mowed, and sowed very thick to
rye-grass ; these means may effectually destroy the
colts-foot, as it is manifest dunging land does destroy clover and French-grass.

I this day (July the 3d) ploughed up broad-clover, and turned up the roots of colts-foot. I observed between earth and air many little buds shot forth
of the bigness of the Midsummer buds in fruit-trees
(in all probability to be the ensuing leaves or flowers
of the next year) from the root ; at five, six, or seven inches depth I observed here and there a shoot,
of a callous body, like the root, one, two, three, or
four inches long. Whether the first or second sort
of shoots were to be leaves or flowers of the next
spring will be fit to be enquired into at spring, but
what is to be observed, is, that in my fallow I turned up the colts-foot roots of a foot long ; therefore
in a winter-fallow I had undoubtedly turned up the
same roots, at least of the same length, and one would
think to better effect, nature being to begin again

all

all the progreſs ſhe had been going on till that time ; but it is manifeſt a ſummer-fallow is of much greater conſequence to deſtroy the colts-foot, than a winter : how comes this then to paſs ? the only reaſon I can give is, that the nature of colts-foot is to thrive and improve in cold wet ground ; the winter-fallow therefore does not deſtroy theſe roots, which are ploughed up, but they live ſtill by reaſon of the coldneſs of the ground at that ſeaſon, and ſtrike freſh roots ; whereas the colts-foot lies ſo dry in the ſummer-fallows, turned up to the ſun, as to die, nothing being more contrary to their nature than a healthy dry ſoil. —— This ground being ploughed dry, and a rain following, whereby the ground was mellowed, I found theſe roots eaſy to be pulled up, at a conſiderable length, with their ſoboles or bud of the next year, above taken notice of ; from which I do infer, that in hiring people to pull up ſuch colts-foot roots, if a remainder does break off, and is left behind, which may grow, yet for the next year it cannot, becauſe, the ſoboles being loſt, it is too late in the year to provide another ; and though it may be thought that ſuch roots as are turned up in a ſummer-fallow will wither of themſelves, yet it is to be conſidered, that ſuch ſoboles as are buried, if the ſeaſon be wet, will ſpring again.

Being at Oxford, I viſited Mr. Bobart of the phyſick-garden, and I told him of the method I took to deſtroy the colts-foot : he ſaid, if I cut the colts-foot often in a ſummer, or whipped it, it would, he believed, kill it ; I ſaid I had ſo heard of fern ; he agreed it to be true, and ſaid all plants were eaſily killed by keeping them under ground in that manner.

§. 24. Common ragwort, Mr. Ray ſays, grows Ragwort. in paſtures and lay-grounds, and about path-ways; the root dies ; therefore it propagates by ſeed, and is to be extirpated before it ſeeds, by cutting it up.

U 3   Hoary

Hoary perennial ragwort, Mr. Ray says, has a perennial root, and throws out new soboles, or buds, at autumn : if so, different methods are to be taken with it to extirpate it.

Nettle.

§. 25. Mr. Ray tells us, that the common stinging nettle is of a lasting nature, —————— but the lesser stinging nettle is annual.

Dyer's-weed.

§. 26. Dyer's-weed makes the milk of the cows that feed on it bitter, as it also does the butter and cheese made of it.

Mullen.

§. 27. Ray and other herbalists say, that mullen grows on clifts and banks, and say nothing of it's growing in warm sunny fields, which it does at Crux-Easton, particularly in one of my fields, where not above thirty roots of it came up in a scattering manner at first, which seeded, and the winds blew it about the ground, and the next year came up thousands ; but I observed those that seeded the year before died, and therefore that it is a weed easily destroyed by cutting off the stem when it is in flower, and preventing it's increase by thousands.

Groundsel good against the worms.

§. 28. Groundsel and savine are good against the worms, commonly called the bots in horses.

Pilewort.

§. 29. In our meads at Easton, on our hills, and hedges, and lanes, we have great plenty of pilewort growing, which is one argument, that such of our lands are moist and strong where it grows.

Spurge.

§. 30. I find by Mr. Ray, fol. 868 and 869, that both the tithymalli or corn-spurges, which grow up in corn fields, are but annual.

Spurry.

§. 31. In the common corn-fields, about Lutterworth, inclinable to a heavy fat sand, I observed spurry to grow wild very plentifully ; I gathered of it, and shewed it to Mr. Bobart of Oxford ; we both wondered so contemptible a plant should be sown in the Low Countries, where Mr. Worlidge, fol. 31. says, they sow it twice a year ; once in

May,

May, to be in flower in June and July, and the second time after rye-harvest is in, to serve their cattle in November and December; he says, hens will eat the herb greedily, and it makes them lay eggs the faster.

§. 32. The knapweed, or matfellon, is chiefly natural to corn-land, in a gravelly soil, and is of a perennial root, as Mr. Ray observes: devil's-bit is also perennial in it's root; it is probable blue-bottles are the same, and all of the scabius sort, seeing they emit new soboles every summer at the root for the fruit of the next year, and seem not to seed early enough, before the corn is cut, to propagate themselves in corn-lands by seed, in which ground they most abound. *Knapweed, scabius, &c.*

It seems plain to me that both knapweed, scabius, and spatling-poppy roots are perennial, as also millefoyle (which infests some pastures) by the many buds or soboles they emit at their roots at this time of year.

§. 33. It's seed ripens very soon, and as soon sheds, after which it dies away root and all before hay-harvest: the ready way to destroy it is to well-dung the meadows. *Yellow rattle grass.*

§. 34. Eye-bright flourishes chiefly in upland barren pasture ground. *Eye bright.*

§. 35. Mr Ray says, lady's finger grows for the most part, in dry, chalky, or gravelly soils, and in all barren ground. *Lady's finger.*

§. 36. Yellow lady's bed-straw, or cheeserening, over-runs almost two of my meads, which have been mowed and not well supported with manure; but my other meads, parted only by a hedge, the soil and situation the same, being fed for two years have very little of it; it grows chiefly in warm places, and in dry pastures, and on hillocks, and balks. *Yellow lady's bed-straw.*

balks.——Therefore where this grows you may conclude your meadows want foil to fatten them,

Silver-weed, or wild tan-fey.

§. 37. Mr. Ray fays, the root of wild-tanfey is good to eat, and fomewhat of the parfnip kind, and that hogs are very fond of it.

Common chickweed.

§. 38. On the 23d of October I obferved a great deal of chickweed, the branches of which carried many buds in order to bloffom, many full bloffoms, many feed-pods with white feeds almoft ripe, and many pods with red feeds full and kindly ripe ; fo it feems it is in the nature of this plant to be always feeding, and fo the lefs fence againft it by any fort of hufbandry.

Crow foot, or ranun-culus.

§. 39. There are feveral ranunculus's common in our meadows, which, when green, blifter the fiefh ; thefe are not touched by cattle, but left ftanding in the fields, and yet, as I am told, are fed on greedily by all forts of cattle, when only dried into hay : Dr. Sloan mentions this to account for the caffavis root, which, being ftrong poifon, by being baked is wholfome bread. fol. 25.

Red-rot, or flower-fun dew.

§. 40. Red-rot (or flower-fun-dew) is faid to take the name of red-rot from it's being fo pernicious to fheep.

Ground-ivy.

§. 41. I obferved abundance of ground-ivy trailing on the ground, and, in gathering it up, I found the trailing joints, being in abundance, had ftruck frefh roots, from whence new leaves came up, as in ftrawberries.

Mallows.

§. 42. Mr. Biffy of Wiltfhire had abundance of mallows that came up in a broad-clover ground, fo as to overfhadow the broad-clover ; he was fatisfied mallow was in the clover-feed, becaufe his brother fowed the fame feed, and had the fame increafe of mallows ; Biffy fays, every bit of the root of a mallow will grow. Note, this 23d of October I obferved plentiful foboles or fpring-iffues from the old roots.   §. 43. Cicu

§. 43. Cicutaria tenui folio, or fool's parſley, Fool's parſley. which grows in rich land, and in grounds that are cultivated, is an annual, and therefore may be deſtroyed before it has ſeeded.

§. 44. In Sheepſhead and Hawthorn fields in Hare's-foot trefoil. Leiceſterſhire, I obſerved ſome ridges ſo peſtered with hare's-foot trefoil growing amongſt the corn, that it ſeemed as bad a weed in the corn as any I had ſeen that year; both grounds ſeemed to be of a clayey ſand.

§. 45. Being at Mr. Raymond's, he aſſured me, Cow-garlick. that cow-garlick was a great whore in corn, a little way from his place in the dry ſandy grounds; and yet it is no whore to them who ſow it in the clays; for there it will not grow; but in his neighbourhood it comes up in the corn in great abundance; Stevens of Pomeroy ſays, it grows in ſome places in ſuch abundance, that the wheat taſtes ſtrong of it, and is thereby damaged 6d. and 12d. in the buſhel.

§. 46. As rye-graſs and natural graſs eat out the Moſs. clovers, ſo I obſerve in the third year of rye-graſs moſs begins to grow on the land, and eat out the rye-graſs and natural graſs, and is the great impoveriſher of meadows; it is very probable it's ſeeds are carried to far diſtant grounds, being ſo imperceptible (as Mr. Ray makes it) to the eye: it is very probable alſo, it, being ſo ſmall, is buried in arable, which may be the reaſon it comes not up but in land lying to reſt, where the ſeed cannot be covered or bound; it is poſſible alſo it comes not up in arable with the corn, becauſe (as many ſeeds do) it may not grow under two, three, or four years time; Mr. Ray obſerves, they are apt to grow either in too cold lands, or too ſcorched-up lands: he ſays, on houſe-tops they ſeldom increaſe on the ſouth ſide of the tiling, as on the eaſterly expoſition, and northerly, which the ſun goes off from by times, and on which the firſt dews of the night

night fall; from whence it may be concluded, land is so much the more or less liable to it as it faces those expositions : but seeing it is so great an enemy to meadow, and other grasses, the nature of it ought well to be observed, and it's seeds planted in pots to see their nature, and thereby one may know how to destroy it :——our experience seems to agree with what Mr. Ray says as to it's inclination to thrive in cold land, it being manifest that, when such cold clay is rectified by ashes or lime, or as he says, ᵇ ashes of which lye has been made, which he advises to be laid on the ground in the month of March, the moss forsakes the ground for some time.

It is no such great wonder that mosses should grow on stones and walls, if we consider how many thousand times less their seeds are than the seeds of most herbs, whereby they have as fit a matrix to cover themselves in, in the crevices of the stones; where usually dust gathers, and are as well buried, in proportion to their bodies, as the seeds of other plants are in earth-mold; nor are we more to wonder, that the mosses from the said seed should thrive and flourish as well as their seeds germinate, if we consider how their bodies drink not only the dews, but are fitted, by the innumerable angles their branches and close-knit fibres make, to be a long receptacle of water, and at the same time to break all the rays of the sun, and how fit for gathering the dust to their roots, as by experience may be seen.

§. 47. That dung, ashes, &c. should kill moss, is, I suppose, from this reason; because the moss having a most wonderful small root, which grows only to the ground by adhesion, is easily suffocated with too much goodness of the dung, and overcome

by

Why dung and ashes kill moss.

ᵇ Muscus, qui hortos & prata humida obsidet, ita ut gramen supprimat, Martio mense cinere aboletur, sed eo quo lixivium fuerit confectum. Ray, Hist. Plant. fol. 122.

by the ftrong penetrating quality of the afhes, as being no ways qualified by rain on the furface of the
ground. For thefe reafons the moft diminutive
plants will not grow on rich ground, fuch as rue,
whitlow-grafs, mofs, and a great many more, becaufe they, being very fmall, and of flow growth,
are eafily over-charged with a plethory, from whence
the fibres of the plant, nay even of it's very feeds
whilft in the ground, muft burft.

WATER and WATERING.

§. 1. IT is but of little purpofe to depend on a pond's holding, becaufe it is dug in a ftrong clay, if there be no great fhade, over it; for the fun and froft will quickly open it, and the water will run away; but fuch pond muft be made with four fquare flopes, and covered with gravel, or a mortar-earth, four or five inches on the tops, which, cattle treading in, will cement with clay, and bind, and will not crack with the fun and froft; but no-thing fuffers more by either than mere clay. *Of making a pond.*

§. 2. I begin to fufpect (in my hill-country farm, where I have no ponds but what are pitched, and where I have my backfide-pond and the ftreet-pond, which both muft necesfarily be fometimes ftained with dung) that, of your great cattle efpecially, it is of confequence to buy thofe that have been bred in the hill-countries, where they have been ufed to want water more than they will with me, and have been ufed to drink our pond and ciftern water; for I find cattle that have been ufed to fpring or river water, do drink very fparingly of our water; and then I am fure they cannot thrive or fat well. *Water proper for cattle.*

§. 3 Foul water, as Grew obferves, will breed the pip in hens, and naftinefs, lice and fcabs in kine; *Foul water pernicious to cattle, &c.*
and

1

and all creatures, swine themselves, which love dirt, yet thrive best when kept clean.

Watering cattle.

§. 4. Farmer Elton, late of Crux-Easton, extolled the convenience of the pond I made in my field to a high degree ; he said, that by means of that pond I need not fear the driest year, for, if I had no grass and did put a hay-reek in the field, my sheep would be all the summer mutton, when others would be carrion.

Farmer Collins (in the Isle of Wight) was speaking of the great necessity of having convenient water for cattle at all times, both for their health and increase of their milk, and how insufficient it was for cattle to be drove to water but twice a day, whereas the cattle would possibly drink five times a day : and he said, that hard weather came one winter when he had lambs, and was forced to fodder his ewes with hay, and the water where they drank was frozen hard over ; three or four lambs of a day died away, and the ewes had not milk for them ; at last he bethought him to break the ice of the pond, which when he had done the sheep came to the water with great eagerness, and went in above their bellies and drank, and no more lambs died.

Water proper for watering plants.

§. 5. Worlidge, fo. 248. speaking of different waters, says, it is a very great injury to most tender plants, to be diluted with cold water from the well or spring ; it checks their growth exceedingly, as may be seen by a bleeding vine, to the naked roots of which if you pour store of spring or cold water, it suddenly checks the ascending of the sap, by means whereof the bleeding ceases, and the wound consolidates again, before the more liberal ascent of the sap : much more then will it check the growth of a weak herb or flower.

Rain and snow-water.

§. 6. Rain-water seldom sinks above a foot deep, but water of snow two or three feet deep, as being

much

much heavier than rain-water; and as it melts slowly and by degrees, from the undermost part of the mass of snow, so it soaks with more ease, not being hindered by the wind or sun.———Therefore (says Monsieur de Quinteney) as I dread much snow upon moist strong grounds, and order it to be removed from about the fruit-trees, so in dry earth I gather it as a magazine of moisture to the southern expositions. fo. 29.

§. 7. Worlidge, fo. 248. says, it is observed to be the best to sow in the dusts, whereby the seeds *Watering seeds.* gradually swell, from the cold dews of the night and from the air, and are made ready to sprout with the next rains. So it is not good to water new-sown seeds till the long defect of showers invite you to it; some seeds, as radish, lettuce, gilliflower-seeds, &c. remain not long in the earth, and therefore may in two or three days, for want of rain, be watered; but tulips, auricula, parsley, carrot-seed, &c. lie long in the ground, and require not so speedy an irrigation.

§. 8. It is better to water a plant seldom and thoroughly, than often and slenderly, for shallow *Of watering plants.* watering is but a delusion to a plant, and provokes it to a root shallower than it otherwise would, and so makes it more obnoxious to the extremity of the weather. Mortimer, fol. 455.

§. 9. The reason, I conceive, why plants or trees once begun to be watered in the heat of the summer *Of watering trees.* must be continued on, otherwise it is worse than if they had not been watered at all, is not because a tree once watered needs it the rather, but because watering in the heat of summer makes the ground subject to chop the more when dry, and therefore such ground must be kept moist.

Mr. Bobart, of the physick-garden in Oxford, says, that it would be a very good way, in dry summers,

mers,

mers, (where water can be had) to water all forts of fruit-trees, for fake of the fruit-buds and bearing fhoots, and fhoots of the wood for the following year, which are all formed in the Auguft before ; which do miferably fail by reafon of the drought.

I have heard it reported more than once, how conftant and great burthens of fruit orchards have had, where the owners had power of throwing the water over them ; of this it feems the antients, particularly Cato, had a great opinion, when (in book 1ft. de Re ruftica) next to the vineyard, he gave the preference to hortus irriguus ; it is no wonder if they foon found out the benefit of the command of water to trees in hot countries ; it feems to be expreffed by Cato, as if an orchard was no orchard without it ; and though our clime ftands not fo abfolutely in need of watering, yet by this hint we may conclude how, in fome hot fummers, and dry grounds, an orchard is of little value without fuch convenience.

§. 10. Want of rain at bloffoming-time often makes the bloffoms drop ; by watering thefe trees have bore abundantly when none others did. Mortimer, fol. 529.

Of watering fruit-trees in bloom.

Of watering apples when the fruit is fmall.

§. 11. This exceeding dry fummer I obferved apples were rather fmaller than ufual, which Stevens of Pomeroy, my tenant, perceiving, and that his trees were well loaden, he in good time began watering his trees often, pouring down leifurely two or three buckets full of water to each tree : which bounty his trees foon began to be fenfible of ; for whereas before, his and his neighbours leaves of their apple-trees were pale and fhrivelled, his foon recovered a ftrong deep colour, and he was very fenfible his apples looked of a livelier fairer colour, and grew larger.

WORKMEN

WORKMEN and WORK.

§ 1. TAKE care to man the hay-harvest with enough people, for I find, by understanding farmers, that it helps to the dispatch mightily, if it be any thing of a good hay-making day, to turn even the grass swarths that same day.

The not well manning a harvest, has either of these three effects, viz. that corn is over-ripe, or being cut down, is not carried in without damage, or is cut down too soon, for fear lest it should all ripen together on you; the disadvantages of the two first are very apparent; and for the disadvantage of the latter, your corn shall yield two shillings in the quarter less than if it had been properly ripe : and two men extraordinary are many ways needed, both to carry on sowing, dung-carting, thatching reeks, or odd necessary things.

§. 2. Whereas men's hands are not only wanted in harvest-time, but in seed-time also, therefore great care ought to be taken by forecasting, to do all works before those times, which otherwise must of necessity be done then; therefore let no thatching, carpentry work, mending of hedges, or other work, whereby the labourer may be called off, be delayed till then; which will not only put you in a hurry for want of men, some of whom may be such indifferent workmen as you would not employ but on necessity, but hereby you are obliged to be often calling off the labourers from the works they should stick close to, whereby you cannot so easily take an account of their works.

Take care how you bring yourself under two dilemmas at the same time in your husbandry : as for example, to be under equal inconveniencies if wood-carting is not performed to-morrow, and ploughing

or

or fowing, when you have but one team to fupply
thefe double duties : or again, to be obliged to keep
folding your whole flock, becaufe you cannot otherwife manage the corn you have undertaken, when
another way you fuftain as great a lofs by the not
having the liberty of making the beft of your lambs
and old fheep, by fatting them to a good advantage : if you run yourfelf into fuch inconveniencies
daily, it will daily take off a confiderable part of
your profits : and though you take the beft care to
free, and make yourfelf eafy from fuch incumbran-
ces, the nature of hufbandry will unavoidably force
fuch difficulties too often upon you ; for there are
critical feafons offering themfelves for fome things
to be done, in which one would be glad to have
three times the number of men and horfes, that are
requifite in courfe, to carry on the bufinefs of the
farm.

Leave
nothing
for winter
that may
be done in
fummer.

§. 3. Avoid all manner of winter work as much
as poffible (except the direct hufbandry of ploughing) all cartings wear out your plough-timber abundantly, foul and wear out your lanes, unlefs frofty ;
and fo many lets happen by bad weather, that man
and horfe often, for a long time, earn not half their
pay : bring not yourfelf therefore under neceffities
of winter work, by picking up ftones for highways,
which you muft be neceffitated to remove becaufe of
your ploughing up the ground; by leaving any ways
undone in fummer, that muft be repaired in winter;
one load of ftones in fummer going farther than two
in winter, and then carting to that end hurts the
ways as much as mends them : let your hedges,
where damage may arife, be therefore well in repair
before winter, that there be no works of neceffity in
wood-carting : let all carpenters work, bricklayers
work, pitching or paving work, be forefeen in fummer, that by bad weather and fhort days they may

not

not lose half their time in winter: bad wet weather in the winter is not fit for any sort of carting, such as wood, dung, chalk, &c. (but to plough white land in the hill-country, and in moderate frosts you ought to be fallowing) and if you leave such work undone, depending on the winter, you will be at a much greater loss to finish it, on account of unseasonable weather, than you will be at a loss how to employ yourself in case the hardest snow and frosts come: for then there may be dung and chalk-carting, carting stones in heaps, which may be took up by the shovel: going to the best markets that are farthest; and no ingenious contriver, be the frost never so long, can be at a loss to invent work for that season fully to employ him.

§. 4. The labourer's lazy time for work, when *When* they want the master's eye most over them, is about *workmen do least* three weeks or a month before harvest, when work *work.* of all sorts grows scarce, hay-making and faggoting, and dung-carting being over, and most other works out of season; then they are apt to spin out their time, and linger it on to harvest, that they may not want employ.

§. 5. I advise every farmer to employ a nimble, *Of jobs.* active, and free-labouring man, in such business as consists in jobs and fractions, and employ the dull heavy man, if such he employs, to single works, such as threshing, &c. whereof an account can be kept; for a lazy lubbard will lose half his time in the vacancies between one work and another, if you employ him in many in the day.

Of the FARM-YARD, &c.

§. 1. MR. Raymond advised me to fence about *Of a mud-* my backside with a mud-wall; he said, *wall.* it was not only ornamental, but the cheapest and moſt ſerviceable of any ; he gave but ſixpence per lugg or pole of a foot high, and two feet and half broad : but indeed, if he made it nine feet high, he gave five ſhillings and ſix pence for nine lugg of that height : he added, that in keeping my cattle warmer by ſuch a wall I might ſave half my fodder.

Of the ſtable.
§. 2. When I ſhewed ſeveral underſtanding farmers my ſtables that were building, and told them I propoſed but four horſes on a ſide, whereas in my farmer's ſtables they allowed ſix horſes to thoſe dimenſions, and would reaſon it to be ſufficient, by ſaying the horſes would not lie down all together, and it was ſufficient for the ſtanding ; they all replied, they hoped I was wiſer than to regard them ; that too narrow room might be the ſpoiling of a horſe, whoſe value might pay for the enlargement.

H O G S.

Marks of a good hog.
§. 1. THE marks of a good hog among the antients, according to Varro and Columella, were a ſmall head, ſhort legs, long bodies, large thighs and neck, and the briſtles on the laſt mentioned part thick ſet, erect, and ſtrong. In Wiltſhire they look on huge heavy lop-ears in a pig, as a very good ſign of his making a great hog.

Spayed and gelt ſhutes.
§. 2. I aſked Sir Ambroſe Phillipps's ſhepherd, whether the country people made any difference in the price between ſpayed and gelt ſhutes, provided, in other reſpects, they were equally good ; he ſaid, they would not draw out the gelt ſhutes unleſs they had a better price, though he knew no other difference, but that the gelt pigs would be the maſters over the ſpayed, and ſo fare better, and conſequently thrive better.

Signs of an unthriving ſhute.
§. 3. A gentleman in my neighbourhood bought half a dozen young ſhutes (of about nine ſhillings value) ;

value) ; when they were bought I thought them big enough for the money, but did not like their shapes, being not long and strait, but their rump bones rising a little ; but what was the worst sight and omen, these hogs, though of little bodies, had long hairs and bristles : he kept them three months, gave them four bushels of vetches, and very good keeping ; then put them up for porkers, and gave each a sack of peas, and would then be glad to sell them for the prime cost, and the price of the peas they had eat, so little did they thrive : the length of their hair I take to be an ill sign, when their bodies are not proportionable, for it shews the hogs have had some check, which notwithstanding hinders not the bristles from growing, no more than sickness does a man's hair or nails : and one had better buy hogs in a backside than in market ; for one cannot see so well what is a proveable hog in a market as one can in the backside, when he is among those of the same litter, and the most proveable pig is cheapest, though dearest at first cost.

§. 4. The breed of pigs I had of farmer Stephens of Pomeroy in Wilts, which were used there to whey and grafs, being removed to Crux-Easton, where their food was corn and wash, did bring but three, four, or five pigs at a farrow, and so the descendants of them continued to do for three or four years, which I impute to their degeneracy, for want of the same food they and their parents had been used to.
Of hogs degenerating.

§. 5. [a] Varro says, we may judge of the fruitfulness of a sow from her first litter ; for she generally brings about the same number ever afterwards.
Fruitfulness of hogs.

§. 6. I kept four sows, but soon grew weary of their farrows, for to a boy or other servant, that is to feed them, a great deal of corn is to be committed,
Keeping sows unprofitable;

---

[a] Sus ad fœturam quam fit fœcunda animadvertunt ferè ex primo partu, quod non multum in reliquis mutat. Varro. fo. 56.

both

both on account of the sows and weaned pigs, and in the favour that must be used to them when they come to be shutes : if such servant either gives them not enough, or your corn waftingly, or neglects them some hours, either thro' idleness, or being otherways employed; in either of these ways, the profit of breeding these creatures is lost; and if we make up the account how much corn the sow eats us, the weaned pigs, and shutes, they eat out their heads; especially considering, that in every year you keep your sow you lose twenty shillings, inasmuch as a pig ought to pay so much, and, when you kill your sow, the bacon is nothing near so good : I infer from hence, that it is no ways proper for a gentleman to be a breeder of pigs, or other young creatures, as poultry, calves, &c. any farther than a conveniency is to be regarded, but rather leave them to farmers wives, who can tend them themselves punctually in all respects; nor can I apprehend the profit to be any thing to them, notwithstanding their offa corn, which they might sell : we say a sow will undo a poor man, and we observe they never keep them notwithstanding they may feed them with their own hand, and see nothing be lost.

I find great inconveniency by having four sows this year, not only on account that the greater pigs are the more neglect d, such attendance must be on the little pigs, but also on account of the harvest coming on, ag inst which time, and in which time, a boy's b finess should be to give the birds disturbance, and break them off their haunts, and drive the drove of pigs early into the field a leasing, at which season his time is lost (which is too precious to fling away) in breakfasting the little ones; besides, at that time a spare hand is very useful, for an hour or two, in the garden, when no weeders can be had.

§. 7. They

§. 7. They count in Wiltshire, breeding of pigs not to make so quick a return as buying in of Welch pigs, and fatting them off with whey as fast as they can: a pig bought in will in six weeks, or two months, be very good bacon, or pork, and pay at least eighteen pence or two shillings per week. In Wiltshire they order it so, that the sows farrow not till May, because their dairy comes not in till then; but he that intends to keep no cows, must order so that his sows farrow six weeks before harvest, that at harvest the pigs may be able to go into the field.

A certain dame was commending the breed she had of sows and pigs; I replied, I thought them to be the smallest sort; she said, the farmer could not abide the great large sort: I asked her what was his fancy for that; she said, that the pigs, that were farrowed in March, of the greater sort, would not make porkers in winter, for they would keep on growing still instead of growing fat.

Besides the trouble of breeding pigs, it is well to be considered, whether you can maintain the young shutes as well as the old ones between the leasing of the harvest and fatting, for, if not, you must be forced to thresh out barley the sooner, when most likely it is the cheapest; nor likely is there more waste corn in the field than the great hogs of a farmer can pick up.

§. 8. Sir Ambrose Phillipps had a hog, which they thought to be gelt, and put him up to fatting, but he never fatted kindly, and, when they came to kill him, they found his stones in his back; his bacon shrunk and eat strong: the shepherd says this is common to lambs, which when, at cutting-time, they find, they fat them up; it is common, he says, also to horses.

§. 9. They give the sows in Leicestershire, that they may take boar the sooner, a good piece of leaven

ven once in twenty-four hours, for two or three times : it is nothing but the green dough made as common leaven.

§. 10. I was going to buy a sow and pigs, and consulted several persons about the managing them, who acquainted me of these particulars, viz.—First, That a young sow, as this was but a year old, would bring but small pigs.——— Secondly, That being a young sow, and having so many as nine pigs, it could not be expected any of them would be so properly fat for roasters, as if she had brought but four or five.——— Thirdly, That this sow had come too early for most farmers keeping, though, if they had keeping for them, it was best of all, because, if not stunted, they would be young bacon within the year. ———Fourthly, That such young pigs, and other lean pigs, should not have their bellies full given them at first of sweet whey, for by that means they often burst their bellies.——— Upon which I asked a Wiltshire dairy-woman about it, and she said, she never knew them break their bellies ; but one of our Hampshire women replied, it was because in their country they skimmed the cream off to make whey-butter, which took off from the lusciousness.

[b] Varro's rule is to save as many pigs as the sow has teats : if she brings fewer, says he, she is a bad breeder, and not profitable to keep, and if she brings more, it is very extraordinary.

If a sow be high in case when she farrows, I am informed, she will be apt to eat her pigs. The first farrow of a sow is accounted the worst.

§. 11. I told a notable dame in Wiltshire, that I thought to give my sow and pigs bean-flour, instead

[b] Parcere tot oportet porcos, quot mammas habeat, si minus pariat, fructuariam idoneam non esse ; si plures pariat, esse portentum. Varro, fol. 56.

of barley-flour ; she said bean-flour was best, and
would breed most milk ; but when she gave them
barley-flour, she used to have some oats ground
with it.

§. 12. Whey is more nourishing to pigs than
skim-milk.

§. 13. I had little pigs of about six weeks old
newly weaned ; my bailiff was of opinion they
would turn up the meadows and corn-land, and dig
worse than older pigs (it was then just the opening
of the stubble) he asked me why I did not ring them,
for by that means the sow would not endure them to
hang on her ; for the pigs, though weaned, did run
after the sow and would be lugging her teats ; he
said it was a common thing to ring the pigs they
designed to wean, in order the sooner to wean them,
for, being ringed, the sow would be hurt by their
sucking, and so forsake them sooner.

The smith came to ring my little pigs ; I attended the operation ; he said he never spoiled a pig in
his life, which put me upon asking the question,
whether pigs were ever hurt by ringing ; he replied,
yes, often ; for, said he, if you run them through
the gristle of the snout, which lies on the bone and
beneath the fleshy part, the pigs noses will often
swell and rancle so as to kill them ; therefore great
care must be taken that the ring be only run through
the fleshy ridge of the snout : again, said he, if the
ring be twisted too close to the snout, so that it binds
too hard, and cannot run round with ease to the
pigs, their snouts will swell, in which case the rings
must be taken off, and the snouts anointed to give
them ease.

Ring not a sow with pig, lest in the dispute she
cast her pigs, nor endeavour to take an oat-hull out
of a cow's eye forward in calf, lest she warps.

X 4   §. 14. May

§. 14. May the 17th, 1700, farmer Elton cut
and fpayed his pigs, which were fixteen weeks old;
the fame day, by the fame gelder, farmer Biggs,
my neighbour, fpayed his, which were fix or feven
weeks old: they did very well, and fell to their meat
prefently; but farmer Elton's pitched, and would
not come to their meat, nor eat of wafh, when they
called them to it. till the fifth day, at which time
they began to feed; the farmer thought he fhould
have loft them; I afked dame Biggs what fhe thought
could be the meaning that there fhould be that difference between their pigs; fhe faid, poffibly farmer
Elton's might be too hoggifh and rank, and then
they are apt to pitch; now I had obferved, before
they were cut, that they were apt to ride one another: upon this, I enquired of an underftanding
farmer, when he thought it was beft to cut and fpay
pigs; he faid, the boar-pigs, the fooner the better,
if it was in a fortnight or ten days, as foon as their
ftones were come down; there was the lefs danger,
and they would pitch the lefs upon it; nay, if a pig
was cut in that time, defigned for roafting it would
be never the worfe: as to a fow pig, faid he, they
cannot be fpayed under five, fix or feven weeks old,
and then is the time for it; in two or three days after
this I came into Wiltfhire, and afked farmer Pain
the fame queftions, and he agreed to what the farmer
laft mentioned had faid.

I had little pigs cut and fpayed the 3d of September; it was agreed it was not fit to defer it, becaufe
the weather would foon grow too cold, and, when
they are cut or fpayed, they muft be kept moving
and walking for three or four hours, left by laying
down too foon, they fhould fwell.

If pigs be cut (or efpecially if fpayed) they ought
not to be fuffered to creep through hedges, left the
thread which fows up the fpaying hole, be drawn

out,

out, or the place bruised ; nor ought they under a fortnight's time, in such case, to be ringed, lest they struggle and hurt themselves.

A sow-gelder that had cut for me, cut four pigs for a neighbouring farmer, and the pigs happened to be broken-bellied, and they died on the spot, their guts coming out at their cods: I asked whether it was usual for pigs to be bursten-bellied ; they said, yes ; and that if they were cut young, they do often not perceive it, but if they did, they should forbear to cut such pigs, or, when cut, should take great care to sew up the skin.

If a boar-pig be cut or gelt, his tusks do not grow, which seems to shew a strange consent of parts between the stones of a boar and his tusks ; and this seems to hold vice versâ ; for this month (September) I broke the tusks of a large, fierce, and most venereous boar, which before was riding all the gelt and spayed pigs in the backside, and would all the days and nights lie close to the sow that was brimming, having at that time seven sows, and would go over walls and pales after them, five feet high, but when his tusks were broke, he begun, from that time, to abate his venery, and carried much less regard to them, and grew dull in his courage ; I take the more notice of this [c], because I observe the antients took the like notice of the relation between the cock's stones and his spurs.

They told me it was common among the pig-jobbers to put off a farrowing sow for a spayed sow, by cutting a slit in her side, and sowing it up again ; I asked what that cheat availed the seller ; they said,

---

[c] Of making capons (says Columella, lib. 4. cap. 1. fol. 185.) semimares, capi, qui hoc nomine vocantur, cum sint castrati, libidinis abolendæ causâ, nec tamen id patiuntur amissis genitalibus, sed ferro candente calcaribus inustis, quæ cum igneâ vi consumpta sunt, facta ulcera, dum consanescant, figulari cretâ linuntur.

such a sow was worth less by two shillings or half a crown than a spayed sow, for there is hazard in spaying.

A sow will not fat, unless spayed before put up to fatting but will be continually riding the other hogs, and hinder them also from fatting ; wherefore it is common to spay them a fortnight before.

It was July the 25th. and the sow-gelder was with me to have spayed my sows (for it seems that is a good time in order to their fatting before harvest) ; but we thought them rank, that is, desirous of the boar, and so we would not let him undertake it, for we look on it to be two to one but in such case it will kill the sows.

It is generally said, that it is good to spay a sow two or three days before her litter of pigs are weaned, because in case she should take harm, the pigs will draw off the venom ; or, without being spayed, she may be fatted at Michaelmass, because being young with pig will not hurt her.

Of turnips for hogs.

§. 15. I was telling a person of great repute in husbandry matters, that I could not make my pigs, in the winter, eat turnips, which was a great loss to me, for I could not keep so good a winter stock as I otherwise should ; but he assured me, he kept, one winter, a great many pigs by turnips ; he said, he mixed some bran with them, and scalded the turnips, but, said he, they will not eat the scalded turnips without bran.

Of grains.

§. 16. In managing hogs a gentleman has a good advantage above the farmer in this respect, inasmuch as in March (when the corn is almost threshed out) great store of drink may be brewed, with the grains of which many pigs may be maintained till the middle of May, when the broad-clover comes in ; and in October another great brewing may be had, to supply a great quantity more of grains, so as to

maintain

I

maintain porkers (if pork in October and Novem-vember fells cheap) till December and January, when it is more likely to fell dear, for pork at the fore-hand of the year, viz. September, October, and November, is likely to be cheap, inafmuch as the gleanings of the harveft do raife the porkers to a great height, at which height they muft be killed, becaufe they cannot be maintained at it.

§. 17. It is a common thing to fow half an acre of goar-vetches for hogs, where farmers keep a great many, and they will eat them greedily, if the goar-vetches run grofs, and you give them to them when grofs, and before they run far in flower. Goar-vetches good for hogs.

§. 18. In Wiltfhire they count vetches too hot a food to give pigs, which is apt to give them the meafles; and therefore they mix corn with them. Mr. Ray fpeaking of the vetch fays, fol. 900. they are ufed in England as food for horfes mixed with peas and oats; and adds, as peas are loofening, and of great virtue, fo vetches are binding, and have no good virtues. Vetches too hot for hogs.

§. 19. I find broad-clover not only excellent for keeping pigs to a height in March and April, in which months the farmers corn is gone, and the dairy not come in, but alfo excellent for heightening up porker fhutes, after the gleanings of the harveft is over, all the months of September, October, and part of November, at which time pork is at the cheapeft, becaufe the harveft has fatted fo many, which people muft fell, becaufe, after the gleanings are over, they cannot maintain them; whereas, by the help of this clover, with fome little other helps, the porker fhutes may be kept on longer. Broad-clover good for pork-ers.

§. 20. I afked fome farmers of experience, if pigs would not take the fame damage by broad-clover as cows; they replied, that the full-grown pigs would thrive exceedingly with it, and be good pork, Bread-clover fwells young pigs.

pork, but that it would scour the young pigs, tho'
of twelve, thirteen, or fourteen weeks old, and
make them swell as big as two, but they never
knew it kill them; on the whole it was agreed,
that hogs will grow very fat by broad-clover, yet
they never care that their young shutes and pigs
should eat much of it, for it not only swells them
for the present, but makes them pot-bellied.

Henbane good for hogs.

§. 21. Henbane is beneficial and nutritive to
hogs (as Dr. Mead observes, in his Essays on
poisons) tho' it kills poultry.

Warm wash in winter.

§. 22. If any person in the winter time keeps
thirty or forty hogs, as I and many hill country
farmers do, I do advise, if they have the building
of their own hog-houses, wherein are their cisterns
for their hog-wash (of which I have one holding
about eight hogsheads) to set up a copper also and
furnace therein, handy to put in the wash, which
may heat the wash for the hogs in the winter; I
find it to be very profitable.

Nuts bad for hogs.

§. 23. A butcher this day (September the 3d)
wanted to buy some porkers and bacon hogs of me;
my corn-ersh was just eaten up by them, so I told
him I would gladly have parted with some of them,
if I had not hoped they would take to the nuts,
which were in abundance in my coppices; he replied, the nuts would hurt them; nuts would make
their fat soft and greasy, so that it would boil away,
and nuts, being so sweet, would make them so
sweet mouthed, that the lean ones would not take
to their wash when the nutting season was over, nor
those, that are to be fatted, to their peas; and they
would lie in the coppices whilst any nuts lasted,
though there were not a tenth part enough to maintain them, or to keep them from pitching: my
cook said, all this was true; she knew it to be so
by experience: I asked her how she knew this: she
said

said she had lived in families that had had the expe-
perience of it, and had heard many say to the same
effect: my woodman and other labourers do agree
in it; but they add however, that, if such bacon
be put in the pot boiling a gallop, it will make it
boil firm.

§. 24. Farmer Collins of the Isle of Wight as- Hemlock-
sures me, that if the pigs meet with a piece of hem- root poisons
lock-root, in their digging up and down, be it ne- hogs.
ver so little, they will be perfectly mad, and jump
as high as an ordinary chimney-piece, and it is
great odds but they die.

§. 25. Mr. Edwards chid his man for suffering Not to let
his pigs to lie at night in the dung of the backside, hogs lie in
and for not accustoming to chace them to their night.
stye: I asked him what was the reason for it; he
said, their lying in the dung was not accounted
wholsome for them; for the heat of the dung made
them so tender, that they would not endure the
cold so well, nor thrive with their meat so well.

§. 26. Mr. Edwards, and my neighbouring far- Of fatting
mer, and I, were discoursing upon hogs; Mr. hogs.
Edwards said, the farmer kept hogs in too good a
condition before he put them up to fatting; the
farmer replied, there would be the more lean, and
therefore the bacon the better; for lean must be a
long time making in a hog, and if a lean hog were
soon fatted up, though you might raise him to
what degree of fatness you pleased yet such fat
would shrink and boil away: the farmer said, the
great cotshill-pea is much the best pea for fatting hogs, and a quarter of them would go much
farther than a quarter of the others, the which they
would not swallow whole, as they would many of
the partridge-peas. The underling hog put up
with the rest, is longest a fatting, being beat off by
the rest, so makes the fattest bacon; that bacon
therefore they generally keep for beans.

At

At Newbury I met farmer White of Catmore; we talked of fatting pigs; I said I believed beans to be as good to fat with as peas; he said, he thought so too, and many persons about him did fat with them; he thought change was very good, which kept them up to their stomachs, and said, you must begin with beans, for after peas he thought they would not eat beans, peas being the sweeter food; he and farmer Stockwell did both seem to agree (that in reason, though they never tried it) the flour of beans or peas would fat better than the whole grain.

I find farmer Farthing, and my tenant farmer Wey of the Isle of Wight, without regard to the price of peas, be they cheaper or dearer, do still fat with ground oats, and barley, and do allow a bushel of barley to a sack of oats; they say, the reason for allowing barley to the oats is to make them both grind, for otherwise, I conceive, the mill could not be set fine enough to grind the oats by themselves: they assure me, the hogs will fat thus much sooner than with peas, but, I suppose, if peas could be ground, it would alter the case, for hogs seem very voracious of peas, and to chuse the pea-stubble beyond any other; they fling also into the trough, when they feed them, if there be many of them, a handful of bay-salt, but if that be not to be had, other salt, which makes them drink very much, and contributes to their quicker fatting.

In discourse with farmer Bristow, I observed, that the smaller peas were sweetest, and discernable so to our taste, and the small grey partridge particularly sweeter than the great partridge, and therefore, tho' the great partridge was always dearest, yet the lesser would fat a hog sooner. He said, his father, who lived near Reading, and the farmers thereabouts, gave their hogs the white boiling pea, and that they fatted much sooner; I answered, undoubt-
edly

edly the blue pea (which of all field-peas is the sweetest) would for the same reason fat hogs soonest; he replied, no; for he could assure me, that about Reading they had tried them, and had found they made the hogs scour; therefore it seems they are too luscious and cloying.

Farmer William Sartain of Wilts came to see me at Easton, June the 8th, and I carried him into my corn, and shewed him several sorts of peas I had sowed, viz. great grey partridge, or Windsor-greys, Burbage-popling, and blue peas; the farmer assured me, that though blue peas, if they boiled well, would sell for most on that account, yet the grey-partridge would fat hogs better than the Burbage-popling, or blue-pea, as he had observed on experience; and he said also, that though the popling and blue pea seemed sweeter, yet the hogs would prefer the great partridge to them, as he had often experimented, by laying all three sorts in distinct troughs before them.

Mr. Smith of Stanton, a very experienced farmer, assures me, that the best way of fatting hogs is thus; viz. to give them, when they are first put up, rough corn, or peas wads, that they may work upon the halm, which when they have done for two or three days, he then gives them threshed peas in troughs, and also a service, once or twice a day, of wash; and this he continues to do for two or three days, and then he plies them in the usual way, with peas altogether and water; by this means they are not at first glutted and surfeited, but kept to a coming stomach, and are by degrees initiated to a full diet.
——However, it is agreed that hogs should be well swilled with wash before they are put up for fatting, otherwise they will make themselves sick for two or three days.

I observed two pigs, after they had been about
three

three weeks in fatting, to look very lank in the flank; notwithſtanding this it was agreed they were very fat; and that pigs would bluff and ſwell much with their feeding the firſt ſix or ſeven days, and look fatter to the eye than afterwards; for, when they gather fat inwardly in their bellies, the weight of it draws down their bellies, and makes them look thinner and lanker.

Of fatting a boar. §. 27. A boar is fit to be killed when leſs fat than a hog; for all the ſoft fat between the fleſh and the horn will be, for the moſt part, boiled away, therefore to no purpoſe to make it very fat.

If any gentleman keeps a boar for fatting, I adviſe him to be provided with another young boar to brim the ſows, againſt the time he put up the old one to fatting; for by experience I find, that, though the fatting-boar be penned up at ſome diſtance from the backſide, and out of the road of the hogs, and hedged out from them, yet the brimming ſows will rig over or under hedges to him, or labour ſo long at the gates till they ſhall open them, and, if they once get to the outſide only of his pen, it does the boar more harm than a fortnight's meat will do him good.

Of a gelt hog and a ſow. §. 28. Mr. Edwards and others I find do agree, that a gelt hog fattens moſt in the back, and a ſow in the belly.

Not to ſend fat pigs a leaſing. §. 29. About Holt in Wiltſhire, the farmers never uſed to turn their forwardeſt pigs into the cornfields, for they, that were near half fat with whey, would never go a leaſing to any purpoſe, but would either come home again, or lie down under the hedges, ſo that they would come home worſe than they went out; therefore they uſually buy lean pigs againſt ſuch time.

Clean ſtraw for hogs in fatting. §. 30. Of hogs, ſays the Maiſon ruſtique, freſh ſtraw often given them doth fat them as much

as

as their meat, and you must take care their troughs
be always clean, fol. 147. Special care must be taken
that their meat be not cold, nor too thin, left it cause
them the flux in their bellies.   ᶜ Columella has the
like observation in regard to keeping them clean.

§. 31. In an acorn year the hogs will not thrive Of acorns.
proportionably on the mast, at the first part of the
season, as they will after wet has fallen, to make the
acorns * chissum, for then they are far more nourish- * Grow.
ing.——They are apt to scour hogs, when eat new
from the tree, and are not then so good, as when they
have laid in heaps to sweat.

§. 32. A sign to know if a hog be sick, is, when Signs of a
he hangeth his ears very much, and for your better sick hog.
certainty thereof, pull from him, against the hair,
a handful of bristles off his back, if they be clean
and white at the root, he is sound and healthful, but
if they be bloody or otherwise spotted, he is sick.
Maison rustique, fol. 149.

§. 33. The signs of a measled hog are blackish Of the
pustules under his tongue, and if he cannot carry measles.
himself upright on his hinder legs, and if his bristles
are bloody at the roots.   Maison rustique.—ᵈ Also
Florentinus in Geoponicis.—ᵉ Didymus tells us that
Democritus prescribed for this distemper in hogs,
bruised asphodel roots to be given to them mixed in
their food, and says it will cure them in less than
seven days.

§. 34. If a pig is hot in his body, which is to be Of the fe-
known from the driness of his dung ; two spoonfuls ver.
of

ᶜ Quamvis prædictum animal in pabulationem spurcitie ver-
sentur, mundissimum tamen cubile desiderat. Columella, lib. 7.
fol. 181.

ᵈ Qui ipsos emunt ex pilis de jubâ evulsis sanitatis ipsorum no-
tas sumunt ; si enim fuerint cruentati, morbum indicere aiunt,
puros contrarium. Florentinus in Geop. fol. 468.

ᵉ In quem casum Democritus physicus asphodeli radicis mo-
dicè tusæ minas tres cibo singulorum suum admiscere jubet, &

of sallad oil in a pint of warm milk, such as comes from the cow, will cleanse him, and bring him to his stomach again. [f] Didymus prescribes bleeding in the tail.

Of the murrain.

§. 35. Mr. and Mrs. Edwards say, the murrain in pigs (for as much as they can observe, and as their doctor for drenching tells them) proceeds from their being in too great proof, and case; many hold that musty corn will give them the murrain; as soon as they observe it in one, they drench all the rest.

It was the 25th of August I had a hog died of the murrain, and many hogs did die about the country; I had some powders to give them in their wash of grains, which I could not get them to eat of, it being stubble-time; my bailiff said, he could not ever, in the like case, get them to eat of grains, but the way was to give them it in skim-milk, and then they would eat it.

This (1705) was a wonderful dry summer, in which for three weeks we fetched water for our cattle; about the latter end of October I had a sow with pigs fell ill, and in a day or two after a fatting hog fell ill and died; we sent to the hog-doctor to drench all the hogs, who said, Mr. Whistler had lost six, and that they died in many places, and the cause of the murrain was the mighty dry summer, whereby the hogs had not water in plenty to drink, nor mire to roll themselves in: therefore after such dry summers drench hogs by way of precaution.

Of the leprosy.

§. 36. Mr. Boyle, in his Advantages of experimental philosophy, recommends antimony to cure the leprosy in swine, it being a great sweetener of the blood, and says also, it is very good to cure the worms in horses.

ante septimum diem integram sanitatem inde recuperaturos testatur. Didymus. fol. 470.

[f] Si febricitent, sanguis è caudâ emittendus. Didymus, ib.

§. 37. A

§. 37. A noted pig-doctor in Hampſhire adviſes me, if ever I bleed a pig in the tail, to cut off
his tail above the hocks, and rub it firſt, it will
bleed the better: pigs by having too little of their
tail cut off, eſpecially in the ſummer, when troubled
with flies, will be knocking it about their hocks,
and keep it bleeding ſo as to bleed to death. Note,
he ſays, the long-legged hogs, as it were double-
jointed at the knee, are of a breed ſubject to the
ſtaggers.

§. 38. We had a young pig of three quarters old;
we killed it for bacon; the farmer ſaid, though I
gave ſix ſhillings per ſcore, the pig eat him as much
peas as he was worth, for, ſaid he, a young pig,
though he makes the beſt bacon, yet fats not ſo faſt
as a pig of full growth, for his food runs into
growth.

§. 39. I bought a hog, and when it was ſwilled,
the farmer commended very much the ſwilling of
it, becauſe it was in no place burnt; whereupon I
aſked him if it was uſual to have them burnt; he
ſaid, where the hog was dirty there would be danger of it's burning, which in that place ſpoiled the
bacon.

The chief or only damage of burning a hog in
ſwilling is, that the bacon will be apt to ruſt there.

Care muſt be taken, after hogs are ſwilled, that
they be not bruiſed.

§. 40. Remember to provide a ſtock of ſalt in
the moſt dry ſeaſon of the ſummer, becauſe it will
come dry to you, and is at ſuch times always cheap-
eſt; for the ſalternes at ſuch times, being able to
make a greater quantity of ſalt than they have
ſtowage for, ſell it the cheaper.

§. 41. A hot fire in a chimney, which heats the
bacon, and then letting that chimney be without
fire again, makes the coat of such bacon slack, and
brings a rust into it.

P O U L T R Y.

Number of
hens to a
cock.

§. 1. COLUMELLA, speaking of cocks,
says, one cock is sufficient to five hens.

Hemp-seed
makes hens
lay.

§. 2. Mr. Ray says, hemp-seed is looked on to
make hens lay, even in winter, but to incline them
to so much fat as to prevent their kindly laying
after; it is pernicious to be given to singing birds
alone, without other seeds; it either kills them
with fat, or makes them dull in singing.—[a] The
antients were of opinion that the leaves of cytisus
made hens lay. As to the age, when hens are in
greatest perfection for laying eggs, they preferred
those of two years old.

Of eggs

§. 3. In pursuance of what I have remarked before in regard to the punctum saliens in seeds, viz.
that it is answerable to the sanguinea gutta in an
egg, and like that is a vital principle, which has
action antecedent to bare rules of matter, and is
owing purely to the will of God, suitable to
Moses in Genesis, I do conceive farther, that the
punctum saliens in a seed, as also the sanguinea
gutta in an egg, have each alike their systole and
diastole, that is, an opening and shutting in a
springy manner, and that, if the egg is heated, or
under incubation, the yelk being immediately attenuated by heat, does insinuate some of it's parts

[a] Cytisi folia viridia ipsas foecundissimas faciunt. Aptè ætate
ad parienda ova sunt anniculæ, maximè vero biennes, minus
his valent seniores. Florent. in Geop. fol. 379.

into

POULTRY. 341

into the opening of the heart or *sanguinea gutta* of
the egg, which in it's reciprocal shutting motion
squeezes the juices into the passages and first lines
already formed, although wonderfully short and
fine, which are the main branches of the bird ; thus
they are lengthened and thickened by each opening
and shutting, till the whole yelk is absorbed ; thus
the flour also in the seed is attenuated by moisture
and heat, till at length it is quite swallowed by the
punctum saliens, which like an engine casts it into
the vessels of the plant : these are the food both of
plant and animal.

Columella lays it down as a rule, that eggs ought
to be set at ten days old, whereas in England they
may be set well at thirty ; the reason is, because the
heat of the air in Italy is strong enough to act so on
the sanguinea gutta as to lengthen the fibres so far,
and to make such progress towards the growth of a
chicken, that the circulation to the extremity of
these fibres cannot be maintained, and consequently
not the nourishment of the chicken without a greater
heat, for want of which there is a failure, if not
committed to incubation ; but the air of our clime
works so slowly, that it scarce forwards it.

I asked a notable dame whether it was true, that
if a hen was kept too fat she would lay an egg
without a shell, and a lesser egg ; she said it was
true : I asked whether she had a hen sometimes
crow-trodden ; she said, her people would say so
sometimes, and such hen's feathers would stare ; it
fell commonly on a hen that was black, but Mrs.
Edwards affirmed, she had known it befall other
hens too ; they said it was incurable. I the rather
mention this, because Mr. Markham affirms it in his
book of husbandry, in his chapter of Poultry.

Y 3 Eggs

    [b] Eggs that are new laid may be known by their
roughneſs and whiteneſs, and if you hold them up to
the ſun, you will find a tranſparency in them, which
is not in eggs that have been ſat on two or three
days. If they are ſat on, Florentinus cautions us not
to ſhake them for fear of deſtroying their vital principle. Varro ſays the ſame, and adds, that addled
eggs will ſwim in water, and good ones will not.

Of ſetting
hens.

§. 4. [c] The antients, in many parts of huſbandry, had a very great opinion of the influence of the
moon, and accordingly in ſetting hens, Columella directs it ſhould be done from the tenth to the fifteenth
day of the moon's increaſe ; which is not only of

[b] Dignoſcantur ova, an quod in ipſis eſt fœcundum habeant,
ſi poſt quartum diem incubationis ad ſolis radium contempleris ;
ſi enim quid fibratum tranſiens apparuerit, & ſubcruentum ſit,
quod ineſt fœcundum erit ; ſi vero pellucidum erit, ceu ſterile
ejiciatur. Sed experimenti ſumendi gratiâ, ova non ſunt concu-
tienda, ne quod in ipſis vitale eſt corrumpatur. Floren. in Geo-
pon. fol. 379, 380, &c.——Ova plena ſint atque utilia necne
animadverti aiunt poſſe, ſi demiſeris in aquam, quod inane natat,
plenum deſidit.

Ova ſi incubantur, ſi habent in ſe ſemen pulli ; curator qua-
triduo poſtquam incubari cœperint, intelligere poteſt ; ſi contra
lumen tenuit & purum uniuſmodi eſſe animadvertit, putant ejici-
endum, & aliud ſubjiciendum. Varro, lib. 3. fol. 72.

As our author has given no directions for preſerving eggs, the
following ſhort note may perhaps not be impertinent. Some
dip them in hot fat, which, if care be taken that they are not
overheated by it, may be a good way ; but as eaſy and cleanly
a method as any, and I believe the ſafeſt, is, to beat up the
whites of eggs to an oil, and then to ſmear over the eggs you intend to preſerve with a camel's hair bruſh dipped in this liquor.
Take care that they are entirely covered with this varniſh, and I
am credibly informed it will keep them freſh above a twelvemonth.

[e] Semper autem, cum ſupponuntur ova, conſiderari debet ut
luna creſcente à decima uſque ad quintam decimam id fiat ; nam
& ipſa ſuppoſitio per hos fere dies eſt commodiſſima, & ſic admi-
niſtrandum eſt, ut rurſus cum excluduntur pulli, luna creſcat, diebus quibus animantur ova, & in ſpeciem volucram confirman-
tur. Columella, lib. 8. fol. 188.

                                        advantage,

advantage, fays he, to the increafe of the chickens
in the eggs, but by this means it will fo fall out, that
the chickens will be hatched alfo when the moon is
increafing, which will be a great benefit to them.

When a hen is ready to fit it may be found by the
feathering her neft, for fhe then begins to pull off
the feathers from her breaft, and to make her bed ;
and before fhe is ready to fit, if you would have her
fit in the place you defire, it is good to confine her
to that place before fhe has laid all her eggs, that by
laying an egg or two there, fhe may be reconciled to
it ; for, if her laying be out, and fhe has chofen another place, it will be hard to get her to fit to what
place you defire ; and it is better to let her fit in the
worft of places fhe fhall choofe, than to remove her
from the place fhe has once chofen. Columella directs to increafe the number of eggs you put under
hens as the weather grows warmer. fol. 187.

I find Pliny, Varro, &c. order, that the number
of eggs you fet under hens fhould be odd, without
affigning the reafon for it ; but Markham, fol. 112.
fays, the eggs will lie the rounder, clofer, and in even-
er proportion together.

§ 5. Many of our turkey-eggs and goofe-eggs
proved addled this year (1706) fo that we had very
ill-luck in hatching our feather'd fowl ; a maid,
who came juft after our ill-luck, faid the reafon
muft be, becaufe we ftill took away the eggs from
the hens as foon as they layed them, whereas, if their
eggs had been left, their defire of fitting had increafed, and they would have fat fooner ; therefore her
miftrefs did let the eggs alone : note, it will be
good therefore to pen up the hens foon after their
laying is over, and make their nefts and put eggs
into them.

§. 6. Chickens do better, and thrive much the
fafter for running about with the hen, not being
cooped

Of fetting
geefe and
turkeys.
See §. 13.

Of breed-
ing chick-
ens.

cooped up; for the hen having her liberty, scratch-
es up emmets, bugs, and worms, more agreeable
food than we can give them; but the hen, having
been cooped up, is very wild when set free, and
rambles at a strange rate, to the loss of her chickens,
nor makes she, when set free, a tender mother.

Of rearing chickens in winter.

§. 7. The princess's poulterer assured me, that
rearing early chickens by a kitchen-fire, as poor people did, was by no means a good way, for it was not
a natural warmth to them, and their flesh would
not eat well; that straw and the warmth of the
hen, but especially good meat in their bellies, was
the best means to support them in cold weather:
for outward warmth signifies nothing, if there be
not a good vital substance; and, said he, in feeding
little turkeys and chickens, you will find by experience they will feed better and thrive faster by peck-
ing off of your finger than from the ground; barley-meal is the heartiest and best food for them, and
cheese-curd a very hard food, that nourishes not nor
heartens, and therefore it is a great mistake in
housewives who give it.

Vetches not good for chick-ens.

§. 8. Farmers agree, that at the time of threshing their vetches, it is common to have the chickens,
almost as big as the old ones, die, being not able to
digest the vetches, which swell in their crops; and
even the biggest poultry will be sick with it.

Of a pul-let with egg.

§. 9. A pullet with egg is accounted very good
meat, but then I conceive it is about the beginning
of February, when they are but young with egg:
for on their first being with young all creatures
thrive, but the embryo growing big it preys on the
mother, and draws the moisture and nourishment
from her, which is the case of the pullets at this
time of the year, viz. the beginning of March.

Of geese.

§. 10. Mr. Cowslade of Woodhay tells me, notwithstanding the objection to geese on their tainting
the

the grafs, they are a great good to cattle, where lands are fubject to murrain; he fays the common of Emburn is the fame fort of land as that of Wood-hay, but in the court-leet at Emburn, fuch are prefented as put geefe in the common: yet the Wood-hay people take the liberty, and it is obferved, where one beaft dies of the murrain at Woodhay, ten die of it at Emburn. Salmon's difpenfatory fays, goofe-dung is excellent againft the green-fick-nefs, fcurvy, jaundice, dropfy, and gout.

Pliny fays of the goofe, they tread in the water; and Worlidge fays, it is obferved of geefe, that in cafe the waters are frozen up (as in fome hard winters they are) about their treading-time, then the moft part of their eggs will prove addled; the reafon is faid to be, becaufe the goofe proves more fruitful when fhe is trod by the gander in the water than if upon the land. fol. 175. Quære how it fares with thofe, who keep geefe where no water is, or where the ponds prove dry in treading-time.

Young geefe will never fat well when they are breeding their young feathers, for their feathers take off from their nourifhment.

§. 11. Of geefe, Columella fays, you fhould allow a gander to three geefe; for they are too heavy to ferve more [d]. *Three geefe to a gander.*

§. 12. The older the geefe, the fooner they lay, for which reafon an old goofe is more profitable in bringing earlier goflings, which yield the more money. Some fay, if the goofe be two years old it is as well as if more, but ducks will breed as well at one year old. *Old geefe breed ear-lieft.*

§. 13. Geefe love not to fit but upon their own eggs, at leaft the better part muft be their own; if *Of fetting geefe. See §. 5.*

---

[d] Singulis maribus ternas fœminas deftina; nam propter gra-vitatem plures inire non poffunt. Colum. fol. 193. & Palladius, fol. 59.

you

you take them from them at firſt, as they lay them, they will lay even to an hundred, till ſuch time as their fundaments ſtand gaping open, not being able to ſhut them, by their own laying. Maiſon ruſtique, fol. 107.

Of pen-
ning geeſe
and ducks
at night.

§. 14. I aſked a notable dame why ſhe penned up the ducks and geeſe, and the ducklings and goſlings at night; ſhe ſaid it was, in the firſt place, becauſe theſe laſt were young, and for fear the hogs ſhould meet with them, and eat them: I aſked her why there was not the ſame danger by day; ſhe ſaid, there was ſome danger, but not ſo much, the old one keeps them then, for the moſt part, in the water, and when they are penned up they are more ſecure from the ſtote: ſaid ſhe, we pen up the geeſe and goſlings much, by day, when young, becauſe the gooſe is not ſo careful as the duck of her young ones, but will keep with the gander and flock, and run up and down with them, inſomuch that the young ones, in following them, will frequently fall down dead on the ſpot: but the duck will keep with the young ones, without regard of the other ducks. I aſked another dame of theſe things next day, and ſhe agreed to it, and added, that, if pigs once took to eat up duck-lings and goſlings, they would never give over till they had eat up old ducks, and geeſe, and gan-der; the ſows particularly, if kept hungry, were very ſubject to it.

Ducks.

§. 15. Ducks, I am informed, generally lay in the night, wherefore a careful dame drives them then into a lower coop, and feels every one of them, in the morning during their laying time, to ſee whether they have laid that night, or whether they are full of egg ready to lay, if ſo, ſhe keeps thoſe in; if ſhe takes not this method, they lay about in ſo many holes, that ſhe is apt to loſe their eggs.

I was ſaying to a certain dame, that I thought
there

there was little profit in ducks and geese, for several
reasons, that there was little they could feed on, but
what the hogs did and could find out ; she replied,
that ducks, whilst pigs feed on corn, would follow
the pigs, and live very well on their dung; I asked
whether it was so with geese; she said, she had not
observed them to do it.

§. 16. This day (April the 24th) my servant was *Of ducks*
wondering to a dame in my neighbourhood that my *setting.*
ducks were not for sitting, notwithstanding they had
layed out their laying of eggs ; the dame replied,
that was no wonder, for she did not expect her own
ducks should sit under a month yet; for, said she,
ducks have two layings of eggs, and do not sit to
hatch till the last, which is about the middle of May;
if you will, said she, have early broodlings of ducks,
you must set the first layings under hens. Neither
the Rei rusticæ scriptores, nor Worlidge speak of
this. —— Note, (April the 12th, 1707) this day I
have two ducks that have been sitting this fortnight,
but this is not very common.

§. 17. Columella advises to put aftermass hay *Of fatting*
under fatting-poultry in their coops, for if they have *poultry.*
a hard bed they will not easily grow fat ; and to keep
them in a warm, close, and dark place, that they may
move as little as possible, for cold and motion are a
great hindrance to their fatting.

§. 18. In cramming turkeys and chickens, said *Of cram-*
the princess's poulterer, be sure you give them time *ming.*
to swallow before you give them more ; for, if you
cram it down too fast, they will not thrive with their
meat : he said further, that the prime season for a
pullet is before she has laid, or a week after, for
after that time the straining herself has so weakened her, that she pines, and her flesh eats not
well.

§. 19. In poultry, if you keep long in the same *Poultry de-*
strain, *generate.*

ftrain, the young ones will degenerate, and oftentimes die before they come to maturity ; it is the
fame with pigs and calves.

P I G E O N S.

Of the pi-
geon-
houfe. §. 1. IN pigeon-houfes, many build a lower
window in the wall under the eaves, to
open and fhut at difcretion, to let the young pigeons
of every latter breed (which are weakeft) out the
fooner, they being not ftrong enough to rife upright through the well of the houfe.

Some fay, there ought to be double the number
of holes at leaft, as you have hen-pigeons, befides
what are to be allotted for the cock ; becaufe the
hen-pigeon, whilft fhe has young ones in one hole,
will be building and fitting in another.

It is a great doubt whether it is beneficial to a pi-
geon-houfe, to keep the holes clean from the dung
and trumpery.

Varro ᵃ calls the pigeon a very cleanly bird, and
advifes to fweep the dove-houfe, and clean out the
filth frequently all the year round ; for the neater it
is kept the livelier the bird, adds Columella ; the
whole place, fays he, and even the holes, ought to
be white-wafhed, the pigeon being particularly fond
of that colour.—The Roman epicures had a cuftom
of breaking the legs of the young pigeons, that, not
being able to move, they might fat the better.

ᵃ Varro (lib. 3. dere ruftica, fol 70.) fays, permundæ funt enim
hæ volucres, itaque paftorem columbaria quotquot menfibus cre-
bro oportet everrere. Columella ait (lib. 8 fol. 190) totus autem locus, & ipfæ columbarum cellæ poliri debent albo tectorio,
quandoquidem eo colore præcipuè delectatur hoc genus avium.
Pulli fractis cruribus citius pinguefcunt, nam fracta crura non
plus quam bidui, aut ad fummum tridui dolorem afferunt, & fpem
tollunt evagandi. ib.

Nam quanto eft cultior, tanto lætior avis confpicitur. Columella, fol. 190.

Didymus

[b] Didymus directs us to hang up sprigs of rue at the entrance, and in many places of the dove-house, which, he says, is good to drive away vermin. The old authors agree in the same thing in regard to hen-houses.

§. 2. It has been a question with many, if dove-house pigeons pair or not, and keep true to their plighted love, which it seems to me they must do, because we often find in their hole a pair of eggs and a pair of hatched pigeons near fledged, which eggs are soon after hatched also, which could not well be, unless the cock fed the young ones whilst the hen sat. *Of pigeons pairing.*

§. 3. We had no rain all April and May, and had never so poor pigeons in that season; the reason seems to be, because the corn in the fields was dry, there having been no rain to moisten it: for young birds must have what is tender of digestion, and so we treat all sorts of poultry. *Dry weather bad for the breed.*

§. 4. Towards the end of the month of June, in the pigeons bennetting time, I entered my pigeon-house to see, in case there were any young ones, what seeds they had in their crops: I took half a dozen young ones; besides what corn they could here and there pick up, I found much charlock-seed, and the seeds of the common creeping crow-foot or butter-cups (in their crops) which is a small, flat, and sharp-pointed seed, (vid. Ray, fol. 581.) and afterwards did observe great flocks of pigeons to light in the fields, where that plant grew plentifully, at the time of it's feeding. *Of their feeding on the seeds of weeds.*

July the 19th I had a pigeon killed in the field, and opened his crop, which was full of the before-

[b] In fenestris & ostiis aliisque pluribus columbarii locis, rutæ ramulos deponito, & suspende; habet enim ruta naturalem quandam contrietatem ad bestias. In Geoponicis ex Didymo, fol. 773. lib. 14.

mentioned

mentioned butter-cup seeds, and fumitory-seeds, and nothing else, saving half a dozen bud-flowers of charlock, and two or three oats; I observed they were very voracious of these seeds; for I had three acres of arable, which had laid down to grass two years, and that had more butter-cups in it possibly than my whole farm besides, in which my whole flight of pigeons lay all day, and in a piece of wheat near my house, which had much fumitory in it; you may see, where these plants grow in fields near pigeons, the seeds picked off: they are therefore of great use in ridding the fields of weeds.

Of feeding pigeons. §. 5. It is not to be doubted, if you in winter feed your pigeons, but others from other dove-houses will come to the table in your dove-house, by observing them sleek, and in good liking, or by smelling the sort and plenty of food they have in their crops, as well as is elsewhere noted of rabbits.

Water necessary near a dove-house §. 6. A pigeon-house will not thrive unless very near water; not but the pigeons can go far for water for themselves, but their returns must be very frequent and quick for their young ones, who are wanting much water, and by carrying it far it will be dried up in their crops before they can bring it to their young.

B E E S.

Of bees in general. §. 1. WHATEVER you do to bees must be in the morning, and not at night by a light; for every bee that is disturbed and strikes against the light, is lost and chilled by lying out.

The honey-bee never draws it's honey from the broad clover, for it's proboscis is not long enough; it is the humble bee that feeds on that. The best provision for bees early against the spring, is by sowing turnips in August, which will flower in the spring,

from

from whence the bees extract abundance of honey : they draw abundance of honey also from the vetch-bloſſoms, but never lie on the pea.

A ſouth-weſterly expoſition is better than a ſouth-eaſterly ; for the ſouth-eaſterly calls the bees out too early in the morning, and in a ſouth-weſterly they will work an hour later at night. If a hive will not ſwarm, ſo that you are forced to raiſe the hive, you muſt be ſure, before winter, to take the prop from under the hive, and though they have worked down into the prop, the combs muſt be cut away, that the bees may lie cloſer and warmer, for the reaſon why a ſmart comes to nothing, is, becauſe they are too few in the hive.

§. 2. This day (September the 15th) I could not but recollect what Pliny ſays of flies, that they breath not from their mouths, but from porous parts of their bodies, in which opinion I was confirmed ; for a bee had fallen into my garden pond, and was labouring at the oar to get out ; I wondered to ſee, from the ſides of his body, divers quick curling ſtreams on the ſurface of the water, which extended two inches long from each ſide of the bee, and each ſtream was diſtinguiſhed and divided from the other like the points of a compaſs ; I ſaw plainly this could not be from his legs, and his wings laboured but little ; I was ſatisfied theſe ſtreams proceeded from the porous portals his labouring breath came out at, which iſſuing with force (for otherwiſe it could not have made ſo long ſtreams) may give ſome account how the vibration of his wings on thoſe portals makes his wind-muſic, and plays thereon as we do on a flagelet. *Their manner of breathing.*

§. 3. The 16th of Jannary was a ſtill fine froſt, and at noon it was fine and warm in the ſunſhine ; I obſerved it to invite many bees out of my hive, eſpecially out of my boxen-hive, which ſtood under my ſtraw- *Of hives.*

I

straw-hive, and in the sunshine I saw them play; I saw here and there one fly out of another straw-hive, but very few; the next day I told between twenty and thirty that lay dead on the ground under the hive, and at the hive door, with a hoar-frost of the night covering them; note, the entry-hole of this hive was very open, wherefore I do infer that such entry-hole, being large, lets not only the cold and wind in, to their prejudice, but the sunshine of the winter to their utter ruin : I do infer likewise that these boarded hives are not so warm in winter to resist the cold, nor so able to resist the sun either in summer or winter, as the straw-hives, because the heat and cold cannot penetrate, where the particles of each injected have their powers broken by such a numerous body of twisted straws, between each of which there is a sort of vacuity, which must needs make the frost and sun break their lines; whereas timber being porous, and yet a continued body, the heat and cold passes through it without interruption; so that, I believe, the sun has too immediate an influence on the bees in those boxen-hives to their great prejudice, both at spring and winter.

Mice and moths pernicious.

§. 4. Mr. Cherry's gardener of Shotsbroke had put, during the winter, a piece of slit trencher before the bee holes, with two little arched holes cut in them, to let the bees just have room to pass in and out; I thought it had been for warmth, but he said it was to keep out the mice, which would soon, in the winter, destroy a hive : he said the moths were likewise very pernicious to bees; for they would get into the hives towards the latter end of summer, and at the bottom of the hive, about the edges of it, lay their eggs, which at the latter end of spring come to great maggots, and crawl up and down the hive from comb to comb, sucking

the

the honey; thus, he says, he has known five or six
hives, in a season, deſtroyed by them; his way is
to lift up the hives, and examine them, after Michaelmaſs, and deſtroy ſuch eggs; he ſays, the
mice get not into the hives all the ſummer long;
for then the bees are ſtrong and lie before the hole
all night, and will not let them come in.

H A Y.

§. 1. I Was taking notice that ſome hay my ſer-
vant had bought for me had loſt it's ſmell,
which could not be from the rain; for none fell
that year in the hay-making time, but it had laid
abroad in the dew without being made into cock:
and this is frequently the caſe of hay below our hill;
for below the hill after it is laid in ſwarth and
tedded, that is, ſcattered abroad, they do not
cock it till they cock it for good and all; whereas
in the hill-country they cock it the ſame day it is
tedded, if it be a hot day.

Of making hay.

§. 2. If you will make aftermaſs broad-clover, I
hold it beſt not to let it lie one night in ſwarth, but
againſt every night to cock it in large cocks to ſecure it from the dews, which, at that time of the
year, fall very largely; for the dews ſoke into the
broad-clover, and thin the ſpirity juice, and thereby make it volatile and eaſily exhauſted by the ſun;
whereas if the ſpirity juice, which is of conſiſtency,
be not thinned by the water getting into it, the ſun
will fix it, by drawing out the watery part from it;
but if it be thinned by adventitious water, by reaſon
of ſuch thinneſs of the body, it will evaporate;
it is true, by laying it in ſwarth night after night,
it will ſooner be hay, but then the hay will be ſpoiled; for the dryneſs of the body proceeds from the

Making broad clo-ver hay.

above precipitate manner of exhaufting the fpiri-
tuous juice by letting in the water. [a]

§. 3. They count the great-burnet hay in Lei-
ceftershire, the beft fheep-hay, and the beft horfe-hay.

§. 4. I was faying, at the appraifement of the
hay in Sir Ambrofe Phillipps's great barn, at which
I was prefent, that I would not make ufe of that
barn for my hay, unlefs the feafon of hay-making
was wet, but put it without door in a reek; to
which the keeper replied, that he owned hay came
better out of a reek than a barn, and that hay reeked
abroad required much lefs making, having a paf-
fage for the air and wind to qualify it.

I was propofing to fet up a [b]reek-houfe for hay
in my meads; feveral of my oldeft and moft experienced labourers feemed to be againft it, but I
could not have a reafon, only they faid, hay never
came fo well out of a reek-houfe as out of a reek,
and one of them faid, the reafon was, it never lay
fo clofe; the timber pofts, bearing againft the hay,
kept it from finking clofe, and fo it lay too hollow; I replied, that then in making the reek,
room of a foot fpace within the timbers fhould be
allowed it for finking, which caution, I take it,
fhould be always ufed in fuch cafes.

§. 5. In making hay-cocks it is of great confequence to fee that the cocks are made with a narrow
bottom, and round head; for where they are made
with a broad bottom and fharp top, pyramidwife,
the cock finks flat, and fquats down, and lies fo
wide, and broad, that rain damages it greatly,
whereas a round top with a narrow bottom will fave
the cock from rain.

[a] For making St. Foin or French-grafs hay, fee note extracted from Mr. Tull, under the article Graffes, §. 50.
[b] Dutch barns had not been introduced, or were but little
known in our author's time.

In

In making hay-cocks, in order to be carted, I find by experience, that they ought to be made large (from a dozen to fifteen to a load, which they ought not to exceed) becaufe the fewer make a load, the fooner they are loaded, and the greater is the difpatch, and, if they are fet out in rows it is the better ; lefs time is loft in going from cock to cock ; the more hay-cocks you make, the more bottoms, and, in proportion to the hay, more lies on the ground, and confequently, if the feafon be wet, it is by lying long on the earth liable to more damage ; a little cock is apter to fall flat, and, if rainy weather comes, what with the bottoms and tops, it all takes wet, there being little in the middle ; again, being light of weight it cannot comprefs itfelf clofe, but is hollow, and fo takes in the rain, and, if you cart in the dew, or when the ground is wet, there is more hay fpoiled by raking in the wet, where are many fmall cocks, than where a few great ones.

§. 6. It feems fit to be confidered in the buying a hay-reek, how far the hay-reek may have heated *Of it's fweating.* when it was made, for, if it heated well, provided it be not too much, the hay will yield more loads, becaufe in fweating it falls fo much the more clofe ; whereas, if the hay was put up over-ripe, it will not fo well anfwer expectations in the quantity, it lying fo much the hollower.

§. 7. An ancient experienced farmer tells me, he always found old hay as good for cattle, till the lat- *Of old and new hay.* ter end of the year, as new ; but then it grew too dry for them.

§. 8. We found it manifeft this year, in hay-mak- *Short hay weighs beft.* ing, that fhort hay of the fame bulk out-weighed long hay abundantly.

W O O L.

§. 1. ONE of my labourers in * mowing complained of the old rowet that choaked
up the scythe, and compared it to the young wool,
which, when sheep have been pretty well kept in
the winter, and then checked in the spring, comes
up under the first wool, and deadens the sheers, so
that it is troublesome to cut.

I immediately went to another, who I knew had
been a shepherd, and had sheared much, and inquired of him concerning such wool; he said, it was
true, that, if sheep are kept well at the forehand of
the year, and have a check in the spring, and then
comes a flush of grass on the first rains, their winter
wool will grow no more, but a young wool will arise,
and cast off the old wool, so that one may almost
wipe it off with one's hands; now if the young
wool is not grown so long, but that the shears slide
over it, or between the young and old, then it is not
troublesome to shear; but if it be grown so long
that the shears must cut it, then it choaks up the
shears, and makes it troublesome; and in drawing
the wool out with one's finger and thumb, to see the
fineness of the thread, it will part.

§. 2. I sold my wool to a fell-monger, and we
happened to fall into an argument what time of the
year wool grew fastest on the sheep's back; he said,
it grew fastest that quarter of the year which was
between Christmass and Lady-day; wondered at
that, because it was the coldest quarter of the year;
but he answered me, it did grow faster then, than
from Lady-day to the 17th of June, which was the
day I sheared, for, said he, the wool stops in growth
long before that, and begins to loosen from it's
root, and a new wool growing thrusts it out.

This

This put me in mind that the fleeces in the eastern counties might be easier plucked, and with less pain to the sheep than we imagine, if they nick the time in doing it, when the wool loosens from the skin of the sheep.

§. 3. May the 19th farmers Box, the father and son, and farmer Isles, farmer Stephens, and young farmer Sartain of Wilts, all agreed, that wool grew faster on the sheep in dry than wet summers (for from the growth of the sheep the wool depends) and that all sorts of cattle fatted then faster, and grew fatter than in wet summers, if they had meat tolerably sufficient; for continual wet outwardly on their coats washes them out, as well as inwardly, and then the grasses are sourer also; besides cattle have more hours for eating in dry than in rainy weather.

Wool on the sheep affected by the weather.

§. 4. There is a particular sort of sheep in Persia of which they are very choice, their wool is as soft as silk, and I am well informed, that to preserve the beauty of it, and keep it to a good curl, they swathe their sheep.

Of swathing sheep in Persia.

§. 5. When a sheep's wool peels away under his belly, the shepherds say, it is, most generally, a sign of an old sheep; not but that a young sheep will be sometimes subject to it: that which will best prevent the like another year, if young, is to keep him up in case.

Of wool peeling off the sheep.

The ewes that lamb about Lady-day, will have their lambs, by the quickness of the grass at that time, so brisk and forward, that with sucking and butting they will have beat all the wool bare from the ewes belly by the time they come to be sheared.

§. 6. Mr. Methwin and Mr. Holliday, clothiers, say the Spanish wool is not near so fine and so good of late years, not above half so fine as it was formerly; the finest, they say, comes from Segovia in Spain; the same they say of Herefordshire wool.

Of Spanish wool.

Z 3

§. 7. Tho'

§. 7. Tho' one farm and another is said to have better and worse wool, yet the rule is very uncertain ; it is according to what sort of sheep a farm keeps, which may occasion a great alteration in it, for ewes carry finer wool than weathers and hogs ; again, the wool is improved according to what grass one gives the sheep, clover-grasses raising a coarser wool ; again, it depends on what sort of hay the sheep have at winter ; the better the hay the finer the wool ; and hill-country hay, if one has enough of it, will bring finer wool than the next farmer shall have, who buys a vale hay.

If sheep are abused in their keeping so as to pitch, their wool, tho' never so short, will handle hard and rough, be curled, and not run into a strait thread, and break off in combing.

§. 8. At Bishops-Cannons and all the Cannons, where the wool is so fine, and the land so good, they keep their feeding as close as may be ; for they count, amongst them, the shorter the sheep's pasture the sweeter ; if so, it must be more so with us, where the ground is poor and sour. The wool from Woodcote farm, which is contiguous to me, will out-sell that from Crux-Easton, because their sheep feed on the downs, and ours on the corn-lease.

§. 9. In Isbrants Ides History of his embassy from Muscovy to China, printed 1706, he says, fo, 189. the mulberry-trees in China are managed in a manner different from all other countries ; for they are kept low, and annually lopped, as the vineyards are ; because, says he, the young shoots occasion the production of the best silk ; and indeed the difference between the silk produced by those worms which feed on the first leaves, and that of the latter growth, when they are much harder, is very considerable. — I note this, because I have made a remark before, how the best wool proceeds from grass growing on
fallows,

fallows, which proceed from a feed of the fame fummer, and there feems to be a great affinity between
wool and filk.

§. 10. Burn-beaking the downs will be a great Burn-beaking prejudicial to the wool.
prejudice to the ftaple of wool; for, though the bulk
of wool may come off the vale, yet it is moft born
and bred on the downs, from whence the vale men
buy their fheep, or otherwife they would not have
fo good wool; and though particular parts of the
vale, as all Cannons, &c. produce a fine wool, yet
the reafon of that is before given.

§. 11. Mr. Bifhop's fhepherd of Dorfetfhire faid, Wool of old fheep fineft.
the older fheep grew, the finer was their wool, and
the leaft of it.

§ 12. Where the ewe-wool is deareft, the lamb- Of ewe and lamb's wool.
wool is cheapeft; for the ewe-wool fells for it's finenefs, but the lamb's wool for it's length.

§. 13. Mr. Bell of Marlborough, coming to buy Of lamb's wool.
my wool, afked me whether I fheared my lambs at
Midfummer, as I did my other fheep; I told him yes;
becaufe, faid he, many will fhear their lambs a month
after; for the wool is fo much the better for being
the longer, the ewe's wool the fhorter the better, the
lamb's wool the longer: I afked how much it might
yield the more for being a month's growth the older;
he faid, a penny perhaps in the pound: I anfwered,
twice fhearing made two troubles and charges, and I
know not whether it would turn to account.

I told my fhepherd what Mr. Bell faid about fhearing the lambs early; and he replied, if the lambs were
late fhorn, they would not at Michaelmafs carry fo
good a body and look fo full, nor carry fo good a
price; fome fhear them fo fhallow as to leave a good
coat behind, becaufe they may look more burley at a
fair.—— Quære therefore, if I fhould not fhear thofe
later which I keep myfelf —Afking my fhepherd this
queftion afterwards, he faid, it would be two troubles

both

both in washing and shearing, and chargeable, more than the profit on the wool would come to, and the sooner we sheared our lambs, the more wool they would have when they were sheep.

Wool of colley-sheep:

§. 14. I asked Mr. Townsend and Mr. Fry, clothiers, the reason why Hertfordshire wool should be the worst in England; they said it was certainly so, and that they affected the sort of sheep they had, as a very large sheep, which, said they, are of the colley sort, that is, black faces and legs, and their wool is very harsh, mixed with hairs, like dog's hair, and not so white as ours.

Black wool.

§. 15. Stevens of Pomeroy in Wilts, desired to have two or three fleeces of my black wool, and made no scruple to give me nine pence per pound for it, though he was loath to give so much for the white fleeces; for, said he, the black fleeces are of more value than the white, and he gave this reason; in the making a dark coloured medley drugget, or cloth, the thread of the white being twisted with the black will effect it without being dyed, and will make much the stronger cloth, in as much as all dyes that dye a dark colour do much rot the worsted: but the dyes of light colours, being only a light staining of them, do not so much hurt the wool.

Curled wool.

§. 16. When the wool-man was weighing my wool, he shewed me the difference of some fleeces in goodness, and particularly the locks of some fleeces that were curled, and said, such wool was not, by a penny in a pound, so fine, as that which was soft and strait, nor would such wool lie fine and smooth in the druggets.

Goodness of wool.

§. 17. I was arguing with my wool-man on the qualities of wool, and insisted that, though they judged according to the fineness of the thread of wool, yet wool of the same fineness might be much better than other wool, because the proof and

strength

ftrength of the thread in one fort of wool, might be better than in another of the fame finenefs, by reafon of better food, being never pinched fummer or winter, and confequently having proof to the very end of the hair : he faid, that wool impoverifhed by ill-feeding or ftarving, at any time of the year, was plainly difcernable ; for it would run off thin towards the ends of the hairs more than fuits with a taper figure. I fuppofe the change towards the end is difcernable as in corn and grafs, when it withers at the top : he allowed my wool was better than my neighbours, for my not pinching them any time of the year.

§. 18. A great dealer in wool affures me, that wool of fixteen fhillings in the tod is eighteen pence in the tod worfe in goodnefs when three years old ; for then it grows ftarkey and dry, and will not lie fmooth in the fpinning ; for the oil of wool waftes very much after two years old.

§. 19. I was with Mr. Anthony Methwin, a **Edge-** great clothier, and entered into difcourfe with him **grown** of wool; the edge-grown wool, I fpoke to him **wool.** on, he affured me, was the worft abufe the woolmen put upon the clothiers, for the young wool of it was all to be flung away, becaufe it could not be worked up in cloth ; he faid, wool that pitched, by reafon of the fheep's poverty, would tear and break in pieces, and great wafte was made of it, that wool managed as I manage mine, was much the better in all refpects, and more profitable to the clothier to buy, and though it might run a little longer for it, would be extraordinary good for cloathing : he agreed with me, that fallows always produced better wool than the very fame ground when laid down to grafs, and faid, the longer a ground laid to grafs, and the older the grafs was, it was the ranker food, and the wool coarfer ; for which reafon

fon the fallows having new young grafs in them, produce fo much the finer wool ; he did, for the fame reafon, affent, that the hop-clover generally fpeaking (efpecially in clay-land) might produce a finer wool than it's natural grafs ; that the thicker and clofer wool handled, and ftraiter in it's threads, and not curled, it was the finer, and laid fmoother in the piece of cloth : That wool, added he, in the fheep, that hangs leaft under the droppings of the other, is the fineft, fuch as the neck and breaft and belly.

Of the pitching-mark in wool.

§. 20. I find the pitch-mark, if it be not worn out before fhearing-time, the wool-men do not like, becaufe, fay they, we have no help but to cut it off, whereas, tho' the ruddle, if the fheep be much ruddled, weighs to our lofs, yet that wafhes out.

Of binding wool, and of it's growing.

§. 21. Wool increafes by lying by, and, if put up hollow, will in two or three years feel very clofe, and be intangled, which is occafioned by it's growing ; but it will not grow till after it's fweating is over, which is not till Michaelmafs.

It is generally agreed, that wool, being bound up very clofe, fo that the wind cannot get into it, will pay intereft in growth till towards the next fpring, but fhould be fold before the March following, left the winds of that month fhould dry it too faft.

Of the wool-loft.

§. 22. The wool-man having bought my wool, and coming to weigh it, affured me, that by the tumbling and removing the wool, and letting in the air to it in the carriage, it would lofe in weight, a pound in the tod, before he got it home : from hence it follows, that to move your wool in the loft, or from one room to another is lofs, or to tumble it up and down in fearch of mice.

Time for felling.

§. 23. When wool-men buy not at the firft hand, when the wool is fheared, they care not to buy in the winter ; for the damp and foggy air gets into

into the wool in winter, which makes it weigh heavier ; therefore the chapman chooses not to meddle with it till spring.

§. 24. I find, by Mr. Brewer, Mr. Methwin, and many more clothiers I conversed with in Wiltshire, that the wool-breakers do, in the first place, separate the fleeces by themselves that run most of a sort.

Of the several parts of the fleece.

Then they sort the different kinds of wool in each fleece by itself, which fleece is never divided into less than four parcels, viz.——The tail-wool is laid aside for lifts for cloth, rugs and blankets.——Half the buttock towards the flank is for the long woosted thread, in serges and druggets, which they call the woosted, and runs the length of the serge or drugget, which, tho' spun to a finer thread, yet is harder than the abb which crosses the woosted thread, and runs the breadth, yet is of a coarser wool : but Mr. Merryman, clothier of Newbury, denies that any of of the buttock is fine enough for the woosted thread. ——What is on the back and ribs is somewhat finer, and makes, in druggets, the thread called abb; which runs cross the chain, called the woosted, and is of a finer wool than the buttock, and twisted in the thread looser.——The neck, and breast, and bottom of the belly, make the thread which in the finest cloth is the chain called the warp in cloth, which answers to the chain or woosted thread in druggets ; but the abb in cloth which answers to the abb in druggets, is all made of Spanish wool, which, being finer, will come closer together, and the finer it is made, tho' the thinner, yet will keep out rain the better : but Mr. Merryman of Newbury, clothier, will not believe the neck and breast fine enough for the chain.

HIDES.

H I D E S.

§. 1 ACCORDING as the beasts were in proof, in flesh and fatness, proportionable is the value of the hides, and such will be the proof of them under the hands of the tanner; for example, as young meat and fat meat plims and increases in the roasting and boiling, but lean and old shrinks, so a hide of a young and fat beast swells and thickens in the tan-pit, and yields a proportionable increase according as the beast is young and fat; but the hide of a lean and old beast shrinks and loses it's substance in the tan-pit, and will not take the tan as a young hide: therefore a murrain hide is of small value, unless it be the back part, to make a pair of boots, to which purpose it is useful, on account of it's shrinking and closing of the pores; the very best of the hides are bought by the bridle-makers, because they are required to be of the best substance: the value of a hide is known by it's weight, by lifting it with the hand, as it weighs heavier or lighter in proportion to it's largeness or smallness, nothing being a greater commendation of a hide, than to weigh much heavier than one would expect from the size of it.

The north-country hides are the best, and thickest, and generally handle best, the reason whereof probably is, because their feed is deepest, and they are maintained always in good keeping, and never pinched.

It is generally agreed, the finer the hide the sweeter the meat of a beast.

§. 2. The skins of the sheep thicken much, after they are shorn: in some time after they will grow as thick again as before. I judge this must proceed

from

from the cold, and puts me in mind, that the hides of all cattle are thicker grained in the hill-country than in the vale, as also of the story (which, as I remember, Herodotus tells) of the Persians and Greeks, that when they were, on both sides, slain in a battle and stripped, the nations were not to be distinguished but by their skulls; for the Persians wearing always turbans on their heads, which kept them very hot, their skulls were much the softer, and would yield to the impression.

RISE and FALL of MARKETS, and their CAUSES.

§. 1. GENERALLY speaking, the ear- *Of buying* lier a thing is bought, when the mar- *early.* ket is open, it is bought the cheaper, for though afterwards many contingencies may have an influence, yet the general condition of mankind, who are not provided with money to buy as early as their occasions want it, or want to sell before there is a general demand for goods, must favour the ready-monied man, who is provided beforehand; thus, for example, they, who at spring of the year first buy barren beasts to fat, or sheep, have the advantage; for they, who sell earliest, either want the money, or winter-provisions, as hay and straw, to maintain them till the grass grows; which is a general case of too many; and they, who buy early, do it because they have money before the generality have it for such purposes, or a remaining surplus of hay, or straw, more than the stock of their farm can spend, which is the case of few, so at such times there must be regularly more sellers than buyers

§. 2. In the summer 1702, there was a great *Plenty of* scarcity of hay and grass, for which reason beasts *one kind of provisions* were *affects all others.*

were not fatted in so great a number as usually;
consequently the breed in England of beasts increased; this year, 17c3, there was much grass and
hay, abundance of beasts therefore were fatted,
which made beef cheap; and fat mutton, by reason
of a bane, was cheap; and seeing beef and mutton
was to be had cheap, people would give but a low
price for cheese and bacon : so that any one kind of
food being cheap, is apt to lower the price of all
other sorts.

§. 3. From the exceeding last year's hot summer, 1719, whereby fewer beasts were fatted, and
hay very scarce the spring following, beef yielded
five pence per pound; this made fat lamb sell exceeding dear, not only at spring but all along June
and July; the reason is plain; because there must
be a great many fat lambs go to make up the failure of each ox's fatting, and meat must be had.

§. 4. On the 16th of September wheat was sinking, and about this time of the year wheat generally falls in price, for the farmers, who live in the
pasture and turnip-countries, do about this time of
the year, tumble out their wheat in the markets,
and glut them, in order to raise money to buy sheep
at Weyhill, and the sheep-markets, as well as to
pay harvesting, and for seeding their ground with
wheat.

Wheat sunk for a few markets, and sheep, notwithstanding it was a great autumn aftermass for
grass, and a great turnip year; the reason of it was,
that money must be raised by most farmers out of
the produce of their farm at this time of the year
(September) to answer their many occasions, and
they, observing wheat to sink, thought fit to lessen
their winter stock of sheep, and keep their wheat,
because hay, through the wet, was generally damaged, and not great in quantity, and so the main-

tainance

Side notes:

Scarcity of beef makes lamb, &c. dear.

Sheep and wheat cheap about September.

tainance of sheep was like to be chargeable; and consequently such sale out of the capital must glut the market and sink the price.

§. 5. From the 24th of September to the 20th of October, 1704, the land was so dry, the farmers stopped ploughing for, and sowing of wheat : Mr. Raymond, and Mr. John Horton of Wiltshire, came to me in a visit, and I was saying to them, surely if this weather held a week longer it would make wheat rise ; no, said they, at such a time it sinks in present, because the farmers send their wheat to market, which they would have sowed, but the next year it will be dear : it is the same case as in a rot of sheep, every one having sheep to sell, for the present they are cheaper. *Of the rise and fall of corn.*

§. 6. Generally it may be foreseen and concluded, that, when the harvest falls pretty late, seed-wheat, of the old year and of the new, will hold dearer, in the hill-countty (in proportion to the following price of wheat when the markets open) than when the harvest comes on early and quick ; the reason is, because, when the harvest falls out late, farmers sow much, in those countries, of old wheat, because they sow early, which goes a great way in the consumption of the stock at the latter end of the year (i. e. September) ; also, when harvests fall out late, the farmers can raise money soon from barley, oats, and peas, because by October those grains are vendible, and so they are not forced to sell wheat so soon, to raise money by that grain alone, to discharge the harvest wages; but when harvest comes early, old seed-wheat may probably sink in price, vice versâ. *Prices of seed-wheat*

§. 7. The nearer the market is to London, the worse the marke is, if wheat be cold or grown. *Cold or grown corn unfit for*

§. 8. From harvest time through the winter (1705) barley was three shillings in the quarter dearer, near Salisbury, Devizes, and the inland towns, *London market. Prices of barley.*

towns, than at Newbury, Reading, and those countries that drove the London trade of malting; the reason was, the great stock of barley, the traders in malt to London had provided the year before, had glutted the London market, whereas the malsters in the inland trade do not provide great quantities beforehand, and therefore, the crops of barley miserably failing this hot summer, barley bore a better price with them than with us.

Bane in sheep makes corn dear.

§. 9. I was observing to Mr. Hawkins, the great Hampshire farmer, it was a saying in this country, that if corn was dear sheep would be dear, and vice versa; he said, the foundation was in the sheep and not in the corn, for, if a bane fell on sheep they would be dear, and, if a bane fell on sheep, corn would be dear, because there could not be a fifth part of the folding that otherwise there would be, and consequently a deficiency of the crop, and therefore dear; but if no bane, and a great breed of sheep, corn would, on the other hand, be plenty.

I add to this, that by a bane year of sheep, it may generally be taken for a rule, wheat will be made dear, because in baning years it is a wet spring; but a baned year makes, for the present, beef and mutton cheap, because such abundance of mutton must be killed, before the bane be too far gone in the fat sheep, but the rot makes both afterwards dearer: the dearest time for mutton and beef is Lent, though it is scarce also the latter end of March and April, but then the plenty of lamb and veal keeps the price from rising.

A bane or rot makes ewes fell well.

§. 10. When there has been a rot of sheep, it may be reasonably expected that ewes will sell best, in order to replenish the breed that is lost.

Scarcity of hay makes lambs fell well.

§. 11. When there is great scarcity of hay against winter, it is to be supposed that lambs will sell best, because they can live best without hay.

§. 12. In

§. 12. In years of warm dry springs, or only of mo- Prices of cattle. derate rains, I obferve, cattle are always cheap, be-caufe the breeding counties, which are always the barren, efpecially Cornwall and the mountainous parts of Wales, tumble out fo many into our mar-kets, being not able to maintain them; on the con-trary, in years of wet and cold fprings there is a good growth of grafs in the breeding counties; therefore thofe counties, rather wanting more mouths for their grafs, do not fend them to our markets, and therefore cattle are dearer; after many dry fprings, that their breed has been drained by our markets, if a cold wet fpring comes, then cattle may be expected very dear, as in this year (1709) was the cafe; for then they can fpare none. Note, though in dry hot fprings there be a greater growth of grafs in deep cold lands, as Somerfetfhire, &c. for which rea-fon it might be thought their demand might fet a good price to the Welch cattle, yet it is to be confi-dered, that in fuch cafe the greater neceffity lies on the feller; for the Welch cattle muft ftarve, if they keep them, whereas no great inconvenience lies on the renter of the deep lands, whilft his graffes grow a little the longer only, if he keep off from buying; it is plain in this cafe the Welchman muft buckle to; whereas in wet and cold fprings, when the Welch-man can keep his cattle, it is as plain the neceffity lies on the buyer.

§. 13. During September, October, and half of Prices of fat hogs. November, fat hogs fold for 4s. 6d. and 4s. 8d. per fcore; but thefe are whey hogs, i. e. fatted with whey, and drove pretty far from the dairy-countries, which driving, and their fort of food, takes away the value of the bacon, fo our hill-country bacon, where the hogs feed on corn moft of the year, and are fatted therewith, yield fix pence or eight pence per fcore the more. About the beginning of Novem-ber I fold for 5s. 2d. per fcore, and thought the price of eight pence per fcore more a good equivalent; but by the latter end of November I found the hogs fatted fold at the market for fix fhillings per fcore, at which I was furprized, peas not rifing in the price; but inquiring into the reafon of it, I found that our hill-country bacon feldom came to it's full price till about the latter end of November or December, when all the whey-bacon is gone, for, whilft that is plenty in the market, it keeps down the value due to the hill-country hogs, though at the fame time they may yield eight pence per fcore more, yet feldom fo much then as they do afterwards : therefore it is good hufbandry not to be too ready to fell our hill-country fat hogs.

A dry fummer makes young pigs dear.

§. 14. This fummer, 1720, young pigs on a fudden grew dear all over England; the time they firft appeared to be fo was about the middle of June, and the reafon for it was (as affigned by the farmers about Holt) becaufe the laft fummer was as hot and dry as had been known for fome years, for which reafon the quantity of whey was much leffened in the dairy-countries, and the crop of corn, particularly peas, run very fhort ; and fo the breed, which would have been otherwife preferved, was fent to market for the fpit.

When to buy cattle.

§. 15. If a dry fpring fhould come, with a fucceeding hot and burning fummer till Midfummer, fo that the firft crop, or burden of grafs, be loft, and being under-ftocked with cattle, you have a hay-reek in ftore, you will have good encouragement to buy ; for in fuch cafe you may buy very cheap, and will be very well paid for the hay they fhall eat ; for you may expect a great aftermafs, the earth not having then yet exerted her ftrength ; for the hot fun thereon will have been equal to a dunging ; but then you ought to buy your cattle half fat, that your aftermafs may finifh their fatting.

§. 16. This

§. 16. This summer (anno 1720) about a month or five weeks before hay-making, there fell so much rain in most parts of England, that the water-meadows were overflowed, and very much stranded, insomuch that in several places they sold the hay to them who would cut and carry it off: in general they made the hay up in reeks, with design to buy-in lean cattle, after Christmass, and early in the spring, for fatting, and so to get them forward in flesh. —— Note therefore, when such wet summers happen, doubtless lean and barren cattle for fatting must after Christmass, and towards the spring, be dear, because a large demand for them for that purpose may be expected.

Lean and barren cattle are dear after wet summers.

§. 17. This year (1704) there was a plentiful spring for grass, but no rain fell all June and July, and so the grass was all burned up; from whence I inferred, first, that beef and mutton would be dear by September; for by that time the forwardest beef and mutton would be spent;—secondly, that barren beasts would be scarce and dear the following spring; because, there having been plenty of grass in the spring, few beasts would * go through; —— thirdly, that cows with calf, that had been early bulled, would be plenty and cheap at Christmass for fatting, and yet not easily to be fatted, by reason of the dry months of June and July.

Consequences of dry weather in June and July.

* Not prove with calf.

§. 18. There had been (anno 1716) a cold dry spring and summer to the very autumn, i. e. the latter end of August, so that there was but a small crop of hay, and the aftermass ran very short, rain coming too late to bring it to any length before winter came, and turnips also failed; whereupon it was the opinion of both Mr. Bissy and William Sartain, two Wiltshire graziers of great experience, that beef would be very cheap till Christmass, because the graziers would sell off their beasts the forehand

Of a cold dry spring and summer.

hand

hand of winter, though but half fat, for want of hay ; but that beef would be very scarce and dear in the spring, and the rather, because very few old cows, that have had damage, or went through, will be turned off to fatting at autumn, for want of hay ; but will be milked another year : this will also make mutton very dear at spring.

§. 19. There is no hopes of a good year for the graziers when grass is plenty at the beginning of spring ; for then they buy their cattle dear, and yet meat will be cheap all that summer ; for so many will buy-in for fatting, that, though the summer should prove never so dry, yet so many beasts will be made half fat by the spring-grass, and must of necessity be fatted out, that beef must needs be plenty.——On the contrary, a good year for the graziers is, when, for want of grass in the spring, barren cattle sell cheap, whereupon fewer buy for fatting ; and then rain coming plentifully, the beasts being bought cheap, and a scarcity of beef in course following, and the graziers having plenty of grass to keep cattle in for a market, makes them pay well.——And note, that in wet forward springs barren cattle may be expected to be scarce and dear the year following, because beasts being well in case take bull and go not through ; the contrary may be expected in backward springs, especially when winter-meat proves scarce.

When grass in plenty the beginning of spring, &c.

§. 20. Last summer (anno 1719) was very hot and dry, and so little rain fell, that the crops of both hay and straw fell so short, that the vale-farmers, for want of winter-provisions for their cattle, sold cows after Michaelmass for thirty shillings a-piece, which ordinarily were then worth 4l. per cow.—— It was as forward and plentiful a spring for grass the succeeding April and May as had been known for many years ; yet cows sold cheap, because the stock

A hot and dry summer occasioned the cheapness and afterwards the great dearness of cattle.

of

of cattle, so few having been fatted, was still too great; but after Christmass beef was so very dear, that, take the whole quarter of an ox, it yielded a groat per pound: bulls also were excessive dear this spring; a bull that ordinarily would yield but 40s. sold for 3l. 10s. or 4l. —— The reason was, because, the wintering of cattle having been very chargeable, the bulls were supposed not to answer the charge of wintering so well as other cattle; so the farmers killed them, though but just wholsome, and sold them for a farthing, and an half-penny a pound, and eat them in their families; so the great slaughter that had been of them the winter before made them very dear in the spring.

§. 21. October and November are the cheapest times for beef, because there is then a glut occasioned by the old cows, which are turned off by the dairy at May-day to be fatted, and are killed in those two months. ^{When beef is cheapest.}

§. 21. October and November are the cheapest times for beef, because there is then a glut occasioned by the old cows, which are turned off by the dairy at May-day to be fatted, and are killed in those two months.

W E A T H E R.

§. 1. THIS year (1712) was hitherto (June the 20th) a very hot summer; it was a dry February and March, then a little rainy the first week in April, then no rain till about mid-May, when we had a hard thunder shower, which went to the roots of the corn; then no rain till the beginning of June, when fell moderate rain, for half a day, enough to go to the roots of the corn; then no rain till this day, June the 20th, when a hard shower, of two hours, went to the roots of the corn. ——This hot summer, with so little rain, had this effect upon my oats, as follows. —— In November I had ploughed up forty acres of white poor land, after it was run to a thick short grass, and had laid down two years to hop-clover, in order that, after it had

A a 3 had

had laid ploughed all the winter, and took the frost
and rain to flat it, the ground might be a fit and
mellow bed to receive the oats : but, notwithstanding the ground was p oughed so early, yet, being a
pretty dry and mild winter, at the middle of February, when the oats were sown, the ground required
much harrowing and though they came up well
and promising, yet, for want of rain to soften the
ground and mellow it (having the disadvantage of
being sowed on land not sufficiently loosened) they
did not strike good roots, but dwindled, and by the
20th of June, when they were shooting into ear,
were very thin, for want of tillowing, and were run
into spindle, and looked very poor and starving.——
The bad condition of these oats seems to be owing
to the drought of the year, and the chalky constitution of the ground, which, being lay ground, was
not sufficiently loosened, though ploughed early,
and dragged in with the best management, in order
to help it's natural defects ; and therefore for the future, it is to be observed, that a crop of corn sowed
on such white earth, after it has laid down so long to
grass, is very much hazarded in case such a hot summer happens ; whereas, if this had been the second
crop sowed to oats, instead of the first, doubtless the
success would have been much better ; for then such
white ground, in the second year of it's tillage,
would have ploughed up fine and rotten, and the
oats, with the drags or harrows, would have been
let in as deep as the plough went, and then, being
rolled, would have endured the heat of the summer,
and the want of rain, as I experimented this same
year, in a crop of oats sowed in the same down, on
a black rotten earth, but poor and wood-seary,
which I had not thought worth ploughing and sowing ; but having sowed it to oats and French-grass
from lay the year before, and the French-grass mis-

carrying,

carrying, I sowed it again to oats and French-grass
this year; the ground turned up like ashes, as deep
as the plough went: I dragged in the oats and
French-grass ten days after the former, yet both the
oats and French-grass endured the drought and hot
summer to a wonder, and held till this 20th of June,
when rain came, the colour of a strong dark green.
—Other fields ploughed up early for oats, after they
had laid down two years to broad-clover, ploughing
up pretty mellow, and, being clay-grounds, endured the heat of this summer very well, and held a
flourishing colour, though sowed not till the first
week in March; yet I was sensible, through the
drought several of the weak tillows were lost. ——
But white land, as abovesaid, having laid to grass, is
more difficult to be brought to a friable temper by
once ploughing than the other sort of grounds here
mentioned, which are of strong clay. — Also, when
wheat has, the year before, been sowed to one earth,
on whitish ground that has laid to grass, I observe,
not only, that such ground is more apt to run to
rowet in the wheaten crop (whereby the earth is
more bound by the roots of the grass) than clay-
ground sowed on one earth, especially if it be a little
stony; but also white earth, in case it ploughs stiff,
does not separate and break, when it is to be harrowed, as the clay, if a little stony; and this I
plainly see by comparing together, this year, several
pieces of barley

Though our spring corn is better in cold clay lands,
in the hill-country, in warm than cold wet summers,
it is apparent to me, not only from this, but from
many years observation, that, tho' spring corn will
hold it's colour in a hot dry summer, in the hill-
country, in clay-lands, yet our clays are seldom so
good and of such depth as to bring to maturity, in
such summers, all the backward tillows, but the

strength

strength of the ground gives off, and the number of
ears is not fulfilled, in such cases, for want of seasonable
rains; whereas in rich clays of the vale, where
the corn is buried deeper, possibly no summer is too
hot.

Effects of a
dry spring.
How to
judge
when
French-
grass,
wheat, &c.
have per-
fected their
growth.

§. 2. This spring (anno 1707) was exceeding dry
from about the 12th of March to the 22d of May;
for but one moderate shower, on or about the 13th
of April, fell, which went not to the roots of the
corn, for it brought up none, and but moderately
refreshed any grass. During this season the winds
were very parching, the sun hot by day, but the nights
cold; my French-grass, on a burn-beaked ground,
sowed the year before, was very hopeful at the beginning
of March, and so on to the middle of March
and the latter end of April, and looked so green,
that I thought I should cut half a load at least on an
acre; but from the latter end of April it began to
fall off, and to turn towards a fillemot colour, and
made little or no growth all the spring: on the 22d
of May rain fell plentifully, and frequent rains after;
I had great expectation my French-grass would recover
it's colour, and also grow in stem and length
of blade, in hopes of which I waited till the 19th of
June, but then found all hopes were in vain; for the
grass altered not in colour, and very little in growth,
from these rains. The very same thing happened to
six acres of wheat I had in very white poor ground,
which having lost it's colour (being within a week
or ten days of earing before rain fell) never recovered
it's colour after, and put forth a yellowish and
very small ear; the same happened to my French-
grasses sowed the autumn before with my wheat.——
From hence I observed that, when the air and the
sun have concocted the juices of plants, and confirmed
and hardened the fibres of the leaves and stems
(which

(which the air and sun do rather in less time than they otherwise would, where there is a poverty of juices) the fibres being so fixed and hardened, that they are not capable of being enlarged, and so not to be extended by more juices, the juices struggling for a vent, discharge themselves into soboles above the roots, if the plant be perennial, providing tender juicy buds for the next year; for thus it was with my French-grass, when I pulled up it's roots: from hence I may for the future judge when the hopes of the year are lost.

§. 3. This spring (1714) was very dry, and the summer very hot and dry; it was very observable, that the increase of rabbits, pheasants, partridges, and hares were very great, and I saw many coveys by July the 20th, near as big as the old ones; so much does the sun favour their increase in number and bulk; and doubtless the increase of the vermin that destroy them, as polecats, stotes, and foxes, hold a proportion; as such summers conduce to the destruction of the fish by reason of the lowness of the waters, so they contribute exceedingly to their multiplication and growth; the last summer being very raw and cold, the miller of Long-parish complained of the small size of his spawn, occasioned by the coldness of the season, and made it his apology for furnishing me with no better trout. *Effects of a dry spring, &c.*

§. 4. This winter (1713) has been the driest and freest from rain and snow I ever knew, and the mildest and most moderate for frosts; and the spring was also cold, and the driest, and the summer the driest, for we had, during the whole spring and summer, but these three rains following, viz. January and February dry, March the 10th, or thereabouts, fell a rain that might possibly go to the sheer-point; then it continued dry till June the 9th, when we had such another rain as the former; it continued *Of a remarkable mild winter and dry spring.*

on

on dry with us (though some storms did scatter in several parts as we heard) till June the 21st, and 22d, when a rain fell, which I believe went to the sheer-point; and by this time the wheat was ripe in most places, and the reapers were set on the white oats, and peas were hacking, and some barley was cut; it is true, generally speaking, the last mentioned lacked above a fortnight of being ripe, the spring having been dry and cold, which kept the grain backward; black oats were fit to be cut, with me, by July the 20th.—From the account before given, of the dry winter, the cold and dry spring, and the hot summer, which periods of time, from the beginning of January to the 28th of July, being above seven months, take in only three moderate rains, it will be fit to consider what consequence it had on all sorts of corn, and the different properties of the land on which it grew.——First, as to wheat; it was generally very good throughout the kingdom, and flourished strangely on all strong healthy lands; nor did I observe any light poor lands suffer thereby, so as I could impute the weakness of the crop to the continued drought; the berry was plump and well coloured, golden coloured and not horney coloured, and no failure of chests in the ear, as there was in the last cold and wet summer; it is true, just on the hardening of the wheat the straw did, in many places, give off, so as to be struck with a blight, and felt tough and rottenish under the hook, but this was so few days before the berry was ripe, and the wheat was reaped, that the wheat being, in a manner, already ripe, the berry did not suffer thereby: what I did particularly wonder at, during the fiery trial the corn did seem to undergo this summer, was, that I had twenty acres of wheat, and the ground being of a very cold clayey nature, I had sowed the wheat under furrow,

I

and

and laid the ground round in fmall high ridges, of feven furrows in a land or ridge, thereby thinking to lay this cold land dry and warm, (though this land had by nature a dry fituation, being on the fummit of my hill-country farm) and the lands being thus laid round were fo dry as to be duft, to the eye, before the beginning of June, infomuch that if I run my ftick in as deep as the roots of the wheat, and turned up the earth, there was no moifture to make a cohefion, but the earth fo turned up fell into the drieft powder, yet did the wheat of this ground flourifh, and grow proud in colour beyond any wheat in my farm, though the land was poor, under the fourth crop, and had no dung or fold to fupport it ; and this wheat proceeded to ear, and brought me ten to eleven chefts in the ears, and perfected the berry, without giving out the fupport of it, till harveft ; and yet the earth feemingly iron whereon it grew throughout the whole fummer ; this evidently fhews the clay land of England ought to be fo prepared by tillage, that the fun may carry on it's bufinefs of burning and drying it, to the greateft degree it is capable of doing.

As to the winter-vetch crop of this year, it bore the tedious drought and heat better than the peas, wherever they both grew in land of the fame kind ; in hill-country land, if the mold was any ways light, weak, or poorifh, they bore up againft the heat, where the peas gave out, were parched up, and were loft in bloffom or kid ; this advantage the vetches had over the peas, by having their roots eftablifhed during the winter, and by the earth's being well fettled and clofed to the roots before the drought came : yet I obferved, where vetches were fowed on one earth, on ftiff land, in our hill-country, which had laid two years to grafs, fuch vetches did give out at bloffoming time, and yielded only top-kids, and the leaf soon blighted after the blossoming time was over; which was occasioned by such land being unfriable, harsh and churlish, and so did not close to the roots of the vetches, to keep out the scorching heat, as did the earth of mellow land, tho' not so strong; parcels of whole land sowed in the same field, tho' of a weaker, yet of a more loose texture, did support the vetches better.

As to the peas crop this year (1714) I observed where the lands were not of a strong clayey or malmy kind, or of a fat sandy mold, they failed extremely both in halm and kid: generally all dry, harsh or hungry ground, all ground that was not well worked with the plough, or where the pea was not sowed early, to establish the root before the drought came, and blossomed late, there was a great failure both in halm and number of kids, and those kids were very short, and but two or three peas in them.

As to the black oat crop, it being generally (especially in the hill-country) sown on either light weak land, or on stronger land after it has been worn out with three former crops, and for the most part being sown on one earth, they were in general very indifferent and poor throughout the hill-country, yet being usually sowed, at least a month before the barley, their roots were so well established, and the ground so far settled to the roots, that, of the two, they escaped better than the barley, though that was sowed in much better ground; in the vale I also observed a great failure of oats.

In regard to the barley-crop of this year, there was a great failure throughout the hill country; for the lands there are generally of a lighter, drier, and huskier nature, and not partaking of the malmy fatness of the clays, or of the mellow, rich, hazle mold of the vales; wanting therefore the stock of vegetable

table spirits to support the root, and not having that mellowness of parts, to clasp about and close to the roots, the barley failed in proportion as the lands did more or less partake of the aforesaid properties, or were later sowed; yet it must be granted, that in the hill-country, where was strong land, or cold clays, if the land was in good heart, worked well with the plough, and sowed early, such land bore very flourishing barley: in the vales, where the earth was of a white malmy clay, of a binding sand in good heart, or of a fat hazle mold, and in good bean and peas land, well worked, and sowed early, there was excellent barley; but wherever, in the vale, the land came short of these properties, was indifferently husbanded, or was sowed late, there was also a lamentable crop of barley.

§. 5. This year (1709) we had a cold April and May, insomuch as between Winchester and Banbury I hardly saw a good acre of corn: but when I went from Banbury all along to Garenton in Leicestershire, I never saw better in my life (so said the country people, in those parts, of their corn) the reason of which must be, that the first lands, being poor and lighter lands, were penetrated by the colds, and had not strength to support the corn against them; but the northern lands, which were ten shillings per acre, did support their corn; therefore a cold April and May will not make a scarcity, if not wet. *Of a cold spring.*

§. 6. I looked on rain always to carry with it fructifying principles; yet it happens sometimes, that rains, being very frequent, do beat the fallows flat and close, so as to prevent the ground from letting in the sun and air, and in that respect they may be prejudicial. *Effects of rain.*

Wet summers (such as in the year 1703) keep that juice, which forms the flour in corn, watery and thin, and hinder it from digesting and fixing into a firm
body;

body; and time loft is never to be regained by any plant in any of it's progreffions, whether as to it's formation of roots or fruit; there are certain pro- greffions limited for every day in the week, as on the hatching an egg, and any interruption is a pre- judice: nature will finifh what fhe has undertaken (with very little regard to the difference of time) whether it be perfect or imperfect.——The wetnefs of this whole winter, which was very rainy, prevent- ed fo many grains being formed in the ear as ufual; for it was matter of fact, the ears were never fhort- er; the wetnefs of May and June prevented the grains in every ear filling before it fhot out of hood; for it was manifeft there were four or five hufks in moft ears, at the bottom of the ear, which were not perfected or filled; and doubtlefs the remainder of June or July, if wet, will make the grain in the ear thin, and the lowermoft grains more efpecially.

It feems a great deal of rain and wet weather to wheat in the ear, and other corn when it is high, is a prejudice; for thofe juices, which form and fill up the ear and grain, and fafhion, and make the blade to grow, feem to be different; inafmuch as, both in corn and fruit, it is worfe the wet years, when the blade and fhoots run longeft: when the corn is up fo high, though the feafon of the year be hot, yet the ground is fo fhaded as to be in danger of being chilled by much rain; it feems the heat and power of the fun muft, the whole time, attend the ground in it's incubation; for none doubts the Weft-Indies being better ground than England, yet runs the corn up to fo mighty a ftubble (to which length it cannot grow till towards the latter part be- fore it's ripening) that to it's length, which runs fo high, and keeps off the benign influence of the fun, Mr. Ray imputes the thinnefs of the grain.

§. 7. This fpring (1711) was wet and cold for the

Of a wet fpring.

the moft part of March and April, and May was
alfo rainy ; the confequence of which, in ripening
our corn at harveft, was this ; the wheat ripened,
and we were reaping it by the 27th of July ; but
the oats ripened not till the 18th of Auguft, when I
began to cut them ; and the barley began to ripen
not till the 26th of Auguft, when I began to cut the
barley ; fo there was near three weeks diftance be
tween the wheat and oat harveft, and near a month's
diftance between the wheat and barley harveft. From
hence I conclude (as it feems to me) with reafon, that
the colder and wetter a fpring happens to be, and the
longer it continues fo, there will be the longer diftance of time between the wheat, oat, and barley harveft ; for the wheat being a hardier grain, and being ftrong and well rooted at the fpring of the year,
is not pinched by a wet and cold fpring, nor kept
back in growth, as the oats and barley are, they being tender grains and their roots weak at that time
of the year ; and (vice verfâ) hot fprings may ripen
the barley before the wheat, as it ftands in more need
of warmth, and is more fenfible of it than the laft
mentioned grain.

§. 8. Laft winter (1702) was a very wet winter, *Of wet*
and May and June following were alfo very wet, *winters.*
which made corn yield very ill : I infer if the next
winter and fummer fhould prove as wet, and yet
not wetter, corn will prove thinner, and yield
worfe, and be dearer than in the former year ; becaufe that year came after a very dry fummer, for
which reafon the corn fared the better ; but it is a
great difadvantage for land to wear wet cloaths
to it's back for two years together : the more
years prove fo unfeafonable, the more and more
will the land be poifoned.

It is a common imagination of the farmers in the
hill-country, when much and almoft continual rains
fall

fall for a good part of the winter, that it will make corn dear, whereas I have commonly found them difappointed in fuch their expectations, and that the lands in the vale do not fo much fuffer, through a rainy winter, as they imagine, nay not fo much as the high hill-country lands, if the ground be of a cold clay: for the vale lands, though they lie low, and thereby fubject to be wet, yet, for the moft part, are warm in their nature, by reafon of a mellow hollow texture, whereby they foon recover and grow dry after the winter is gone off, the fun and wind piercing into them, efpecially if the ground of the vale be good, as it ufually is much better than that of the hills: in fuch cafe, by it's own vital heat and fpirit it refifts the chill of the winters, and foon recovers itfelf again; whereas lands of the high hill-country, efpecially the clays, being of their own nature much poorer, and more out of heart than thofe of the vale, do more in that refpect fuffer by winter cold rains, and, by reafon of their heavy and clofe obftinate texture, do much longer retain the water in them after the rainy feafon is over; by which means I have often obferved, that if cold rains return on the back of the former, the corn of fuch cold clays on the hills, being ftill fickly through the former wet, often dies; whereas that of the vale fooner recovering (as I faid before) the chill of the former wet, has got fome days ftrength and refrefhment to bear up againft the cold poifon of the fecond rainy feafon which fo foon returns after the former.

That winter wet is not reckoned to harm wheat by fogging the roots of it, anfwerable to the wetnefs of a March month, has this reafon for it; becaufe the pores of the roots are, in a manner, quite choaked up in the winter, nor is the winter water active, becaufe there is not fun enough to attenuate it's

parts,

parts, and to make them penetrate the tubes and roots of the wheat; whereas, when the month of March comes, the sun has got strength, and has opened the porous roots of the plants, and has attenuated the juices, which are therefore drank in greedily, and at this time the sun has not yet got power enough to qualify this dropsy by it's heat, by drying up the waters, &c.

§. 9. I observed, at one end of a field, that my barley looked much more sickly and thinner (when sowed a month or six weeks) than the rest, but remembered that very patch had been dunged the year before for the wheaten crop much more than any part of the field, at which I wondered; but was told, that that patch was sowed, and before it was harrowed wet came, so that the ground was chilled and did not harrow well; so much the good condition of corn depends on these two things. *Of rain after sowing.*

§. 10. I do conceive the coldness of the nights, (where the ground is cold clay, and the country high situated and hilly) does most contribute to the coarseness of the corn; for the summer days (tho' the coolest) are somewhat refreshing to corn as well as man, but the nights are many times of so cold a degree as to check the vegetable progression; especially, when there has been rain from a cold corner, and a cold soil for the corn, such cold of the night being of a degree beyond what the corn can support itself under, it is pinched thereby. *Of cold nights in hill-country.*

§. 11. On several years experience I find, that on our high hills, situated near a vale (especially in the spring time of March, April, and perhaps May, when the air is cold, dry, and windy, and of a harsh astringent temper, as usually it is at those times of the year: or, in fewer words, when the weather glass imports dry weather, for to that temper of the air I conceive the cause following is assignable) *Cause of rain falling in the vale.*

able) it is to be obferved, that though there be large floating clouds boding rain, that rife and pafs on one after another, watering liberally fome parts of the earth over which they pafs; yet that fuch clouds at thofe times of the year feldom empty themfelves on our hills, but on the vales, whilft we, envioufly, at a diftance look on our neighbours happinefs: this feems to be, becaufe the air, being, as before mentioned, dry and thin, has more elafticity in it, and confequently gives a greater refiftance to the clouds driven on by the winds, fo that the clouds are eafily diverted and turned afide into the ftronger channel of the wind in the vale under the hills, and therefore our expectation from the clouds rifing from the horizon big with rain, at thofe times of the year, are generally vain: whereas I obferve, on the contrary, when the air is loaded with moifture, as may be fenfibly perceived by the dampnefs of moft things, and by the weatherglafs being low, that fuch clouds before mentioned fhall keep their fteady courfe towards us, in an impartial manner, according to the tendency of the air and wind at that time; fo that every cloud moves in a direct line without making a curve, or yielding to the vortex of the vale, and then we have a fhare of the rain with our neighbours. This feems to depend on the yielding temper of the air, whofe tenfion, by the moifture, being unftrung, and it's elaftic power being loft, the clouds meet with lefs refiftance, and fo purfue a more fteady direct courfe, and are lefs drawn off and follicited by the collateral current of air in the vale, but take their courfe purfuant to the direction of the wind behind them, the air before them eafily yielding.

Indication of rain. §. 12. From conftant experience I have concluded, that, if the air be fultry and gloomy, without a breath of wind, or very little, the fky full of light wool-

wool-pack clouds boding no rain, yet in such cases fierce showers are very near, suitable to the gloominess and sultriness that forerun: for the clouds moving towards you, though not above the horizon, according as they are larger, stop the current of the air; whence such a closeness happens, that breathing, on such approaching weather, is not so easily performed, and from the atmosphere being full of ponderous clouds, it happens that the heat of the sun-beams, on us, must be very intense, when they are collected and contracted into narrower spaces, and either pass through the concave clouds, or are reflected from them, or break through the narrow interspace only between the clouds, which makes those scalding uneasy heats: then in such cases, tho' no threatening cloud appears in sight, yet be assured that rains are not far distant, and in an hour's time you may be likely to be surprized; then govern yourself accordingly for that whole day, whether it be in harvest or haymaking time, or when any business may suffer by rain, and lay not yourself open to the power of fierce rains to hurt you, but be on your guard, and forecast the most advantageous game you can play, on the certain expectation of hasty showers; and let not the fallacious opinion of the labourer, in harvest or hay-making, deceive you, who thinks rain is far off, because no cloud is near, and a pretty clear sky.

§. 13. It is an instance of great providence, that in the hot climates God sends rain but seldom, unless the first and latter rain, to bring up the corn and ripen it, and to bring it out of the hose; for did it rain frequently there, as in England, &c. the corn would run up to such a height as to lodge and rot.

Of rain in hot climates.

WEATHER.

§. 14. By what I can collect from the antients, they certainly thought the moon had a considerable heat, more or less, according to it's increase, or decrease, and in that sense the expression of Columella must be understood ; – sol & luna coquunt, for Virgil applies the same to the sun.

" Glebasque jacentes
" Pulverulenta coquat maturis solibus æstas ;"

and what else can that verse in the Psalms signify ; " The sun shall not burn thee by day, nor the moon by night ?" With regard to it's power and influence, sublunary things seem to have a force and strength increasing as the moon increases, and a force and strength decreasing as the moon decreases ; and this is more visible or intelligible in things weak of themselves, which are more easily affected, such as are seeds sown, which are young and tender, children ill, sick persons, persons weak in their understandings, and consequently in the spirits, persons weak in their eyes, and consequently in the local animal spirits of that part, which have not a good influx ; thus we see it is in a moon-blind horse ; but, if ground be strong, I believe it is not much in the power of the moon to affect the seed, as strong constitutioned persons are not affected much with weather, good or bad, whereas valetudinarians must live by rule ; for I apprehend the influence of the moon to be no more than what she has by her borrowed light ; the increase or decrease of which, when the sun is withdrawn from us, may sensibly affect things weak, to their comfort or discomfort ; and the juices in the plants and seeds, and spirits in our bodies, may rationally and experimentally enough be allowed to move brisker, or the contrary, as her borrowed light is greater or less: persons who, through a laxity of muscles stammer, are observed,

the

the wind being south, or south-west, which relaxes,
more to stammer; but such winds affect not the
speech of other persons, who at other times pro-
nounce distinctly.

§. 15. The wind moving the plants, and blow- Of the
ing them to and fro, seems, as Sir Francis Bacon wind.
has observed, to be the same towards strengthening the fibres and solids of plants, as exercise
is to us.

ENEMIES to HUSBANDRY.

§. 1. MR. Bishop of Dorsetshire, his shepherd, Of foxes.
and his carter told me, that in lamb-
ing-time, and whilst the lambs might be in danger
of the fox, they send out a couple of fellows with
horns all night to walk about, and blow and halloo,
and on these nights stake down a couple of dogs,
at fit distance, in a bleak cold place, which will
make them bark all night; but that way, the
shepherd says, will not always do, but a lamb
however will be lost sometimes; nor can the same
dogs abide it for above two or three nights; for
then they will be so cramped as not to be able to
get over a stile for two or three days afterwards:
these men, who walk about, have six-pence a
night, and meat and drink; they must not walk about,
with a dog, for by so doing the sheep will be set
o'bleating and running as much as if the fox was
amongst them; so that they would not know when
the fox came, which by the disturbance among the
sheep may be known; nor will they, after he has
been with them, be quiet from bleating till every
ewe has got her lamb.

Another, a gentleman farmer of that county, af-
sured me, he drew his flock together within two
acres of ground almost as close as if he had folded
them; and set four dogs, staked down at each cor-

ner, to keep off the fox by barking all night, and yet the foxes ftole away that night two lambs, and bit a third.

Hares.

§. 2. I obferved in the barley feveral full-grown ears withered lying along in a track of the field, which feemed t be a great fpoil; I took them up, and found the hares, to make a more convenient track, had bit the ftraws off at the ground.

Moles.

§. 3. The fquare of timbers I faw in the Ifle of White, to cut mole-hills off, were fix feet and a half in length, and the plate of iron about two inches broad, and fharpened as a knife is, from the back to the edge; and made after this fafhion, *a* the joifts, if one

may fo call them, acrofs, which are floped all away upwards, fo as with the flat fide they lie on the ground and are fharp; all the pieces of timber are much of the fame bignefs, about half a foot broad, and four inches, or better, thick, and the plate of iron fet on the uppermoft fide of the lowermoft bar, marked *a a*, hangs a quarter of an inch with the fharp edge over that bar of timber.

Mice.

§. 4. In taking down a reek-ftaffold of wheat, I obferved (as at other times) the mice for the greateft number by much lay on the fouth weft fide of the reek, from which corner comes moft rain and moift air, of which they may drink; this reek was carried up to a center like a cockpit, thatched as well, to my neighbouring farmer's judgment and mine, as ever we faw a reek; yet thefe mice had opened holes in the center top, and hollowed it in fuch manner, in order to come at the water, that, being a wet winter and fummer, much rain had fallen in and done confiderable damage; fo that the top thatch of reeks is to be looked after, where mice are fufpected to be.   To

To my great surprize I find, that mice will not eat the hulled hop-clover seed, but will scoop out all the flour of the broad-clover seed and, to amazement, will not leave one seed in a bushel, but what is thus scooped, in a short time.

§. 5. This day (April the 24th) I observed the rooks, in my garden, to pull up the beans when they were come up green ; they pull at the green stalk, and, if the ground be loose, the bean-seed but little wasted comes up with it.   Corn was almost all sowed now throughout the country, which I believe made them apter to fall on the beans : and in the afternoon of this day I observed the barley just coming up out of the ground, and a parcel of rooks lying thereupon, with their heads going apace up and down from the ground ; I went to the place, and found they had been pulling up the blades of corn, with which often, especially with a little scratching, came up the seed itself, little wasted, and only swelled, the blade but just appearing : note, my ground being rolled, they could not so well draw the grain after the blade, and on that account grew, I believe, sooner weary : the reason why they fell on the barley was, I suppose, the same for which they fell on the beans, viz. all corn being sowed, they could, for a few days, make better wages in fishing after the corn thus than in looking after the loose grains above ground.

In Wiltshire, at Holt and thereabouts, I observed boys keeping off rooks from peas in the fields after they were come up ; upon inquiry I found it was necessary, if peas came up before other corn was sowed, which was usual in those parts.   It is not so in our hill-country, because we are sowing black oats in abundance before our peas appear ; but if I sow the great cotshill-pea, which I intend to do, which must be sowed very early, and come up before other

B b 4   corn

corn is fowed, I muſt have, I find, the rooks kept off, or elſe, if I ſhould go from home for three or four days without taking care about it, they may be all pulled up before I return.

Rooks and pigeons.

§. 6. The deſtruction that pigeons and rooks make is incredible ; a neighbouring farmer aſſures me, that he has known an acre ſowed with peas, and a rain coming ſo that they could not be harrowed in, every pea was fetched away in half a day's time by the pigeons.

I ſowed wheat very early (viz. by the 3d of Auguſt) which was before the wheat harveſt opened ; the rooks, having no other corn to prey on, laid on it, and devoured a great quantity : but they do moſt harm, when, in the winter-time, the ſnow lies on the green wheat, and is firſt going off ; for having had no food for ſome time, they fall then very greedily on the wheat.

ᵃ Rooks, if they infeſt your corn, are more terrified, if in their ſight you take a rook, and, plucking it limb from limb, caſt the ſeveral limbs about your field, than if you hang up half a dozen dead rooks in it, ; this Mr. Ray ſays in two or three leaves of Remarks on huſbandry, fol. 194, in his Etymology of words.

The grain of my wheat began to harden in the ear, and the rooks to gather to it : I was ſaying to my bailiff, that it would be hard to keep them from it, unleſs two men compaſſed it with guns ; but he anſwered, it was a field of whoſe haunt the rooks might be eaſily broken, for, ſaid he, there is only a dead hedge for a few * lug on one ſide, all the reſt is

* Fole.

ᵃ Among the many contrivances to frighten rooks, ſays Mr. Tull, as feathers ſtuck up, the limbs of rooks ſcattered about the ground, dead rooks hung on ſticks, the gun, or a boy to halloo or throw up his hat, or a dead rook in the air, I have found the laſt to be the moſt effectual.

quick

quick hedge, and if you frighten them there, they will fly off to another haunt ; a rook does not like to come to corn, but where there is a dead hedge, for they muſt be out upon the watch (and they do not care to light upon a quick hedge) to tell tidings ; but crows will often light on the quick : I obſerved this year towards harveſt, that the rooks gathered much about thoſe corn grounds where my ponds were, to rendevouz and drink, and ſo to the corn again ; therefore break them of their haunts early there, before the corn ripens.

Rooks will not pull up the lenten corn till ſeed-time is over, and there is not grain for them ; and they ſeldom care for peas in the grain, nor barley as long as they can come at oats : for the oat ſtripped of it's huſk is much ſweeter, and tenderer to be bruiſ-ed than barley, but when it comes up into blade, then they will moſt fall on barley ; being laſt ſowed and a fuller bodied grain, there is more flour left in the barley than in the oat ; when they fall on the barley in the ear it is in light ground that is hollow, where it is * more-looſe ; if peas were ſowed late, without doubt they would ſooner fall on their blade, and pull them up than other corn, becauſe of the bulk of their grain, in which there is more flour to be found unexhauſted ; and I do remember, they fell on goar-vetches, that were ſowed in May, with that voraciouſneſs that it was very hard to ſecure half of them : in ſome grounds, which they take to, one may gather in the compaſs of a yard a handful of blades they have pulled up : ——it is true, pi-geons love peas beſt, which may proceed from the weakneſs of their bills that they cannot unſhell the oat, and from the heat of their crops, which may di-geſt a pea better than the rooks can.

* Looſe a root.

It had been an exceſſive dry ſummer from April to this day (7th of July) and tho' there were no worms nor bugs, by reaſon of the drought, to be

met

met with, yet the birds did not fall on the cherries, which I and others wondered at, but probably it was becauſe there was ſo much corn ſown about the houſe: but, where the ſummer is ſo very dry that rooks cannot come to worms, nor the plough go to turn them up, they will fall on the corn before it is half ripe, even when they can have but a green juice in the ſtraw to chew, therefore are to be prevented.

Rooks and ſparrows.

§. 7. A farther evil there is in rooks, that their neſts, when their breed is over, is a harbour to the latter brood of the ſparrows, which bird chooſes then, when the weather grows warm, and the air mild, to build ſub dio, and not to ſtive herſelf up in neſts under the eaves of a houſe.

Snails.

§. 8. In September I found many ſnails eggs laid at the roots of plants I pulled up: the 21ſt of October in rainy weather I obſerved a multitude of white ſnails or ſlugs, crawling on the ground, under the cabbages in the garden, moſt of which were not half ſo long as my nail, and in thickneſs no bigger than a pin's head; ſo that I concluded them newly hatched from the September eggs; therefore it is ſeaſonable to deſtroy the old ones before September, in order to deſtroy the brood. Quære, if they lay eggs any other months of the year; if ſo, to be chiefly taken off before ſuch laying alſo.

In February I planted cabbages, and by the latter end of March had moſt of them eat up by white ſnails, or ſlugs, of which ſort of ſnails we picked up a quart or more in a morning early for many mornings; the country was this year much infeſted with them; this evil ſeems to have proceeded from the very mild winter, which did not deſtroy the eggs they lay every autumn in abundance at the roots of all manner of herbs: the ſame is to be expected another mild winter, therefore look after them early in the ſpring.

Worlidge (fol. 262.) ſays, that ſnails are of both ſexes,

sexes, and couple from spring until Midsummer and after, and lay their eggs in the ground; you will find them with their bodies buried in the warm dust, and only their shells above the ground; when you take them out you must rake out their eggs and destroy them, or else some will be hatched the same year, and some in the spring following.

§. 9. Ants, in the hotter regions, are reckoned Ants. among the pests of the field, as in Italy, Spain, and the West-Indies. Mortimer, fol. 253.

One Timothy Skrine (a very industrious and laborious person in planting orchards, and my neighbour in Wiltshire, who from an estate of ten pounds per annum, improved it that way to fifty pounds per annum) came to see me in Hampshire, and walking out with me in my meads, and observing the emmet-casts, he told me, he had tried many ways to destroy them, being much troubled with them, and particularly the opening their hills in winter, which they would rebuild again; (I suppose at winter they lie lower than people usually dig after them, therefore that way is unsuccessful); but that the best way, as he has by experience found, is to fling abroad their hillocks in the month of June, in their breeding time, when they lay their eggs, before they come to be flies: I suppose this destroys their breed, puts them on endless labour to find them out, till they are hunger-starved, and, the brood being destroyed, the old ones (who are not, I imagine, long lived) decay, and die in a short time; or perhaps they leave their habitations out of resentment for the cruel usage of their young, God having with his first blessing at the beginning implanted in all creatures an earnest desire of propagating and protecting their species; and we see the most fearful of them will venture their lives for their young ones; and it has been known, when persons would destroy rookeries

by

by firing at the old ones daily, it could not be done, but, when the nests with young ones have been brought down, and burned under the trees, they have all deserted.

Worms.   §. 10. I made a gravel walk in my garden, and underlayed it with white mortar earth rammed in, and layed strand on it; both coats were above a foot thick, notwithstanding which the worms, in a few days time, made their holes through; I cannot suppose it possible for the worms to thrust or bore through such a solid with their snout; but having observed what a power they have with their mouth to pluck at grass, do believe, in the same manner they use their mouth in pulling away the earth in little crumbles, which they still tumble downwards under them.

I made a little court with a gravel walk in the middle, and grass-plots of turf on each side of the walk: the worms came through the turf in vast numbers, and were very hurtful to it; the days being very rainy for a season, which brought them out at nights; my servants visited them with candle and lantern, and caught great quantities of them, till at length they grew so cunning that on stepping on the turf, though at a great distance, they would feel the turf shake, and shoot into their holes; besides, they would not, at their usual hours, come out of their holes, nor then, as they usually did before, lay out with most part of their bodies, but with their noses only: observing the improveable wisdom of these insects, I thought to be cunninger than they, and made sure of taking those that lay within my reach on each side of the walk; for the gravel walk laid lower than the turf, and, being a solid, did not shake the turf, so I carried, as I stood in the walk, my candle and lantern over the turf as far as I could reach, but the worms being used to the light shot
into

into their holes as soon as ever the rim of light came over them; I suppose they have no eyes, but God has given them an exquisite feeling to supply that defect, in many respects, in order to self-preservation. Light being a fluid body makes a different configuration of the particles of the air, which they can distinguish by the feel as a blind man can by use some colours; at last I found the way to destroy them was, to visit them very early in the morning, in copulation, when I found they had a stupor; which puts me in mind of that saying of Pliny, omne animal post coitum triste.

I have a clay so obstinate about my house, for a quarter of a mile's compass, and withal so flinty, that I am sure a mole could never come within that space, and yet, if a stick be put in any place and stirred about, the worms will rise and come forth, for fear of the mole, which seems to be purely owing to the enmity God has set between the worm and the mole from the beginning; for it must proceed from somewhat innate, that a creature, which had never, in the grounds here mentioned, experience of harm in this kind, should blindly use this stratagem.

It is a common proverbial saying of the countryman, that at whatsoever country-farm a colony of rooks planted themselves, and made a rookery, it is a sign of good luck and good fortune attending that man; and on men growing unfortunate and low in the world, the rookery has been observed to forsake such farm: for both which observations some good reasons may be offered; viz. it is certain where a man is a good husband to his land and improves it, the worms also (a great food to these creatures, especially at some times of the year) multiply, and grow also to a much greater bulk and fatness; the strength of land being discernable by the large size of worms

as

as from the growth of plants, and the beetle kind, on whose grubs or maggots, therefore called rook-worms, the rooks do greatly feed, (as is apparent by their following the plough) do not only grow in such ground much fatter and larger, but those flies of the beetle kind, by the wisdom God has given them, do covet and choose to nest their fly-blows in such land as will best nourish and provide for them; and the same instance of the wisdom of these creatures may be given in many like cases; but, where an ill husbandman comes, the contrary to this soon comes to pass, upon which, no wonder if they say, let us go hence.

Upon viewing a farm in the Isle of Wight, to purchase it, we were afraid the farmer, according to the liberty he had by his lease, would have ploughed up the cow-lease; farmer Collins said, if it was his he should hardly do it; for, said he, good sweet cow-pasture ground, that has laid to grass a long time, is (in the Isle of Wight) very subject to the worm, which will eat up the corn; it was a surprize to me to hear him say so, and therefore I enquired more particularly about it; he said, the worm was very small, with a black head, like a fly, and when their wheat, about March, should promise exceeding well, it would die away on a sudden; take up such green wheat by the root, and just above the root and grain, within the earth, one may observe the stalk almost bit in two, and very commonly the worm upon it, and fresh ground is very subject to it, for the two or three first crops; I asked him if it ever fared so with their barley; he said, he never knew the barley to receive damage by it, but he had known the peas receive the same damage as the wheat. Mr. Rowler, an experienced yeoman, was present, and confirmed what Collins said.

§. 11. If

§. 11. If ground be infested much with rook- Rook-
worms, ploughing it up will cure it of them for worm.
some years.

§. 12. I was at lord Pembroke's, and his lord- Of the eggs
ship was difcourfing about infects and their eggs, of infects.
and propagation ; he faid, that many of their eggs
which were laid late, did lie out all the winter, and
were not brought to perfection till fpring ; therefore
it is obferved, that, where there is a cold winter,
there is a lefs increafe of thofe infects.

§. 13. The wifdom of God is very manifeft in Nu mag-
that contemptible infect we call a maggot, and in the got.
fly that blows it in the nut : I do not remember that
ever I faw two maggots in a nut, though moft nuts
in a bunch are faulty where one is fo ; it feems the
maggots of the whole bunch are the blowing of one
and the fame fly, and that all the nuts of the fame
bunch would have been blown, if fome accident had
not difturbed the fly at the time of her incubation,
for that a flefh-fly does at the fame time lay many
eggs is certain : again, it may feem ftrange, that one
and the fame fly fhould difcern (it being an act of
almoft the fame inftant of time) where fhe blowed
her maggot, fo as not to lay another in the fame
nut; yet it feems ftranger, that every other fly fhould
difcern where a former had blown a maggot, fo as
to avoid laying her fly-blow on the fame nut; otherwife it would afterwards happen that many maggots
would be in the fame nut, and the provifion of
maintenance fall fhort : where the fly-blow is injected, when the nut is very fmall and tender, a canker grows over and clofes, and confifts of a rotten fubftance ; and here it fhews wifdom alfo in a
maggot, that it can difcern that eafier place of entrance.

§. 14. I obferved this day (the 11th of Auguft) Caterpil-
a multitude of young caterpillars on the leaves of lars.

my,

I

my turnips half-grown ; all the faid half-grown
leaves they had almoft eaten up : note, the fummer
being very hot from April to this day, I conclude
the latter brood of autumn was ripened alfo the fame
year, the eggs of which would otherwife have laid
in the ground till next winter, thefe will be deftroyed the next cold rains : from hence I conclude we
fhall have the fewer infects next year : it was a new
thing to me at this time of the year to meet with
fuch an enemy.

I obferved this year (1709) in my walks among
apple-trees and codling-hedges, that fome apple-
trees were fmitten with the blight, as the country
people call it, when their leaves are eaten up with
the caterpillar, whilft I obferved that the reft were
under a flourifhing and green verdure, and untouch-
ed by the caterpillar ; and I was told by the owners
that fuch trees were moft years fmitten ; this occafioned fome fpeculation and fcrutiny, but I foon
judged the reafon of it ; for I perceived a difference
in the colour and fhape of the leaves, between the
blighted and unblighted trees, and upon inquiry
found them to bear different fruits, and, if of the
fame fort there were any blighted (which rarely happened when others efcaped) I found, by reafon of
the different ages or unthriving condition of thefe
trees, they had put out their leaves earlier or later
than the others, and foon perceived that fome trees,
by bearing fweeter leaves than others, were more
fuitable to the tooth of the caterpillar, or by bearing
earlier or later, were more fuitable as well as more
tender at the time the caterpillar was to be fed, and
that fuch fly laid her eggs on fuch trees (by the
wifdom appointed fuch infects by Providence) on
which the worm (i. e. the caterpillar) when hatched
and grown to maturity, might have it's beft maintenance.

§. 14. A

§. 15. A notable fellow (though a labourer on-ly) in husbandry, drove a yoke of oxen from the neighbourhood in Wiltshire where I have concerns (viz. Bradford and Trowbridge) : I walked him about to shew him my corn, and an occasion offer-ed to discourse on peas : I asked him if they were not often eaten up by a caterpillar in Wiltshire; he said, in case the peas grew into a good halm, and blowed well, they never doubted a good crop of peas in their neighbourhood, for he never knew peas hurt by caterpillars in their country; but about fourteen years ago there was a winged fly, a sort of locust, which did them damage : I replied, I sup-posed they sowed peas so early as to escape the dan-ger of the caterpillar by their forwardness before that insect came; he said, that was not his meaning, but the true reason for the escape of the peas, about them, was, because so many elms, maples, and oaks grow about their grounds, which the fly (the parent of the caterpillar) who knows the tooth of her brood, prefers before the pea, and in the leaves of the said trees lays her eggs : I take notice of this, because it is agreeable to my own observation in former papers. And here the hand of God is very wonderful, to in-struct the butterfly to choose such plants, to lay it's brood in, as are best suited for their nourishment, whereas the butterfly judges not of it, nor chooses it, by taste, leaves of plants not being the food of those flies, but the juices of flowers and honey-dews.

§. 16. The green-louse or locust falling on the broad side of the pea-kid, and thereupon the grain not thriving, seems an argument that the sap, which nourishes the pea withinside, is conveyed to the grain, and strained through the fibres of the kid : for otherwise there is no reason why the pea should suffer by this, seeing the spine, to which the pea ad-heres by a thread, is preserved entire, and is joined

[margin: Caterpillars and flies.]

[margin: Grass louse or locust.]

to the main stalk; through this therefore the sap
might be conveyed directly, and without any prejudice to the pea, were it not first to be strained
through the fibres of the flat side of the kid.— This
to be referred to what Malpigius has said of the sap's
circulating through the leaves to the fruit.

The 13th and 14th of June, in pulling up whea
in ear, and sowthistles, I did observe among the upper part of the roots of most of the wheat and sowthistles, knots or clusters of grass-lice, or green locusts (though these appeared whitish, being under
ground, and as yet but just come to their shape) and
amongst most of these clusters I observed a fly at her
incubation, which seemed very turgid of a whitish
matter, she being then blowing these insects; her
wings were black, and the fly was plainly the same
as the locusts, only it had wings: I found at no root
more than one fly.

Cuckow-
spit.

§. 17. On May the 22d was the first cuckow-
spit I had observed, which was on a woodbind joint;
till within a day or two of that time there had been
no rain or dews all April and May, and so whatever
insects of that kind were laid in the joints of plants
could not live, but must be scorched up.

In the history of Works of the learned, for April
1707, I find Monsieur Poupart has given an account of the cuckow-spit, or spring-froth; he says,
as soon as the little creature comes out of it's egg, it
goes to a plant, which it touches with it's funda-
ment, and fastens there a white drop of liquor full of
air; it drops a second near the first, then a third,
and so on, till it covers itself all over with a scum or
froth; this froth keeps it from the heat of the sun,
or spiders that would suck it; note, this is not agreeable to my observation made in another place, nor
can I agree with Mr. Poupart: for it is nothing but
the nightly dew, which falls on the fork, or joint of
the

the plant, which the little insect with his proboscis, as with a bellows, works into froth.

§. 18. Being acquainted that a great blight was Of the fly in apple blossoms, &c. upon the apples, where I observed no leaves eat up by the caterpillar, I judged such blight must be of another sort, and upon enquiry (when none of the apples were bigger than gooseberries, and the more backward much less) I found this blight was on the blossoms ; for I found the blossoms had been closed up, and a cement bound the rims of their leaves together, and in the hollow inclosure was a fly, brown, and of a hazle colour, of hard wings like the beetle kind, of legs not shelly like theirs, and more nimble, of a neck as big as horse-hair, and as long, near, as his body, at the end of which he bore a very small head between two slender horns: where these blossoms were scorched up by the sun and looked black, by reason of the time which had passed since their more early blowing, there I found the fly perfect, as before described ; but in those blossoms whose leaves were less dried, scorched, and sun-burnt, which I took to be blossoms of more backward trees, there I found the fly as yet imperfect and unripe, with a yellow soft skin and helpless, but in a quick motion of it's body, it's legs and wings being as yet swathed up in this outward coat, which was by heat to ripen and crack : I perceived, by the degrees of the forwardness and backwardness mentioned of this insect, that the fly which blowed them, must have several days for reigning, to do this mischief, distant in time from each other : it was no cobweb as I could find, that cemented these leaves together as above mentioned ; but I conceive it to be done by the heat of the sun drawing away the tenuous parts from the dew of the flower, whereby the gummy substance quickly joined these leaves : it may be the fly took a blighting mildew

air

air for the doing it : I believe this mifchief was done before the bloffom opened itfelf fully, becaufe the clofure and figure of it was in all like a bloffom whofe leaves clofe at top before they are expanded. When the infect grows to maturity, he eats a hole and goes forth : a vaft mifcarriage fell on the fruit this way, more than in all other ways befides ; I found it the fame in all gardens and orchards. Note, coftermongers and cyder-men may enrich tnemfelves by an early forefight of this, by buying up the apples ; for the fcarcity is to be forefeen before the flower is full bloffomed, whereas we do not ufually underftand this mifchief till it is obvious to every eye.

Expla-

Explanation of Terms in Husbandry, used in the foregoing Observations.

A

AFTERMASS. Aftermath, lattermath, second crop of grass mowed in autumn.

Ana. Of each an equal quantity.

B.

Brashy. Full of small stones.

Barton. The yard, the farm-yard.

Burnbeak, burnbate. To cut up the turf, and burn it in hillocks on the land.

Brit. To shed, to fall.

Backside. Farm-yard.

Bennets, bents. Spiry grass running to feed.

Bennet:ng-time. When the pigeons eat the grass-seeds.

C.

Cotyledones. Rinds, husks.

Chitt. To sprout out, to grow.

Chase-row. In planting quicksets a single chase is a single row ; a double chase means another row planted below the first, not directly underneath the upper plants, but under the middle of the intermediate spaces.

Chissum. To put forth roots, to grow.

Cues. Shoes for oxen.

Chocky. Chalky, dry.

Couples. Ewes and Lambs.

Cow-lease. See Lease.

D.

Declivous. Shelving, sloping.

E.

Earth. To one, two, three earths; to plough the ground once, twice, or thrice ; to sow after one, two, or three ploughings.

Edge-grown. Coming up uneven, not ripening all together.

Ershe. Stubble.

Elm. See Helm.

F

Fallows-stale. Ground that has been ploughed some time, and lies in fallow.

Flue. Weak, sickly.

Finnowy, vinnowy, vinnewed, vinney. Mouldy.

Foliomort, fillimot. Colour of dead leaves. Reddish yellow.

Fusty. Musty.

G.

Gripe. Armfull, from Gripe.

Grip. To lie in grip ; to lie on the ground, before it is bound up in sheaf.

Grip. To grip, or grip up ; to take up the wheat, and put it into sheaf.

Gnash, Crude, raw.

Grete, Mold.

H.

Hulls. Chaff, the hull, the rind.

Helm. Halm, or straw prepared for thatching.

Helm To helm, to lay the straw in order for thatching.

Heirs. Young trees in coppices.

Hayn, or hayn up. To hedge in, to preserve grass grounds from cattle.

Heal. To cover in; to heal seed with harrows, to cover it in.

Hee-grass. Stubble of grass.

Hog-sheep. Young sheep.

Hog-fold. Fold of young sheep.

Hint. To lay up; to put together.

Horse-lease. See Lease.

I.

To joist. To take in cattle to keep at a certain price per head or score.

Idiosyncrasy. A peculiarity in nature or constitution, a temperament whereby an animal body hath a peculiar inclination to, or

aversion

aversion against, some particular things.

K.

Knot-fine. Very fine. To knot fine, to turn up fine under the plough.

Knotted sheep. Sheep without horns.

Kittle. Subject to accidents, uncertain.

L.

Lugg. A pole in measure, 16¼ feet.

Lease, lea, lay, ley. Grassy ground, meadow-ground, unploughed, and kept for cattle.

Linchets. Grass partitions in arable fields.

M

Mores. Roots.

More-loose. Loose at root.

Mamocks. Leavings.

Malt-rashed, Overheated, burnt.

Meliorate, To enrich, to make better.

Mixen. Dung, dunghill.

Muck. Dung.

O.

Oughts. Leavings.

Oils. Barley oils, the beard or prickles.

P.

Præcocious. Early ripe, forward.

Pitch. To waste, sink in flesh.

Pur-lamb. Male-lamb.

Peal. Loose its hair.

R.

Rath-ripe. Early ripe, rather, sooner.

Rashed. See Malt.

Rime Hoar-frost.

Rowet, rowen. Winter-grass.

Rafty. Rusty.

S.

Sull.

Spalt. To turn up; it spalts up from below the staple, i. e. the bad ground turns up in ploughing from below the good mold, which is difficult to be avoided when the land is ploughed dry.

Suant. Kindly, even, regular. Probably from the French word Suivant.

Shutes. Young hogs, or porkers, before they are put up to fatting.

Stale-fallows. See Fallows.

Soboles. Buds for the next year's increase.

Succedaneous. Substitute to, or supplying the place of something else.

Sheep-flate. Sheep-walk, sheep-lease.

T.

Tine. Tooth or spike. To give two tinings, three tinings, &c. to draw the harrows over the ground twice or thrice in the same place

Tilt or Tilth. See Earth. To give land one, two, or three tilts, is the same as to plough to one, two, or three earths.

Tilt or Tillage. To be in good tilt, is to be in good order, or in good tillage.

Tillow. To spread, shoot out many spires.

Trig. Firm, even.

Thorough. To go thorough, not to prove with young.

Tupp. Ram.

Tupping-time. Ramming-time.

Thief. Young ewe.

V.

Vetches-goar. Early ripe, or summer vetches.

Viliorate. To make worse, impoverish,

Vinnow. Mouldiness.

W.

Woodseer-ground. Loose, spungy ground.

Warp. Miscarry, slink her calf.

CON-

CONTENTS

Of the SECOND VOLUME.

Hogs

CONTENTS.

End of the SECOND VOLUME.